W9-BUE-631

JUDAISM

RELIGION AND ETHICS

BY

MEYER WAXMAN

New York · THOMAS YOSELOFF · London

First Printing October 1958
Second Printing January 1960

Library of Congress Catalogue Card Number: 58-9391

Thomas Yoseloff, Publisher
11 East 36th Street
New York 16, N.Y.

Thomas Yoseloff Ltd.
123 New Bond Street
London W. 1, England

Printed in the United States of America

JUDAISM
Religion and Ethics

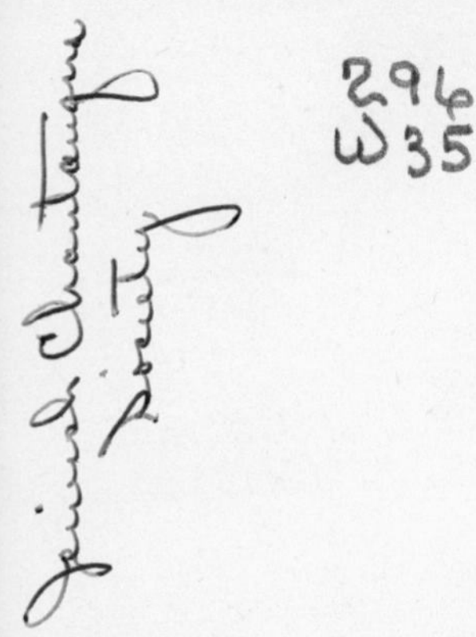

TO THE SACRED MEMORY

OF

millions of Jewish martyrs to whom the practices and beliefs here presented were the breath of life, this volume is reverently dedicated

PREFACE

This book consists of two parts, one dealing with the religious aspect of Judaism, namely with the practice of precepts and commandments, as well as with the principal views and beliefs of Judaism, and the other with the ethics of Judaism. The first part was originally published as a work in itself and underwent two editions. In the third edition, it is combined with the second part treating of ethics in order to present a complete view of Judaism in both its aspects. The author finds it therefore necessary to explain the method and purpose of each of these parts.

He feels that in this period of Jewish history, when Jewish life and Jewish thought are undergoing many changes, it is desirable to provide a succinct statement of the traditional Jewish pattern of religious life and thought for the average Jew and the non-Jew as well (Part I). Such a formulation may serve, at the least, as a backdrop against which the varied patterns of our own day may be viewed. It is true that there are many works on the subject of Jewish religion, but the author believes they fail to meet this need.

Most of the works in the field are elementary in their treatment and limited in their scope. The frequent use of the words "customs and ceremonies" as a book title is perhaps sufficient to indicate the fact that many of the works have failed to treat the subject in a fundamental manner. To the Jews of the past, and to a large number, perhaps still a majority, of the Jews of our day, observance of the Sabbath, of the festivals, the prayers were and are the warp and woof of an integral mode of Jewish life and belief, rather than a series of "customs and ceremonies." To consign these vital elements of Jewish life to the realms of sociology and anthropology is to ignore the hallowed role they have held in our long tradition.

Similarly, many of the works in the field are over-narrow in their approach. By and large, they tend to ignore the doctrinal part of Judaism. The views of Judaism on God, man, life, and the world are omitted or cursorily treated. This is a fundamental failing, for it is impossible both in terms of Jewish religious history and in terms of logic to divorce observances from their intimate relation to the Jewish view of the cosmos.

There is, in addition, another class of books on the subject of Judaism whose value is limited by a partisan approach. Whether they be written from a conservative, reform, or reconstructionist point of view, all representing deviations from the standard type of Judaism, they tend to mirror the views of their writers and their groups. Inevitably these works make selection from the great body of Jewish religious material and emphasize the aspects that most closely conform to their point of view. Perforce, too, other phases of importance are glossed over or omitted. On the whole, the note of apology rings in these books.

The author, however, has sought to avoid writing as a partisan. He has attempted rather to present the point of view mirrored in the long history of Judaism as it is embedded in the sources to which all works must resort. If the result is rather close to the orthodox viewpoint, it is because the bulk of Jewish history and the sources themselves point in that direction. There is here no attempt at apology or justification of a point of view. The material presented is based upon the sources and every detail can be corroborated by statements from the great authorities of our tradition.

It is also thought necessary to open the work with a general statement upon the nature of Judaism, pointing out the uniqueness of its character as distinguished from other great religions on the one hand, and its total integration with the fate and destiny of the Jewish people on the other. Hence, the introductory chapter "What is Judaism" seeks to emphasize that Judaism is a totality embracing all the variegated aspects of Jewish life.

As for the second part, the writer, in undertaking to deal with the subject of Jewish ethics, placed for himself four purposes. The first purpose is to present to the reader the principles of Jewish ethics, as well as their application in practice. He thought it best to devote a large part of the work to brief, though embracive, discussions of the leading virtues that man is to acquire in order to lead an ethical life, as well as the vices one must refrain from following. The presentation is based on the original Jewish sources, concepts, and views on such matters scattered through the wide Jewish literature from the Bible on. The author believes that in delineating a phase of the spiritual heritage of a certain group or people, whether it be its religious beliefs, or conceptions, or the practice of right conduct, it is always necessary to draw the material from the literary sources as well as the tradition of that group. It is then that the views, concepts, and also the modes of practice can be presented in their purity without any admixture of ideas which, though they may appear similar and deal with the same subject, yet differ in essence from the content of the ideas and concepts held by that group.

The second is to remove certain erroneous conceptions regarding the Jewish attitude toward non-Jews and the imaginary corresponding actions resulting from such misconceived attitude. These erroneous conceptions born of age-long prejudice against a unique people, which struggled desperately throughout the ages to preserve its integrity and spiritual heritage in spite of persecution and tribulation, are not exterminated even today. An attempt to correct the thinking of people interested in ethical conduct may help to modify the prejudicial view.

The third purpose is to endeavor to point out the Jewish

contribution to world ethics. While it is true that the ethical principles presented here as well as the modes of their application in practice are shared by all ethically minded men, they were first pronounced by Judaism and in the course of ages have influenced human thought and conduct, directly and indirectly. These principles have not only been accepted by the religions spiritually close to Judaism, but their echoes are heard also in the ethical teachings of the great modern philosophers, such as Immanuel Kant and others.

Finally, the author aims to present certain aspects of ethical action, due to the destiny and fate of Jewish existence, the carrying out of which is primarily the duty only of the Jew, both of the people as a whole and of its individual members.

The very aim the author had in mind, namely, to present Judaism in the above-mentioned aspects to all intelligent men and women, Jews and non-Jews, who evince a desire for such knowledge, determines the character of the work. Efforts, therefore, were made not to tire the reader and to avoid technicality and abstruseness. Notes have been reduced to a minimum, Hebrew terms and phrases transliterated, and technical matters have been expounded in nontechnical language.

In addition, the author found it necessary to append a glossary of the terms and of the sources drawn upon for the material presented in the book. The glossary offers a brief but fairly embracive description of the leading works given as sources, touching upon their character, origin, and the parts of which they consist. The glossary, besides widening the reader's knowledge of some aspects of Jewish literature, may also serve to some readers as an impetus to further study in the field of Judaism.

CONTENTS

THE ETHICS OF JUDAISM

JUDAISM AS A RELIGION

Introduction

WHAT IS JUDAISM?

I

GENERAL FEATURES

Many are the definitions of religion. To the average man, whether he is affiliated with the official institutions of the various religions or not, it means a belief in the existence of God, the Creator of the world, who exercises some kind of providence over the destiny of man and to whose will or commands he has to adjust himself. To the philosopher or theist who is traditionally minded, it implies a belief in, or assumption of, the existence of a first ultimate cause whose rationality is the source of the order and the system in the universe. To the more liberal modern thinker or the moderate humanist, the essence of religion consists in the desire of men to integrate and organize their personality as a whole, namely, to combine their emotions, impulses, sentiments, and ideas into a coherent unity. In the past, these thinkers argue, this unity was accomplished by positing the existence of an external power who acted as a guide in life and brought about that wholeness of character. In the present day, since the scientific outlook upon the world makes such beliefs impossible, unity can be attained by devotion to ideals and values which occupy an important place in human life. They admit, though, that this unity can best be attained by clinging, in a modified form, to the leading religious conceptions of the past, namely, by following the teachings of a great religious personality and even maintaining a relation to some cosmic factor the conception of which helps to develop the integrated personality. To the complete humanist religion is entirely a human affair which needs, in view of the modern outlook upon the world and life, no support from external and supernatural forces, and consists solely in devotion to ideals, such as pursuit of truth, creation of beauty, and achievement of social amelioration.

The religious quality of such devotion inheres in the intensity and the whole-heartedness of feeling expressed therein and in the high value placed upon human good. Some poetically minded humanists recognize the importance of certain religious rites and ceremonies as symbols for human aspiration and advocate their retention, but all agree to the complete human character and nature of religion and dispense with all supernatural support in any form.

However, in spite of these various meanings and interpretations of religion which are now in vogue, the fact remains that it is the standard type of religious view, i.e., the one which looks upon religion as a manifold relation between God and man, which has exerted the greatest influence upon the destiny of man through the ages and is still the most prevalent in the life of humanity. It was this type of religion which served as the uniting cord in the complex of human life and activities almost from the very appearance of man on the face of the earth. As Bergson correctly stated, while art, literature, and all other expressions of the human spirit were not always factors in the life of man, religion was always with him, even in the very dawn of his life. It was this type of religion which followed man during the many millennia in which he struggled towards a constant betterment of his material position in the universe and a continuous expansion of his spiritual and intellectual powers. And it is this type of religion which, as said, is still dominant today, for while the various meanings and definitions of religion referred to are the share of individuals or of small groups, the great masses of all peoples on the earth are still swayed by the central group of ideas of the religions belonging to the standard type.

Since this type of religion was and is so intimately and integrally connected with human life in all its complexity and variety, it follows that like life itself the conditions of its development were primarily of a social nature. While we cannot deny that religion in its higher forms includes also many functions aiming at the satisfaction of the spiritual needs of the individual, such as the desire for salvation or the mystic craving for uniting with the All or the Ultimate Power, yet it is very questionable whether religion could have developed in a state of human isolation. Wherever it made its appearance it was within a definite social group. Consequently, the various historical religions bear the marks of the life of the group in which they originated, both the marks of differentiation from that of other groups as well as of similarity, for since human nature is similar as well as different, it follows that both the life and the religion of the various groups should partake of both phases. Accordingly, we note that on the one hand, in the measure that the life of the various groups of humanity becomes more similar and common, religion or religions likewise share in this tendency and strive towards universality, while on the other hand, it is also clear that no religion can divest itself of its original character and attain complete universality. In fact, the two great religions, the daughters of Judaism, Christianity and Islam, claim that universality. Yet even these two religions which were adopted by many nations which possess various cultural patterns have not attained their goal, for the Christianity and Islam of each group professing them display considerable differences in character and conception from that of other groups.

Moreover, the success of these religions in becoming to a degree universal is primarily due to the fact that they came to the nations from the outside, and were not indigenous to their lives, and in reality, they never amalgamated thoroughly with the essence of the life of the various peoples and always retained somewhat of the nature of a superimposed religion upon a life and a culture of a different character. It is, of course, true that through the centuries these religions became a factor in the development of the life and culture of those who adopted them, but the underlying substratum of the earlier culture continually projects itself into the later strata of their history. Otherwise we could not explain the numerous manifest contradictions between the teachings of these religions and the frequent grave aberrations from them in the conduct of these peoples.

The case is different with Judaism, which is a religion indigenous to a definite group and which developed with the group over the course of millennia. Though it is this religion which nursed within itself the kernels of universalism which were adopted by the other two religions, still it always retained and continues to retain that peculiar connection with the life and destiny of that people. As said, Judaism was the first to impart a universal aspect to religion, but that in no way affects its individual character permeated by the spirit of the people which professes it, for its universalism—as will be explained later—is of a peculiar stamp.

Furthermore, no religion of a people can consist of mere beliefs and sentiments. These may constitute the spiritual aspect of its soul. But like every soul, it must have a body in which it can clothe itself and become an efficient factor in life. This body consists of institutions and laws which contain rules of conduct and practice embracing a great part of the daily life of the devotee. The institutions and ceremonies supply vividness and dramatic force to the sentiments, aspirations, and beliefs, and help to solidify them into a concrete and stable part of human life. The frequent practice of religious rites not only serves as a symbol of the ideas and ideals which religion aims to inculcate but deepens their significance and integrates them into a solid mass which ultimately forms a layer of the very personality of the religious man.

From all that has been said, it follows that in order to evaluate Judaism, a religion which was so closely integrated for many centuries with the life of a people of a *sui generis* character, it is not enough to point to a certain number of principles and views as is often done and say this is Judaism. To grasp the meaning of Judaism, one has to survey the principal stages of its development and its gradual growth through the constant interaction between it and the life and destiny of the people. This interaction was as heterogeneous as the life and vicissitudes of the Jewish people, for Judaism, in spite of its fundamental belief that it is of a divinely revealed character in a more or less complete form, is simultaneously a religion of life and of an essentially practical nature. Its purpose was to guide, shape, and mould the life of a group in its various manifestations. And as it discharged its function through the ages it was in turn affected, moulded, and shaped by that life as well as expanded and enlarged by the reception of many extraneous elements arising out of the variegated historical vicissitudes of the people. As a result the line of demarcation between religion and secular life in its manifold aspects was obliterated, and we can no longer distinguish between the elements which we usually label as distinctly religious and those we subsume under the name of national culture. Any attempted separation only results in an incomplete understanding of the essence of the complex phenomenon which we call Judaism. We therefore shall endeavor to present in the following chapter a conception of Judaism with a view to its wholeness as it was crystallized in the history of Israel.

II

THE NATURE AND CHARACTER OF JUDAISM

In attempting to present the essence of the nature and character of Judaism, an historical phenomenon three and one half millennia old which has saved the Jewish people from extinction and simultaneously has exerted considerable influence upon the course of civilization in general, one must draw his data primarily from its own sources. It is only its own traditions, recorded in its cherished and sacred writings, which have become part and parcel of the spiritual and mental outlook of the people of Israel upon the world and life, that can reveal to us its true nature. All other documents and sources, "finds" or discoveries upon which historians and critics build up theories and hypotheses aiming to attribute to Judaism, in certain periods of its development, traits which are at variance with the traditions, are, to say the least, of doubtful worth.

We must remember that history together with the affiliated studies are not exact sciences the results of which can be verified by numerous experiments. Many of the historical theories, even if supported by archaeological finds and discoveries, are based on interpretations and suppositions, and as such always remain hypotheses and seldom attain certainty and even probability. Consequently all "finds" in excavations and archaeological discoveries cannot invalidate an indigenous tradition of a people.

Whatever parallels to the principal contribution of Judaism, namely, monotheism, Oriental scholars claim to find in records of other nations antedating its manifestation among the Jews, cannot in reality minimize the originality of that contribution. Neither the poems of Ichnaton to the sun-god extolled to exaggeration by the late Egyptologist, Breasted, nor the Babylonian hymns to Sin, the moon-god, adduced by the same scholar and by Hugo Gressman and others as a proof for the origin of monotheism elsewhere, rise above mere flashes of a conception of the Godhead somewhat higher than the ordinary polytheistic notions. Aton is still identified with the sun, which has greater power than the other numerous natural forces, nor is the conception of Sin expressed in the Babylonian hymns on a much higher plane. The best that can be said of these poems and hymns is that they represent glimpses on the part of some religious spirit into a higher realm of religion, usually designated as henotheism,[1] but do not approach monotheism. That these expressions were merely

[1] Henotheism is a term used by scholars to designate a state of religion intermediate between polytheism and monotheism, namely, when a people assigns supreme power to one God, usually its national God, while admitting the existence of other gods in a more or less subordinate position. The term was coined by Max Müller who himself gave to it at different times several meanings. Other scholars likewise introduced into it various nuances, but the above definition is the most general.—See Hastings' *Encyclopaedia of Religion and Ethics,* Vol. VIII, pp. 810b–811a.

occasional leaps into a more elevated stratum of spirituality and not an organized religious trend which exerted influence on the lives of the Egyptians and Babylonians can be seen from their ephemeral character. Ichnaton's reforms and views were like the fluttering of the passing wind and left no trace in the life and religion of Egypt, while the sentiments of Babylonian hymns were only the expressions of an individual priest and never attained recognition by larger groups.

The monotheism of Judaism not only presents a systematized and well-organized set of ideas, but is the very foundation of the life of the people, of its nationhood, and the spirit and power of its existence through the ages. In none of the passages of the Old Testament, even in those frequently designated as anthropomorphic and very often cited by scholars as proof for the incomplete conception of the Godhead in early periods of Jewish history, is monotheism really impaired. Only prejudice, conscious or unconscious, reads into them that meaning.[2] Nor can we leave unchallenged the various assertions made by numerous scholars that the creation idea was borrowed from Babylonian mythology.

It may be admitted that a detailed description of the creation of the world, an act which in its general conception is universal, should incorporate some features which find parallels in the religions of neighboring and related Semites, the parallels being expressed primarily in a phrase or a name. But the essence of the creation conception as well as its entire setting, as told in the Book of Genesis, is purely monothe-

[2] As an illustration of that prejudice we can cite the statement of Breasted. "The very name Yahveh, being a proper name like Apollo or Mercury, implied the existence of other gods with similar personal names; and in the first commandment that Yahveh laid upon the Israelites He Himself recognized the existence of other gods ,when he said: 'Thou shalt have no other gods before me'" (*Dawn of Conscience,* p. 352). The misinterpretation of the commandment is patent to every objective reader, for a lawgiver, speaking in the name of God to a people living in a world where the belief in many gods is the order of the day, could not use any other language, but warn them not to fall into the ordinary human habit and follow the ways of others by having other gods. Only by reading into these very plain words the preconceived notion could any such admission of the existence of other gods be wrung from them. As for the meaning of the name Yahveh see below.

istic, and stems from the very concept of the unity of the Godhead. To the religious men in all times, God is not an abstract First Cause or a principle of motion, but a Being who is active and has a definite relation to the world and man. Consequently, it follows from the very concept of one God that the world is His handiwork. And since monotheism is the very foundation of Judaism, creation necessarily follows. In the entire story of creation, both in the first and second chapters of Genesis, there is no reference to other participants in that grand act,[3] nor is there any mention of any struggle with resisting forces, as is the case with other descriptions of creation in the literature of the Babylonians. There can therefore not be any authentic basis to the theory of borrowing or to the view that the story of creation in Genesis was composed under the influence of Babylonian creation myths.

Likewise there is a considerable lack of substantiation for the theories and views by almost all Biblical scholars who espouse the critical view that pure monotheism was attained by the Jews only in the 8th century B. C. E. through the influence of the Prophets. These theories popular among scholars—also many Jewish scholars—cannot claim either certainty or even probability. In fact, the very basis upon which they are founded, namely the documentary theory which broke up the Pentateuch into various sources composed at different dates much later than the one assumed by tradition, and shattered numerous sections and verses into fragments, has of late been discredited by many scholars. On the whole, there is noticeable a general trend towards a more conservative view regarding the composition of the Pentateuch, attributing to it an earlier date and more wholeness and unity of composition. However, the real weakness of the view which draws a dividing line in the history of Judaism recognizing in

[3] There is only one expression in the first version of the creation of man in Genesis I which is in the plural, verse 26, which reads: "And God said, 'Let us make man in our image and after Our likeness.'" But the usage of the plural in this verse is most likely a *pluralis majestatis,* for it is not repeated either in this version of the creation or in the second version of creation of man in the second chapter.

it two stages, the pre-Prophetic and the Prophetic, and designating the former as henotheistic and only the latter as monotheistic, consists in the fact that it contradicts the words and the content of the Prophets themselves as well as their action.

We are told in the First Book of Kings (XIX, 15) that after Elijah's sojourn at Mt. Horeb, he was told by God to go to Damascus and anoint Hazael as King of Aram. Whoever the compiler of the Book of Kings was,[4] he drew his material from earlier records, and there is no doubt that this story dates from the time of Elijah who lived in the first half of the 9th century. The antiquity of the content of this passage is proved by the fact that the events in connection with which the various commissions were given by God to Elijah before his translation are told again in the Second Book of Kings, Ch. VIII, 7–15 and Ch. IX, 7–9, though in the first instance the name of Elisha is substituted for Elijah. The mere positing of an act like this, namely, interference on the part of a Prophet in the most important political affair of a neighboring nation stronger than Israel, proves that the belief in a pure monotheism, i.e. in a God who rules the world and is as powerful in any part of it as in the land of Israel, was not only already centuries old in the days of Elijah but fundamental. Were the case otherwise, were that conception a mere evolution from henotheism to monotheism just taking place at the time of Elijah, such a commission would be unthinkable. A Prophet who had only recently reached such a religious notion would not have dared to undertake a mission like this, nor would such an act be recorded by any contemporary writer. And certainly we cannot attribute the story of the act to the later compiler or redactor as the injection of a later concept into an earlier time, for why should he invent an act which by its very character is unique in the entire history of the Old Testament? It has, as far as I know, no parallel in any other ancient literature. There are, of course, numerous hymns and

[4] According to the Talmud the compiler was Jeremiah (*Baba Batra*, 14b). The modern critical view differs little from the Talmudic inasmuch as it assumes that the compiler was a contemporary of Jeremiah and a follower of his school. See Driver, *Introduction to the Old Testament*, p. 190.

songs of praise in Egyptian and Babylonian literature where certain gods, whether Amon, Ra, Bel, Marduk, etc., are extolled because they gave victory to the arms of the respective kings who conquered kings and rulers of other nations, removed them from their thrones, and set others in their place. But in all these the god helps the arms of the worshippers and subdues the weaker god of the conquered nation. But nowhere are we told that such an act was performed by a messenger of a god in a neighboring country in peaceful times. And if we add to it the simplicity of the narrative which tells of the act in a matter-of-fact manner as an ordinary occurrence, we may conclude that such an attitude can stem only from a centuries-old conviction in the hearts of at least a large stratum of the people, that there is only one God in the universe whose command must be obeyed by all nations if He chooses to utter it.

Greater support for our thesis can be derived from the words and prophecies of Amos. He is considered by all Biblical scholars as the first of the great Prophets whose utterances were preserved and who, according to the scholars, were the original expounders of the doctrine of monotheism. He is also the first of the Prophets who injected the idea of exile [5] into Judaism and into the history of the Jews. In his warnings to his people to avoid sin and not to transgress the commandments of God, he threatens them with the dire punishment of exile. This threat is of great significance and a fact pregnant with importance to which little attention has thus far been paid by Biblical students. It is a unique phenomenon in the history of nations that a people or its leading spiritual representatives should dare think of such a fate. Every nation of antiquity indeed attributed to its god or gods the power to punish it in various ways by pestilence, drought, etc., but never thought of punishment by exile for two reasons. First, a limited and a national god has no power over any other na-

[5] It is true that exile and expulsion are mentioned in Leviticus XXVI, 33, and also in Deuteronomy XXVIII, 36. The critics, however, assign both of these books to later dates than Amos, Deuteronomy to the last quarter of the 7th century and Leviticus to the exilic or even post-exilic period.

tion to make it agree to the settlement of another people in its midst. Secondly, and which is more important, exile meant not only the punishment of the people but also of the god himself, for the moment the exiled god comes within the domain of another national god, he must be subjected to him. It is only a universal God who can decree exile for His people and not suffer by it.

Moreover, the concept of exile carries within it the idea of the extension of divine providence over the people in a foreign land and God's ability to exercise His power throughout the world. For the exile spoken of by Amos as well as by all the other Prophets never implies dissolution and assimilation of the people, but signifies only a temporary chastisement, and is constantly accompanied by promises of a return, even if that may be extended only to a remnant. Consequently, the idea of preservation in foreign lands by divine power follows necessarily from the utterances of chastisement by this and other Prophets to their people. We shall later see that the coupling of the two apparently contrary ideas, exile and return, exercised a powerful influence upon the development of the history of the Jewish people. For the present, we may draw from the statement of Amos, who was followed by the other Prophets regarding the exile and the return of the people, the plausible conclusion that monotheism in its pure form was not a novel idea attained ultimately by the Prophets, but was centuries old, known to wide circles in Israel as the very foundation of their religion. Otherwise, the threat would have been useless, for it would have been unintelligible to the people. That this was not the case is evident from the vehement protest of Amaziah, the High Priest of Beth-El, who sent to King Jeroboam the following message: "Amos hath conspired against thee in the midst of the House of Israel; the land is not able to bear his words. For thus Amos saith, 'Jeroboam shall die by the sword and Israel shall be exiled from his land'" (Amos VII, 10, 11). We note that he does not say that his words are baseless, but emphasizes the fact that they spread terror in the land, for people will be disheartened, which shows that the belief in a universal God was widespread and age-old.

Though we have gone somewhat at length in the matter of deducing proof for the plausibility of Jewish tradition against current theories, it should be emphasized that the authenticity of the entire tradition was never doubted by the Jews nor does tradition show any inner contradiction, nor is the language in any place ambiguous regarding monotheism being the special heritage of the Jews. The Bible speaks explicitly in numerous places of the divine revelation at Sinai, and this event was never doubted even by the most liberal thinkers in Jewry, either by those who belonged to the body of the Jewish people or by those of the various sects which arose from time to time, such as the Sadducees in ancient times or the Karaites in the Middle Ages. Moreover, the divine origin of the Torah including the laws was established as a fundamental dogma of Judaism by all leading Jewish theologians, even by those who in their time were considered liberal and even radical, as Maiominides and others who followed him.[6] It is true that the philosophical theologians attempted to interpret certain features in the Sinaitic revelation as well as explain a number of laws in a more rational way than the literal meaning of the words convey. But these do not in any way throw doubt on revelation as a fact, nor on the view that the laws are divinely ordered, though they asserted that a number of them could be attained by human reason.

It is because the views of the critics, spoken of above, have become so popular in wide circles, both scholarly and nonscholarly, among Jews and non-Jews, and have even been in-

[6] Though Hasdai Crescas, a leading Jewish philosopher, and his disciple, Joseph Albo, an outstanding dogmatist, differ with Maimonides in regard to counting divine origin of the Torah among the fundamental dogmas of Judaism, yet the difference is only a formal and not an actual one, for they too consider both revelation and divine ordering of the law as elemental in faith, but they place them for certain reasons as necessary corollaries from other dogmas. See the writer's essay "Maimonides as a Dogmatist" in the *Year Book of the Central Conference of American Rabbis,* 1935, also his essay (in Hebrew) on "Albo's Theory of Dogmas in Judaism and its Relation to his Contemporaries Hasdai Crescas and Simon Duran" in *Hatekufah,* Vol. XXX–XXXI, pp. 712–745.

corporated in several Jewish histories, that the attempt has been made to prove on historical and logical grounds the plausibility of the tradition and to assert that its authenticity is by no means shattered by the evidence on which the critical and scientific views are based. The fact remains that of all the nations, including those of antiquity, whose attainment in material and secular culture greatly surpassed that of Israel, only this little nation on the shores of the Mediterranean emerging comparatively late from a nomadic state was the one which conceived the idea of monotheism in its present form and made it the very essence of its life and history. And simultaneously, it evolved laws and ideals which were out of time and place, the nobility of which nobody can deny, and many of which humanity cannot attain even now, millennia after the Prophets announced them. Neither environment nor contact with neighboring nations can explain these phenomena, nor even the type of prophecy among the Jews which is unique in the history of religion. As a result, we may say that if one finds it difficult to accept the doctrine of their supernatural origin, he will have to find a place for them within the frame of the natural and attribute them to natural revelation, whether in the form of special genius or otherwise, but they will still remain inexplicable.

We were trying to establish the veracity of the tradition even from the point of view of historical science, namely, that the firm belief in one universal God with all that follows from it was indigenous in Israel from the moment it stepped forth on the arena of history. But that does not mean that this idea in its purity became immediately the share of every Jew and that it did not pass through a period of struggle for the complete dominance of the life of the people. On the contrary, almost all the books of the Old Testament, the historical as well as the prophetic, testify to the bitter struggle monotheism had to wage during the entire period of the First Commonwealth in order to become the share of the people as a whole.

It was only natural that it should be thus. An idea like monotheism, even if divinely revealed, could only become the firm conviction of the few and select, while the people as a whole could only have a vague idea of it. By its very nature monotheism, thrown into a world of polytheism, could only appear to the mass of a people, just emerging from a state of nomadism, as an ideal which they sincerely endeavored to attain, but from which they all too often fell short. It is little wonder that the Israelites, situated in an environment in which the religion was pagan, and its culture and civilization materially higher than theirs, and which possessed many attractive features appealing to the passions and physical appetites, constantly succumbed to the lure of the civilization of the neighbors. Hence the struggle and hence the swaying of the religious pendulum among the mass of the people between pure monotheism and one adulterated with pagan elements. It was left for the national catastrophe, the Exile, to accomplish the cure and make the religious heritage which was with them from the very beginning of their history the share of the entire people including even its lowest stratum.

Turning to the implications of the fundamental concept in Judaism, namely, the belief in one universal God as the factor in the life of the people which moulded its entire history and made it a people *sui generis,* we note the following. First, as stated above, out of the idea of one God, there follows as a corollary the creation of the world and man. For the very essence of God is activity, and since in addition all forces in nature are subservient to God, for He is the only all-powerful, it follows *eo ipso* that He is the Creator. Providence is another corollary, for a Creator is interested in His work, as the Psalmist says: "He that planted the ear, shall He not hear? He that formed the eye, shall He not see?" (Psalms XCIV, 9).

Likewise is the election of Israel a corollary of that fundamental concept, for when in a world of nations sunk in idolatry there rises only one small group possessing the unique idea of a universal God, it has full right to conclude that it was elected by divine providence for that task. This idea of election was strengthened by a subsidiary concept which is, that since all nations are essentially alike in the eyes of God—

for He is the Creator of man and Supervisor of nature and human activity—yet He chose to reveal Himself only to a small group. This group is then elected by His will. The nature and character of that election were determined by the following reason. The other nations are strong, powerful, and wealthy, while this elected nation suffers. The election could not be for power and material well being, but for a noble and moral purpose. There must also have been a cause for the election of this particular nation and tradition relates the cause. The ancestors of the nation were distinguished for their moral life, intense spirituality, and religious conception. Abraham, on whom, according to tradition, the exalted God idea in its full glory dawned first, was sorely tried time and again in order to test his sincerity, and he was not found wanting Hence he was chosen as the father of that stock which was destined to be elected, as the Torah distinctly says: "For I know him that he will command his children and his household after him, and they shall keep the way of the Lord to do justice and judgment, that the Lord may bring upon Abraham that which He hath spoken of him" (Genesis XVIII, 19). Hence followed the covenants at Sinai and other places between God and the people.

Election for a moral and religious purpose requires that the elected shall lead a distinct type of life calculated to realize the purpose and demonstrate its value. This cannot be accomplished without a set of laws, precepts, and regulations, and hence the Law with its numerous particulars which embraces all phases of the life of the Jews. There are, undoubtedly, as mentioned, similarities in the laws with those of other nations at the time, but even these are, if not externally, at least inwardly, different in content and essence.

Again, a covenant implies a duty on the part of the one who accepts it to carry out its stipulations, and a neglect of that duty brings the necessary reprisals. Hence, we meet with constant threats of punishment, both in the Pentateuch proper and in the Prophetic books. One of these punishments was, as pointed out previously, a unique note in the history of nations, namely, exile. It was this threat which cast its shadow upon the people early in its national life, which forms one of the principal factors in the subsequent tragic history of Israel and of Judaism.

The fact that Prophet after Prophet repeats this threat of exile together with the concurrent promise of restoration contributed to the formation of the peculiar character of the Jewish people through history, which displays two apparently contradictory phases yet seemed to have been simultaneously complementary. On the one hand, exile became a form of life in which the people not only managed to survive, but to which they managed to adjust themselves, and unlike other nations, which disappeared in foreign lands, thrived, and at times, even grew in strength. In other words, Israel made the conditions of its existence independent of land and boundaries. On the other hand, the hope for restoration to its former land and its striving to resettle there became an important factor in the existence and survival of Israel in the Diaspora. Thus we see that the life of the people presented the double aspect of being both dependent upon and independent of its former land. This unique phenomenon is inherently connected with several other ideas indigenous to Judaism which are in reality its substratum and source. The principal one is the idea of Messianism.

In that grand idea, which can be considered the second important Jewish contribution to the progress of humanity, there are to be noted two primary phases. In the earlier one, promulgated primarily by Isaiah, the restoration element is not in evidence, for the Jews at the time were still in their land, and exile was only foretold but not realized. It is an exalted vision of a future when all humanity will share the great religious ideals to which Judaism aspired and which it strove to realize in its own life, namely knowledge of God, justice, and righteousness, and consequently also peace, for when real justice dominates there is no cause for war. In other words, the divine selection of Israel for spiritual and moral purposes will extend to all nations. In fact, the original selection itself also was not intended for the exaltation of Israel alone, but rather for the exaltation of all humanity through its instrumentality. The Messianic vision represents the projection of that aim.

But soon the exile of the Ten Tribes took place and it was only natural that the promised restoration which was always joined to the threat of exile should become an integral part and an important element of the Messianic vision. And thus even Isaiah himself, after he drew the grand vision of the ideal future, when justice supervised by the scion of the House of David will reign throughout the world, delivered a prophecy of restoration [7] which is primarily national and less ideal in its content, and was considered a preliminary step in the realization of the grand vision. He in turn was followed by other prophets. As time went on and exile also overtook Judah and it became a permanent feature in the life of the people, the prophecies of restoration expanded and the future was drawn not only as a mere restoration but as a glorious time for Israel, both in a spiritual and temporal way.[8]

Thus the two phases, the universal rise to a high spirituality and the glorious national restoration, were amalgamated in an idea of Messianism which persisted in Judaism without essential change through the ages. That there were currents within Jewish life during the Second Commonwealth which attempted to separate the two concepts with the resultant establishment of a new religion is well known.

As a corollary of these ideas there developed the idea of

[7] There is no need to attribute the verses 11–16 in Ch. XI of Isaiah to another and later Prophet as is done by most modern commentators. The chapters in the Prophetic books do not necessarily represent single prophecies. They may contain several short ones which were delivered at different times. These verses represent the content of a prophecy spoken after the exile of the Ten Tribes into Assyrian provinces and hence Elam and Shinnar are included among the places of the Diaspora. As for the mention of upper and lower Egypt as places of Jewish settlement, it is possible that there were already Jewish colonies there even in the time of Hezekiah. It is well known from Josephus that Psametichus, King of Egypt, in the time of Josiah had Jews as mercenary soldiers in his army. Why then can we not assume that Jews settled in Egypt a generation or two earlier?

[8] See Isaiah Chaps. LX, LXI, LXII, which probably belong to a later Prophet.

the eternity of Israel, which was not only emphasized by the Prophets but was shared by the people themselves. This idea helped to make the Jews a people whom exile does not impair, for they rested secure in the belief in a divine guarantee that not only will they be restored but that they are destined for a great role in the history of humanity, even if the time for that role is designated only indefinitely by the term "the end of days." Such a nation cannot disappear.

It is this group of ideas which laid its impress upon Judaism and which served Israel during its long history as a tower of strength. For though accepting exile and attempting to adjust itself to its conditions—the people never made a serious attempt until recent times to return to its land—yet the firm and convincing hope of restoration and vision of its glorious future made it look upon exile as a passing phase in its life. Extent of time did not matter, for was it not given eternity? Armed by this spiritual strength it survived all attacks and all attempts to destroy it.

From the foregoing sketch of the logical coherence of the ideas within Judaism, all stemming from the fundamental concept of monotheism and together forming a distinct view of the world and life, we can draw the following two conclusions. First, that there is really no break or rift in Judaism between the earlier and later periods of its history, as is often asserted by many scholars who see in it two distinct types, the Biblical and post-Biblical, or as some call it, Judaism proper. All these ideas, which were dominant in Judaism throughout its history and form its backbone, already received their full expression in Biblical times. If there is any difference between these two periods, and difference there is bound to be, for Judaism, like all historical phenomena, went through a process of development, it is a difference in degree and not in kind and essence, as will be shown shortly. Secondly, in Judaism there is really no separation between the elements which, in the life of other nations, are considered as part of religion proper, and those which we call national. As we have seen, the tradition of the people emphatically insists that the very emergence of the group as a nation, the conquest of the land, its view of itself as a spiritually selected people, of its destiny in the future, its function in the history of humanity, its assured continued existence even in foreign lands, its very political and economic state laws, nay, even its military laws, all stem from divine acts or commandments. Unlike any other nation, it has no record of legislative assemblies or regal lawgivers, and furthermore, most of the laws are considered only as a means for the realization of that spiritual distinction embodied in the idea of selection. Nor were the few military heroes admired and honored in the memory of the people because of their physical prowess, but because of their being instruments in the hand of God to carry out definite purposes in the divine scheme of things. Even the greatest military king, David, who converted the small kingdom of Israel into a fair-sized empire, was honored by the later generations more as the "sweet singer of Israel," as the author of the Psalms, than the mighty conqueror and fearless leader on the battlefield.

Yet, though these phases already have their origin and expression in Biblical times, the full fruition of Judaism as a complete way of life, as an amalgam of religion and essence of nationhood, took place in the immediate post-Biblical period. It is then that Judaism reached its climax and became what it was during the millennia. The difference, as said, was one of degree, consisting primarily in the intensity and extent of the hold the complex group of these ideas, and especially the Law, had upon the life of the people.

We have already noted that Judaism in the Biblical period was engaged in a severe struggle to make its fundamental ideas the share of the mass of the people who were constantly lured away by the blandishments of foreign civilizations into pagan beliefs and practices. It stands to reason that the Law, namely, those precepts and commandments which appertain to other phases of life besides the socio-ethical, was not observed to a great extent by the people at large. But with the Exile, contrary to expectations, the situation was changed. The sojourn in a foreign land sobered the people and weaned them from the allurement of paganism and brought about a clarification in the minds of the people of their conception of monotheism and the whole complex of ideas inherent in it. And since after the return, political life was reduced to a minimum, the people turned to the spiritual values in order to continue in integrity the role as a selected and distinct people. Of course, that change of emphasis was not accomplished without any struggle, as is evidenced by the activity of Ezra and Nehemiah, but after that was over, the process was completed. Henceforth, there was no more rebellion against the Law and its numerous details; on the contrary, there arose an insatiable desire to know more and more about the Law, to observe all its details, and if necessary, to expand it and add to it so that it might embrace all phases of life. As a result, the Torah became the constitution of the national life, and the scholars became legislators, and consequently, the amalgamation of religion and national life was complete.

True, as long as there was a political life of whatever proportions in existence, there were struggles against the completeness of amalgamation and the all-encompassiveness of Judaism. From time to time, there were outbursts of secularism and pure political tendencies. The Maccabees who, with great zeal and fortitude, entered an unequal struggle with the Syro-Greeks on behalf of religious freedom, ultimately became kings under whose rule the political aspect played an important role. There arose the party of the Sadducees which apparently had a more secular view of life. Yet there was no rebellion against the Law nor was there a rift between the religious and the national elements. The Maccabees were not only kings but simultaneously high priests; the Sadducees never rebelled against the Law and undoubtedly observed it zealously, but sought to circumscribe its area. The Pharisees never minimized the values of national life and were as zealous in the defense of their country as the Sadducees, but they championed a complete amalgamation in Judaism of religious and national elements. What is more, they transformed, in accordance with the spirit of the Torah itself, these national and political tasks into religious duties and commandments of such degree that at times their performance took precedence over purely religious duties. As an instance we can cite the law, dating from Hasmonean times, which allows the waging of war, even an offensive one, on the Sabbath.

With the loss of the remnant of political life in the year 70 C. E. the circle of Judaism was widened and became all-inclusive. For almost two thousand years, the world witnessed a remarkable phenomenon, how Judaism, which is to all intents and purposes a religion, yet penetrated the deepest recesses of the life of a people and with its mantle of holiness covered every element of life, even the most secular and most ordinarily human, including the desire for settlement in the ancient home. It became a complex in which religion, race, and the memory of a distant land were so inextricably bound together that henceforth none could separate the elements. A people, scattered to the four winds of the world, yet lived constantly in the shadow of a former distant land. Not only does that land together with the historical phase form the very bases of the most important holidays of its calendar, but that land intruded itself in numerous ways in the life of the people and penetrated to its very heart. The people prayed regularly for rain in the fall and dew in the spring, not because it was needed by them; the rain would only have increased the mud in the crooked streets of the ghetto wherein they were confined, and the dew would have been of little value to the soil of the lands wherein they dwelt. Yet they did pray semi-annually for these gifts for the sake of the land wherein they had formerly dwelt, where these gifts in the proper season were of primary importance, prayed even though the soil did not belong to them and the accrued benefits were enjoyed by others. The people still thought of the land as theirs, possession by others and the law of conquest notwithstanding. Even such a secular element of culture as language was wrapped in the mantle of holiness, and Hebrew was for centuries known as *Leshon ha-Kodesh*, the holy language, and its use was considered by a number of Rabbis a quasi-religious performance. There were numerous pious Jews who, in their desire to impart additional sanctity to the Sabbath, abstained from using on that day the ordinary vernacular and spoke only Hebrew.

It is superfluous to say that the integrity of the Jewish people, its existence, survival, and all that these imply in their numerous manifestations, were considered fundamental parts of Judaism. For is not Judaism the share and heritage of Israel, both the nation and the religion being interminably joined together as, to use a well known Rabbinic phrase, the flame and the light which it emits? Were the one to be extinguished, the other would also disappear. We can thus see how Jewish nationhood is inextricably bound with Judaism. Consequently, it follows that one who is a Jew by birth is *eo ipso* a sharer in the whole spiritual and cultural complex which we call Judaism, not only through physical laws of heredity, but from the religious and legal point of view as well. One born a Jew may repudiate that heritage and transgress most or all of the commandments of his religion, but Judaism does not repudiate him. He is, of course, considered a transgressor, but is to all intents and purposes a Jew and holds certain rights. Even conversion does not sever a Jew entirely from Judaism, for he still has some rights, such as the right of inheritance, unless deprived thereof by a special act of court.[9] Judaism has thus absorbed also the element of race, for though the tie of the individual to the group in which he was born is considered today a secular matter, Judaism superimposed upon it a religious bond.

It does not, however, follow from this that Judaism does not welcome proselytes. It accepts any one who wants to join the group and embrace its ideals, aspirations, laws, and is ready to suffer if necessary for their sake. It is felt that these will ultimately be absorbed in the House of Israel.

It was this unique character of Judaism which, as noted, is a complex of a number of phases in which the secular and the purely religious were so integrally amalgamated that no

[9] *Shulḥan Aruk, Ḥoshen Mishpat,* Sec. 281.

separation can be successfully effected, which dominated the life of Israel for the larger part of its history, and laid its impress upon its numerous manifestations. Consequently, no one born a Jew can ever divest himself from Judaism entirely no matter how much he may strive to attain this complete emancipation, for much of the spirit of Judaism, physical tendencies, even abilities and inclination, come by heredity. This can be accomplished only by generations of total assimilation, a process in which the continual diminution of Jewish blood is an important factor.

However, the very variegated character of Judaism, in which phases originally of different nature are blended, encouraged attempts in modern times on the parts of groups of Jews to separate the elements, disregard some, and emphasize others at the expense of the former. The Reformists minimized the value of the Law, excluded the element of Jewish nationhood from Judaism,[10] and emphasized the ethical and a part of the religious aspect. On the other hand, there arose some who cling tenaciously to the national element in Judaism, emphasize the value of language and literature, and other elements which are more secular, but in the type of Judaism which they advocate the religious element has a strange flavor. In their attempt to reconstruct and to revaluate, the laws are turned into mores and folkways, and the source from which there stem all the important and leading religious ideas, namely, the concept of the Godhead, is emptied of its content and turned into something indefinite, the function of which in life and history cannot be determined. Between these there are several other attempts to separate the elements in Judaism in greater or lesser degree. There is no doubt that the values these groups emphasize are parts of Judaism, but by no means has any one representative of any group the right to say, "This is Judaism." It may be the conception of Judaism of his group

[10] For a succinct but comprehensive account of the principle of Reform Judaism in its original pristine nature, see the author's work "A History of Jewish Literature," Vol. III. In the last two decades, however, a number of its leaders have changed their attitude towards nationalism, but this does not change its central position.

which, of course, will prove erroneous by the light of the Old Testament in its entirety—not by single quotations—the entire Talmudic, Rabbinic, and philosophic and theological literature, and above all, by that of the greater part of the long history of the Jewish people. Judaism is that which, as stated, contains all the elements in an integral form. It was thus through the ages and will undoubtedly continue to be in the future. With the rise of political life in Palestine and changed economic conditions, modifications in laws may become necessary and the position of the elements in Judaism may change, but the fundamental character of the all-embraciveness of Judaism will remain even if that character will only be the share of a part of the Jews.

PART I

THE INSTITUTIONS OF JUDAISM

Chapter I

THE SABBATH

1. General Characteristics

Of the many religious institutions established by Judaism, the Sabbath is the most important one. In fact, it is one of the principal contributions of the Jews to humanity at large. It is through the medium of the two great daughter-religions of Judaism that civilized nations the world over set aside one day a week as a day of rest, pleasure, and meditation. Even the highly civilized nations of antiquity, such as the Babylonians, the Egyptians, the Greeks, and the Romans, had no conception of a Sabbath. An attempt was made by an unfriendly non-Jewish scholar to deny the origin of the Sabbath and to derive it from a quasi-similar festival or days of rest of the Babylonians, but this theory was thoroughly refuted by almost all Semitists of authority.[1]

The Greeks and Romans were even hostile and antagonistic to the idea of a weekly day of rest. The Sabbath was the most frequent target of the quips and epigrams of the Roman poets and satirists. Characteristic of this attitude is the statement by the famous Stoic philosopher and moralist, Seneca, who says: "Jewish superstition, especially the Sabbath, is reprehensible, for by refusing to work every seventh day, they (the Jews)

[1] The Babylonian days of rest followed the four phases of the moon during the month, namely, the 7th, 14th, 21st, 28th, and consequently were not fixed at the end of the week but were changeable and took place on any day of the week. On the whole, they were considered evil days, and work was prohibited because the days were unlucky. They were days of fasting and propitiation rather than days of rest and joy. See Fr. Hommel, *Die altorientalischen Denkmäler und das alte Testament,* p. 18; also Hastings' *Encyclopaedia of Religion and Ethics,* article, Sabbath, Vol. X, 889–891.

lose a seventh part of their life in idleness, and many important matters are neglected." [2]

The Jewish people cherished the Sabbath as the most precious gift of their religion, and the entire literature is filled with maxims and proverbs extolling its value and worth, several of which we will quote here: "With the arrival of the Sabbath, there arrives rest to the body and the soul" (Sanhedrin 38a). "On the Sabbath one experiences a sixtieth part of the pleasure prepared for the righteous in the world to come" (Berakot 56).[3] The famous modern essayist and social philosopher, Aḥad ha-Am, said: "Much more than the Jews observed and preserved the Sabbath, the Sabbath preserved them."

2. The Sabbath as Symbol of Human Equality and Dignity

The Torah offers two different reasons for the institution of the Sabbath. The first, as stated in the version of the Ten Commandments in Exodus (Exodus XX, 11), can be termed the cosmic, inasmuch as it emphasizes its connection with the creation of the world, saying: "For in six days the Lord made heaven and earth, the sea, and all that in them is, and resteth on the seventh day; wherefore the Lord blessed the Sabbath day and hallowed it." The holiness of the Sabbath is, then, according to this version, primordial, hailing from creation. The Deuteronomy version offers an historical basis. "And remember that thou wast a servant in the land of Egypt, and that the Lord, thy God, brought thee out thence by a mighty hand and by a stretched-out arm; therefore, the Lord, thy God, commandeth thee to keep the Sabbath" (Deuteronomy V, 15). This verse implies that by resting on the Sabbath we recall the beginning of our history, the Exodus, for in Egypt we could not rest, as we were slaves and not free men.

[2] Quoted by Theodor Reinach in his *Texts d'auteurs Grecs et Romains relatifs au Judaisme,* p. 362. The passage is found in a Ms. treatise on superstition by Seneca.

[3] On the meaning of the concept of the world to come, see Pt. II.

Without discussing the various theories advanced in explanation of the two reasons given for the observance of the Sabbath, we may note that both reasons presuppose an ideal substratum or a premise, that is, the value of man as man. Man is not to be lowered to the status of work-animals for whom time has one meaning without distinction. Man must rest in order to rise spiritually. Hence the Torah says more by way of a symbol—for it is impossible to take it literally, as the term rest does not apply to God—that even God rested upon completion of creation. And when man subjects his fellow-man, enslaving him and depriving him of his elemental right to rest, it is a sin against God as well as against the inmost nature of man. Hence, in order to emphasize the latter view of the Sabbath, God commanded us to observe the Sabbath so that we may remember the Exodus which freed us from bondage, for the destiny of man is to be free; and when, through political and social conditions, some are subjected by their fellow-men and are enslaved by them, then they possess at least one fundamental right which, by divine command, cannot be taken from them—the right to rest. This idea is embodied in the very words of the commandment concerning the Sabbath, which read: "But the seventh day is the Sabbath of the Lord, thy God; in it thou shalt not do any work, thou, nor thy son, nor thy daughter, nor thy man-servant, nor thy maid-servant, nor thine ox, nor thine ass, nor any of thy cattle, nor any stranger that is within thy gates, that thy man-servant and thy maid-servant may rest as well as thou" (Deuteronomy V, 14). Here we have a clear enunciation of the principle of the equality of all men no matter what their station in life may be. Men may differ, through conditions, as far as labor is concerned, but they are equal in regard to rest—this right belongs to all.[4]

[4] The rest enjoined for animals is based primarily on the fact that animals cannot work by themselves and their labor involves also the labor of men, and, of course, there is also the element of mercy. That equality is emphasized in the law of the Sabbath can be deduced from the fact that in the Deuteronomy version of the Decalogue the enjoinment of rest for servants is repeated at the end of the verse with the addition that "they may rest as well as thou."

The Sabbath, then, is the primary source whence, through the ages, the idea of human equality was derived, an ideal for the attainment of which humanity has struggled for millennia.

3. Types of Labor Prohibited on the Sabbath

Since the essence of the Sabbath is rest, or, in other words, cessation from work—the verb *Shabat* means to cease—it follows that the observance of the Sabbath consists primarily in abstaining from work. In fact, the Torah enjoins Israel a number of times not to desecrate the Sabbath by performing any labor (Exodus XX, 10, XXIII, 12, XXXI, 15, XXXV, 2; Deuteronomy V, 14), and in two places (Exodus XXXI, 15 and XXXV, 2) it even prescribes the penalty of death for wilful and public desecration. But the question arises, what does the term *work* connote? The Torah is not explicit on that subject. It only mentions two instances of labor forbidden on the Sabbath, one directly, and the other, indirectly. The first is the prohibition against kindling fire on the Sabbath (Exodus XXXV, 3), and the second is a record of a man who was condemned to death for desecrating the Sabbath during a journey in the desert. The desecration is described by the ambiguous term *Mekoshesh Eẓim.* The word *Mekoshesh* denotes to gather or to cord and also to splinter. There are, therefore, two opinions in the Talmud, one interpreting the term as splintering wood and the other as cording, both of which acts were considered prohibited. These instances are, of course, insufficient. The Oral Law, the function of which is to explain more explicitly what is implicitly contained in the Biblical injunctions, accordingly found a method of defining the term labor,[5] and, as a result, the Mishnah enumerates thirty-nine classes of labor which are prohibited on the Sabbath. The kind of labor which heads each class is called *Ab*, i.e., father

[5] The method is by analogy, namely, the term labor or *Melakah* is found in the description of the construction of the *Mishkan* (Tabernacle). There the term includes a certain number of labors without which the Tabernacle could not have been set up and equipped. That number consists of thirty-nine types or classes of labor. Hence it was concluded that the same term in regard to the Sabbath is similarly inclusive of the same number.

or head of family; the other labors included in the class are called *Toladot,* i.e., descendants. The members of the class possess an essential resemblance to the head, e.g., grinding is considered the head of a class, but the cutting of vegetables very fine—not to be used for food—is considered a descendant. All these labors are equally forbidden and if wilfully or publicly performed are severely punishable. The difference between *Ab* and *Toladah* exists only when labors are performed erroneously on the Sabbath either through ignorance or forgetfulness. In such cases, during Temple times, the sinner was obliged to bring a sin offering. The difference between *Ab* and *Toladah* was then evident; if one performed two labors, an *Ab* and a *Toladah,* he brought only one offering, while if they were both of the grade of *Ab,* he brought two.

The thirty-nine classes of labors, as enumerated in the Mishnah, bear the stamp of the simple industries prevalent in Biblical times, such as planting, sowing, reaping, cording, weaving, sewing, writing, building, and similar labors. But by analogy and similarity numerous types of labor can be included under these classes.

In addition to the thirty-nine classes prohibited by Biblical command and by the Rabbinic interpretation of the term "labor" in the Pentateuch, there are a number of lighter types of labor or even of quasi-labors which are prohibited by Rabbinical ordinances. The reason for their prohibition is that they constitute "a fence around the law," namely, were they permitted their performance would ultimately lead to the desecration of the Sabbath. The technical term for such prohibitions is *Shebut,* i.e., these labors are prohibited because they may result in breaking or disturbing the rest on the Sabbath.

We will cite a few examples of these types of labors: (1) It is forbidden to ride a horse or any other animal on the Sabbath even when the animals do not belong to the rider—the Torah itself enjoins rest for animals one owns—not because riding in itself constitutes labor, but because the rider may have to break off a branch from a tree in order to whip an obstreperous animal. (2) It is prohibited for a Jew to order a Gentile to perform any work for him. Moreover, if the Gentile performs the task expressly on behalf of the Jew even without being asked, the Jew is prohibited from enjoying its fruits. (3) Doing business on the Sabbath, that is buying and selling merchandise, even when no labor is involved, is likewise prohibited. It is quite evident that in the enacting of these ordinances the Rabbis had an eye rather to the spirit than to the letter of the law, for some of these quasi-labors, such as buying and selling, violate the very intention of the Sabbath, which is to rest from all occupation aiming at material benefit or pursuit of gain. In regard to riding or traveling modern conditions undoubtedly invalidate the original reason for this prohibition, yet it is still observed and with justice, for once traveling is permitted on the Sabbath, it becomes difficult to draw the line between a journey for pure pleasure and one for the pursuit of gain. An institution like the Sabbath which aims at the elevation of human life cannot allow deviations based on subjective distinctions.

It is worthwhile to note that these prohibitions, though called Rabbinical, are not ordinances enacted by rigorous pietists, but have their roots deep in Jewish life, some having been observed even in Biblical times, for they arose from the proper conception of the nature of the Sabbath.

Thus, Amos, in reproaching the people for their greed, says to them: "You say impatiently, 'When will the new moon be gone that we may sell corn, and the Sabbath that we may set forth the wheat, making the *Ephah* small, the *Shekel* great, and falsifying the balance by deceit'" (Amos VIII, 5). From this statement it is clear that the people in his time, even the greedy, abstained from doing business on the Sabbath. Again, Nehemiah ordered the gates of Jerusalem closed to the Tyrian merchants on the Sabbath so that the people should not buy on that day (Nehemiah XIII, 15–22).

While we do not intend to enumerate the thirty-nine classes of labor and discuss them in detail, we will make one exception and describe one type more adequately because of its influence on Jewish life, at least in the near past, that is, carrying a burden on the Sabbath. Carrying things on the Sabbath is, like many other kinds of labor, not specifically mentioned in the Bible, although one Talmudic interpretation finds reference to it in the verse in Exodus XVI, 29, but it is included by the bearers of the Oral Law under the thirty-nine principal labors. However, this prohibition was in force even in Biblical times, for it was understood that the carrying of burdens violates the Sabbath rest, both in its literal and in its spiritual meaning. We therefore find Jeremiah thundering against such violators of the Sabbath, saying: "Thus saith the Lord, 'Take heed to yourselves and carry no burden on the Sabbath day, nor bring it in by the gates of Jerusalem'" (Jeremiah XVII, 21). Likewise Nehemiah tells us: "I set some of my servants at the gates that no burdens should be brought in on the Sabbath day" (Nehemiah XIII, 19). And while it is true that these prohibitions refer to carrying of burdens for the purpose of selling their contents, yet it can be safely inferred, especially from the words of Jeremiah, that the carrying of any burden was considered a violation of the Sabbath.

Every labor, though, has certain limitations in quantity and quality. Since the carrying of burdens is a most frequent and significant type of labor, the Mishnah devotes two chapters to determine the quantitative minimi for different types of burdens (Sabbath, Chaps. VIII, IX). Carrying, however, also has a spatial limitation, as it is prohibited only in certain places, primarily in a public thoroughfare. Accordingly, a Tanaitic statement (*Tosefta* Sabbath) says that there are four places for which regulations in regard to carrying or moving any objects were established. These are: *Reshut ha-Yaḥid* (private places); *Reshut ha-Rabim* (public thoroughfare); *Karmilit* (a place the status of which is neither the former nor the latter); and *Mekom Petur*.

Under the first are included all places belonging to a private person which are fenced around to the height of approximately two cubits.* In such places all objects may be carried or moved. The second includes public streets, sixteen cubits wide, which are visited by multitudes. In such places, carrying, moving, or throwing of objects is prohibited, and transgressors are subject to punishment. Moreover it is forbidden to transfer things from one place to the other, i.e., from a private place to a public, and vice versa.

Of the other two, *Karmilit* embraces all places which are fenced around but do not reach the required height and have a minimum width of four *Tefaḥim.* The term is furthermore applied to places which are wide and long and not fenced around, but are not frequented by people, such as rivers, lakes, seas, and fields. In all of these, carrying, moving, and throwing of objects as well as transferring them is prohibited by a later Rabbinical ordinance, but the transgressor is not subject to punishment. The *Mekom Petur* includes places which are higher than three *Tefaḥim,* but are narrow, less than four *Tefaḥim* wide. These have the same status as a private place which is fenced around, but in this case it needs no fence and may even be located in a thoroughfare. There are, of course, certain variations in these regulations into the particulars of which we cannot enter, but this is the general outline of the laws regarding the carrying of burdens on the Sabbath.

We must not, however, overlook the fact that the prohibition against carrying on the Sabbath, even things of light weight, resulted in considerable hardship upon the people. Consequently, the Rabbis endeavored to find legal means to somewhat mitigate the difficulties. And as a result, we have a device known as the *Erub* by means of which carrying of burdens necessary for the maintenance of the comforts of life are permitted even in a public street. The importance of the *Erub* can be gauged from the fact that a whole tractate of the Talmud is devoted to the discussion of its particulars. It performed a very useful function in the life of the Jews of the

* Literally ten *Tefaḥim,* a *Tefaḥ* being the size of a fist or the breadth of the palm. A cubit, about nineteen inches, consists of six *Tefaḥim*—ten *Tefaḥim* is 1 and 4/6 cubits.

near past inasmuch as it lessened some of the rigors of the Sabbath. In fact, while conditions in modern urban life make the establishment of the *Erub* impossible, it is still employed in many Jewish communities in the East, and was also utilized in numerous towns in Eastern Europe before the War.

The device of the *Erub* consists in changing the status of the streets of a town from that of public to private property, i.e., from *Reshut ha-Rabim* to *Reshut ha-Yaḥid,* by affixing at the end of each street a wire supported on two poles, thus achieving the effect of an entrance or a door. The street is then considered fenced around, for the two rows of houses are then regarded as fences. Consequently, it loses the status of a public thoroughfare where carrying of objects is prohibited. It is, of course, understood that this device applies primarily to small towns where the streets have the aspect of court-yards—the type of town where the majority of the Jews in European countries lived—and not to large, wide plazas where multitudes of people pass. The name *Erub* is derived from the root *Arab,* to mix or to combine. In this case, it denotes the fact that legally the individual houses or the street form a continuous fence and the houses are considered as jointly-owned property.

In addition to this type of *Erub,* there is also another called *Erub Teḥumim,* which likewise aims at a mitigation of another phase of the Sabbath law, referring to the distance one is permitted to walk on the Sabbath. *Tehum* means a boundary or a limit in space. It is stated in the Pentateuch in regard to the Sabbath: "Let no man go out of his place on the seventh day" (Exodus XVI, 29). This statement is not explicit, for it could not be taken literally as it would turn the Sabbath into a day of gloom instead of one of joy. The interpretation of the Oral Law is that the term "place" in the verse means the distance one covers when taking a walk for pleasure, and the Rabbis determined that distance to be 2000 cubits—about three fifths of a mile—on either side of the town he resides in. In other words, he can walk through the entire town, no matter how large, plus 2000 cubits on either side. Beyond that it is not considered a walk but a forced hike which wearies and disturbs the rest. However, if one needs or desires to walk beyond the limit of 2000 cubits, a legal device is available. Before sunset on Friday, an amount of food sufficient for two meals may be placed at the end of the 2000 cubit limit thus symbolizing the transference of residence. Consequently, one is permitted an extension of 2000 cubits from the new point of residence. One need not, however, remain there through the entire Sabbath but may return to his town or village after depositing the food.

Allied to the laws of *Erub* are the regulations concerning the removal and carrying of certain vessels and objects even in the house. The technical term for the prohibition to remove or carry such objects is *Muktze,* derived from the verb *Kotzah,* meaning to move, separate, or to devote to a definite purpose. It signifies that the use of the object or vessel is devoted primarily to weekday affairs. The principle involved in such prohibition is to inculcate the sanctity of the Sabbath and its distinction from the week days. Were the tinkering with and the moving around of such objects permitted, complete Sabbath rest would hardly be observed; these actions would bear the aspect of work. In addition, such occupation may also lead to actual violation of the Sabbath as men in carrying around such objects or vessels may inadvertently repair them if any were broken or experiment with their use and thus perform work on the Sabbath. The prohibition belongs then to the class of Rabbinic ordinance known as "fences around the law."

The regulations of this ordinance are generally as follows: All vessels the use of which is for such acts permissible on the Sabbath, as utensils for food, e.g., cups, plates, knives, and the like, may be moved or carried around in any manner even if the purpose is only for the sake of the vessel itself, i.e., in order that it should not be spoiled. All these constitute Class I.

Class II. Vessels the use of which is primarily for such acts which are not permitted on the Sabbath, such as tools of crafts and the like, can be carried around only if one makes use of them for his own needs or if he has need of the place they occupy, e.g., one may use a hammer to crack nuts but not if the purpose is for the sake of the vessel itself, namely for its protection. On the other hand, objects which are not vessels and are used primarily for acts prohibited on the Sabbath, such as stones, bricks, coins, and similar things, are not to be carried around at all. Likewise, candlesticks in which candles were lighted at sunset on Friday are not to be removed, for their use was devoted to an act prohibited on the Sabbath, but candlesticks in which candles were not burned on the Sabbath can be carried around under the conditions of vessels in Class II.

4. Sabbath and Human Life

Though the Sabbath is holy, matters involving human life take precedence over it. The law was given in order to foster and improve life, and the Sabbath is no exception to the rule. It is said in the Talmud (Tractate *Yoma,* 85): "The Sabbath is instituted for the sake of Israel and not Israel for the sake of the Sabbath." Consequently, it is allowed to desecrate the Sabbath for the sake of a gravely sick person, when all kinds of labor are permitted, if need be, on the advice of a physician. Moreover, the desecration of the Sabbath is allowed even if the gravity of the illness is doubtful, as when physicians differ, one admitting the urgency and the other denying it. The opinion of the former is followed, for the rule is that even in a doubtful case the laws of the Sabbath are rescinded.

When desecration of the Sabbath becomes urgent the necessary labors may be performed not only by a Gentile or a minor, but even by great scholars and leaders in Israel. This is done to demonstrate forcefully that the laws of the Torah were given in order to preserve life and not to cause, even indirectly, any injury to life or limb. The case of illness was cited only as a typical and most frequent example, but the law also applies to all instances where safety of life or limb is concerned and even includes those where apparently there is only a loss of property which might indirectly result in danger to life, as in the case of a fire in one's home or in that of a neighbor. It is, however, to be emphasized that the breaking of the Sabbath is permitted in this case because of the possible danger to life and not because of loss of property.

5. Sanctification and Distinction of the Sabbath (Kiddush and Habdalah)

It is a Biblical commandment to sanctify the Sabbath, for the Rabbis interpret the words, "Remember the Sabbath day to keep it holy" (Exodus XX, 8), to mean that it is enjoined upon us to sanctify the Sabbath day by an evident act upon its entrance and its departure. Hence, the ceremonies known as *Kiddush* and *Habdalah.*

The *Kiddush* is recited at the entrance of the Sabbath before the meal on Friday eve. As its name signifies, it is intended to emphasize the sanctity of the Sabbath, and therefore consists of the recitation of a passage from the Bible (Genesis II, 1–3) in which the sanctity of the Sabbath as a day of rest is first mentioned and a short prayer in which thanks are offered to God for His gift to us of the holy Sabbath. The recitation of the *Kiddush* is usually made over a cup of wine, but if wine is not available, it may be made over the Sabbath bread (see below). Though the *Kiddush* is inherently connected with the Sabbath meal, yet it is customary to have it pronounced also by the cantor in the synagogue over a cup of wine at the close of the Friday night service. This custom arose out of the fact that in Talmudic times the synagogue had a few adjoining rooms where poor travelers were accommodated at the community's expense, and it was for their benefit that the *Kiddush* was recited. The custom has been retained and rightly so, for the public *Kiddush* imparts dignity and distinction to the Sabbath.

The *Habdalah* recited in the synagogue at the close of the evening service or at home at the exit of the Sabbath over a cup of wine or other beverages—with the exception of water—

consists of a few verses culled from the Book of Isaiah and the Psalms and a short prayer of thanksgiving for the spiritual distinction of holiness bestowed upon Israel and the seventh day, the Sabbath. Two other benedictions are pronounced, one on light and the other on spices. The reason for the former is that attention is thereby drawn to the benefit of light and fire which are indirectly gifts from God. There is also a supplementary reason based on a legend regarding the origin of fire which says that when Adam was driven out of the Garden of Eden late Friday afternoon he sat in darkness Friday night, which caused him great anxiety, but Saturday night God endowed him with a special knowledge and caused him to generate fire by friction.[6] The custom, however, is an old one, antedating the legend, and the real reason is the one given above. Moreover, it was always customary in Jewry to pronounce a benediction over any form of pleasure, and since the kindling of a fire was prohibited on the Sabbath, the lighting of it after an interruption is regarded as a new form of pleasure.

As for the benediction on spices, various reasons are offered, none of which is satisfactory. The most plausible is the one which ascribes it to a desire to bridge the transition from the rest enjoyed on the Sabbath to the labor of the week by some mildly pleasant ceremony. The benediction on light is pronounced over a candle or torch lit for the occasion. The spices are, as a rule, placed in boxes of wood or silver adorned with some design, known by the name of *Hadas*.[7] This custom served through the ages as an impetus for the development of Jewish art, as many silversmiths and craftsmen distinguished themselves in the art of constructing these boxes and in their design. Some exceptionally artistic specimens are found in a number of Jewish museums.

The Sabbath is distinguished and sanctified in numerous other ways in addition to those described above, primarily by

[6] Tr. *Pessaḥim*, 54a.

[7] The word *Hadas* means myrtle and since this plant formed in Palestine one of the principal spices, the name was applied not only to the myrtle proper but to all spices, and, as stated, even to the spice-box.

dress and food. Even the poor made an effort to have special clothes for the Sabbath. Attention is also given to the meals. Two loaves of bread over which grace or the *ha-Motzi* is pronounced are required at each of the three Sabbath meals. The requirement, though nominally based on a Rabbinic interpretation of two words *Leḥem Mishneh* in Exodus XVI, 22, arose from a desire to have food in abundance on the Sabbath. These loaves bear the name *Halot*, a name given in the Pentateuch to the loaves used in the Temple, such as the showbread and those used with certain sacrifices.

As no fire is to be kindled on the Sabbath, the food is prepared Friday and kept warm. In the course of time, various types of rich foods were developed and eaten exclusively on the Sabbath. In Central European countries and later in those of Eastern Europe, this food had a special name, *Cholent*, originally derived from the French word, *Chalet*, the food which was immortalized by Heine in his poem, *Die Prinzessin Sabbath*.

6. Intellectual Enjoyment

Sanctity cannot be attained without intellectual improvement. Accordingly, the Sabbath day is devoted partly to instruction and learning. In early times, the lecture, *Derashah*, was the most important part of the service. It centered about the reading of the Law (see below). The Pentateuch and part of the Prophets were read, translated if necessary, and interpreted. The interpretation usually concerned itself with the legal, moral, and historical aspects of the text.[8]

This was the first attempt in the history of education to initiate adult education on such a large scale. In later times, when education spread and learning developed to a degree where every Jew was at least able to read the Hebrew text of the Bible and understand large portions of it, while a majority had access to various parts of the extensive Jewish literature,

[8] For the details on this matter see the author's "A History of Jewish Literature," Vol. I, Chaps. III, VI.

the entire Sabbath day was primarily devoted to study. To the synagogue came various groups, each of which devoted itself to the study of a certain subject. Some studied the Pentateuchal portion of the week with its commentaries; others, the Agadic portions of the Talmud or the Books of the Midrash; still others, chapters of the Mishnah; and the learned, treatises of the Talmud. Each group had a teacher, but almost all the members participated in discussions. Those who did not wish to study availed themselves of the sermon, which was usually preached in the afternoon before the *Minḥah* service by special preachers called *Maggidim* (i.e., speakers). These imparted spiritual and religious instruction in an inspiring and popular way.

This form of education is still carried on in many Jewish settlements in various parts of the world and in numerous congregations in this country, though unfortunately, with diminishing results. These various ways of observing and sanctifying the Sabbath imparted to it the unique importance it holds in Jewish life, and justifies the statement, quoted above, that it helped to preserve the Jews in their integrity as well as in the distinctness of their way of life.

Chapter II

THE FESTIVALS

1. Rosh ha-Shanah

We will discuss the cycle of festivals in the order they take place during the year and we will accordingly begin with Rosh ha-Shanah (New Year).

It is not definitely known when this festival, which falls on the first day of the month of Tishri, became the first day of the New Year. The Bible (Leviticus XXIII, 24; Numbers XXIX, 1) merely refers to it as a festival which is to take place on the first day of the seventh month—taking Nisan in the spring as the first month as expressly stated in Exodus XII, 1.—Nor is it indicated in the eighth chapter of Nehemiah, where a description of the celebration of the holiday is given, that it marks the beginning of the year. Without entering into the very complicated discussion of whether the ancient Jewish calendar was reckoned according to the solar or lunar year, we can say that there is enough ground to assume that even in early times Tishri began the practical year. Since agriculture was the main occupation of the people, Tishri, which was the beginning of the farming year, had a strong claim to consideration as the first month of the year. However, the order of the months beginning with Nisan was continued according to an earlier calculation which was based either on astronomical observation or on the fact that Nisan, the month of the Exodus, had a distinct historical importance. There are several references in the Bible which confirm the notion that the month of Tishri was regarded as initiating the practical year. Exodus XXXIV, 22 speaks of the festival of Succot as occurring at a time when the year completes its cycle, and Deuteronomy

XXXI, 10 similarly speaks of the same festival as coming at the end of the year, and hence the time is simultaneously the beginning of a new year. Since Succot falls on the 15th of the month of Tishri, it obviously could not begin the year; consequently, both passages are to be understood to mean that the holiday occurs in the month which begins the year, which *eo ipso* is the terminus of the preceding year. Furthermore, the solemnity with which the observance of this first day of the seventh month is endowed in the commandments cited above shows that special importance was attached to the day. In both of the references mentioned above, it is enjoined that trumpets should be blown on the day. In Biblical times, the trumpet or *Shofar* was sounded on important public occasions, such as calling the people together or summoning them for battle. We may therefore assume that the purpose of the blowing of the *Shofar* was to notify the people that a new year had entered. However, be that as it may, an old Mishnaic statement, hailing probably from Soferic times (ca. 350–330 B. C. E.), speaks of the first day of Tishri in a very matter of fact manner as the beginning of the civil year, thereby indicating that it probably acquired that status some centuries earlier.

The character which Rosh ha-Shanah assumed during the ages as a day of spiritual inspiration and reflection as well as the first day of a period of repentance must also go back to ancient times. Evidence for this assumption is afforded by the proximity of the Day of Atonement, which even in early Biblical times was the supreme day of spirituality and repentance. This view of Rosh ha-Shanah was undoubtedly strengthened during the period of the Second Commonwealth, which was marked by a deepening of the religious spirit and its penetration into the consciousness of every Jew. To a people as religiously-minded as the Jews were at that time, the beginning of a year must have evoked reflections on their conduct of the past year; and since the Jewish belief in divine providence was complete, it readily came to be believed that the beginning of a new year was the proper time for a line of demarcation in that providence as far as each individual Jew was concerned, and Rosh ha-Shanah thus became the day of judgment. Hence the Mishnaic statement (Tr. Rosh ha-Shanah, Ch. I, 2) which bears all signs of antiquity that "On Rosh ha-Shanah all people pass before God in judgment like sheep before the experienced eye of the shepherd."[1]

The principal ceremony connected with this festival, the performance of which is enjoined by Biblical precept, is the blowing of the *Shofar*. This ceremony, however, lost its original Biblical simplicity and grew somewhat complicated in the course of time. The reason for it is that the words of

[1] That Rosh ha-Shanah was very early considered a day of reflection and repentance can be inferred indirectly from the very passage in Nehemiah VIII, 1–13 which most Biblical critics use to prove that in the days of Ezra Rosh ha-Shanah was neither regarded as the beginning of the year nor invested with a spiritual character. It is there told, after the story of the public reading of the Law is related, that Nehemiah and Ezra the scribe told the people: "This day is holy unto the Lord, your God; mourn not nor weep, for all the people wept when they heard the words of the Law." He further urged them to eat and drink, "for this day is holy unto our Lord; neither be ye sorry, for the day of the Lord is your strength." The Levites on their part kept on repeating: "Do not be grieved" (verses 9–11). Now two questions may be asked. First, what passages of the Pentateuch were read, and second, why did the people cry so bitterly? As for the first, it cannot be assumed that the passages contained a catalogue of sins, or one of the two long passages in Leviticus XXVI, 14–46 and Deuteronomy XXVIII, 15–69 known as *Tokhaḥot*, i.e., passages presaging severe chastisement for transgressions. These passages do not belong to the readings on the holidays nor do they have any relation to them. The reading most likely consisted of the passages regarding the first of the seventh month and of the Day of Atonement, which is the next passage. The people then being reminded of the importance of the day, especially by oral explanation, for as stated in verse 8, the reading was accompanied by interpretative comments, bethought themselves also of their sins which were numerous. Hence their weeping and their desire to fast. As a result, they had to be pacified by their leaders.

It may therefore be safely assumed that the character of the first day of Tishri as New Year and as a day of judgment is not, as the critics say, a late innovation, but its origin can be traced at least to the time of Ezra and probably even to earlier times.

It is worthwhile also to point out that the Aramaic translation of the Book of Job (Targum) remarks on the words, "And there was a day when the sons of God came to present themselves before the Lord" (Ch. I, 6), that it was New Year when judgment was proclaimed in heaven. Translations of Job were circulated in writing at the beginning of the Common Era (Tr. Sabbath, 116), while the content was current orally for centuries before. The remark is therefore an additional proof for the antiquity of the character of Rosh ha-Shanah.

the commandment are not explicit, though they are repeated twice. In Leviticus XXIII, 24, it says: "In the seventh month on the first day of the month, ye shall have a rest day, a memorial of blowing trumpets" (Zikron Teruah). Again in Numbers XXIX, 1, it is said: "It shall be unto ye a day of *Teruah.*" The *Teruah* is mentioned a third time in connection with the sounding of the *Shofar* on the entrance of the Jubilee year. The Rabbis, therefore, deduced from the repetition of the term *Teruah* and by the method of analogy that in all blowing of the *Shofar,* both on Rosh ha-Shanah and on the entrance of the Jubilee year, there shall be three *Teruot.* The *Teruah* consists of a number of short blasts, and as a *Teruah* was never sounded alone but was preceded and followed by long extended sounds known as *Tekiah,* the order of the blowing of the *Shofar* is given in the Mishnah as three triads of sounds each consisting of a *Tekiah, Teruah,* and a *Tekiah.* This was the ancient order. In later times, doubt arose as to the exact nature of the *Teruah,* whether it symbolizes a wail or a sigh, or both, and in order to overcome any doubt, one of the Rabbis of the Talmud introduced a more complicated order, namely, he tripled two sets, one consisting of *Tekiah, Teruah* (a wail), *Tekiah,* and the other of *Tekiah, Shebarim* (a sigh), and *Tekiah,* and introduced a third set consisting of four sounds, i.e., *Tekiah, Shebarim, Teruah,* and *Tekiah,* which is likewise tripled. We have then a total of thirty sounds, which removes any doubt, for whether *Teruah* is the sound of a sigh or a wail or both, we have three triads of each.

Formerly, the *Shofar* was blown in connection with the *Musaf Amidah* *, a set after each of its three sections, but for one reason or another—probably because of some calamity which assailed the Jews—the time of the blowing of the *Shofar* was changed to before the recitation of the *Musaf* service, immediately after the reading of the Law. But in order that the old custom should not be entirely forgotten,

* ***Amidah*** **is another name for the prayer usually called** ***Shemoneh Esré.*** **See Ch. III.**

the later Rabbis decreed that the *Shofar* should be sounded again during the *Musaf Amidah*, either ten blasts (i.e., four after the first section and three after each of the other two sections), or even thirty blasts, namely, twelve after the first section and nine after each of the other two. Mystical tendencies, leavened by folk imagination, pictured the day as a day when the heavenly court actually sits in judgment and Satan acts as procureur, and portrayed the blowing of the *Shofar* as a call to battle to overcome the evil passions, or as they expressed themselves figuratively, to confuse Satan in his role as accuser. As a result, ultra-pious people introduced additional *Shofar* blowing after the prayers so as to make the total number one hundred.

The *Shofar* is made from a ram's horn, preferably in curved form. It must be whole, have no cracks or holes in it, so that the sounds emitted shall be clear and penetrating. All Israelites are obliged to hear the blowing of the *Shofar*, and while the ceremony is being performed two benedictions are pronounced, the first emphasizing the command to hear the sound, the second thanking God for preserving us in life, a benediction (see below) recited on the first day of every festival and on other occasions when performing special precepts.

The particular character attributed to this festival which makes it not only the beginning of a New Year but a day of judgment gave rise to a number of folk customs and ceremonies which are of a purely symbolic nature and bear no obligatory character. These are connected with the festive meals and are at least more than a millennium old. It was customary for the heads and fellows of the Academies of Babylon, among them Hai Gaon (d. 1038), to eat on the eve of Rosh ha-Shanah certain vegetables and fruits, the Hebrew or Aramaic names of which signify blessings and good wishes for a happy year. In Western Europe the head of a calf or fish and honey in which the bread is dipped serve the same purpose. The first symbolizes the desire for a leading part in the affairs of life, and the second for sweetness and pleasantness. Appropriate Hebrew phrases expressing the wishes are said while partaking of these foods.

Another ceremony, also of a symbolic nature, is the ceremony of *Tashlikh* which consists of a short prayer recited on the banks of a body of water which reads in part: "And thou wilt cast all their sins into the depths of the sea" (Micah, Ch. VII). Hence the ceremony is called *Tashlikh* (Thou wilt cast). That the prayers of these days as well as of the Day of Atonement as a whole possess special solemnity, and that it is one of the two festivals observed even by those who are not as a rule faithful or assiduous observers of religious precepts and ceremonies, goes without saying.

8. Day of Atonement

The ten days of penitence, which begin with Rosh ha-Shanah, culminate with the Day of Atonement.—The seven intervening days are not distinguished by any special religious ceremonies except by the recitation of certain additional prayers which are of later origin and the content of which is conducive to religious reflection and meditation. The celebration of this day is explicitly enjoined by Biblical command which says: "On the tenth day of the seventh month there shall be a day of atonement; it shall be an holy convocation unto you, and ye shall afflict your souls and offer an offering made by fire unto the Lord. And ye shall do no work on that same day, for it is a day of atonement, to make an atonement for you before the Lord, your God" (Leviticus XXIII, 27, 28). It then goes on to warn those who will desecrate the day, either by not abstaining from work or by not afflicting themselves, with the dire punishment of being cut off from their people. The holiness of the day is further emphasized by the special name it bears, "Sabbath of Rest." The same injunction in similar terms is also stated in Leviticus XVI, 29–31 at the end of a long description of the Temple service to be performed on that day. The affliction and prohibition of work are mentioned again in Numbers XXIX, 7. However, nowhere is the nature of the affliction given. Oral tradition interpreted the term affliction to mean abstaining from such things the absence of which causes pain or lack of comfort to the body. Accordingly, the Mishnah (Yoma VIII, 1) says that on the Day of Atonement one is prohibited from eating, drinking, bathing, anointing oneself with oil—a necessity in those times and conditions of life—and from wearing shoes. Abstaining from these things is considered an affliction.

Since the commandments regarding affliction and rest from work make the day the most spiritual of the year, it was naturally surrounded by a halo of solemnity and religious ceremonies. In Temple times, the service in the Temple was the most solemn and most lengthy, lasting the whole day, and was performed solely by the high priest. In later times, the day was spent entirely in the synagogue in prayer, meditation, and reading of the Law. The spiritual solemnity of the day is further distinguished by the addition of another service to the four services held on the Sabbath and festivals, making a total of five—figuring from sundown to sundown.—The fifth service, called *Neilah*, i.e., the closing service, is held in the late afternoon. In the Talmudic period it formed a regular feature of every public fast, but in later times (see below), it was omitted on all other fast days and retained only on the Day of Atonement.

There is another feature of the Day of Atonement which deserves consideration. The service on the eve of Yom Kippur is popularly known not by the usual name, *Maarib*, but *Kol Nidré*, though curiously enough, *Kol Nidré* itself is not part of the service nor even a prayer. In reality, it is a legal document and consists of a declaration that vows, promises, or even oaths which may be made by any member of the congregation during the coming year shall be null and void if the one who makes them changes his mind for one reason or another.

This ceremony is not enjoined by law or precept, and unfortunately its intention has been frequently misinterpreted by non-Jews. It arose not from a light attitude towards vows and promises, but on the contrary, from an attitude of excessive respect and high regard for vows or promises which a man makes. The Torah says: "If a man vow a vow unto the Lord or swear an oath to bind his soul with a bond, he shall not break his word. He shall do according to all that proceedeth out of his mouth" (Numbers XXX, 2). This statement was considered by the bearers of the tradition of the Oral Law as a command to fulfill vows and oaths for the transgression of which punishment is meted out—in some cases, flagellation—and a considerable number of rules and regulations were thereupon evolved covering all kinds of vows and oaths. However, being conscious of the frailties of human nature which often prompt a man to take a vow or make a promise, or even swear in haste or anger without due premeditation, and in order to avoid tragic consequences which might ensue as a result of such acts, as was the case with the vow taken by Jephthah (Judges XI, 34–40), certain privileges for the annulment of vows were extended by the bearers of the Oral Law to those who took an oath inadvertently. Such extension has a basis in the Torah itself which allows annulment of vows made by women under certain conditions. It was therefore established that a well known scholar or a court of three laymen may, at the request of the maker of the vow, absolve him from his vow, provided the scholar or the court determines that it was made with a certain justified reservation, though it might have been subconscious rather than conscious. This proviso justifies the court in assuming that had the results or the consequences been known to the person at the time he made the vow, he would not have done so. Consequently, the vow was taken with an unexpressed contingency, and thus there is legitimate ground for the change of mind and the annulment. The law of annulment has many rules and regulations and is encumbered by limitations into which we cannot enter. Later scholars penetrated more deeply into the complicated matter of promises and vows. They noted that people all too frequently make them, but either through certain conditions or forgetfulness they cannot fulfill them. Therefore, in the desire that people may avoid transgressions and consequent punishment, they asserted that one can state a condition at the beginning of the year that all vows and promises which he might make during the coming year and which he may not be able to fulfill are annulled by him in advance. It is for this reason that the *Kol Nidré* was introduced on the eve of the Day of Atonement when the whole congregation is present. The language of *Kol Nidré*, which is Aramaic, proves that this custom was introduced not later than the middle of the Gaonic period when Aramaic was still in vogue. However, in the beginning, it was not approved of by all scholars, for we find some authorities opposing it. Towards the end of the Gaonic period (10th century) it gained ground, and the Gaon Saadia (892–942) enjoins it. In the communities of Western Europe and later in Eastern Europe, it was in general use at least for a millennium. Its prevalence was most likely due to the hard conditions of life, the persecutions and discriminations which frequently caused people to make promises or take vows under duress.

There are two versions of *Kol Nidré*, the one spoken of above intended for the coming year, and the other which states that repentance is made for all vows of the past year. This form is based on the previously mentioned modification in the law of vows introduced by the Rabbis which allows annulment of a past vow either by a scholar or by a court of laymen. In this case the whole congregation acts as the court, though the reason for the change of mind is not given. The first version is used by the communities of Western and Eastern Europe following the Ashkenazic rite, and the second by all those following the Sefardic or Portuguese rite.

It is explicitly understood that this annulment is valid only in cases of vows and oaths which are made in private life, mostly in regard to religious matters, but no annulment can be made of vows and promises made to another person, or to a court, or to the government, and certainly not by a community. Accusations formerly made against the Jews for this declaration are totally groundless. Its sole intent was, as stated, to absolve one from sin when forgetfulness or unpreventable conditions made fulfillment impossible.

The solemnity and awe with which this essentially legalistic declaration is invested are partly due to the form in which the declaration is given, namely that it is recited by the entire congregation which acts, as said, as a public court, while the leading scholars of the community with the Scrolls of the Law in their hands stand at the side of the cantor, thus adding dignity and order to the court, but primarily it is due to the melody in which the *Kol Nidré* is chanted. In the course of the ages this melody has gradually absorbed into it all the bitterness of the Jewish fate, the protest at the constant suffering, and the cry of a martyred people.

The Day of Atonement is distinguished at its departure, like the Sabbath, by the reciting of the *Habdalah*. However, no benediction on spices is pronounced.

In spite of the holiness attached to the Day of Atonement, and in spite of the oft-repeated injunction in the Pentateuch regarding "affliction" on that day, it does not apply in cases when fasting would in any way endanger life or health. Accordingly, a sick person is allowed to break the fast at the advice of a physician or even at his own insistence that he must have food. His opinion is recognized even against the opinion of the physician.

9. Succot (The Feast of Tabernacles)

The festival known as Succot is designated in the Pentateuch by two names, *Hag ha-Asif* (The Feast of the Ingathering), as it is said: "And the Feast of the Ingathering which is at the end of the year when thou hast gathered in thy labors out of the field" (Exodus XXIII, 16), and *Ḥag ha-Succot* (Leviticus XXIII, 34). The same name is repeated in Deuteronomy XVI, 13. These two names indicate the double aspect of the festival. It was undoubtedly observed in very early times, even before the Exodus, as a nature festival, celebrated at the time when the grain and the fruits are gathered in and thanks rendered to God. The Pentateuch added to it the historical aspect and says: "Ye shall dwell in booths seven days; all that are native Israelites born shall dwell in booths, that your generations may know that I made the children of Israel to dwell in booths when I brought them out of the land of Egypt, I am the Lord, thy God" (Leviticus XXIII, 42, 43). This, as said, is the second aspect, but the first, namely rejoicing and giving of thanks, is continually emphasized in all passages referring to the festival and is symbolized by the ceremony of taking the *Ethrog*, the *Lulab*, the myrtle, and the willow branches. The historical aspect blends properly with the earlier one, for were there no Exodus there could be no rejoicing and giving of thanks at the ingathering of fruits and grains. Accordingly we will see that both aspects are symbolized by various ceremonies clustered around this festival.

Succot consists of two festivals, Succot proper which is to last for seven days according to the Bible, and *Shemini Aẓeret*, i.e., the eighth day, which is a festival in itself. In Palestine both were celebrated, and are even today, for the same number of days. In the lands of the Diaspora, for reasons which will be explained (see section on calendar) one more day was added even in the time of the Temple, thus making a total of nine days. It is still being celebrated in the same manner by all Jews outside of Palestine except by those who are affiliated with the Reform party. The extra day is added on to the second festival, *Shemini Aẓeret*, but Succot proper still consists of seven days.

Though this festival consists, as said, of nine days, yet only the first two and the last two days are really *Yom Tob* or holy days, the intervening five days being a semi-holiday and known as *Ḥol ha-Moed.* These days partake both of the nature of the week days and of holy days, that is, the principal ceremonies connected with this festival are also observed on *Ḥol ha-Moed,* but no cessation from work is enjoined. (For the regulations governing rest on the holy days see section on Yom Tob.)

Two principal ceremonies are observed on Succot, namely dwelling in booths and the taking of the *Ethrog, Lulab,* and the other plants. As regards the first, the obligation consists primarily in spending as much time as possible in the *Succah.* In early times, in Palestine, where the climate is mild, the words of the Bible, "Ye shall dwell in booths seven days" were construed more literally, and people not only ate in the booths but also slept there and spent most of their time there. Later, and in other lands, the term "dwelling" was confined primarily to the eating of the meals in the *Succah,* though very pious people also sleep there.

The *Succah,* as its very name indicates, was primarily intended to resemble a hut built by sojourners in the desert, made of any material and covered by a roof of things growing from the earth, such as grass, plants, and the like, its principal purpose being to give shade during the day. Accordingly, the rules and regulations covering its construction as given in the Talmud retain these characteristics. The important feature is its covering. As said, the *Succah* must be covered with products growing out of the soil; the covering must be placed loosely so that the sky may be seen through it, and at night, the stars, for otherwise, it would lose the character intended. On the other hand, it must not be too loose, for then it would give no shade, and the rule is that the sunny portion of a *Succah* must not be larger than the shady portion. The Pentateuch does not specify the dimensions of the *Succah,* but the Oral Law, taking into consideration human needs and habits, fixed the following dimensions: Its height must not be more than twenty cubits since a Succah of greater height must have solid walls and a solid foundation. Again, it must not be lower than ten

*Tefaḥim,** approximately two cubits, for then it is not even a decent hut. No limits are placed on its length or width, but a minimum of a cubit and a Tefaḥ are required for each. These small dimensions were fixed so as to enable one to observe the ceremony even under difficult conditions. A *Succah* must have at least three walls; the fourth may be open with only a pole placed on top to resemble a door. Even the third wall may be a partial one: However, all these rules give only the minima. In practice the walls of a *Succah* often formed parts of a room in the house, with the ceiling and roof above it so constructed that they could be removed for the duration and a covering of branches or other permissible materials placed there.

As said, the term "to dwell" was in time limited primarily to the meals in the *Succah,* and it is therefore required that one have at least two meals a day there. As emphasized hitherto the laws lose their force when their observance might cause injury to life and health. Consequently, sick people are not obliged to eat in the *Succah.* Furthermore, if for one reason or another, eating there cause acute discomfort, such as in the case of inclement weather or other causes, one is not obliged to go to the *Succah.*

The second important ceremony observed on this festival is the "taking" of four plants and pronouncing an appropriate benediction over them. It is expressly enjoined in the Torah which says: "And ye shall take you on the first day the fruit of goodly trees, branches of palm trees, and the boughs of thick trees, and willows of the brook, and ye shall rejoice before the Lord, your God, for seven days" (Leviticus XXIII, 40). The commandment enjoining the ceremony evidently emphasizes the thanksgiving aspect of the festival, for these plants symbolize the blessing bestowed by God upon His people in causing an abundance of products. The wording, however, is not clear, for while the first part speaks of the observance of the ceremony on the first day only, the second part mentions "rejoicing" for seven days which evidently re-

* For the measure of a cubit and a *Tefaḥ* see above p. 34 note.

fers to the "taking" of the plants. The bearers of the tradition of the Oral Law in the time of the Temple explained the precept to mean that on the first day the ceremony is to be observed by every Jew everywhere, while in the Temple it is to last seven days.[2] After the destruction of the Temple, Johanan ben Zakkai, the founder and head of the Academy at Jabne, passed an ordinance that henceforth the ceremony should be observed everywhere for seven days, and it has thus been practiced throughout the centuries.[3] Nor are all the fruits and plants specifically indicated in the verse. Two are explicitly mentioned, the palm branch and the willow, the other two are referred to only generally. Tradition, however, early decided that the "fruit of the goodly trees" spoken of in the verse is the *Ethrog* (Peri Etz Hadar), the finest citrus fruit which grew in Palestine. "The branch of the thickly grown tree" is the myrtle (Hadas), the leaves of which grow so thick that they cover the trunk of the tree entirely. Accordingly, it was established that the plants be taken in the following order: an *Ethrog*, a tall palm branch, three short twigs of the myrtle, and two twigs of the willow tree. The *Ethrog* is held in the left hand, while the *Lulab*, the myrtle, and the willow twigs tied together are held in the right hand and a benediction is pronounced. This ceremony is to be performed by every Jew before or during the morning service on each day of the festival except Saturday, when the plants may not be carried through the streets to the synagogue.

Since the original purpose of the ceremony was to symbolize the abundance of the produce of the earth which is a blessing bestowed by God, it follows that these plants should be the finest specimens of their genera. Accordingly, there are a number of rules regulating their size and appearance. The *Ethrog* must be of fair size without defects. Cracks, spots, or perforations disqualify it. The *Lulab* must

[2] The basis of the interpretation are the words "before the Lord" which the commandment "for seven days" includes. The Rabbis then said, "We must take the plants seven days only before the Lord, i.e., in the Temple.

[3] As a Rabbinical commandment.

not be cleft and its leaves must be joined, and must be about three quarters of a cubit high (four Tefahim). The myrtle and the willow twigs with a minimum height of half a cubit (three Tefaḥim) must be fresh and their leaves full.

OTHER CUSTOMS CONNECTED WITH THE "TAKING" OF PLANTS

Succot is primarily a thanksgiving festival for a nation which, in the period of its early history, subsisted principally on agriculture. There are, therefore, other customs which symbolize the expression of thanksgiving for God's blessings. In early times the plants were also held in hand during the services and when *Hallel* was recited (see below) and when the words, "Give thanks to the Lord, for He is good because His mercy endureth forever" (Psalms, CXVIII, 1), were pronounced, the *Lulab* was pointed towards the six points of space to symbolize His goodness which is present everywhere. Another custom which was practiced in the time of the Temple was that on each of the seven days of Succot the Altar in the Temple was encircled by a number of people with *Lulab* in hand chanting words of praise to God, and on the seventh day it was encircled seven times. The custom was retained for centuries, with some modifications, in all lands of the exile, and is still practiced in traditional synagogues. During the procession short poetic prayers known as *Hoshanot* are recited, for they are based on the words of verse 25 in Psalms CXVIII, "*Ana Adonai Hoshia na*" ("Save, I beseech Thee, O Lord").

10. HOSHANNAH RABBA

The seventh day of Succot bears the name *Hoshannah Rabba* because of a special ceremony connected with it. The ceremony, though not mentioned in the Bible, is very old and was practiced in the Temple during the time of the Second Commonwealth in somewhat different form. Tradition assigns its institution to the Prophets. The ceremony expresses a phase of the thanksgiving aspect of the festival as a whole. Succot not only completes the cycle of agricultural labors but also presages the beginning of a new cycle for which rain is a prime necessity. Since the rainy season in Palestine usually begins a short time after Succot, a ceremony was introduced which symbolizes a plea for future abundance. It consists in "taking" on that day during the services willow branches, for willows which grow at the banks of brooks are a symbol of abundance of water. The ceremony in the time of the Temple was performed with great pomp. Leading men among the priests went out daily and cut a number of tall willow branches and placed them on the Altar of the Temple reciting at the same time verse 1 in Psalm CXVIII—the words, "O, Give thanks unto the Lord; for He is good: because His mercy endureth forever." On the seventh day they circled the Altar, carrying these branches in their hands. The day was called the *Day of the Arabah* (Willows). This ceremony is still observed with some changes. The *Bimah* is encircled with the *Lulab* in hand seven times, but when the special prayers called *Hoshanot* are recited the willow twigs are held in hand until the end of the service. Hence the day was called *Hoshannah Rabba* and even the bundle of twigs is popularly known as *Hoshannah.* In general, later mysticism surrounded *Hoshannah Rabba* with a halo of importance. It is considered the final day of judgment which began with Rosh ha-Shanah. On that day the "decree" of the fate and destiny of the individual is supposed to be issued.

11. Shemini Aẓeret and Simḥat Torah

The eighth day of Succot bears the name *Shemini Aẓeret* and is considered, as mentioned, a special festival. Though the *Succah* and the *Ethrog* are discontinued, the joyful note which characterizes Succot is maintained. The Torah emphasizes the feature of rejoicing on Succot, as it says: "And thou shalt rejoice in thy feast, thou and thy son, and thy daughter, and thy man-servant, and thy maid-servant, and the Levite, and the stranger, and the fatherless, and the widow that are within thy gates" (Deuteronomy XVI, 14). And again: "Thou shalt surely rejoice" (ibid. 15). Tradition also included the eighth day among the days of rejoicing, and the Mishnah accordingly says: "Rejoicing is obligatory for eight days" (Mishnah Succah, Ch. IV, 8). This statement gave rise to a number of ceremonies (see below). The eighth day, though, had in early days a distinguishing mark of its own which was expressed in the service where a short prayer for rain was introduced. In fact, the plea for rain was expressed symbolically during the entire festival of Succot, first by the ceremony of the *Arabah,* as stated above, and second, by the libation of water on the Altar, a ceremony which is not mentioned in the Bible but was practiced during the Second Commonwealth and which seemed to have enjoyed popular favor despite the opposition of the Sadducees. On the eighth day the symbolic ceremonies were discontinued and replaced by the prayer, and this feature was retained even after the exile in all lands of the Diaspora. Curiously enough, it has assumed additional importance. Religious poets gave it special attention, and a large number of compositions are dedicated to the supplication. A special service known as *Geshem* (rain) is held on that day which is joined with the *Musaf* service read on festivals. This service is endowed with a peculiar solemnity as expressed in the attire and in the chant of the cantor which are similar to those of the High Holidays. The reason for this solemnity is that, according to a figurative statement in the Mishnah, this day is one of the four heavenly days of judgment, for on it the decree of providence regarding the amount of rain for the coming year is issued. The retention of this ceremony in the lands of the Diaspora testify to the exceptional place the memories of Palestine and the hope of the return to the land have always held in Jewish life.

However, the feature of rejoicing was destined to become of greater importance. It ultimately gave rise to a number of ceremonies and even gave to the second day of this festival in the Diaspora, where it is celebrated for two days, a special name, *Simḥat Torah.* Neither the name nor the ceremonies connected with it are mentioned in the Talmud or even in the Gaonic times. They undoubtedly originated in times when the annual cycle of the reading of the Law was definitely established and became prevalent (see below). This phase of the celebration marks the completion of the reading of the Pentateuch from the beginning of Genesis to the end of Deuteronomy. The exuberance of joy displayed on that day are the external signs of the love and loyalty the Jews entertained during the ages towards the Torah. There are two formal ceremonies marking the celebration. The first is called *Hakafot,* in which the members of the congregation with the Scrolls of the Law in their hands march around the *Bimah* seven times during the morning and evening services. Short liturgical pieces are recited and sung at the time. The second ceremony consists in calling as many people as possible to participate in the reading of the Law.—It is read twice, morning and evening.—Minors who ordinarily are not called are also accorded that honor on that day. The most scholarly person in the congregation is called last to read the closing portion in Deuteronomy and is given the title, *Ḥatan Torah* (The Groom of the Torah). In time it became customary to read the first part of Genesis also to indicate that the study of the Law never ceases, and the one called to read that portion is entitled *Ḥatan Bereshit* (Groom of the Beginning of the Torah). The people, especially in the towns of Eastern Europe, invented many ways and forms to express their joy in the Torah, and special attention was paid to the children who came to the synagogue with flags depicting Biblical or religious scenes in their hands. In general, it was, and still is, a day of merry-making and hilarity.

12. Passover

Whether Passover had any other origin or aspect in pre-Mosaic times cannot be definitely known. Its clear-cut historical character as a celebration of the most momentous event in Jewish history, the Exodus, and the birth of the Jewish nation is all-dominating. In five out of ten times where the observance of this festival is enjoined in the Law (Exodus XII, 15–20; XIII, 3–11; XXIII, 15; Leviticus XXIII, 5–8; Deuteronomy XVI, 1–5), this character is emphasized, and the reason for its principal features stated. These features are, first, a prohibition against eating or possessing leavened bread, and second, an affirmative precept, to eat Matzot, i.e., unleavened cakes. The reason for these two precepts is, that at the time of the Exodus, the Jews could not prepare leavened bread because of their hasty departure and ate *Matzot*. The aim of the lawgiver was to keep this event constantly in the mind of the people, and hence the repeated injunctions and admonitions to remember the Exodus and the redemption from slavery. The third feature, the sacrificing of the Paschal Lamb, need not be discussed here. The Torah warns against the transgression of the prohibitive commandment and says that anyone who will eat leavened bread will be "cut off" [4] from the congregation of Israel, the punishment being extended even to the non-Jewish stranger in the land.

The momentousness of the event celebrated by the festival as well as the severe punishment attached to the transgression of the precepts imparted a special importance to Passover, and it was observed by the people through all ages with a scrupulousness of detail and ceremony which in turn gave rise to numerous laws, rules, and regulations concerning the various phases of its observance.

[4] The meaning of the word "cut off" (*Karet*) is not entirely clear. Various interpretations are advanced in the Talmud; one says that it means that the transgressors will die childless, another says that he will die at an age earlier than three score and ten—the usual span of life. Both views are unsatisfactory. Originally it might have meant social ostracism.

First of all, oral tradition and its bearers, paying scrupulous attention to every word of the passage in Exodus XII, 15–20, noted that not only *Ḥometz,* i.e., leavened bread, is prohibited, but leaven in general, as expressed by the term *Maḥmeẓet* in verse 20. Consequently, the prohibition was extended not only to bread leavened and baked, but even to dough or flour in the process of leavening. This may include grain which, under certain natural conditions, such as immersion in water, tends towards leavening. Secondly, the term was made to include also mixtures of leaven, namely, when any leavened object is mixed with other foods or dissolved in them, the whole is prohibited. And while in the Talmud there is a difference of opinion regarding the amount of leaven which makes a mixture unfit for use on Passover, some contending that one sixtieth part of leaven in a mixture should not affect the whole, the severer opinion nonetheless prevailed, that even an infinitesimal amount of leaven if mixed or dissolved in any amount of food disqualifies it.

It is this view which brought about the rigors in connection with the observance of the Passover, for though it was accepted that the actual term leaven was applied only to five kinds of grain, namely, wheat, rye, barley, spelt, and oats, and not to rice, millet, sesame, or legumes, yet all other foods, if not carefully guarded, might have, at one time or another, been mixed with particles of leaven. Consequently, all food used on Passover must be specially prepared and guarded from any mixture or solution of leaven.

The same rigorous attitude was adopted towards retaining as well as possessing on Passover any food which may have leaven or even a particle of leaven. Such food is prohibited forever, not only as food but even to be used in any wise which might bring profit or enjoyment. As a result of this attitude and regulation all traces of leavened food are obliterated and the house is cleaned thoroughly. As far as dishes are concerned, special sets dedicated to Passover use only are employed. Silver tableware, which cannot be so easily duplicated by Jews of moderate means, is immersed in boiling water for a few minutes so that any taint of leaven which might have been absorbed should be exuded by the force of the heat.

However, the punctilious carrying out of all the regulations to destroy all traces of leavened food in one's domain could be accomplished only in a limited economy. But when commerce developed among the Jews and many merchants had large stocks of food which might have been leavened or fermented and its destruction or removal would entail great loss, later legal scholars evolved a device whereby the law could be observed and the loss obviated. This consists in a formal sale of all food to non-Jews for the Passover week with a provision for resale at the end of the holiday. It is no doubt a kind of legal fiction, but in view of the fact that the bills of sale are made out in accordance with the letter of the law, and taking into consideration that most of the food is not really *Ḥometz*, but rather types of admixtures, no harm is done by this legal device. How seriously this commandment, namely, that *Ḥometz* should not be seen or found in a Jewish home during Passover, was regarded by the Jews can be proved from the fact that we have numerous records in Responsa of cases of great loss suffered by merchants when, for one reason or another, that device was not used. Merchants of food—especially of fermented liquors—often poured such liquors worth great sums into the rivers on the day before Passover without hesitation. These facts prove, of course, the great economic need which made the introduction of this device a necessity and justify its enactment from all points of view.

There is another ceremony connected with the enjoinment to destroy and remove the *Ḥometz*, and that is *Bedikat Ḥometz*, the symbolic search for *Ḥometz* on the eve before Passover. I say symbolic, for in olden days a real search was instituted in all corners of the house or storehouse. In later times, however, the removal of *Ḥometz* took place several days before Passover, but in order that the commandment of *Bedikat Ḥometz* be not forgotten, a figurative search is instituted. With candle in hand, the head of the house searches for bread and collects a few crumbs which are burned the following morning. On the day preceding Passover, the last meal of *Ḥometz* is eaten not later than about nine-thirty in the morning. This limitation is another evidence of the exceptionally serious attitude which was adopted towards the precepts enjoined in regard to Passover. After the meal, the crumbs of bread set aside the night before are destroyed by fire. Short benedictions are pronounced during the process.

The second commandment regarding Passover is the eating of Matzot. The Torah does not give any specific description of the Matzot, nor does it say anything about their preparation. Oral tradition, however, added a number of rules and regulations. First of all, it interpreted the words: "Seven days ye shall eat unleavened bread (*Matzot*)" (Leviticus XXIII, 6) as an obligation to eat *Matzot* during Passover. Since it was impossible to construe it literally, for a man may, either by personal choice or because of physical condition, feed only on vegetables or fruit and very little bread, the obligation was limited to a minimum. A Jew must eat, at least on the first night of Passover, a piece of Matzah the size of an average olive, in order to discharge that obligation, and as this is the performance of a precept a special benediction is pronounced. Secondly, the Matzah, in order to be entitled to that specific name, must be baked only from flour of the following grains—wheat, barley, rye, oats, and spelt—and without salt. Again, it was argued that since the Bible in one place (Deuteronomy XVI, 3) calls Matzah the "bread of affliction," it must be prepared in the simplest way, as the poor would prepare it, namely, of flour and water. If any other liquid is used, such as wine, milk, or the whites and yolks of eggs (Matzah Ashirah), it may be eaten, but not as the obligatory portion on the first night of Passover.

The most popular feature of Passover is the cluster of

ceremonies which attend the meal on the first night of the festival. In the lands of the Diaspora the ceremony is repeated on the second as well, and on both nights it is observed with special pomp. On this account it received later the name *Seder*—a name unknown in Talmudic times—which signifies that there is a fixed order and system in the observance of the details and ceremonies accompanying the meal.[5] The origin of the special attention given to the meal goes back to the time of the Temple and was due to two factors. The first was the eating of the Paschal Lamb which was obligatory upon each family or group who gathered together for that meal, and hence the meal by its very nature was a group meal and, consequently, formal. The second was the injunction of the Torah that the story of the Exodus be recited on the first night of Passover, which was done in the presence of a group, while the children were encouraged to ask questions regarding the event and the various ceremonies attending the formality of the meal. Eating of the Paschal Lamb was accompanied, as the Bible says, by the partaking of bitter herbs (Moror), the usual way of eating roast lamb in those days. Again, at formal and joyful meals, wine was drunk both in connection with the *Kiddush* and otherwise. It was therefore accepted that at this grand and festive meal four cups of wine be drunk—no more, no less. In time it became an obligation. When the Temple was destroyed certain ceremonies were added as a reminder of those times and thus the *Seder* was evolved. It seems that this took place very early, for a number of the old *Mishnot* give the entire arrangement, and some of the statements even refer to customs which were prevalent at least half a century before the destruction of the Temple. It can be assumed, then, that at the beginning of the Common Era, the *Seder* was much similar to its present form.

We will present the order of the *Seder* ceremony and offer

[5] The term *Seder* is not found until the 11th century. It is suggested however, that it has its origin in the expression found in the *Tosefta* (*Berakot*, Ch. IV, 8) where in the discussion about the ceremonies of a formal festive meal it is said, "This is the *Seder* of the formal meal."

explanations of the various ceremonies subsequently. The table is arranged festively. At the head of the table a plate with three Matzot is placed, and another containing the following items: a piece of roast meat, an egg, *Moror, Ḥaroset,* and a vegetable. The seat of the head of the family is furnished with cushions and he sits half reclining.

The *Seder* begins with the *Kiddush* over a cup of wine. The next step is the ablution of the hands with the omission of the usual benediction, and this is followed by eating a small portion of some vegetable, such as potato, cucumber, etc., dipped in salt water, after the recitation of the proper benediction. The head of the family then breaks the middle Matzah and reserves half of it for the end of the meal as the *Afikomon* (dessert).

With these preliminaries over, the *Seder* continues with the recitation of the *Hagadah,* which opens with the four questions propounded by the youngest child at the table. The questions concern themselves with the ceremonies of the *Seder,* and judging from their content, they are very old. They are: Why is only Matzah eaten this night? Why only *Moror?* Why the ceremony of dipping food in liquids twice? (See below.) Why do you sit leaning on cushions? The *Hagadah* which purports to be a detailed answer to the questions is then recited. At the end of the recitation of the *Hagadah,* the second cup of wine is drunk.[6]

The meal begins with a few ceremonies; first, two benedictions are pronounced—the *ha-Motzi* and a special one over the Matzah, followed by the eating of a portion of the *Moror* dipped in the *Ḥaroset.* This is supplemented by a *Moror* sandwich and a statement is made that this is done as a memento of a custom practiced by Hillel in the time of the Temple.

[6] The four questions are given in the standard version which is found in the early Codes—Maimonides and Vitri—but the version in the Mishnah does not give the last question and instead has the following: Why do we every night eat all kinds of meat, whether cooked, potted or roasted, while this night of Pesach only roast meat? This question was asked when the Paschal Lamb, which was roasted, was eaten, and no other meat was permitted.

At the end of the meal the *Afikomon* (dessert in Greek) is produced and is followed by grace, after which the third cup of wine is drunk.

With the completion of the meal, the second part of the recitation of the *Hagadah* begins. It opens with the recitation of four verses, two from Psalm LXXIX, 6, 7; one from Psalm LXIX, 25; and one from Lamentations III, 66, all of which contain a plea for the destruction of the enemies of God and Israel. It is customary to open the door while these verses are recited. This is followed by the reading of the larger part of *Hallel*—Psalms CXV–CXIX, and also Psalm CXXXVI, together with a poem of praise to God called *Nishmat.* It is also customary to fill a cup of wine symbolically called the Cup of Elijah the Prophet. The fourth cup of wine is then drained. This practically completes the *Seder.* In later times, however, several more poems composed by poets in Palestine and other places were added.

In attempting to understand the meaning and rationale of the ceremonies connected with the *Seder* we must bear in mind two things. First, that the Exodus was the momentous event in Jewish history and the perpetuation of its memory by numerous symbolic ceremonies is continually enjoined. Consequently, ceremonies which were practiced during the time of the Temple, in accordance with the sacrificial cult, were retained even later, though in modified form, in order to retain the pristine character of the feast as much as possible. Second, that Passover was believed to be the time set for the future Messianic redemption of Israel just as it was in the time of the first deliverance. Hence the insistent retention of the ancient ceremonies which express the deep longing of a martyred people for redemption.

It is with these things in mind that we can understand the significance of almost every ceremony. The Torah states (Exodus XII, 8) that the Paschal Lamb shall be eaten roasted and with Matzot and *Moror.* It was probably eaten in that way at the time of the Exodus and the custom was continued during the time of the Temple when the Paschal Lamb was also sacrificed. However, to assuage the pungency of the bitter herbs, a mixture of various crushed fruits and wine (*Ḥaroset*) was used in which the herbs were dipped. Hillel, a famous scholar, who lived at the beginning of the first century, C. E., because of his interpretation of the verse in Exodus XII, 8, enjoining the eating of *Moror,* ate not only the roast with *Moror,* but the Matzah with it as well. When the Temple was destroyed the Rabbis retained as many of the customs as possible. It was not possible to retain the Paschal Lamb for it was a sacrifice which could be brought only to the Temple, but the eating of the *Moror* was made obligatory by Rabbinical ordinance, and consequently a benediction is pronounced over it. The *Moror* was then endowed with a meaningful interpretation, to wit, that it serves as a symbol for the bitterness of the suffering which the Jews had undergone in Egypt. Similarly a symbolic meaning was imparted to the *Ḥaroset* which was retained,[7] namely, that it resembles clay and reminds us of the fact that the Jews in Egypt were compelled to work in clay to make bricks.

However, it was also thought necessary to have at the *Seder* ceremony symbols of the Paschal Lamb as well as of the other sacrifices, *Shelomim* or *Ḥagigah* brought on each of the three principal holidays when the Jews came on their pilgrimage to Jerusalem. It therefore became customary to place on the *Seder* plate a piece of roast meat and an egg—the egg was substituted for the second piece of meat—to serve as a reminder of the former sacrifices, the *Paschal Lamb* and the *Hagigah.*

In early times it was customary, at a formal meal, to eat vegetables dipped in vinegar or salt water as an appetizer. Similarly, it was customary, as a result of the laws of purity which were observed in the times of the Temple, to wash the

[7] According to the Mishnah (Pesaḥim X, 3) *Ḥaroset* is not a *Mitzvah,* but was used merely as a means to lessen the bitterness of the herb.

hands before tasting food.* Both of these ceremonies were retained even in later times in order to keep the formality of the feast in its full glory. Since the usual vegetable used for the purpose in Babylonia—as mentioned in the Talmud—was called *Karpas* in Syriac, which means celery or parsley, the ceremony is denominated *Karpas* in the program of the *Seder*.

In the Eastern lands in olden times, chairs were little used and people sat on the floor. Important guests at a grand feast were seated on couches and leaned back on cushions. Since Passover is the festival of freedom, all people at the meal were seated on couches propped up by cushions to display their dignity and importance. Later, when chairs were introduced, only the head of the house followed this custom.

Of the four cups of wine which are drunk at the *Seder*, the first is for the *Kiddush* and the third for grace after the meal, which was formerly recited over a cup of wine at any meal partaken of by three men. The other two cups are a mark of joy at the event of freedom. Agadists and sermonizers attempted to supply another reason for the prescribed number and saw in it a symbol of the four phases which distinguished the Exodus. Be that as it may, in the course of time the four cups of wine became the most prominent feature of the *Seder* and it was considered a necessary condition for its performance and was raised to the rank of a *Mitzvah*. It is stated in the Talmud that even the poorest of the poor must obtain the necessary amount of wine, and if he cannot afford it, he is supplied with it by the community. In the time of the Temple it was desired that people should thoroughly enjoy the Paschal Lamb which was the main symbol of the Exodus and not partake of other foods. It was therefore said that there is to be no dessert after

* However, as stated above (p. 65) no benediction is pronounced on the ablution for there is a difference of opinion among scholars whether ablution is necessary before the eating of fruits or vegetables or not.

eating the meat of the lamb. The dessert was called in the vernacular *Afikomon,* a distorted Greek word. In order that this ancient custom be remembered, the meal is concluded with the eating of the *Afikomon.*

Passover was believed to be the time set for the future redemption of Israel, and since the Jews looked forward through the centuries to this happy time, that longing was symbolized by the cup of Elijah who, according to Malachi III, 23, and numerous passages in Talmudic and Agadic books, will precede the Messiah. To emphasize this hope and longing, the door is opened as if to welcome Elijah. The verses recited then voice the cry of Israel for redemption and its prayer that punishment be meted out to its cruel enemies. We can forgive a martyred people which in a moment of joy at a past redemption, coupled with expressions of passionate longing for a future one, allows itself to say a few harsh words about its enemies who are always present in one place or another.

Passover, thus, through its web of numerous ceremonies which remind us so strongly of the past and point towards the hope of the future and which bring change in the ordinary monotony of life, occupied an important place in Jewish life and, in the past, was awaited with eagerness, especially by the young. In spite of the burden of labor and cost it involved, it was, and still is, cheerfully greeted by all, even by the poor who are helped to meet its obligations by the community. It was the custom of old in Jewish communities to establish a fund for the purpose of helping the poor defray the special cost of Passover. This fund is known as *Maot Ḥittim,* i.e., money for the purchase of wheat, since Matzah made of wheat flour was the principal expense, but the fund was not limited to Matzah only, but covered all other items. As a result, the evening of the *Seder* was the most cheerful evening in the home of rich and poor alike.

13. Shabuot

This festival which is celebrated on the sixth of Sivan is designated in the Bible by several names. First, it is called *Hag ha-Kaẓir* (Exodus XXIII, 16), then again, *Yom ha-Bikkurim* (The Day of the First Fruits) (Numbers XXVIII, 26), and finally, *Hag ha-Shabuot* (Feast of Weeks) (Deuteronomy XVI, 16). All three names denote the same aspect of the festival, namely a day of rejoicing and praise to God at a season of agricultural importance in Palestine. The harvest of wheat and the beginning of the ripening of the fruits of the trees occurred at the same time and this led to the use of the first two names for the festival. The name Shabuot is given to it because it marks the end of a seven week period between the beginning of the harvest in the fields, especially that of barley, and its close with that of wheat. These seven weeks begin on the first day of the Passover when, as a sign of thankfulness, the *Omer,* a measure of barley, was brought to the Temple as an offering. From that day, the days were counted for seven weeks or forty-nine days, and the fiftieth day was the festival of weeks, Shabuot. The custom of counting the days between the two festivals was continued even after the destruction of the Temple and is practiced today, though no *Omer* is brought nor are there days of harvest. The counting is done at the evening service, and the six weeks between the end of Pesach and Shabuot are popularly called *Sefirah* days, i.e., numbered or counted days.

In the time of the Temple, Shabuot was marked by a special ceremony of bringing *Bikkurim* to the Temple, namely, owners of orchards all over Palestine brought their first fruits as an offering. The ceremony was performed with great pomp and hilarity, inasmuch as the people gathered in groups for that purpose and marched together, accompanied by song and playing of fifes and beating of drums.

All this, however, belongs to the distant past though in present day Palestine attempts are being made to reinstitute the ceremony of *Bikkurim* in a modern form. In later times, the Shabuot festival underwent a complete metamorphosis and was endowed with a spiritual and historical aspect, being designated as a celebration of the giving of the Law (Matan Torah) and it is in this connection mentioned in the prayers. The festival, however, has no distinguishing ceremonies, for the early ceremony of *Bikkurim* could not possibly be retained. However, it is customary among the learned and very observant to devote the entire night preceding the holiday to the study of the Torah, and a text-book known as *Tikkun Shabuot* was compiled for that purpose. Some relic of the earlier character of the festival was also retained in a custom which was practiced by many to decorate the homes and the synagogues with flowers, ferns, and leafy twigs.

14. General Rules Covering the Festivals

Yom Tob is, like the Sabbath, a day of rest, and work is prohibited, with this distinction, that all work done in preparation of food for the day, such as cooking, baking, and the like, is permitted. It follows, of course, that kindling of fire is also permitted, the rule being that since kindling of fire is permitted for the preparation of food, it is also permitted for other purposes. Hence, when smoking was introduced there was no objection to its use on the holidays except on the Day of Atonement. However, the food prepared must be for that day only; no preparation of food for any other day, even for the second day of *Yom Tob* or the following Sabbath, being permitted. The question then arises as to how food can be prepared for the Sabbath when the holiday falls on Friday. The Rabbis in this case invented a legal device known as *Erub Tabshilin* (mixing of foods). It consists in taking a portion of bread or fish or meat on the afternoon preceding the festival and setting it aside for the Sabbath. This ceremony is construed as a declaration that the preparation of food for the Sabbath was begun before the holiday, and consequently, the preparation of the food on the holiday is a continuation of that of the day before. It is, of course, a legal fiction, but the festivals, on the whole, bear a more lenient character. Carrying of burdens on the holidays is permitted, but the prohibition against a long walk beyond the fixed limits holds good also for the holidays. Those who had to go beyond that limit had to use the above-mentioned device, the *Erub Teḥumin.*

The status of *Hol ha-Moed,* i.e., the intervening days between the first and last days of the holiday, was given above. It may be added that in post-Talmudic times when the economy of the Jews changed primarily to a trade and commercial economy, almost all labors were permitted on *Hol-ha-Moed.*

15. Semi-holidays

There are several semi-holidays in the Jewish calendar which in turn can be divided into two classes differing in the degree of their importance. To the first class belong Hanukkah and Purim. Both commemorate important events in Jewish history in the post-Biblical period, the former, the victory of the Hasmoneans over the Greco-Syrian king, Antiochus IV, which victory ultimately resulted in liberating Judea from the yoke of foreign subjection, and the latter, the saving of the Jews of the Persian Empire by Mordecai and Queen Esther from the destruction planned by Haman. Both differ little from the ordinary week days as regards work and occupation and are only distinguished by ceremonies peculiar to each.

Hanukkah lasts for eight days, its distinguishing ceremony being the lighting of candles each evening to commemorate the rededication of the Temple to the worship of God by Judah Maccabee in the year 165 B. C. E. after it had been for a time devoted by the Greco-Syrians to the worship of Zeus and other Greek gods. This rededication made possible the relighting of the Menorah of seven branches which was an important fixture in the Temple. There was also at the time a general feast of dedication for eight days participated in by the people, jubilant at both the military victory and the purification of the Temple. This feast was most likely celebrated by ceremonies of illumination. Hence the ceremony of lighting the candles for that number of days symbolizes the lighting of the holy candlestick as well as the general illumination. However, in order that interest should not lag as the days pass, it was established by the School of Hillel that the order of the lighting of the candles should be gradual, namely, one on the first night, increasing the number daily by one until it reached eight.

Hanukkah is also distinguished in its morning service by the recitation of *Hallel* (Psalms CXIII–CXVIII). The people, though, added to Hanukkah something of their own besides the prescribed ceremonies. It was marked by a certain spirit of hilarity; parties were given and games of chance including cards were played. Especially was that hilarity manifested among the children who were usually given gifts of money which in European countries bore the special name of *Hanukkah Gelt*. They also invented a game of chance consisting of the spinning of a metal or wooden top (dreidel) on which Hebrew letters are engraved, the winnings being determined by the letter on which the top rests.

With the rise of the Jewish national movement known as Zionism, Hanukkah assumed a new dignity and value as the national element was added to the religious. Its days became days of Zionist propaganda and a number of public meetings and parties are held during that week. The heroism of the Maccabees in liberating their country from foreign subjection became a source of inspiration for Zionist endeavor.

The story of Purim as well as the derivation of its name are well known. The story is told in the Book of Esther, and the name is said to be derived from a foreign word, most likely from the Persian *Pur* which means casting of lots

(Esther III, 7). It is celebrated on the fourteenth day of the month of Adar. The principal ceremony connected with the day consists in the reading of the Scroll of Esther at the evening service of the thirteenth and the morning service of the fourteenth. Another ceremony which is prescribed in the Scroll itself is the exchange of gifts and the distribution of charity. However, since the Scroll designates it as a day of cheer and joy, it subsequently became a day of public festivity, though there is no cessation of work. It is usually climaxed by a festival in the late afternoon known as the *Seudah.* In European countries, where the general carnivals consisting of parades, mimic plays, and masquerades took place at about the same season of the year, the celebration of Purim was influenced by the customs of the environment. Consequently on this day plays were produced by amateurs, representing scenes from the events related in the Scrolls, and at times, also from other Biblical events. The amateur players were known as *Purim Spielers,* Purim actors. In some communities in the mediaeval ages children used to burn a straw effigy representing Haman, a custom borrowed from the carnival ceremonies.[8] From that there spread a milder form of expression of both protest against the Jew hatred typified in Haman as well as of the hilarity which is still practiced in the synagogues, consisting of a blaring of various instruments by the children whenever the name of Haman is mentioned during the reading of the Scroll. Besides, Purim became a day of excessive feasting and also drinking in a goodly measure, which in turn resulted in the preparation of special dishes and pastries. Needless to say that there was much jesting on that day and expression of witticisms. Due to these features, Purim left a great impression in life and literature. It gave an impulse to the development of dramatic art among the Jews, and also to an incipient theatre. In literature it helped to develop the drama, the parody, and other kinds

[8] On the carnival ceremonies see *Encyclopaedia of Religion and Ethics,* article—Carnival.

of humorous literature.[9] In general, in former ages, it somewhat relieved the otherwise gloomy ghetto life.

16. Rosh Ḥodesh

The first day of the month, often the first two days of the month (see below), have some slight holiday characteristics. In Biblical times, it was considered of great importance, the Prophets often coupling it with the Sabbath (2 Kings IV, 23; Isaiah I, 13). From a verse in Amos (VIII, 5), it can be inferred that even commerce was abstained from. However, this must have been a custom prevalent in certain localities and has no legal sanction. In the Talmud it is explicitly stated that *Rosh Hodesh* does not differ from any ordinary day.[10] Still, a relic of the old custom was left in the fact that some women abstained from unnecessary work on the first of the month, a custom which is mentioned in the Talmud and lingered for a long time, but has now fallen into desuetude. The only distinguishing mark of *Rosh Ḥodesh* is in the prayer service which is distinguished by the recitation of the *Musaf* and *Hallel.*

17. Fifteenth of Shebat and Lag B'Omer

These two days, the fifteenth of Shebat and *Lag B'Omer* (i.e., the 33rd day after the *Omer* has begun to be counted), which possess a touch of festivity, are hardly distinguishable by any ceremonies or special customs. Even the time of their origin is not definitely known. There is no reference to the festival of the 15th of Shebat in earlier literature as it was instituted much later, and was intended to keep the memory of *Eretz Yisrael* fresh in the mind of the Jews. It may, however, have its origin in a statement of the *Mishnah* bearing

[9] On Purim literature, see Waxman's "A History of Jewish Literature," Vol. II, p. 606 ff. and 658 ff.

[10] Babylonian Talmud, *Ḥagigah* p. 22 Palestinian Talmud, *Taanit,* Ch. 1.

upon a legal matter. It says that that day marks the beginning of a year of growth for the trees,[11] and hence the custom to partake on that day of the fruits which grow in Palestine was introduced. At present the day is celebrated in modern Palestine as Arbor Day, on which many young trees are planted.

Lag B'Omer is mentioned in the Talmud (Yebamot 62b)[12] as the day on which a plague which raged among the numerous disciples of Rabbi Akiba ceased, but no reference to the day as one of festivity is made. However, in later times, it assumed that character primarily because it serves as a break in the semi-mourning days of *Sefirah* (see below).

The festive aspect of *Lag B'Omer* was manifested primarily in the schools. In the towns of Eastern Europe Jewish schools were closed for the day, and the pupils, accompanied by their teachers, spent the day picnicking in the woods where they engaged in games of a military character, carrying homemade bows and arrows and shooting at targets. This offers a clue as to its origin, which probably was a celebration of some military victory in the War of Bar Kokhba, which Akiba and his disciples enthusiastically supported. The enigmatic words of the Talmud that *Lag B'Omer* marked the cessation of a plague among Akiba's disciples may refer to this military victory which kept down the casualties among them to a minimum. All this is pure conjecture as we have no records, but the memory of the people must have retained some dim recol-

[11] Rosh ha-Shanah for trees is a term used in the *Mishnah* (*Rosh ha-Shanah* Ch. I, 1), primarily as a legal term in regard to giving of tithes (Maaser) from fruit, namely that the year for giving of tithes for the fruit of trees is reckoned from that date, the time of their bloom; for the different tithes vary according to the years in the seven year cycle (Shemitah) as follows: The first year, two tithes are given, known as first and second; the second is to be brought to Jerusalem and eaten by the owner, the first is given to the Levites. The second year, the process is repeated, but that year a tithe for the poor is substituted for the second tithe. The process is repeated in the second triad of the circle. Hence if trees bloomed before the 15th of Shebat of the third year, the tithes are given as of the second year and not as of the third.

[12] According to an improved reading in that passage which shortens the time of the disciples' death to two weeks before Shabuot, i.e., Lag B'Omer instead of the ordinary reading which says that the plague lasted from Passover to Shabuot.

lection of such an event and commemorated it through the ages.

18. Fasts and Days of Mourning

There are five public fast days in the Jewish religious calendar, not counting the Day of Atonement. They all commemorate historical events, four in connection with the loss of independence and the destruction of the Temple, and one in connection with Purim. They occur as follows: (1) *Asarah be-Tebet* (10th of Tebet), the day on which the siege of Jerusalem by the Babylonians in the year 588 began; (2) *Shibeah Asar b'Tamuz* (17th of Tamuz), the day on which the Romans broke into the city in the year 70 C. E.; (3) *Tisha b'Ab* (9th of Ab), the day of the destruction of the Temple, both in 586 B. C. E. and in 70 C. E.; (4) *Ẓom Gedaliah* (3rd of Tishri), the day on which Gedaliah, the Jewish governor, appointed by the Babylonians after the fall of Jerusalem, was killed; and (5) *Taanit Esther* (13th of Adar), in memory of the fast proclaimed by Queen Esther when she was informed of the decree of Ahasuerus ordering the destruction of the Jews.

All these fasts with the exception of *Tisha b'Ab* last from sunrise to sunset, and only eating and drinking are prohibited but no other comforts. *Tisha b'Ab* is a day of mourning, and its rigor is similar to that of the Day of Atonement. It lasts from sundown on the eighth of Ab to sundown on the ninth, and besides food and drink, bathing, anointing oneself with oil, and wearing of shoes are prohibited. At the evening and morning services *Ekha* (The Scroll of Lamentations) is read. It has also been customary for centuries to lower the lights in the synagogue and for the worshipers to sit in stockinged feet as is the custom in mourning for the dead. Several of these customs were modified in modern times, though in Oriental communities they are strictly observed. At the morning service, the phylacteries and prayer shawl are omitted to indicate grief and are put on instead at the afternoon service.

At the morning service numerous religious poems and elegies composed by poets of the Middle Ages are recited.

The expression of grief at the destruction of the Temple and loss of national independence symbolized by the observance of *Tisha b'Ab* is, to a degree, extended to the eight days preceding the fast. These days of mourning, including the fast day, are known as the *Nine Days*. During these days, observant Jews abstain from eating meat, drinking wine, and from cutting their hair, and likewise weddings and engagements are deferred for other dates. Even the Sabbath falling at this period has a gloomy air, though the restrictions regarding the eating of meat and drinking of wine are suspended in honor of the Sabbath. In certain communities of Germany it was known as the "Black Sabbath." Its general appellation, however, is *Shabat Ḥazon,* so named after the portion from Isaiah, Chapter I, which is read at the service and which begins with the words, "*Ḥazon Yeshayohu*" (The Vision of Isaiah), in which the Prophet chastises Jerusalem for its sinful ways and prophesies its destruction. These regulations regarding the Nine Days go back to early times as we find them stated in the Mishnah (Taanit IV, 7) compiled about 210 C. E. In later times, in the communities of Germany and Eastern Europe, some restrictions, especially in the deferment of weddings, were extended to the three weeks preceding the fast, from the 17th of Tamuz to the 9th of Ab, thus giving to the period its name in the language of the people, "The Three Weeks."

Another period in which a mild form of public grief is expressed consists of thirty-three days out of the forty-nine days between Passover and Shabuot, which are known as the *Sefirah* days on account of the counting of the *Omer* at the time. The principal restriction is the deferment of weddings during that time. There was, however, great variety in fixing the beginning of these days. Some communities counted from Passover to *Lag b'Omer,* and some from the first of the month of Iyyar to the third of Sivan, *Lag b'Omer* itself excepted. The origin of that custom cannot be definitely established. The usual reason given is that grief is expressed at the memory of the numerous disciples of Akiba, who, as stated above, died in a plague during that period. The Talmud, however, which mentions that event, does not enjoin any restrictions. It is possible that the folk-mind harbored some dim recollection of a disastrous defeat in the course of the War of Bar Kokhba against Rome in which Akiba and his disciples took a leading part. But it is also possible that the custom became prevalent in the 12th century in Franco-German Jewry after the massacres of the First Crusade and later spread to other countries.

19. The Jewish Calendar

The Jewish year is a lunar year consisting of twelve lunar months, the months being determined by the time of the revolution of the moon around the earth. That revolution is accomplished in 29 days, 12 hours, and 793 parts of an hour divided by the number 1080. Up to the year 363 C. E., as long as the *Sanhedrin,* the Jewish Supreme Court and highest religious authority, existed in Palestine, the day of the beginning of a new month was determined by that body according to the birth of the new moon. Witnesses who noticed its almost indistinguishable appearance testified to the court on the same day, and the entire court or a committee thereof declared that day *Rosh Ḥodesh,* i.e., the first day of the month. But if for one reason or another, the witnesses could not report on that day but did so on the next, the day following the appearance of the moon was declared *Rosh Ḥodesh.* Consequently, there were months of 29 days when testimony of the birth of the new moon was given on the same day, and months of 30 days, namely, when witnesses failed to report on the 30th day, and the day was then counted to the preceding month. The declaration of *Rosh Ḥodesh,* technically called *Kiddush ha-Ḥodesh* (the sanctification of the month), was broadcast by lighting of bonfires on high places and waving of torches from stations on mountain tops so that the people throughout Palestine might know when the month began by official reckoning in order to prepare for the holidays which take place in certain months of the year or for general reckoning. In the six months in which the holidays or semi-holidays occur, messengers were sent by the Court immediately after the declaration of *Rosh Ḥodesh* to the nearby Jewish communities of Syria to inform them of the exact day so that they might know when to declare the holiday. These months were Nisan- Passover; Ab- fast day on the 9th; Elul- Rosh ha-Shanah; Tishri- Day of Atonement and Succot; Kislev-Hanukkah; Adar- Purim. No information was necessary in Sivan for Shabuot as its date was determined by the counting of forty-nine days from the first day of Passover.[13] It is, of course, understood that in Temple times there was no *Tishah b'Ab.*

The more distant communities throughout the Diaspora which could not be reached by messenger added an extra day to the holidays, viz. Passover was celebrated for eight days instead of seven, Succot nine days instead of eight, Shabuot and Rosh ha-Shanah two days each instead of one. In this way they guarded themselves against any possible change in the fixation of the first day of the months in which the holidays take place. This, then, is the origin of the additional day as celebrated by Jewry in the Diaspora with the exception of the Reform faction in late modern times, and is accordingly called *Yom Tob Sheni Shel Galuyot,* i.e., the second day of the holiday celebrated in the Diaspora.

In the year 363, Hillel the Second, the Nasi or head of the *Sanhedrin,* realizing that, due to political and other conditions, the continued existence of the *Sanhedrin* was uncertain, rescinded the earlier method of determining *Rosh Ḥodesh* by observation and testimony and established a permanent calendar (*Luaḥ*) according to reckoning and calculation. Its principal features are as follows: Since it is impossible to begin a month in the middle of a day or an hour, the year was divided

[13] The question arises how did these nearby communities celebrate Rosh ha-Shanah on the exact day, since on that day no messengers could be sent. The answer is given that as a rule they celebrated it on the 30th of the month of Elul which they declared the first day of Tishri, for most years Elul had only 29 days even in Palestine.

into twelve months, six of which consist of twenty-nine days each and six of thirty days, thus making a total of 354 days. This equality of division of the month is, however, theoretical and not always observed in practice. Account had to be taken of the 793/1080 of an hour which completes the lunar month and which amounts to close to forty-four minutes and three and one half seconds. In order to account for that portion of time which during the year accumulates to a little over one third of a day and also because of certain other factors, such as the rule that Passover and Rosh ha-Shanah must not begin on certain days, the equality of the division of the month is frequently disturbed.[14] It was decided according to mathematical calculation to choose the months of Kislev and Ḥeshvan and assign to them at fixed intervals various numbers of days. In certain years, both of these months have thirty days each, thus making seven months of thirty days (plena) and five of twenty-nine, and the year of 355 days. In other years, the regular order prevails, i.e., one of these months has thirty days and the other twenty-nine days, and the year has the regular number of days, 354; and in still other years, both of these months have twenty-nine days each, which means that in that year seven months have twenty-nine days and only five have thirty, resulting in a short year of 353 days.[15] There

[14] Rosh ha-Shanah cannot come on Sunday, Wednesday, or Friday, for in the first case, *Hoshannah Rabba* would fall on Saturday, and the rite of taking the willow branches could not be performed, and in time it might be forgotten. In the other two cases, Yom Kippur would come either on Friday or Sunday which would cause great hardship, having the Sabbath and Yom Kippur follow each other—both days on which labor of any kind is prohibited. If Rosh ha-Shanah cannot come on any of these three days, it follows eo ipso that Passover cannot come on Monday, Wednesday, or Friday. If the birth of the moon of Tishri happens to fall on any of the three days, Rosh ha-Shanah is postponed for a day. All these cause a change in the number of days in the years in making some to consist of 355 days instead of 354.

[15] Since the calendar is well established according to calculation by many scholars of many generations, printers of calendars in present days usually place on the title page certain letters which indicate the character of the year, namely, whether it is regular or has seven full (30 days each) months, or vice versa, seven defective (29 days each). The letter *Ḥet* signifies defective; *Shin* means full, while *Kaf* denotes regular. These letters are preceded and followed by two others, the first indicating the day of the week on which the first day of Rosh ha-Shanah falls, and the last that of the first day of Passover.

was, however, another difficulty to be straightened out in order to make the Jewish calendar a workable one, and that was to reconcile the lunar year with the solar, which being 365¼ days is longer than the former by eleven and one fourth days. Were this not done, the Jewish holy days would circle around through all the seasons of the year as is the case in Islam, and Passover would sometimes come in the spring and sometimes in the summer, and at times, in the fall, etc. But the Bible says distinctly that Passover is to come in the spring and Succot at the ingathering of the fruits, i.e., at the end of the summer. In order that this be avoided, the device of intercalation or the adding of a month to the year was resorted to. Formerly, this was also enacted by observation. When the lunar year fell behind the solar for some time and Passover was about to take place considerably before spring, the Court decided to add another month. When the permanent calendar was established by calculation, a cycle of nineteen years was taken as a basis and seven years of that cycle were declared to be leap years consisting of thirteen months each in the following order: the 3rd, the 6th, the 8th, the 11th, the 14th and the 19th years of the cycle.[16] The additional month was placed, as in early times, between Adar (12th month) and Nisan (1st month) and is called *Adar Shéni* or *we-Adar* and is always of twenty-nine days' duration. The leap year is technically called *Shanah Meuberet,* i.e., a pregnant year, and the adding of the thirteenth month, *Ibbur,* for the addition is figuratively expressed as if the year is impregnated with another month.[17]

[16] The total number of 7 × 29 amounts to 203, while the total of 19 × 11 equals 209. The difference is made up by the other factors, spoken of above, which bring about an additional day to a year and also, if necessary, a day is added to the first Adar.

[17] The order of the months is as follows: Nisan—30 days; Iyyar—29; Sivan—30; Tamuz—29; Ab—30; Elul—29; Tishri—30; Ḥeshvan—30 or 29; Kislev—30 or 29; Tebet—29; Shebat—30; Adar—29, in a leap year 29 or 30; Adar Sheni—29.

Chapter III

INSTITUTION OF PRAYER

20. Introductory

Prayer is one of the oldest religious institutions. There is hardly any religion in the world of which prayer is not the most important component. Its origin lies in the very nature of the human soul. Man, feeling forsaken in the vastness of the universe, turns to God for protection. At other times, man desires to offer his thanks to God for the good He has bestowed upon him, or he longs to commune with Him, and he expresses this desire and longing in prayer. At still other times, he is weighed down by a sense of guilt and sin, and he lightens his burden by confessing his sins before his Maker. There are, accordingly, several types of prayers—a plea for intercession on man's behalf, a prayer of praise, or of confession. Underlying all types is the belief that the relation of man to God is as that of a son to his father, and he can, therefore, turn to Him in accordance with the moods of his soul.

It follows, of course, that Judaism which emphasizes the Fatherhood of God should place a high value upon prayer. The Bible is replete with prayers of all types and the Book of Psalms is nothing but a collection of prayers uttered by the noblest singers and pious men of Israel. Yet we find no reference in the Biblical books, with the exception of Daniel which is of post-exilic origin, to prayer as a regular daily institution. Nor is the duty to pray considered one of the 613 precepts. It is assumed to be a Rabbinical ordinance (see below). In Biblical times prayer was a personal matter. People prayed whenever they were moved to do so. Thus we find prayers by Moses (Exodus XXXII, 11–14; Numbers XII, 13; XIV, 14–20);

by Hannah (I Samuel Ch. II, 1–11); by David (I Chronicles XXIX, 10–20), besides the Psalms ascribed to him; and by Solomon (I Kings VIII, 23–53). We are also told that after the victory of King Jehoshaphat over his enemies, the people gathered in a valley which was later called *Emek Berakah* (Valley of Blessing), for there they blessed and praised God.

Berakah and *Tefillah* are the terms most frequently used in the Bible for blessing and prayer, respectively—the first is derived from the root *Barokh,* i.e., to kneel, and the second from *Palel,* to address a judge or high power.—We also find the terms *Hallel* (praise) and *Shebaḥ* (adoration) mentioned in the Bible.

The number and frequency of the terms shows us that prayer was prevalent in Israel even in early times, but as said, it had not yet become an institution determined as to time, number, and form.

The beginning of the institution of prayer is to be traced to the time of the Babylonian exile. During that period, when many of the previously existing forms of public worship had been eliminated, such as the Temple and public sacrifices, there arose on the part of the individual Jew an intense desire to come into close contact with God and commune with Him. As a result, prayer became a daily affair, and we read in the Book of Daniel: "And his (Daniel's) windows being open in his chamber towards Jerusalem, he kneeled upon his knees three times a day and prayed and gave thanks before his God as he did aforetime" (Daniel VI, 11). From this statement we can infer that at the time when the book was composed, the custom of praying three times daily had already become prevalent and established. The tradition in the Talmud ascribes the establishment of the institution of daily prayer to the Great Assembly whose activity lasted for over one hundred years, approximately from the last third of the fifth to the last third of the fourth centuries B. C. E.[1]

[1] According to the Talmud only the morning and afternoon prayers are obligatory for they were connected with two daily public sacrifices, the *Temidim* which were brought in these hours. The evening service is a matter of choice or voluntary (Reshut). There was, it is true, a difference of opinion

Be that as it may, there is no doubt that the institution of regular daily services was in existence during the larger part of the period of the Second Commonwealth, for a very early *Mishnah* (Tamid V, 1) tells us that important portions of the morning prayer were recited in the Temple. From the time immediately after the destruction of the Temple, we have the fixation of the leading part of the three daily services, the *Shemoneh Esré* or the Eighteen Benedictions. From the text of several of the benedictions we may assume that the fixation only was enacted in the Academy at Jabne, but that the recitation of the benedictions was in vogue much earlier. It can, therefore, be said that a great portion of the daily prayers was recited by Jewry for at least a period of 2000 years. That prayers were added in later centuries and the prayer-book underwent a process of growth is superfluous to say, but even the complete prayer-book, slight modifications notwithstanding, has a history of close to 1000 years.

The first attempt to organize the various prayers into some kind of formal system was made by the Gaon Natronai, son of Hilai (ca. 860), who is reputed to have sent to the Jewish community in Alessano, Spain, the order (Seder) of the daily prayers. However, since the text of that *order* is lost, we do not know its nature. It appears, though, from references by later authors that the order was not a complete one, as it contained only the principal prayers together with the more important benedictions for other occasions, such as those for grace after meals. His disciple, Amram Gaon, left us a complete *Seder* or *order* of prayers. This work contains the text of the prayers for the whole year together with the laws relating to liturgy. Saadia Gaon (892–942) compiled his own *Seder* which contains the text of the prayers as well as the laws governing them and a number of sacred poems, mainly his own. Maimonides also gave a standard text of prayers for the entire year in the first part of his Code, though in a succinct

on this matter, but the above opinion prevailed at the Council in Jabne held at the end of the 1st century C. E. There is, however, a part of the evening service, the *Shema,* which all agree is obligatory. Besides, it has been the practice of Jewry for at least 1800 years to pray three times daily.

manner, and Rashi compiled a *Seder* of prayers which set forth the order and the laws affecting them, but the text is only referred to. The first four collections represent one of the two main forms of the Jewish liturgy, namely, the Spanish or Sefardic, while the last represents the German or Ashkenazic form. The first seems to stem from Babylonia, since the orders of the Gaonim Natronai and Amram were written at the request of Spanish communities, while the last emanated primarily from the schools of Palestine with which the Franco-German and Italian Jewries were in contact. However, the differences between these two forms are not essential, for both contain the same principal prayers, the difference consisting in variations in their phraseology, in the sequence of the minor prayers, or in the omission or addition of a number of liturgical pieces.[2]

The disciple of Rashi, Simḥa of Vitri, compiled a more complete prayer-book containing not only the laws governing the prayers and their texts, but also a large number of sacred poems for Sabbaths and holidays. He called his collection *Maḥzor,* i.e., a cycle of liturgy for the entire year. Since he (Simḥa) found imitators who added still more poems, and collections frequently became too voluminous, it became necessary to divide the liturgy into separate collections, one containing the prayers for week days and the Sabbath, and the other, prayers for the holidays only as well as numerous sacred poems. The first bears the earlier name *Seder* or the more popular form *Siddur,* and the second *Maḥzor.* With the rise of the Reform and Conservative movements, many changes were introduced in the prayer-book, and, as a result, the size of the collection was greatly reduced, especially in

[2] In addition there are several minor forms of liturgy, the Italian or the Roman, which is a combination of both the Spanish and the German forms, the Romanian, the order of liturgy used mainly by the Jews of Greece or of the Byzantine Empire, including the communities of the Balkan countries, and that of Avignon, an order of prayers followed by four communities in the south of France of which Avignon was the leading one. But with the exception of the Italian, which is still in use by the communities of that country, the other two were replaced either by the Sefardic or the Ashkenazic order of liturgy.

the Reform ritual. But even in the Conservative synagogues where the traditional prayers are recited, the collection is limited to one volume, the *Siddur,* since the sacred poems are reduced to a minimum, except on the high holidays when a *Maḥzor* is used.[3]

THE ORDER OF PRAYERS

21. Week-day Prayers

There are three daily services, morning (*Shaḥarit*), afternoon (*Minḥah*), and evening (*Maarib*). The limits set for each of these services are as follows: For *Shaḥarit* from sunrise to a third of the day, which varies from 10 A. M. to noon according to the season; for *Minḥah* from 12.30 P. M. to sunset; and for *Maarib*—the entire night.

The morning service is, on the whole, divided into five parts: (1) Introduction and morning benedictions; (2) Psalms and Doxologies; (3) the *Yoẓer* including the *Shema;* (4) the *Amidah* or the Eighteen Benedictions; (5) Prayers of supplication. The *Yoẓer* and the *Amidah* are the most important parts and constitute the body of the service, while the other parts are mainly supplementary. The *Yoẓer,* named thus after its first benediction or section which begins and concludes with thanksgiving to God for the creation of the luminaries, includes the *Shema* together with two benedic-

[3] The first *Siddur* printed was the one containing the Roman or Italian form. It was published in the year 1486 by the printer, Solomon of Soncino. The first *Siddur* according to the Ashkenazic rite appeared in Prague in 1516. It bears on the title page the motto, "A *Siddur* according to the Polish rite," which is practically the same as the German. The Spanish *Siddur* was printed eight years later, in 1524, in Venice. Since then numerous editions of the *Siddur* have appeared but with little change except for additions of a few prayers bearing the stamp of the teachings of the Kabbala.

However, the spread of the Kabbala among the Jews of the Slavonic countries, especially since the rise of the Ḥassidic movement, brought about two new versions of the *Siddur,* even among the Ashkenazic Jews, which are in vogue among the Ḥassidim. One is called the *Nusaḥ Sfard,* and the other *Nusaḥ Ari* (i.e., Isaac Luria, founder of the system of the Lurianic Kabbala). Both retain in the main the German order of prayers with slight changes in the position of several prayers and in phraseology. These changes are borrowed from the Spanish ritual. The *Nusaḥ Ari* contains a number of changes in phraseology introduced by Luria.

tions preceding and one following. The *Shema* consists of three passages from the Pentateuch: (1) Deuteronomy VI, 4–9, emphasizing the unity and love of God and the observance of the precepts; (2) Deuteronomy XI, 13–21, stressing reward and punishment as well as the duty of teaching the Torah to the children; (3) Numbers XV, 37–41, containing the injunction to put fringes (Ẓiẓit) on the garments and the admonition to remember the Exodus. The two benedictions preceding the *Shema* are the *Yoẓer* proper and the *Ahabah*. The latter refers to the election of Israel, to God and the Torah, God's eternity, and His promises to the people of Israel, and concludes with a plea for redemption.

The *Shemoneh Esré* (Amidah) consists of two parts; the first part contains the first three and the last three benedictions, and the second part the twelve middle benedictions. The six benedictions in the first part of the *Shemoneh Esré* are recited at all services, while the twelve middle benedictions are recited only on week days. The former are of ancient origin and deal with general religious subjects. Thus, the first benediction of the first triad called *Abot* mentions the greatness and goodness of God and His promise to the patriarchs; the second called *Geburot* describes God's potence as expressed in relation to man, primarily in the promise of resurrection; the third called *Kedushah* speaks of the holiness of God. The last three benedictions—*Abodah, Hodayah,* and *Shalom*—contain a plea for life and divine goodness, as displayed in daily human affairs, and a plea for peace respectively. The twelve middle benedictions are both of a religious and national character as more than half are pleas for redemption, restoration of the Davidic dynasty, rebuilding of Jerusalem, and the preservation of the scattered communities of Israel in the Diaspora. Some of these benedictions date from the time prior to the destruction of the Temple, some were added immediately after, as the entire order was established around the year 90 C. E. at the Academy of Jabne. A nineteenth benediction known as *la-Malshinim* (Against Informers) was added somewhat later. However, since it was a later addition, the name *Shemoneh Esré* was not changed.

Of the two preceding parts, the first is a group of benedictions called *Birkot ha-Shaḥar* (Morning Benedictions). On the whole, they do not form an actual part of the service and used to be recited privately immediately upon rising. These contain (a) a short Doxology of God wherein His unity, providence, and man's trust in Him are emphasized; (b) a rhymed version of the Thirteen Articles of Creed; (c) a group of short benedictions thanking God for creation of the world, light of day, and various providential acts in regard to the individual and Israel; (d) several short prayers eulogizing the greatness of God and the littleness of man, culled from liturgical pieces in the Talmud. These conclude with the first verse of the Shema.[4] (e) The final part consists of a number of passages from the Bible, *Mishnah,* and *Gemara* relating to sacrifices. These passages were inserted as a substitute for the sacrifices so that the institution might not be forgotten. Some rituals also contain the Biblical story of the *Akédah* (Sacrifice of Isaac, Genesis XXII, 1–19).

The second part, the inclusion of which dates from early times, is called *Pesuké di Zimra* (Recitation of Psalms) and consists of Psalm CV, 1–15; 1 Chronicles, Ch. XVI, 20–36; and Psalms CXLV–CL. These are prefaced by a prayer dating from early Gaonic times and known as *Barukh she-Omar* (Praised be He Who Spoke). The Psalms are succeeded by several other Biblical passages, namely, 1 Chronicles, XXIX, 10–13, Nehemiah IX, 6–12, and Exodus XIV, 30–XV, 19 and are concluded with a Doxology. The last part, succeeding the *Amidah,* is called *Taḥanun* (Supplication), so named primarily because in early times people recited prayers privately. In time it was standardized and now consists of 2 Samuel, XXIV, 14, and Psalm VI, which is a plea for mercy. This

[4] The recitation of the verse from the *Shema* at this part of the service originated in time of persecution in Babylonia when public service was forbidden and the *Shema* could not be recited. It was then thought advisable to instruct the people to recite at home at least that verse which speaks of the unity of God together with a few preceding short prayers which express the principal ideas contained in the longer service. The custom was continued even after the persecution ceased.

Psalm is recited with bowed head and covered face, a modification of the former custom of prostration. An added plea for the preservation of Israel is joined to the supplication. On Mondays and Thursdays to the *Tahanun* is added a group of prayers of a supplicatory nature called *we-hu-Raḥum,* as it opens with the verse: "May He, the Merciful, forgive our sins" (Psalms LXXVIII, 38). The prayers are of ancient origin and anonymous. On the whole, they consist of a combination of Biblical passages and verses excerpted from various books. At the conclusion, Psalm CXLV is recited again and is succeeded by a short *Kedushah* to which a number of verses from Biblical passages are added. The verses of the *Kedushah* are also read in the Aramaic translation. From the 13th century on, it became customary to recite *'Alénu* as the final prayer. *'Alénu* is taken from the New Year service in which the exaltedness of God, creation, selection of Israel, and the hope for the Kingdom of God are stressed.

The *Kedushah,* which is recited by the cantor or reader when the service is public or communal and is repeated by the congregation, follows the third benediction of the *Amidah.* It is omitted when the *Amidah* is recited privately. This divine sanctification consists of three Biblical verses: Isaiah VI, 3, Ezekiel III, 12 with the addition of a few words from Verse 13, and Psalm CXLVI, 10. The first two verses repeat the sanctification pronounced by the angels and the third proclaims the Kingship of God. These verses are prefaced by a short passage calling upon the assembled to sanctify the name of God on earth just as it is sanctified in heaven by the angels. The introductory passage varies in length and language according to the kind of service, shorter on week days and longer on Sabbaths and holidays. The verses of the *Kedushah* are also recited in connection with other prayers before the *Amidah,* in the first benediction of the *Yoẓer,* and in the concluding prayer *U-Bo le-Zion.* These are qualified by special names, as the name *Kedushah* without qualification is limited to the one in the *Amidah.*

22. Priestly Benediction

The priestly benediction is recited by the cantor before the last benediction of the *Amidah.* It consists of the verses in Numbers VI, 24–26. Formerly, these benedictions were pronounced by the priests who ascended the pulpit at every service, but the custom was discontinued in the lands of the Diaspora except during the morning holiday service. In Palestine, though, the daily blessing by the priests is still followed.

23. Afternoon and Evening Services

The *Minḥah* service is comparatively short. It consists of Psalm CXLV, known as *Ashré,* the *Amidah,* the short *Taḥanun;* 2 Samuel, Ch. VI, 24, Psalm VI, and the *'Alénu.* The Amidah is repeated by the reader in public service.

The *Maarib* service consists of the Shema preceded by two benedictions, the first stressing the coming of night, and the second expressing the election of Israel and the importance of the Torah. It is succeeded by two benedictions, one a prayer for redemption, and the other a plea for protection during the night as well as for peace in life. The German ritual has an additional prayer. This part is followed by the *Shemoneh Esré* which is not repeated by the reader. The service is concluded with the *'Alénu.*

24. The Kadish

The *Kadish* is a short prayer recited several times in each service, both at the conclusion of each of the parts of which the service consists and at the very end. Due to the fact that at the end of the service and once or twice in the service proper it is usually recited not by the cantor but by mourners, it assumed special importance. However, in spite of its recitation by mourners, it is not primarily a prayer for the dead. It consists of two elements, a Doxology, in which the name of

God is sanctified and exalted, and a plea for the realization of the Kingdom of God. On account of the first element it is called *Kadish,* sanctification. Its nucleus is the phrase: "Let His great Name be exalted and blessed forever and unto eternity." This is taken from Daniel II, 20, with slight change. The prayer, as a whole, seems to be very old, for it is mentioned in the Talmud under the title, "The Great Name," and reference to its frequent daily recitation is made by the Tanna, Rabbi José, a disciple of Akiba, who lived in the first half of the 2nd century. Besides, its plea for the Kingdom of God to come is echoed in the early Christian prayer, *Pater Noster,* which is quite plausible to assume was modeled after the *Kadish.* The *Kadish* in early times was recited in the synagogue mostly at the conclusion of public study or after the sermon of the preacher. Later it became a regular feature of the service. As such, several other statements were added, a plea for peace and also one for acceptance of the prayers. Since it is repeated several times, certain distinctions in usage were introduced. When recited between parts of the service, it is known as a half *Kadish*—the plea for peace is omitted. When recited at the end of the service before *'Alénu* which was added in the 14th century, and by mourners, the complete form is used. Since the *Kadish* became such an important part of the service, another version was composed for the conclusion of the public studies in the synagogue, known as *Kadish d'Rabanan* (a Rabbinic *Kadish*), in which prayers on behalf of scholars and students are added. It is not known definitely when the *Kadish* became the special prayer for mourners, and various reasons are advanced for this appropriation. The real reason seems to be that the Kingdom of God is so closely associated in the entire Talmudic and Rabbinic literature with the Messianic times when resurrection will take place, that a plea for its realization was considered indirectly a plea for the resurrection of the departed. Hence the recitation by the mourners. In fact, the Sefardic rite joins with that plea also one for the coming of the Messiah. A special version of the *Kadish* is recited at funerals.

25. Sabbath and Rosh Hodesh Services

There is, as a rule, on the Sabbath as well as on the holidays, an additional morning service called *Musaf* (an addition), making a total of four services for the day. However, since the additional service follows closely upon the morning service, it may be considered an extension of the former. Since the Sabbath and holidays begin on the preceding evening, the order of the services begins with the *Maarib* and ends with *Minḥah* on the following day.

The main difference between the week-day services and those of the Sabbath and holidays consists in the content of the *Amidah* which has, instead of the usual eighteen benedictions, only seven. On the Sabbath and holidays with the exception of Rosh ha-Shanah, the *Amidah* consists of the first and last triads and one middle benediction dealing with the importance of the day. Introductory passages which vary with each service are added to this middle benediction.

The other parts of the Sabbath services are, with few changes, the same as on the week days. Thus, the Friday night service consists of the *Shema* and its preceding and succeeding benedictions unchanged except for the addition, at the end of the fourth benediction, of the verses in Exodus XXXI, 16, 17, where the observance of the Sabbath is commanded. This is followed by the *Amidah* in which the middle benediction is prefaced by a passage on the holiness of the Sabbath and the Biblical verses Genesis II, 1–3. The cantor repeats only the seventh benediction and a short version of the other six. Before the concluding prayer of *'Alénu, Kiddush* is recited by the cantor, as stated above (p. 38). In some rituals, such as the Sefardic, the German, and in a large number of American congregations, the hymn of *Adon Olam* or of *Yigdal* is sung by the congregation at the close of the Friday night service. In the 17th century, an introductory part known as the *Kabbalat Shabbat* was added to the service. This comprises Psalms, XCV–XCIX inclusive plus Psalm XXIX, the hymn of *Lekha Dodi,* and Psalm XCII, which is entitled "Song of the Sabbath Day." This Psalm was the original introduction, but in the 16th century, the mystics of Safed who used to receive the Sabbath several hours before sunset, adopted the custom of reciting the above-mentioned Psalms, and one of their circle, Solomon ha-Levi Alkabetz (ca. 1500–1570), composed the hymn *Lekha Dodi* (Come My Friend) with his name in the acrostic. The influence of these mystics was great and the custom spread throughout Jewry, and, as a result, the Psalms together with Alkabetz's hymn were incorporated in all prayer-books.

The Saturday morning service is, on the whole, divided into the same parts as the week day service, with the addition of Psalms XXXIII, XXXIV, XC, XCI, CXXXV, XCII to the second part, *Pesuké di-Zimra,* and of the concluding hymn known as *Nishmat.* The *Yozer,* besides containing the ordinary benedictions preceding and succeeding the *Shema,* also has additional hymns, such as *El-Adon.* The Sabbath benedictions in the *Amidah* are preceded by a short poetic introductory piece called *Yismaḥ Moshe,* glorifying the Torah and the Sabbath, to which are joined verses 16 and 17 of Exodus XXXI. The *Kedushah* is similar to that of the week-day service with some additional short passages.

The morning service is followed by the *Musaf,* consisting primarily of *Ashré,* Psalm CXLV, and the special *Amidah.* In the Ashkenazic ritual, Musaf is preceded by a memorial prayer known as *Ab Haraḥamim* (Merciful Father), recited since the Crusades in most Orthodox congregations on behalf of Jewish martyrs, and also by an Aramaic prayer on behalf of scholars and the community, dating from Gaonic times in Babylonia.

The main change in the *Musaf Amidah* consists in the addition of the introductory passages to the middle or Sabbath benediction. The passage called *Ata Tokanta* (Thou Hast Established—the Sabbath) emphasizes the special sacrifice denominated *Korban Musaf* (Additional Sacrifice) brought in the Temple on the Sabbath. The service concludes with *'Alénu* preceded by *En Ke-Elohenu,* a hymn in praise of God, sung by the entire congregation, and is followed by the Psalm of the day, XCII. In many congregations *Adon Olam* or *Yigdal* is sung.

The *Minḥah* service on the Sabbath begins with *Ashré* and is followed by the prayer known as *U-Bo le-Ẓion Goel* and the *Amidah* which differs in its introductory passage to the Sabbath benediction and is concluded by *'Alénu.* The passage called *Ata Eḥad* extols God, Israel, and the Sabbath.*

The *Maarib* service on Saturday night is distinguished from the daily service by several additions. A special benediction for the departure of the Sabbath called *Ata Ḥonantonu* is inserted between the third and fourth benedictions of the *Shemoneh Esré* and in addition Psalm XCI and the larger part of *U-bo le-Ẓion* is recited. It is concluded by the *Habdalah* and *'Alénu.* Some congregations add to the service a group of short prayers and selection of verses which is collectedly known as *We-Yitten Lekah,* because it begins with that verse (Genesis XXVII, 28). These prayers are more often recited at home.

The services of the first day of the month (Rosh Hodesh) differ from those of the week-day primarily by the inclusion of a *Musaf* service in the morning which begins with *Ashré* and *U-bo le-Ẓion* and is followed by an *Amidah* of seven benedictions. The seventh benediction deals with the importance of the day, preceded by an introductory passage and the verse in Numbers XXVIII, 11. In addition, *Hallel* (see below) is recited, as well as a special short prayer for the nation and its redemption inserted in the *Amidah* of all the services between the seventeenth and eighteenth benedictions. It is called *Yaaleh we-Yabo.*

26. Festival Liturgy

In regard to prayers, the three great festivals, Passover, Feast of Weeks (Shabuot), and Tabernacles differ but little from each other except in minor details. In fact, they differ

* For the reading of the Law on Sabbath morning and Minhah services see sec. 28.

only slightly from those recited on the Sabbath. The main difference consists in the content of the *Amidah.* As on the Sabbath, the morning service includes also the *Musaf*. The *Shaḥarit,* i.e., the morning service proper, is the same as that of the Sabbath with the exception of the *Amidah* if the festival falls on the Sabbath, but if it falls on a week day, then the additional hymns in the *Yoẓer* are omitted and the week-day form is followed. Likewise *Maarib* and *Minḥah* services are the same as those on the Sabbath except for the *Amidah.** The holiday *Amidah,* as stated, consists of seven benedictions, the seventh devoted to the significance of the day. This benediction is preceded by two introductions, one of which speaks of the selection of Israel and their sanctification by observing these holidays, the other, the above-mentioned prayer, *Yaale we-Yabo.* The *Musaf Amidah* likewise has several introductions. In the principal one, *u-Mipne Ḥatoenu,* reference is made to the exile, to the sacrificial offerings in the Temple, and a plea for national restoration is offered. Though we generally count only three principal festivals, there are, in reality, four, namely, *Shemini Aẓeret,* on the last two days of Succot, which is considered a special holiday and is thus specifically mentioned in the *Amidah.*

Passover and Succot, as mentioned, have four and five days respectively of semi-holidays called *Ḥol ha-Moed.* These have the festival *Musaf* service, but in the *Shaḥarit* and other services week-day liturgy is used.

The *Hallel,* which forms an important part of the festival services and is also recited in the morning services of the first day of the month and Hanukkah, consists of a group of Psalms from CXIII–CXVIII inclusive, the first verse of which begins with *Halleluyah* and speaks in praise of God, His greatness and glory. These Psalms used to be recited in the Temple on the festivals and on festal occasions, especially during the time of the sacrifice of the Paschal Lamb. The complete *Hallel,* however, is recited only on the first two days of Pass-

* In addition, the reading of the Law is omitted in the festival *Minḥah* service.

over, two days of Shabuot, nine days of Succot, and the eight days of Hanukkah. On the last six days of Passover and on the first day of the month, Psalms CXV and CXVI are omitted, and it is usually called the incomplete *Hallel.**

27. The High Holiday Services

New Years prayers are, on the whole, distinguished by a note of supplication, a plea for life and health. Still, with the exception of the *Amidah,* there is very little change in the standard prayers recited at the three services. The main change is in the *Amidah* of the *Musaf,* which contains nine benedictions instead of the seven of the Sabbath and holidays. However, the *Amidah* of the other services, though the number of its benedictions is seven, contains several special introductory passages inserted in the third benediction which dwell in various ways on the aspect of the day. These passages repeatedly emphasize God's providence and plead for the coming of the Kingdom of God, for the cessation of evil from the earth, the restoration of Israel, and the establishment of peace on earth. The prayer of *Yaaleh we-Yabo* recited on all festivals in the *Amidah* is also recited on Rosh ha-Shanah. The body of the *Musaf Amidah* is divided into three parts, *Malkiot,* i.e., verses and passages glorifying the Kingship of God, *Zikronot,* i.e., reciting memorable Biblical events in which God displayed His beneficence, and *Shoforot,* i.e., which speaks of the significance of the *Shofar* on certain occasions. Each part consists of ten verses, four from the Pentateuch, and three each from the Prophets and Hagiographa. Each of these parts is also prefaced by introductions and short hymns, one of which is the well-known *'Alénu* later incorporated in the daily service as the closing prayer. The parts conclude with benedictions. Inasmuch as the benediction of the day is combined with that of *Malkiot,* there are only nine benedictions instead of ten. In addition to all these prayers, a group of short supplications (forty-five in number), known as *Abinu Malkénu*

*** In fact verses 12–18 of Psalm CXV are retained in the incomplete *Hallel.***

(Our Father, Our God), is recited. The supplications cover every phase of life of the individual and the nation, that of the latter predominating. *Abinu Malkénu* is recited twice on Rosh ha-Shanah, once at the close of the *Shaḥarit* service, and again, after *Minḥah.* It is also recited during the ten days of penitence after the *Amidah,* morning and afternoon, and also on fast days.

Yom Kippur is a day of prayer and supplication, and has, as mentioned above, five services instead of four, for the *Neilah* is added in the late afternoon. The order of prayers on that day differs only in the *Amidah* which contains, besides the seven benedictions and the special introductions of the New Year service, a distinctive feature, namely, a confessional (Widui) known as *Al-Ḥet,* recited at the end of the benedictions at every service except *Neilah.* The *Al-Ḥet* is a long catalogue of all kinds of sins which a man may have committed willingly or inadvertently. It is in reality a collective or group confession. *Abinu Malkénu* is again recited at the close of all services except the *Musaf.*

28. The Reading of the Law

The reading of the Law during public services dates from the time of the Great Assembly, the early period of the Second Commonwealth. In fact, in the Talmud it is ascribed to Ezra, the titular founder of this Assembly.[5] Reference to such practice is found in the Book of Nehemiah Ch. VIII, 5–18, where we are told that Ezra read from the Law to the assembled people, and it is said: "They read in the Book, in the law of God, distinctly, and gave the sense, and caused them to understand the reading" (ibid. vs. 8). This reading, we are told, was repeated daily during the eight days of the Festival of Tabernacles (vs. 18). It is not definitely stated whether it became a permanent institution immediately or later. However, from the manner in which the Law was read, we can

[5] On the activities of the Great Assembly see Graetz' *History of the Jewish People,* Eng. trans. Vol. I, Ch. XIX; Waxman, "A History of Jewish Literature," Vol. I, Ch. II.

determine the purpose of the reading and why it was later enacted into a permanent institution. The purpose was to teach and instruct the people in the observance as well as the understanding of the Law. In fact, a Talmudic comment interprets the terms of the above-cited verse as follows: "The Law of God" means the Pentateuch; "distinctly (Meforosh)" means with an Aramaic translation; "gave the sense" means with a pause at the end of the verses; "and caused them to understand the reading" means they read with accents and proper pauses, for it is these which help us to understand the meaning of the verses.[6] It can therefore be said that this institution was the first attempt on a large scale to introduce adult education. It must be noted, though, that while the features enumerated in this Rabbinic comment may be attributing later conditions to earlier times, as for instance the use of accents, undoubtedly some of the other features enumerated, such as the translation, accompanied the public reading of the Law from its very beginning. It is well known that the vernacular of the Jews during the Second Commonwealth differed greatly from the Biblical Hebrew and possessed a large admixture of Aramaic, the language spoken by the Jews in the Babylonian exile. Consequently, a translation into the vernacular was needed when the Law was read, and as a translation cannot be literal but must contain comments and interpretative remarks, the reading of the Law served as a fountain-head of the two literary streams which began to flow in the early times of the Second Commonwealth, the *Halakah* and *Agada*.

The reading of the Law was first instituted for the Sabbath and the holidays, days of rest, but later it was extended also to two week days, Monday and Thursday, which were market-days in the cities and towns of Palestine when the villagers crowded into the larger centers for shopping purposes. It was done for the benefit of the villagers living in small settlements who had no public service on Saturdays, or more probably, had no learned man among them to read the Law.

[6] *Talmud* tr. *Nedarim,* 36b.

As education spread and learning multiplied, and a literature was produced, the reading of the Law lost its original character, but the institution remained an important part of the service.

The Torah is now read on the following days and in the following services: On Monday and Thursday during the morning service; twice on the Sabbath, morning and afternoon. On the first of the month, in the morning; on all festivals including New Year, in the morning, with the exception of the Day of Atonement when it is read twice, in the morning and in the *Minḥah* service.

There prevailed in early times two different divisions of the Torah as regards the reading of the Law. In Palestine the Torah was divided into smaller sections known as *Sedarim* of which there were one hundred and fifty-four, and the reading of the Torah was completed in three years. In Babylonia, the Torah was divided into larger sections called *Parshiot*, popularly known as *Sidrot*, of which there are fifty-four, and the reading is completed in a year, so that each week has its *Sidra*. The division is as follows: Genesis contains twelve *Sidrot*, Exodus eleven, Leviticus ten, Numbers ten, Deuteronomy eleven. On the festivals no special *Sidra* is read, but portions of *Sidrot* where the holidays are mentioned are read. As there are only fifty-two weeks in the year, and furthermore, when a holiday falls on the Sabbath the weekly portion is not read but rather the one appropriate to the holiday, there are, as a result, more *Sidrot* than weeks. It was therefore thought advisable to read two *Sidrot* on a Sabbath several times during the year. This device is unnecessary during a leap year when a better numerical balance is achieved.

Formerly, the practice was to call a number of people to read the Torah, each reading a section, but for centuries now the practice is to have a reader chant the entire portion of the week while the people who are called merely listen. They do, however, pronounce two benedictions, one preceding the reading and the second at the conclusion. The benedictions express thankfulness to God for giving the Torah to Israel.

The number of people called and the order of the reading on various occasions are as follows: On the Sabbath morning seven people are called, and as said, the entire portion of the week is read. On Sabbath afternoons only three persons are called, and only one-seventh of the next week's portion is read, and the same procedure is followed on Mondays and Thursdays. On the first day of the month and on semi-holidays four people are called, and selected portions of the Pentateuch dealing with the affairs of the day are read. On all the festivals including New Year five people are called and the readings are selected from various parts of the Bible which have reference to the events of the day. On the Day of Atonement, at the morning service, six people are called and in the afternoon three, and the readings are selected accordingly.

In addition to the reading of the Torah there were instituted for each Sabbath and the holidays readings from the Prophets, the content of which refers to incidents related in the portion of the week. These are called *Haftorot* (closing sections), namely, they conclude the reading of the Torah. The one called to read the prophetic portion is called *Maftir* (one who concludes) and is also given a section of the Pentateuch to read, thus adding one to the standard number. On the Sabbath, the reading consists of a repetition of some verses read before. On the festivals or when the first of the month falls on the Sabbath, a second Scroll of the Law is taken out and a number of verses from Numbers XXVIII dealing with the sacrifices on holidays and *Rosh Ḥodesh* is read by the *Maftir*. The reading of the *Haftorah* is preceded and succeeded by special benedictions.

There is a certain order observed in the calling of the people to the Torah. The first to be called is a *Kohen,* i.e., Aaronide, the second a Levite, then an Israelite follows. It was customary to call a scholar as the third, but now there are no fixed rules. One called to the Torah must be over thirteen years of age. Occasionally a *Maftir* is given to a younger child, usually to a boy who is about to be confirmed. Both the Torah and the Prophets are read in a chant in accordance with the accents with which the words are supplied.[7]

There are four Sabbaths in the year which bear special significance. They begin with the two Sabbaths before Purim and end with the one before Passover. These are Sabbath *Shekolim, Zakar, Parah,* and *Ḥodesh.* The first is in commemoration of the *Shekel* which every Jew throughout the world paid as his tribute to the Temple. It was collected on the first of the month of *Adar.* The second Sabbath is based on the identification of Haman the Agagite as a descendant of Agog, King of the Amalekites, the inveterate enemies of Israel, who was killed by Samuel (I Samuel, Ch. XV). It is called *Zakar* because verse 17 in Chapter XXV of Deuteronomy begins with the words, "*Zakar et Asher Asah Leka Amalek*" (Remember what Amalek did unto you), and it is intended to remind us of the deeds of Haman. *Parah* (cow) is connected with the Red Heifer ceremony, the ashes of which were sprinkled upon the unclean in order to purify them, and inasmuch as those that were unclean could not eat of the Paschal Lamb, the Jews hastened to purify themselves before Passover. *Ḥodesh* is in connection with the first of Nisan, the month in which Passover falls and which is considered, as the Pentateuch states, the first of the months of the year.[8] On these four Sabbaths, there is a special reading from appropriate sections, such as Exodus XXX, 11–15, where the first half *Shekel,* a contribution for the Tabernacle, is mentioned; Deuteronomy XXV, 17–29, where the deeds of Amalek are stated; Numbers XIX, 1–22, where the rite of the Red Heifer is given; and Exodus XII, 1–20. The sections are read for the *Maftir* usually in a separate Scroll, and there are also special *Haftorot*

[7] The main purpose of the accents was to serve as signs of punctuation, yet each sign serves also as a note, and consequently there developed several chants in which the Law and the Prophets are read.

[8] As can be seen, only the Sabbaths *Zakar* and *Ḥodesh* have special significance which stems directly from the holidays which they precede, while that of the other two, *Shekalim* and *Parah,* lies primarily in the desire to keep alive the memories of Jewish life in Palestine as much as possible. This demonstrates once more how great was the hold of Palestine upon Jewry.

for these Sabbaths the content of which refers in some way to the event of the day.

In addition, the Five *Megillot* or Scrolls are also read in the synagogue—Esther and Lamentations on Purim and the ninth of Ab respectively, Song of Songs on the Sabbath during the Passover week, Ruth on Shabuot, and Kohelet or Ecclesiastes on the Sabbath during the Festival of Tabernacles.

29. Occasional Prayers and Benedictions

The fundamental thought of the Jewish religion that man is to express his gratitude frequently to God for His multifarious benefits is not limited to the stated daily services, but is interpreted in a broad manner. Such expression is required on many occasions, and especially on those when joy or pleasure is experienced. Those expressions of thankfulness which acknowledge God's creation of things as well as His providence are usually given in brief benedictions pronounced primarily at the time of the enjoyment of food and drink of various types.

They are as follows: The benediction on vegetables which grow directly from the soil is: "Blessed art Thou, our God, King of the universe, the Creator of the fruit of the soil." On fruits, the formula varies to "Creator of the fruit of the trees." On things which grow neither in the soil nor on trees, as fish, meat, etc., as well as liquids, the benediction varies to, "He by Whose word everything comes into existence." Wine, however, is distinguished by a special formula, "The Creator of the fruit of the vine." And likewise there is a special formula for bread which reads, "He Who produces bread from the earth." For other types of food made of flour, as cakes, pastries, etc., the formula is, "The Creator of various kinds of food."

There are also two benedictions pronounced after partaking of these fruits or foods. One called *Berakah Aḥaronah* is recited after the eating of choice fruits (seven kinds) or pastries, or drinking of a substantial portion of wine. A shorter one is pronounced on other fruits and foods, such as meat and fish, which reads: "The Creator of souls and bodies Who provided them with things they need, and the Creator of all things alive, blessed is He, the Ever-living One."

The enjoyment of the sense of smell is also preceded by a short benediction; if the sweet smelling spices grow on the tree the formula is: "The Creator of spice trees"; if herbs, the word herbs is inserted. On the enjoyment of a new fruit or on donning a new garment, the benediction pronounced is: "He who kept us alive and in existence up to the present." Natural manifestations have their benedictions. At the sight of lightning: "He who continues the work of creation"; on hearing the rumble of thunder: "He whose might and strength fills the world." Even the sight of a distinguished scholar or great political figure has its benedictions. The first reads: "He who gave a portion of His wisdom to men"; and the second inserts "His honor" instead of wisdom. News or events, good or bad, have their benedictions; the former: "He who is good and does good"; and the latter: "The true and impartial Judge," indicating a calm submission to the judgment of God.

30. The Meal

The meal occupies an important position in the religious ritual. It is preceded by the lavation of the hands with its proper benediction, and the breaking of bread with the *ha-Motzi.* The main feature is grace after meals, which is long and consists of four benedictions. The first is an expression of thankfulness to God in His capacity as provider. The second contains thanks to God for giving Palestine and the Torah to the Jews. It is of ancient origin, hailing from the time before the destruction of the Temple. The third is a prayer for redemption and the restoration of Jerusalem; and the fourth contains prayers and expressions of gratitude for the general benefits God bestows upon man in His kind providence as well as individual good wishes for the family or the host and hostess.

When the meal is partaken of by three men or more, the pronouncement of grace is preceded by an invitation by one to perform the ceremony. He says, "Let us thank God for the meal," and the others respond, "Blessed is He of whose substance we partook." This particular way of saying grace is called *Zimun,* namely invitation—in the vernacular a *Mezuman.* At weddings, or at meals in a mourner's house, or at feasts of circumcision, special benedictions which refer to the event of the day are added to the regular grace. At such occasions grace is usually recited over a cup of wine.

31. Ẓiẓit, Tefilin, and Mezuzah

There are two distinctive religious symbols, namely, *Ẓiẓit* (fringes) and *Tefilin* (phylacteries), the former pertaining to dress, and the latter employed in connection with prayer. It is explicitly stated in Numbers XV, 37, that the children of Israel shall wear fringes on the four borders of their garments. It was later interpreted to mean that the commandment is obligatory only upon one who has a garment which is square, but if it is of different shape, there is no obligation to attach the fringes. The *Ẓiẓit,* while preferably made of wool or threads of spun flax, can be made also of other materials, such as silk. Formerly these fringes were dyed blue. The fringes are placed at the four corners of the four borders of the garment and consist of four threads which usually are folded in two so that there are really eight threads.

Since we, as a rule, do not wear that type of garment, substitutes had to be found in order that the law should not be abolished altogether. These are called *Talit* and *Talit Katan* or *Arba Kanfot.* The *Talit* or the prayer shawl is a square piece of cloth made of wool, linen, or silk, which has the fringes placed at the four corners of its borders. The *Talit* is usually worn at services by men or boys after confirmation.

In order to make the wearing of fringes accessible to all males of any age as well as a permanent feature of dress, the

Arba Kanfot was introduced. It is a small square piece of cloth with fringes at the corners of its borders and is worn under the upper garment.

The *Tefilin* are not expressly commanded in the Torah but are implied by logical interpretation of the words in Deuteronomy VI, 8: "And thou shalt bind them (referring to the words of the command in the previous verse) on thine hand, and they shall be as frontlets between thine eyes." (The word *le-Totofot* translated frontlets means literally an ornament which used to be worn on the head.) A very old tradition, often called Sinaitic, took the words literally as implying that the most important teachings of the Torah should in some way be constantly before the eyes of every Jew and introduced some means to realize that ideal. Accordingly, there were selected four important passages of the Bible which are placed in two small boxes of parchment and placed on the hand and on the forehead by means of leather straps. These are worn during the morning prayers, the time when the Jew communes with God.

The first two passages are Exodus XIII, 1–11 and 11–16, where the Exodus from Egypt is emphasized, and the commandment to commemorate the event during the generations by sanctifying the first-born as a reminder of the tenth plague brought upon the Egyptians is stated. Verse 16 of the second passage reads: "And it shall be taken on thy hand and for the frontlets between thine eyes, for by the strength of hand the Lord brought us forth out of Egypt." The other two passages are Deuteronomy VI, 4–10, the *Shema,* where the unity and love of God as well as obedience to the Torah are stressed, and XI, 13–21, where divine providence is emphasized and the commandment about the phylacteries is repeated. These four passages written on pieces of parchment are placed in the head frontlet or phylactery in four compartments, but in the phylactery of the hand all are placed in one compartment.

The Jewish house is also decorated by a religious symbol called *Mezuzah.* It is explicitly commanded in one of the above-mentioned passages, Deuteronomy XI, 20: "And thou shalt write them (i.e., important passages of the Torah referred to in previous verses) upon the doorposts of thy house and upon thy gates." Accordingly, two of the passages, namely Deuteronomy VI, 4–8, the *Shema,* and Deuteronomy XI, 13–21, are written on a piece of parchment and placed in a case which is nailed on the doorpost of the house. The parchment with the writing is called *Mezuzah* because in Hebrew *Mezuzah* also signifies doorpost.

CHAPTER IV

DIETARY LAWS

32. CLEAN AND UNCLEAN ANIMALS

Judaism is a religion which embraces all phases of the life of the Jew. It is no wonder, then, that there are numerous precepts which deal with his daily life in the home. And first of all, there are those called the dietary laws. Of the numerous animals, domestic and wild, namely quadrupeds, fowl, and fish, the Jew is restricted to a small number distinguished by certain characteristics which mark it as "clean." Of the quadrupeds, only those are considered clean, i.e., permitted to be eaten, whose hoof is cleft and who chew their cud. As a rule, animals which possess one of these marks also possess the other, with the exception of the camel which chews its cud but does not have the cleft hoof, and the pig which, on the other hand, has the cleft hoof but does not chew its cud. It is to be noted that these animals are all herbiverous and not carniverous or predatory, symbolic of the fact that life must be gentle and not violent, for the view was held that the nature of the food determines a man's character.*

The Torah does not specify the characteristics of the fowl which are considered clean, but enumerates twenty-four species prohibited as food. Tradition, however, did find some identifying marks. The general one is that any bird which places its foot upon its food before eating is unclean. Birds which have an extra toe in the back and a gizzard which can be peeled are clean. However, the bird need not possess all three marks; one of these coupled with its manner of eating is

* We may be reminded of the biologist Büchner's dictum, "Der mensch ist was er isst" (A man is what he eats).

sufficient. It is to be noted in this case as in the former that birds possessing these characteristics are not predatory.

As for fish, the Torah distinctly states that only fish which have scales and fins—and usually the fish that have scales also have fins—may be eaten. All other species of fish are prohibited.

33. Preparation of Kosher Food

In order to eat the meat of an animal, quadruped or bird, it must first be slaughtered in a definite manner which consists in cutting the organs of the esophagus and the windpipe. In the case of a quadruped, both organs or at least the larger parts of them, must be cut; but as for birds, the cutting of one organ is sufficient. Fish may be killed in any manner.

The knife with which the slaughtering is done must be not only sharp but without any blemish. The smallest dent can disqualify the slaughtering. Consequently, the slaughterer, before performing the act, examines the knife with the greatest scrutiny, running it three times over his finger and three times over his nail. This care is taken so as to obviate any unnecessary pain to the animal. For the same reason, the cutting must be done adroitly and within a limited space of the throat. Any digression from this procedure disqualifies the slaughtering and the animal is declared unfit for food. When one slaughters a bird or one of the few undomesticated quadrupeds which are classed as clean, the slaughterer is to cover with earth the blood which flows out of the body immediately after the slaughtering.

After slaughtering, the animal is not yet fit to be eaten until it is examined to determine its state of health during life. If any signs of disease are evident, it is pronounced *Terefah,* i.e., not to be eaten just as if it were not slaughtered but killed violently by a carnivorous animal. There are numerous rules governing these matters, but in general it can be said that when any of the important organs, as the brain, the windpipe, the esophagus, the heart, the lungs, or intestines is found perforated or with evidence that it had been perforated, the animal is pronounced *Terefah.* Consequently, the animal is examined by experts before it is pronounced Kosher. However, taking into consideration that the other organs are not as subject to injuries as the lungs, which are the most likely to be diseased, the examination is primarily centered on the lungs, while the other organs are looked at casually, and if anything is noted, they are then examined more carefully.

Due to the special adroitness necessary for the performance of ritual slaughtering and the knowledge of the laws of hygiene needed in the examination of the body of the slaughtered animal, ritual slaughtering is considered a profession for which proper preparation is necessary. The one who prepares for this profession must pass an examination in the presence of Rabbis, both in theoretical and practical parts, and he is then given a certificate as *Shoḥet.* The certificate is called *Kabbalah,* a term which signifies that the *Shoḥet* has undertaken to follow the rules and regulations established by law.

The meat now must go through still another process before it can be eaten. The purpose of the process is to draw out the blood from it as well as to remove parts of the fat of the animal which are forbidden. Consequently, after slaughtering, veins containing blood are removed together with parts of the prohibited fat of the quadruped. In addition, there is the sinew in the hind part of the animal which, according to Genesis XXXII, 33, is prohibited and which must be removed. In former times, there were men who specialized in the removal of these sinews and thus prepared the flesh of the entire animal as Kosher. Under modern conditions, as a rule, the hind part is not used by Jews who observe the dietary laws.

Again, since the eating of blood is prohibited, it follows that meat which contains blood is also prohibited. Hence, it must undergo a further process of preparation before it is ready for cooking. This process consists in soaking the meat in water for half an hour and then salting it and keeping it in that state for an hour. The soaking softens the fibres of the meat and enables the salt to draw out the absorbed blood. During the salting the meat is placed on a perforated inclined board so that the exuded blood may run off and not be reabsorbed by the meat.

The prohibition against tasting blood extends also to eggs, for some frequently have drops of blood in them. Consequently, if such a drop or drops are found, the egg is disqualified. Only eggs laid by birds which are clean are permissible for use, for the eggs of unclean birds are likewise considered unclean. It was therefore determined on the basis of experiment to assign marks of distinction which are as follows: If an egg has one end round and the other oval and the yolk is surrounded by a white liquid, it is considered clean; but if both ends are round or oval and the yolk is outside of the white of the egg, it is prohibited.

34. Other Dietary Laws

The prohibition against seething a kid in its mother's milk is repeated in the Torah three times (Exodus XXIII, 19; XXXIV, 26; Deuteronomy XIV, 21). Tradition inferred from this that not only does the commandment refer to boiling a kid in its mother's milk, but that it is all-inclusive and prohibits the eating of meat in general with milk or mixing the two in any way or form. Furthermore, even the deriving of profit by selling the mixture to a non-Jew is prohibited. From such interpretation there ensued the complex regulations connected with this matter. The general rule is that a mixture of the two may be considered Kosher only if one, i.e., the milk or the meat exceeds the other sixty times, e.g., if a drop of milk falls on a piece of meat or in a meat soup, and if the meat or soup contains sixty times its quantity, the mixture is Kosher, and the same applies, of course, if a piece of meat or soup falls into milk; otherwise it is *Terefah*. This rule applies also to all utensils in which the meat or milk is boiled, for it is assumed that they are saturated with particles of either. Consequently, if a spoon used for milk soup is placed in a hot pot of meat soup, the soup must contain enough liquid to displace sixty spoons in order to be Kosher; and similarly, if the spoon is used with meat. The rule, however, applies only if the meat or soup is hot, but if they are cold, e.g., if cold meat and cheese touch each other, or if a cold piece of meat falls into cold milk, all that is necessary is to wash the meat. The reason is that the process of absorption starts only in high temperature. When the proper measure of sixty times the spoon or of the meat or of the milk is not found, the entire mixture is *Terefah,* and even the utensils containing it may not be used. In order to make the utensils Kosher again, they are to be dipped in boiling water several times so that whatever is absorbed therein is exuded.

The measure of sixty times was adopted because it was thought that the taste of anything can be felt in a mixture up to that amount but no further. Because of these rigors against mixing meat and milk in all their ramifications, all Jews who observe the dietary laws have two sets of dishes, tableware, and pots, and keep them strictly apart.

Chapter V

THE FAMILY AND ITS INSTITUTIONS

35. The Place of the Family in Judaism

There is no religion or nation in which the family occupies such an important place as in Judaism. In fact, according to the Bible and Jewish tradition, the entire nation sprang and developed from a single family. And furthermore, the development proceeded not from all the members of the family, but from those whose character displayed traits of nobility and righteousness. Tradition thus indicates the value placed by Judaism in its very beginning upon character as the most important element in family life. Consequently, the highest values are placed upon sanctity, purity, and stability of the family. The laws relating to these subjects are numerous and occupy a considerable part of the legal portions of the Pentateuch and the Talmud, and their general purpose is to ennoble the life of the family and its institutions.

36. Marriage

Marriage is the basis and the source of all family life. Small wonder then that its value is continually emphasized in the entire Jewish literature beginning with the Pentateuch. According to the Book of Genesis, marriage was instituted by God Himself at the very beginning of creation of man. The words: "It is not good for man to be alone" (Genesis II, 6), impart to the association between man and woman an importance above the level of mere satisfaction of a biological necessity and emphasize the element of companionship through their entire life. Later we find the divine command, "increase and multiply," considered by authoritative Judaism an expressed precept, one of the 613 precepts obligatory upon Jews to obey. The propagation of the species was thus placed as the primary purpose of marriage and Talmudic law states that a man is obliged to have a minimum of children in order to fulfill this precept. The minimum is two, one male and one female. The Prophets often describe the relation between God and Israel symbolically as a marriage-tie or covenant, and constantly emphasize the element of love and the impossibility for a husband to forget the wife of his youth, a figure which reflects the high conception of the marital tie.

The Pentateuch does not prohibit polygamy, and we also know that the kings, David and Solomon, had many wives like most of the Oriental kings. However, even during earlier times, monogamy was the ideal marriage, as is evident from the very symbolism used by the Prophets in comparing the relation of God to Israel to that of a marriage. The same ideal is reflected in the poem dedicated to the industrious wife in Proverbs XXXI, 10–31. From early post-exilic times, monogamy was the rule and polygamy the exception. The Prophet Malachi storms against those who take an additional wife, and says: "The Lord hath been a witness between thee and the wife of thy youth against whom thou hast dealt treacherously. Yet, she is thy companion and the wife of thy covenant" (Malachi II, 14). Such utterances indicate that monogamy was the general practice, and those who acted otherwise were considered sinners. There is not a single reference in the literature produced during the Second Commonwealth that any Hasmonean prince practiced polygamy. According to Josephus,[1] Herod indeed had nine wives, but from the apology which Josephus offers for him, namely that it was permitted by law, we can conclude that it was not the practice. Besides, Herod was not the ideal Jewish prince. And certainly in Talmudic and post-Talmudic times monogamy was the rule. Of the numerous Tannaim, Amoraim, and

[1] Antiquities XVII, 1, 3, & Wars I, XXIV, 2.

Geonim, we know of no one who had more than one wife. The Agadic statement that forty days before a male child is born a heavenly voice announces: "The daughter of a certain man is destined to be the wife of the child who is about to be born," [2] as well as the saying which speaks figuratively of match-making as one of the numerous occupations of God Himself [3] reflect the attitude of Judaism towards monogamy. Jewish mysticism calls the unmarried man or woman a half person—*Plag Gufa* (literally half a body), meaning that both together make a complete person. It buttresses this view by a mystic notion of marriage. According to it all souls in their pre-existent state consist of masculine and feminine elements. When the time comes for the descent of the soul, it splits in two, the masculine descending into a male child and the feminine into a female child. Later in life, when the time for marriage arrives, these two halves are again united. There is, however, a condition attached to this union, namely the worth of the man. If he is worthy, he obtains as his wife the woman who possesses the second half of his soul, if not it may be any other woman.[4] This allegory expresses not only the high regard for monogamy but also asserts that the proper marriage is founded on the harmony of souls and characters. Still, in the early Middle Ages, in Oriental countries under the influence of Islamic environment, cases of bigamy or even of polygamy were not unknown among the Jews, and probably also made their appearance in European countries. Rabbi Gershom, known as the Light of the Exile (940–1028), then ordained that any breach of monogamy be punished by the severest type of excommunication and the ordinance was accepted by entire European Jewry as a fixed law.

37. Prohibited Alliances

The Pentateuch prohibits any intimate relation between twenty-one consanguines under the pain of death, either by

[2] T. B. *Sotah* 2.
[3] *Leviticus Rabba,* Ch. VIII.
[4] *Zohar,* Pt. I, p. 91b.

decree of court or by heavenly judgment. Of the Biblical prohibited alliances, some run to the third degree, both downwards and upwards, as for instance, the prohibited relation between a man and his mother-in-law's mother; while some run only to the second degree, as nephew and aunt. Later, twenty more consanguines with whom marriage or intimate relation is prohibited were added by the early Rabbis. In the case of sixteen of these, the prohibition is one degree removed, i.e., to the third downward or upward, where Biblically it stops at the second degree, but four continue indefinitely. These are (1–2) the two grandmothers on the maternal side, i.e., father's mother, her mother, and so on indefinitely, and mother's mother, her mother, etc., (3) step-grandmother, and (4) the wives of the grandsons and great-grandsons on the male side. On the female side, the prohibition stops with the third degree, i.e., the wife of the daughter's son. However, a marriage between uncle and niece is permitted and likewise between first cousins.

38. Minority and Majority Ages

In Jewish law there is a slight difference in regard to attainment of majority between male and female. The minority of the former extends to the age of thirteen, while that of the latter terminates at twelve, at the time when she displays signs of puberty. However, at that age she does not attain the full status of majority, only a partial one. That period of transition extends for six months and a day during which time she is called a *Naarah,* i.e., a young woman, but at the end of that time she acquires the status of full womanhood and is called a *Bogeret,* i.e., matured. During the periods of minority and young womanhood (*Naarut*) she is under paternal authority in regard to marriage, and only the father has a right to give her in marriage—with her consent, of course. In case she takes the initiative and is married without the consent of her father, the marriage is invalid. However, in the case of an orphan the situation is changed; the minor is given in marriage by her mother and brothers, and the marriage is valid by Rabbinical ordination, while the young woman attains her majority immediately and has full right to marry by her own initiative.

The betrothal and marriage of a male minor by his own initiative is invalid and has no legal status. The above statement regarding the paternal right to give in marriage a minor daughter as well as one who is in the transitory stage (*Naarah*) is the legal view, but Jewish authorities always looked with disfavor upon such marriages, and the most authoritative code, that of Karo (the *Shulḥan Aruk*),[5] says that it is a religious duty not to marry off a minor daughter until she is able to choose the man herself. It therefore goes without saying that when a woman attains her majority, marriage must take place with her full consent and any forced marriage is null and void.

The attainment of majority by the male at thirteen gives him the complete status of a man, both legally and religiously. Legally, his commercial transactions of whatever nature are valid, and likewise, his betrothal and marriage contract are valid. He is also held responsible for any deeds of infringement or transgression of the law and is subject to all the prescribed punishments for the various acts.

Religiously, he is from that date on considered a full-fledged Jew and is obliged to perform all affirmative precepts as well as to take care not to transgress any of the prohibitive commandments. He is henceforth counted as a member of the quorum necessary for the conduct of a public service, and is entitled to be called to the reading of the Law.

The most distinguishing feature, however, in this entrance of the boy into the religious fellowship is the act of putting on phylacteries at the week-day morning prayers. Up to the age of thirteen, the young are exempt from this duty, but from the thirteenth year on, this obligation is imposed upon him.

In early times this entry of the young man into the full

[5] *Shulḥan Aruk*, Part *Eben ha-Ezer*, Ch. 37, 8.

membership of the community of Israel, assuming all duties and obligations, was considered a natural and ordinary event not marked by any special ceremony. In later times, however—the exact date cannot be determined—the event assumed a more ceremonial aspect and was given a special name, *Bar Mitzvah,* which means that henceforth he receives the yoke of the *Mitzvot*. Simultaneously, the day began to be celebrated as a family festival marked by a few ceremonies. On the Sabbath of the week during which the boy becomes thirteen years old, at the morning service in the synagogue, the celebrant is called to the reading of the Law and is given the *Maftir* passage of the Torah, and he then reads also the Prophetic portion with the benedictions preceding and following it. Being called to the reading of the Law and the chanting of the *Haftorah* serve as a kind of public ceremony of initiation into the religious community. Formerly, the father of the *Bar Mitzvah* pronounced a special benediction while reading his portion of the Torah, in which he thanks God for his release from the responsibility which he hitherto bore for the conduct of his son.* Occasionally the celebrant or the *Bar Mitzvah* boy delivered in the synagogue or at a family feast in honor of the event a short speech of a religious nature.

In our own days, especially in this country, due to circumstances, primarily to the influence of the confirmation ceremony adopted by the Reform wing of Jewry, the celebration of the *Bar Mitzvah* event assumed undue importance with all Jewish factions. It is practically considered the most outstanding event in the religious life of the young Jew, and frequently forms the only link which connects him with the religion of his people. Many parents who otherwise neglect the Jewish education of their children do not fail to celebrate

* It is mentioned by Moses Isserlis (1520–1575) in his Gloss to Karo's Code (Shulḥan Aruk) Pt. I, Sec. 225, where he quotes Jacob Möllin (1365–1422) as well as Mordecai ben Hillel (d. 1298) for the opinion that the father should pronounce a special benediction on the day when the son becomes *Bar Mitzvah.* From this we can deduce that the beginning of the celebration of the *Bar Mitzvah* can be traced to the 13th century. Reference to the feast on that day is also mentioned by Solomon Luria of Poland (1510–1574) in his commentary on the tractate *Baba Kama* of the Talmud.

the *Bar Mitzvah* of their sons and see that they should be prepared for the occasion, namely to chant the *Haftorah* in the synagogue.

39. The Marriage Ceremony

The act of betrothal (*Kiddushin*) which gives the pair the status of a married couple consists in the bridegroom placing a ring on the finger of the bride in the presence of at least two witnesses and pronouncing the formula: "Thou art betrothed unto me with this ring in accordance with the law of Moses and Israel." The ring, however, is not, according to the strict meaning of the law, a necessity. A coin may take its place. Formerly, the marriage ceremony was divided into two parts: the *Erusin*, or betrothal, and the marriage proper. The first consisted in the *Kiddushin* ceremony and was performed earlier than the marriage proper. And while the woman was considered married, inasmuch as intercourse with another man was considered a crime, severely punishable, she did not yet have the full status of a married woman in regard to other matters, such as the duties of the husband towards her until she actually came to live with him, or after the *Ḥupah* ceremony. For centuries, however, this division of ceremonies has not been practiced. Now the betrothal and marriage ceremonies are combined. The pair are brought under a canopy and a benediction called *Birkat Erusin,* referring to the sanctity of betrothal and marriage, is pronounced over a cup of wine. Following this, the *Kiddushin* ceremony is performed with the pronouncement of the abovementioned formula. The *Ketubah* is then read. The *Ketubah* is the formal marriage document in which the willingness of both parties to enter into the contract of marriage is expressed and some of the mutual duties specified. Besides, the husband obligates himself to give to the wife a certain sum as the *Mohar,* i.e., dowry. This sum was fixed in early times as 200 *Zuzim,* about $50 if the bride was a virgin and 100 *Zuzim* if a widow or divorcee. The *Ketubah* money is paid on divorce or on the death of the husband when the widow leaves the house. It is customary to increase the endowment to any amount the groom may see fit; usually it is doubled and the *Ketubah* is read that way. After the reading seven benedictions are pronounced over a cup of wine. Because of this number, the benedictions are usually referred to as *Sheba Berakot,* i.e., seven benedictions. There is an ancient custom to break a glass at the conclusion of the wedding ceremony. The reason given is to remind the cheerful throng of the destruction of the Temple by an admixture of grief—though of a slight nature—over the loss of a glass which in former times was usually a very expensive one. At present, however this has lost significance. At the wedding feast, the seven benedictions are again recited after grace. The ceremony is, as a rule, performed in the presence of ten men, a *Minyan,* i.e., a quorum, but this is not an absolute necessity.

As it is stated in Leviticus XXI, 7, a *Kohen,* i.e., an *Aaronide,* is not allowed to marry a divorcee and the injunction has been observed even in exile through the ages.

40. Marital Life

Although Jewish law enjoins a number of restrictions upon the rights of the married woman, for it gives to the husband the right to the profits of her labor and the enjoyment of the income of her private property, still the place of the woman in the family is an honorable one. The entire Jewish literature, the Bible, the Talmud, and the post-Talmudic works, continually extol the value of a happily married life and make it dependent upon the respect paid by the husband to the wife. The Book of Proverbs contains an extensive poem, arranged alphabetically, in praise of the virtuous woman (Proverbs XXXI, 10–31), and in another place it says: "Whoso findeth a wife findeth a good thing, and obtaineth the favor of the Lord" (ibid. XVIII, 22). Ben Sira declares: "A good wife is the best of gifts."[6] The Talmud, in laying down the

[6] Proverbs of Ben Sira, XXVI, 13.

conditions of a happily married life, says: "One who loves his wife more than he loves himself and honors his wife more than he honors himself, he can be sure that peace and harmony will reign in his house; as the verse says, 'And you will know that peace is in thy tent'" (Job V, 24).[7]

Judaism insists on modest conduct on the part of the married woman, and such conduct is exceedingly praised by the sages, while the reverse is reproved severely. A certain standard of conduct is even called the law or code of the Jewish woman (Dat Yehudit). The one who transgresses it is subject to punishment, inasmuch as the husband may divorce her without giving her the fixed sum designated in the *Ketubah*. Among the breaches of the standard of conduct are, going out in public with uncovered head, spinning or weaving in the street, thereby attracting the attention of the passersby, and flirting with strangers.[8] Some of these, especially the first breach, seem too stringent to the modern man and woman, but we must not forget that these rules were formulated in an Oriental environment.

Likewise, mild continence in marital relations is urged, and in reality not only urged but excess is prevented by laws concerning prohibition of intercourse during the menses. The Bible explicitly states that intercourse is forbidden for a period of seven days from the beginning of the menses. Rabbinic law is severe in this matter and decrees that seven days must elapse from the day the flow ceases entirely, and only then can intercourse be resumed. The severity of the Rabbinic law causes an extension of the prohibited days to various numbers depending upon the complete cessation of the flow. The Bible also prohibits intercourse during seven days after the birth of a male child and fourteen days after the birth of a female child. Later law imposed here also the rule of seven days of purity, but if the flow has not stopped, the prohibition may extend to fourteen days in case of the former, and twenty-one days in case of the latter.

[7] Talmud Babli, *Jebamot*, 62.
[8] Talmud Babli, *Ketubot*, 72b.

However, even after the termination of the seven days of purity, intercourse is permitted only after immersion of the woman either in the waters of a river, or a well, or in a place where water is collected, either rain water or water drawn from a river or a well. The collected water must contain at least 240 gallons (literally 40 *S'ah* or a space of three cubic cubits filled with water). There are numerous laws and regulations connected with it, both in regard to the observation of the days of menses and those of purity, as well as the construction of the *Mikweh,* i.e., the ritual bath, and the manner of immersion. But these are primarily for specialists; we only give the general outline.

These laws were scrupulously observed by Jewry for millennia and are still observed by a large number of Jews. In former times, and even today, there is hardly a well-established community which does not maintain a bathhouse with a *Mikweh* constructed according to regulations. The observance of this rite is called *Taharat ha-Mishpaḥah* (the purity of the family), and there is no doubt that it contributed much towards raising the family life to a higher level by introducing moderation in marital relations and that it is also advisable from a biological point of view as testified by authorities.

41. Divorce

The attitude of Judaism towards divorce can, on the whole, be considered a liberal one. The Pentateuch states explicitly that "when a man hath taken a wife and hath married her, and it came to pass that she find no favor in his eyes because he had found some uncleanness in her, let him write her a bill of divorcement, and give it in her hand and send her out of the house" (Deuteronomy XXIV, 1). From the literal meaning of the verse it follows that the only condition for divorce is adultery on the part of the woman, or unseemly conduct in matters of religion, such as conversion to another faith, or open transgression of important precepts which may be subsumed under the term uncleanness. And this is the opinion of the school of the early Tannaim (Beth Shammai). However, the School of Hillel held a more liberal view and allowed divorce for other reasons, such as inattention to matters of the household or a general incompatibility of character. Akiba went further and allowed divorce for even a personal change of attitude of the husband towards his wife.[9] The accepted opinion, though, is that one cannot divorce his first wife except for uncleanness, i.e., conditions stated above, but has greater latitude in case of the second wife. It is said of one who divorces his first wife that "even the Altar weeps because of him." [10]

However, both the severity and the lenience assume a different aspect if we attend to other phases of the Jewish law of divorce. According to Jewish law the husband is the only one who has the right to divorce his wife. A court has no right to grant a divorce, nor can the wife sue for one. What is more, according to Talmudic law, she can be divorced even against her will. But from the 10th century on, that is since the decree of Rabbi Gershom, it was established that no man can divorce his wife without her consent, and it is in that way that Jewry has conducted itself for close to a thousand years. Consequently, the conditions necessary for the validity of a divorce mentioned above lose their importance since a divorce is valid only by mutual agreement. Only in exceptional cases can the court interfere either at the request of the wife on account of certain diseases, or at the request of the husband for definite reasons, and force the husband to a divorce or the woman to accept one. Otherwise it is the husband of his own free will who gives the divorce with the consent of the wife.

The divorce bill is written and issued by the court, which sees that all regulations are observed. The principal regulations are as follows: (1) Divorce must be by a bill in writing, no oral statement suffices. (2) The writing must be done, as stated, at the bidding of the husband. (3) It must be written

[9] T. B. *Gittin*, 90a.
[10] Ibid. 90b.

according to a certain version which states the purpose clearly and in no ambiguous words. (4) The bill must be written with intention for the particular man and the particular woman. (5) It must be signed by two witnesses. (6) It must be given into the hands of the woman or placed in one of the vessels she uses frequently. (7) It must be given to the woman before two witnesses. In addition, the exact date must be stated, year of creation, month, and day. From the strictly legal point of view, the bill of divorce can be written in any language and in any script. However, it was decided to use the standard version handed down from Talmudic times which is in the Hebrew script and in the Aramaic language, and for many centuries no one has dared to introduce any changes. The bill must be written clearly in a legible handwriting and with proper spelling, and in general, with great carefulness so that no possible mistake in the reading of a word may ensue. Consequently, there are numerous rules and regulations in regard to the writing of the bill any breach of which may invalidate it. The witnesses must not be related to one another nor to any of the principals.

The husband does not necessarily need to hand over the divorce himself; he can do so through an agent. In view of the numerous rules and regulations attached to the execution of the divorce, the act is carried out before a court of three men of which a Rabbi well versed in the Law is a member. On the receipt of the bill of divorce, the woman is paid by the husband the sum stated in the *Ketubah,* the amount fixed by law, as well as any additional sum he may have promised at the wedding.

Traditional Jewish law requires for a legal divorce that the bill be executed according to all regulations and does not accept a civil divorce in lieu of it, but the practice today is that no Jewish divorce is issued unless a civil divorce has previously been obtained.

According to Biblical law, a man may remarry his divorced wife provided she was not married to another in the interim. If she was he cannot remarry her. A *Kohen* or an Aaronide cannot remarry his divorced wife. The husband may remarry immediately after the divorce but the wife must wait three months after she receives the bill of divorce. This is done in order to establish definitely the paternity of the child to which she may give birth after her second marriage. It is thought that this period would establish definitely when pregnancy began.

41a. Yibum (Levirate Marriage) and Halizah

It is stated in the Pentateuch (Deut. XXV, 5–10): "If brethren dwell together, and one of them die and have no child, the wife of the dead shall not marry unto a stranger; her husband's brother shall go in unto her and take her to him to wife, and perform the duty of an husband's brother unto her. And it shall be, that the first born that she beareth shall succeed in the name of his brother that is dead and his name be not blotted out of Israel. And if the man like not to take his brother's wife, then his brother's wife shall go up to the gate unto the elders and say: 'My husband's brother refuseth to raise up unto his brother a name in Israel; he will not perform the duty of a husband's brother unto me.' Then the elders of the city shall call him and speak unto him; and if he stand and say: 'I like not to take her'; then shall his brother's wife draw nigh unto him in the presence of the elders and loose his shoe off his foot, and spit in his face and say: 'So shall be done unto the man that buildeth not up his brother's house.' And his name shall be called in Israel the house of one that had his shoe loosed."

We have an explicit statement that if a man dies childless, his wife is not allowed to marry any other but her brother-in-law, unless he refuses to marry her. He must then release her by the ceremony of *Ḥaliẓah.* We are also given the reason for such injunction, namely, that the Levirate marriage must take place in order that the name of the deceased shall not be blotted out of Israel, which indicates both the great importance attached by the Jews to the continuation of the family through the descendants, and the dread of disappearing from the world without leaving any vestige. In transferring the marital duties to the brother and in naming the first-born child after the dead man, there is a symbolic continuation of the original family. The practice of this kind of marriage, called *Yibum* from the noun *Yabam,* brother-in-law, though enjoined in this passage by a mandatory law, goes back to patriarchal times, as is evidenced by the passage in Genesis, XXXVIII, 2–10. We are told there that when Er, son of Judah, died childless, his brother Onan married the widow, and when he too died childless, she waited for the younger brother Shelah.

The law of Levirate marriage, though given in comparative detail, is not explicit enough in certain particulars, and the Oral, or Talmudic law, had to supplement it. Accordingly, we have the following regulations. The duty to marry the brother's widow rests only upon the brother of one father and not upon the brother of one mother. It devolves upon him under all circumstances, though he be only an infant of a day or less, or even illegitimately born (*Mamzer*). However, if that brother was born after the death of the husband, though the mother-in-law was pregnant at the time, the widow is free to marry a stranger. If there are several brothers, the duty rests upon the eldest, but if, for one reason or another, he cannot fulfill it, then any other brother may assume the duty.

The childlessness of the deceased must be complete. If he had a child, son or daughter, from another woman, whether legitimate or illegitimate, the widow is free. Again, if the widow was pregnant at the time of the death of her husband, and she gave birth to a child who died immediately after birth, she is free, provided the child was not prematurely born. It is, of course, understood that if the widow was the niece of her husband, i.e., the daughter of his brother, that the law is abrogated in this case. There are also other cases which bring about abrogation of the law, but we cannot enter into such complicated matters, as they are of little practical value.

According to the Biblical law, there is no need in the case of the Levirate marriage for an official ceremony of *Kiddushin,* but an early Rabbinical ordinance requires such ceremony. Biblically, *Yibum* is preferable to the release by the ceremony of *Ḥaliẓah,* as is evident from the text of the passage quoted, in which the ceremony is intended as a means of degradation of the brother-in-law who shirks his duty. However, as early as Talmudic times, opposition arose to the Levirate marriage and *Ḥaliẓah* was preferred. In later times actual *Yibum* fell into desuetude and the widow was freed by *Ḥaliẓah.*

The ceremony of *Haliẓah* is, on the whole, performed according to the form laid down in the Bible. The brother and widow appear before a court of three judges. These co-opt two more, even laymen not versed in the law. After brief preliminaries, ascertaining by documents or witnesses the absolute childlessness of the deceased, as well as the authenticity of the brother, court asks the couple whether they both agree to *Ḥaliẓah.* The answer given in the affirmative, the brother is ordered to don a leather shoe made for that purpose, and the widow slips it off, spits on the floor,* and repeats the verse of the Pentateuch quoted above: "So shall be done," and the court and the others assembled repeat three times "One who had his shoe slipped off" (Haluz ha-Naal). It is customary to have ten people witness this ceremony.

No *Ḥaliẓah* is performed before ninety days have passed from the time of the death of the husband. This time limit is necessary in order to ascertain whether the widow is pregnant or not.

There is no doubt that this law of *Ḥaliẓah* often causes great hardship to the widow, as when the whereabouts of

* It is to be noted that the Sadducees insisted upon interpreting the words of the Bible, *We-Yarkah be-Fanav* (Deut. XXV, 9), literally "to spit in his face." The Pharisees said that *be-Fanav* means "in his presence."

the brother is unknown, or when he is still in his infancy, or when he is a man of mean character and utilizes the plight of the woman in order to extract a sum of money from her. As a result, attempts have recently been made by scholars to devise legal means, through insertion of a condition in the marriage contract, which should obviate the ceremony. However, such attempts have not yet met with common approval of scholars and Rabbis.

42. Duties of Parents to Children and Vice Versa

The father has certain duties towards his children which he must perform to the best of his ability. In addition to support during the years of minority, the most important duty in regard to the sons was the provision for teaching of the Torah, in other words, to give him an education. This was for centuries considered the prime duty of the father, or in case of an orphan that of the mother, and no Jew or Jewess shirked that duty. Even the poorest of the poor scraped together some money to pay for the teaching of their sons. Another duty is to teach their sons a trade or a profession by means of which they should be able to earn their living.

The most important duty of the father towards the daughters is to give them in marriage. This duty too was scrupulously observed in the Jewish family for centuries. When the daughters began to grow up, the principal problem of the parents was to marry them off. To help the parents solve the problem or to marry off an orphan girl was considered the highest type of benevolence. There was hardly any *Mitzvah* greater than *Haknosat Kallah* (to help marry off a young woman).

The duty of the children to honor their father and mother is explicitly stated in the Ten Commandments. However, while the commandment is brief and general, later Jewish law is specific. It obliges the son to show the parents proper respect, such as not to contradict the statements of his father, nor to interrupt his speech, nor to occupy his seat at the table, and similar marks of respect. The son is also obliged to give him personal service if necessary. And if the parents have no means of support, the son or sons are obliged to support them. In case of refusal, the Jewish court enforces the performance of this duty. This, of course, cannot apply to a married daughter since she is not financially independent. However, an unmarried, widowed, or divorced daughter has the same obligations as the son towards the parents.

43. Mourning

The duty of mourning falls upon seven relatives mutually, namely, father and mother, children, brothers and sisters, even if only of the same mother, and husband and wife. These mourners are obliged to rend the garments they wear at the time of the death of the relative. The rent is larger when the dead are parents, for such mourning is of a severer nature. On the day of the death the mourner is relieved of the performance of religious duties, such as prayer and putting on of *Tefillin*. That day is called the day of *Aninut*. After the funeral the seven days of mourning or *Shib'ah* begin, during which time the mourners sit on low stools and do not do any work unless there is great necessity because of poverty or exceptional loss, in which case they may engage in work after three days. Mourners are also forbidden to bathe, cut their hair, perfume their bodies, wear shoes, or study, except portions in which suffering is referred to, such as the Book of Job. A part of a day is considered a whole day. Consequently, the mourning is in reality carried on only for six days and one hour. If the burial took place before sunset, this is also considered a day. On the Sabbath of the week of mourning, public signs of deep grief, such as removing the shoes, not changing clothes, or sitting on low seats, are dispensed with, but other things of a private nature are observed. The holy days have the force of annulling mourning, e.g., if the burial took place an hour before the holiday, the mourner is not obliged to sit *Shib'ah*, but if the death occurred on *Hol ha-Moed*, mourning is completed after the holidays. From the seventh day to the end of the month the relative maintains a lighter type of mourning, during which he does not cut his hair or wear new clothes, nor is he allowed to marry during that period. If a holiday intervenes, this form of mourning is annulled. If one was not present at the death of the relative but was informed within thirty days, he is obliged to sit *Shib'ah,* but if the news came later, the severer form of mourning lasts for one hour.

43a. Circumcision

As is well known, one of the most important precepts of the Torah is that every Jewish male child must be circumcised on the eighth day after its birth. The duty to see that the act of circumcision is performed at the proper time rests upon the father. It is considered one of the most important affirmative precepts, for as stated in the Torah: "And ye shall circumcise the flesh of your foreskin, and it shall be a sign of the covenant between Me and you" (Genesis Chap XVII, v. 11). And further: "And the uncircumcised man child whose flesh of his foreskin is not circumcised that soul shall be cut off from his people; he hath broken My covenant" (Ibid., v. 14). It is then clearly stated that the uncircumcised Jew is excluded from the community of Israel, since he is not a son of the covenant. Consequently, if the father, for one reason or another, did not have his son circumcised, the son himself is obliged to have the act performed on him when he reaches maturity. Otherwise, he will be subject to the penalty of *Karet.* [1] In case the father willfully neglected to circumcise his son, the Jewish court has the right to step in and order circumcision against the will of the father.

The time for circumcision is, as stated, the eighth day after birth, and can take place any hour between sun-

[1] For several views on the meaning of the term "cut off" or *Karet* as the term is called in the Talmud, see above, p. 60, note.

rise and sunset. It was, however, usual to have the circumcision in the morning hours to prove that the parents are anxious to perform the Mitzwah of entering their son into the covenant of Israel. If, however, the child was born during the twilight hour—a time which is doubtful whether it is part of the day or of the following night, he should be circumcised on the ninth day, which is in reality a doubtful eighth, for if the twilight hour is considered night then it is only the eighth day, as according to Jewish reckoning the twenty-four hour day begins at nightfall.

If the child happens to be sick, circumcision is postponed until the end of the seven days after he is declared cured from the sickness. This seven day extension, after the child is declared well, is allowed only when the sickness affects the entire body, as a fever, etc., but if only an external organ is affected and that is not of a serious nature, circumcision is postponed only up to the date when the child is declared cured of the malady, and then circumcision is performed immediately.

Every Jew may perform the act of circumcision provided he is capable by proper training to perform such operation. Most codifiers even allow a woman to perform circumcision. However, it is customary to have it performed by a professional person, called a Mohel.

The act of circumcision consists in cutting off the foreskin and then tearing or cutting the membrane which remains after the skin is cut off. This is called *Periah;* this must be done, for otherwise the top of the virile organ may be covered again by a new foreskin. If the *Periah* is not performed, it is not considered proper circumcision. In addition there is *Metzitzah,* i.e., the act of drawing off a part of the blood from the organ so that it should not congeal and cause a permanent injury. Formerly it was done by the mouth. This was discontinued and is now performed by an instrument.

Two benedictions are recited at the circumcision, one by the Mohel and the other by the father. The first is pronounced before the operation begins, and the second between the cutting and the *Periah*. The text of the benedictions is given in every prayer-book and need not be quoted here.

The act of circumcision must take place on the eighth day even if it happens to fall on the Sabbath, for this Mitzwah takes precedence to the Sabbath and even to the Day of Atonement. There is, however, a slight difference when the ceremony is performed on the Day of Atonement, for in addition to the two bendictions a third one is pronounced over a cup of wine, and a drop of wine is even put into the mouth of the child. On the Day of Atonement, this part is omitted and similarly on the ninth of Ab, for no one is permitted to drink the wine. On the other fast days, the benediction is pronounced, for the mother is not obliged to fast and may partake of the wine.

Circumcision is performed on the Sabbath only when it is done on the proper day, i.e., on the eighth day, but if for reason of sickness, it was postponed, it cannot take place on the Sabbath or on a holiday, and likewise when circumcision is performed on the ninth day or on the doubtful eighth, in the case stated above, the Sabbath or holiday cannot be desecrated, and it is postponed for the following day.

43b. Redemption of the First Born Son

It is a Biblical precept that the father is obligated to redeem his first-born son, as it is stated: "And all the first-born of man among thy children shalt thou redeem" (Exodus, XIII, v. 13). The Bible itself states the reason for the redemption, for it is said: "And it came to pass when Pharaoh would hardly let us go that the Lord slew all the first-born in the land of Egypt, both the first-born of man and the first-born of beast; therefore I sacrifice to the Lord all that openeth the matrix, being males, but all the first-born of my children I redeem." (Ibid., XIII, v. 15). The verse seems to mean that the fact that the first-born males, whether of man or of beast, were spared by God, placed upon all the first-born males divine proprietership or sanctification, as it is said in an earlier verse: "Sanctify unto me all the first-born, whatsoever openeth the womb among the children of Israel, both of man and of beast; it is Mine" (Ibid. XIII, v. 2). It is also clear from these verses that the purpose was to inculcate in the hearts of the children of Israel the memory of the Exodus at the occurrence of events which bear some relation to it.

From the fact that it is stated twice in the verses which refer to the first-born, that it must be the male child who opens the matrix or the womb, it was deduced that the first-born child of the mother must be redeemed but not the father's first-born, and it is so stated in the Mishnah (Tractate Bekorot, Chap. VIII, v. 1), and this is the law.

However, the duty of redeeming the child rests only upon the father, the mother is not obligated to redeem him. If for any reason the father did not redeem his child, the son upon reaching maturity is obligated to redeem himself.

The act of redemption, generally known by the name of *Pidyon ha-Ben*, consists in giving a Kohen the sum of five dollars [1] and the father pronouncing the following benediction: "Blessed art Thou, God our Lord, who sanctified us and commanded us to redeem the first-born son."

The date set for redemption is the thirty-first day after

[1] The amount of the sum fixed for redemption is deduced from the statement in the Book of Numbers (Chap. III, v., 46-49) that Moses was told by God to take from each of the two hundred and seventy-three first-born Israelites who exceeded the number of Levites who substituted for the first-born, the sum of five Shekolim as redemption money, and turn over the sum collected to Aaron and his children, i.e. the Kohamin.

birth, and not before. The reason for it is that up to that date, we are not certain of the child's capability to survive. If the father happened to redeem his son before the passing of thirty days and the child died during that time, the Kohen is obligated to return the money to the father, for before that set date, there is no obligation of redemption. If the chiid lives and the Kohen still possesses the money the redemption is valid. The Kohen may return the money as a gift.

Kohanim and Levites are exempt from the obligation of redeeming their children. The reason for this exemption is, as we are told in the Bible, that they were chosen at the time when the Tabernacle was set up to be the servants of the Sanctuary instead of the first-born male children of Israel upon whom that duty originally rested. It is therefore reasoned that if their sanctification exempted the first-born Israelites at the time, it follows that it exempts them from such obligation, And not only is the father exempt from the act of redemption when he himself is a Kohen or a Levite, but also if his wife is the daughter of a Kohen or a Levite, for as was pointed out, redemption is dependent upon the child being the first-born of the mother and her status then absolves the father from that obligation.

PART II

THE PRINCIPAL VIEWS OF JUDAISM

Chapter VI

GOD AND THE WORLD

44. Conception of God

Of the numerous concepts and general abstract notions which the human race has developed in its long course of progress, the concept of God is the most important and the most prominent one. All races, scattered in space through the breadth and length of the earth, and in time, from the dawn of history to the present day, had and have some kind of conception, more or less perfect, of God. They all believe in the existence of a Being or even of more than one who is superior to, and above, the created things. How this concept or notion developed and came into fruition is the business of anthropologists, ethnologists, historians, and psychologists of religion to investigate. What interests us is the point of departure of the Jewish people in this matter from all other civilized nations of antiquity. While all the others, including the Greeks, arrived at a purer conception of the Godhead by contemplating the external world, the Jews, on the contrary, reached an understanding of the world through the concept of God.

The monotheistic God-conception is an elemental trait in the character of the Jewish people, or so to say, an intuition inherent in their mind. The revelation at Sinai with all its majesty as described in the Book of Exodus, Ch. XX, was only a means to clarify and fix in the mind of the entire people the pure conception of the Godhead which was present only in the minds of the select few, the outstanding ancestors of the nation, the Patriarchs, and less pure in the minds of the group as a whole. We have already noted that notwithstanding the various theories which Bible critics and historians advance regarding the development of monotheism in Israel, all these theories and suppositions as well as the deductions from archaeological discoveries cannot explain the unique phenomenon expressed in the Jewish conception of the Godhead.

It is because of this religious intuition par excellence that we do not find in the entire Old Testament any attempt to prove the existence of God. It was considered an axiom regarding the truth of which no doubt could enter one's mind. In the two places of the Bible (Psalms XIV, 1 and LIII, 2) where it is said: "The fool hath said in his heart there is no God," the meaning is not that God does not exist—that thought could not occur to anyone—but that there is no providence, as is quite evident from the context. Similarly, Job, writhing in pain, complains bitterly against God's injustice or indifference to the suffering of the righteous, but utters no word which may intimate doubt in His existence. The many passages found in the various parts of the Bible in which nature in its full glory and majesty is exalted and described as the handiwork of God are not intended as proof for His existence, but merely to point out the manifestations of His greatness. It is in this matter that we are to understand verses 2 and 4 in Psalm VIII: "O, Lord, our Lord, how excellent is Thy name in all the earth, Who hast set Thy glory above the heavens," and "When I consider Thy heavens, the work of Thy fingers, the moon and the stars, which Thou hast ordained." The same meaning is expressed in many similar passages.

This God of Judaism is not an abstract principle as in Greek philosophy, but a living active Being whose activities are constantly emphasized throughout the Bible. The title "a living God" is bestowed upon Him many times (Deuteronomy V, 23 et alia). He is thus endowed with the qualities of personality.

There are a number of names applied to God in the Bible, most of them of a general nature, such as *Elohim,* or the singular *Eloha* or *El,* all of which were common Semitic names for God or gods. The name *Elohim,* though plural in form, by no means signifies even a remote reference to a plurality of gods but is used as a plural of majesty, such as *Baal* and *Adon.* There is, however, a special name used only in the Bible and by Judaism called the Tetragrammaton, namely the four-lettered name, YHVH. This is more than a name, for according to definite uses made of the name in the Bible, the veneration placed upon it by tradition and the interpretation of the greatest Jewish thinkers through the ages, it signifies a certain manifestation of His existence, or it may he His existence itself—namely, that He is the basis of all existence. It is undoubtedly derived from the verb *Havoh,* to be, or to exist. However, we are not certain of the right reading of the name for the Jews out of reverence read the Tetragrammaton as if it were written *Adonai,* i.e., our Lord, and similarly, it is punctuated in the Bible with the vowels of that word. According to this punctuation it is read in English Jehovah. But Judah ha-Levi maintains that the Tetragrammaton is really a verb and should be read *Yahveh,* i.e., one who brings forth existence. He is followed in that reading by German scholars.

God is one and unique, simplicity itself. The unity of God in all its phases is the fundamental thought in Judaism and is repeated numerous times in the entire Jewish literature beginning with the Decalogue and extending through the entire Bible, Apocrypha, and Talmudic and Midrashic literature. The thought is epitomized in the statement of Isaiah XLIV, 6: "I am the first, and I am the last, and besides Me there is no God."

If God is conceived as endowed with the qualities of personality, then His activity follows as a necessary corollary from that concept. His first and most important form of activity was manifested in the creation of the world which is His handiwork. Nature, in accordance with this view, is not an independent mysterious power as the Greek philosophers thought, but is, by the very condition of coming into existence, dependent upon God, and serves primarily as an instrument for the continuous manifestation of the divine creative power. This view also imparted dignity to human life, for man is freed from subjection to nature and fear from a blind fate which hangs over him like a Damoclean sword, as the ancient pagans believed.

Creation is one of the manifestations of divine activity. Another is His revelation in the life and conduct of man or His providence. (See below.)

45. Attributes of God

Neither in the Bible nor in Talmudic literature is there any attempt made to describe the essence of the Godhead in a philosophic manner. This essence is usually described by the attributes. However, of the numerous appellations we find in the Bible as well as in later literature, we can distinguish a few which offer an approach to a conception of His essence or of His nature and character. All others which bear an anthropomorphic character, namely, ascribing to Him characteristics which are human, such as warrior, mighty, etc., are only metaphors used by the lawgiver and the prophets in order to convey to the people at large some idea of the majesty of God and His relation to the world. The people, as a whole, in earlier times and even in our own day, do not think in the abstract but in the concrete. Consequently, images and metaphors had to be used in order to impart some notion of the Godhead and especially of divine activity in this world. For the same reason, numerous anthropomorphic expressions are employed to indicate this activity and relation, such as God sees, hears, rises, goes forth, and many others. Those attributes, on the other hand, which indicate a closer approach to the conception of the nature of the Godhead are all of an ethical nature, which point to the fact that God is conceived by Judaism not only as manifesting Himself in nature and in history, but also as an ethical personality. These are enumerated in Exodus XXXIV, 6, 7: "The Lord passed by before him (Moses) and proclaimed, 'the Lord, the Lord God, merciful and gracious, long-suffering and abundant of goodness and truth. Keeping mercy for thousands, forgiving iniquity and transgressions, and that will by no means clear the guilty, visiting the iniquity of the fathers upon the children and upon the children's children up to the third and to the fourth generation.'" These are usually the thirteen attributes which denote the nature of the Godhead. Of course, it is to be understood that even these do not reveal His essence and only describe His nature in relation to the world and man. In other words, these are what later Jewish philosophers called the active attributes, namely, abstracted from God's activity in this world, mainly His providence. It is also to be noted that even in these attributes there is a ring of anthropomorphism, for merciful denotes emotion which is a human trait. The Jewish religious philosophers of the Middle Ages devoted much effort to explaining these terms and succeeded to a great extent. The important point is the ethical character of divine activity from which it follows that in Judaism God is conceived as an ethical personality par excellence or as the source and fountain of all morality. In spite of His omnipotence, His activity could not be other than ethical. This attitude is typically expressed in Abraham's plea to save Sodom from destruction even if there should be found therein only a few righteous men, saying: "That be far from Thee. Shall not the judge of all the earth do right?" (Genesis XVIII, 25). That such ethical attributes are inalienable to the Godhead is constantly emphasized in the Bible. To name only a few: "For He put on righteousness as a breastplate" (Isaiah LIX, 17); "For the righteous Lord loveth righteousness" (Psalms XI, 7), and in many more places. Besides the above-enumerated ethical attributes, there is still another frequently applied to God, namely, holiness, or in the adjective form, holy.

Holiness is likewise a manifestation of God's nature. In general, the term holiness implies distinction, importance, and dignity or exaltation above others. In regard to the Godhead, this attribute is used in the Bible in connection with a manifestation of His power, righteousness, and majesty. Whenever these are manifested, He is described as holy, for His name is then hallowed among men. Thus Ezekiel, speaking of the promised redemption of Israel, says: "When I bring you out of the peoples and gather you out of the countries wherein you have been scattered, and I will be sanctified in you before the heathen" (XX, 41). Similarly, when God punishes the wicked—which is a manifestation of justice—He is sanctified, as the same prophet says: "Thus saith the Lord God, 'Behold, I am against thee, O Sidon, and I will be glorified in the midst of thee, and they shall know that I am the Lord when I shall have executed judgment in her and shall be sanctified in her' " (Ezekiel XXVIII, 22). Even when He punishes the righteous for a sin committed, He is sanctified, as in the case of the death of the sons of Aaron, where it is said: "I will be sanctified in them that come nigh to me" (Leviticus X, 3). Since the attribute holy signifies manifestation of divine power, Isaiah, who speaks more than any other prophet about the close relation of God to Israel and the frequent revelation of His power in the life of the nation, uses often the title "Holy One of Israel" in regard to God. Especially frequent is its use in the latter part, Chaps. XL–XLVI, in passages where redemption is the theme. Thus: "Thy redeemer, the Holy One of Israel" (XLI, 14); "The Holy One of Israel, thy Savior" (XLIII, 3); "Thus saith the Lord, your Redeemer, the Holy One of Israel" (ibid. 14); and in numerous other places. In the legal part of the Pentateuch, the concept holiness is inherently connected with dignified ethical conduct in which the distinctness of the person or the group is expressed. To all laws forbidding incestuous relations or other prohibited intercourse, such as the relations with a betrothed or married woman as well as unnatural ones which typically express the violation of the distinctness and sacredness of the human personality, there is appended the injunction: "Sanctify yourself therefore, and be ye holy, for I am the Lord, thy God" (Leviticus XX, 7). The same formula is appended after the dietary laws, which likewise form a mark of distinction of the group, saying: "I am the Lord, your God. Ye shall therefore sanctify yourselves, and ye shall be holy, neither shall ye defile yourselves with any manner of creeping things that creepeth upon the earth" (ibid. XI, 44). The laws of high social ethics are also prefaced with the words: "Ye shall be holy, for I, the Lord, your God, am holy" (ibid. XIX, 2).

From all these it is evident that God is considered the archtype of all moral conduct to be imitated by the Jews, as expressed in the early Tannaitic statement: "God said to Moses, 'Tell the children of Israel, My children, just as I am merciful, so shall ye be merciful, and just as I am holy, so shall ye be holy' " (Sifra Ch. XI).

46. Creation

The world, says Judaism, was created by God. According to accepted tradition which is continually reiterated throughout post-Biblical literature, it was created from nothing. Belief in the creation of the world is a primary article in Jewish faith, and in creation from nothing a secondary one, though of great importance.[1] However, not all dogmatists agree on that point.

Creation was taken as a fact in the Bible, and no reason is given as to why the world was created or for what purpose. The Rabbis frequently stated its purpose, and mediaeval philosophers attempted to supply the why. According to the latter, creation follows inherently from the nature of God

[1] According to the right interpretation of Article IV in Maimonides' Credo, only the creation of the world in general by God is asserted therein but not *ex nihilo*. In fact, Albo says distinctly in his *Ikkarim* (Book I, Ch. I) that Maimonides did not count creation from nothing as a dogma. Albo himself counts it as a secondary dogma (ibid. Ch. XXIII). Other dogmatists, though, counted it a primary dogma. Cf. Waxman, "Maimonides as a Dogmatist," Year Book of Central Conference of American Rabbis, Vol. XLV pp. 408–409.

who is essentially good, and since, according to the Jewish view existence is good in itself—in contradistinction to the Hindu and Greek view—creation is a necessity as an overflow of His goodness. This view finds support in the Pentateuch, for after every stage in creation it is stated: "and God saw that it was good." As for the purpose or rather the goal—since according to the view stated no purpose is necessary—man is that goal, as it is said: "He created it (i.e., the world) not in vain; He formed it to be inhabited" (Isaiah XLV, 18). The Rabbis, however, basing themselves on this verse, elaborated the thought and introduced a moral purpose in the creation of the world. It is not only man but the righteous man for whose sake the world was created. Verse 13 in Ch. XII in Kohelet says: "Let us hear the conclusion of the whole matter, 'Fear God, keep His commandments, for this is the whole of man'" (*Ki Ze Kol ha-Adam*). The Rabbis interpreted the last words as follows: *Ze Kol*, etc. (Kol may mean whole or all) means all the world was created for the sake of the man who fears God and obeys the commandments.[2] This ethical purpose of creation is expressed more clearly in another Agadic statement which says: "God created the world conditionally, namely, that if the Jews should accept the Torah, it would continue to exist, but if not, it was to return to chaos." [3] The meaning of the dictum is that if there is not at least one group of people dedicated to the observance of the moral laws enjoined in the Torah, the world has no raison d'être and it were better that it turn back into chaos than continue its existence.

47. Providence

From the premise that the world is the handiwork of God and that He constantly manifests His power both in nature and in life, it follows that He exercises providence over the process of events in this world. Accordingly, the Bible emphasizes numerous times that God observes all events and hap-

[2] Talmud Babli, Berakot, 6a.
[3] Talmud Babli, Abodah Zara, 5.

penings in the world and that nothing which takes place, no matter how insignificant, escapes Him. Frequently, this providence is expressed in the figurative language of the time by the word *eye*, as in the verse: "The eyes of the Lord which run to and fro throughout the whole earth" (Zechariah IV, 10).

The idea of divine providence served as an important factor in the spiritual and moral development of humanity, but its penetration into the consciousness was slow. And it is due to the prophets of Israel and their continuous emphasis of this doctrine that it ultimately prevailed. It was they who supplied meaning to history and introduced into the constantly changing complex of life's events a certain order and a type of unity, or better still a certain form of the law of causality.

The conception of history of most of the peoples in the ancient world was a very confused one. The numerous events which took place in the world were looked upon as a jumble of happenings brought about by chance without unity and orderly sequence. Even the Greek thinkers who knew of a law of causality left ample space to fate and chance. The Prophets fought against such a view and inculcated the idea that history is a process of causes and effects. Thus says Amos: "Will two walk together except they be agreed? Will a lion in the forest roar when he hath no prey? Will a young lion cry out if he have taken nothing? Can a bird fall in a snare upon the earth where no trap is set for him? Shall one take up a snare from the earth and have taken nothing at all? Shall a trumpet be blown in a city and the people be not afraid?" (Amos III, 3–6). Amos thus proves in a simple and clear manner that events or actions do not take place even in the life of animals without cause, and the corollary is that so much more is there a cause for great events in the life of the human group. He emphasizes that the cause of all changes in the life of nations is God, as stated in verse 6, which is the climax of this remarkable passage.

Divine providence taught by the Prophets is *eo ipso* an ethical purposive one, for since God is the archetype of morality, it could not be otherwise. Hence, the fundamental principle of that providence, or still better, of history in general—at least as far as it is manifested in the life of nations—is the one known as the cause and effect relation between sin and punishment. Time and again, Prophet after Prophet inculcated this principle as a way of explaining the life of the Jewish nation, and in their efforts to enunciate it, they equated the validity of the laws of the moral world with that of the laws of nature. For while the Prophets believed in God's constant manifestation in nature and made it His handiwork and dependent upon His will, they did not deny the stability of nature and the permanence of its laws which He Himself had established.

They therefore assert that just as it is impossible to transgress the laws of nature without suffering the necessary consequences, it is likewise impossible to transgress the laws of morality and escape unscathed. Punishment in this case follows necessarily just as in the former. Again, Amos leads in the inculcation of this principle, saying: "Shall horses run upon the rock? Will one plow there with oxen?* For ye have turned judgment into gall, and the fruit of righteousness into hemlock" (VI, 12). The meaning of this parable is that just as horses cannot run on the rock but plod their way up slowly, for otherwise they would break their necks or fall from exhaustion—since they break a law of nature—so must those who disparage justice or trample upon righteousness be punished. And this principle ultimately became the substratum of the prophetic view of the fate of Israel as well as of the general situation in the social and political world. It is especially developed by Isaiah in numerous prophecies which assert the necessity of punishment for all sinning nations including Israel. In a broader sense, all nations, even the mighty ones, are only instruments in the hands of God. If we see a powerful nation conquering other peoples, it is not by its own

* This is the translation of King James which follows the text. But according to a slight emendation by Luzzatto, this part of the verse will run: "Will one plow the sea with oxen?"

might that it is able to do so, but by the will of God who makes it possible for the nation to accomplish its deeds for a definite purpose, mainly to punish the conquered for their sins. This is stated clearly in the words of Isaiah: "O Assyrian, the rod of my anger and the staff in their hand is my indignation. I will send him against an hypocritical nation and against the peoples of my wrath will I give him a charge to take the spoil and to take the prey and to tread them down like the mire in the street" (X, 5, 6). He continues to tell us that when the time of Assyria will come, it will be punished in turn. The thought is repeated by this Prophet several times, and is likewise expressed by other Prophets in their continual reproaches and warnings to Israel against the consequences of their deeds.

This view was accepted by later generations and became an integral part of Jewish tradition and belief. Moreover, in the course of time, the individual soon came into his own— not that the Bible totally disregards the problem of the individual but it does not emphasize it prominently except in the Book of Job.— And as a result, the question of providence was extended and became more complex and its function more embracive. Consequently, the problems connected with it also became more numerous, for life does not always confirm the theory that the punishment fits the crime. It is therefore not to be wondered at if we find in the later literature, such as the Talmudic and Midrashic, a product of centuries of life under various conditions, different views on this all-important subject of providence. There are some which extended it to embrace every move of man. Thus the statement of one Rabbi reads: "A man does not even strike a finger here below unless it is decreed from above" (Hulin, 7), and in another statement it is said: "Every action of man is controlled by heaven—except the fear of the Lord" (Ketubot, 30), meaning that man is free to choose between right or wrong. Some views allow a man wider latitude, but none deny God's relation to the world as expressed in providence.

However, these phases of providence and the problems they entail are inherently connected with other fundamental views, such as reward and punishment and freedom of the will, which are discussed subsequently.

CHAPTER VII

MAN AND ISRAEL IN RELATION TO GOD

48. MAN

We will now turn to man, the value and worth of his personality as reflected in Jewish teachings. We have already noted the important position of man in the world according to Judaism, but it teaches more than that. First of all: "Man," says the Pentateuch, "was created in the image of God" (Genesis I, 26; V, 1). One of the great Tannaim, Rabbi Akiba, said: "Man is beloved by God for he was created in His image, and this love is of great advantage to him" (*Abot* Ch. III, 18). Without entering into the theological difficulties in which the statement may involve one and into the discussion of the various explanations of the meaning of the "image of God," we may point out the important implications bearing upon the dignity and importance of man which are embodied in the words.

The first implication of this view is the equality of all men in their elemental worth, for every man without distinction bears the impress of the divine image. It was so understood by the Rabbis of old, for we find statements to that effect. Rabbi Akiba said: "The words, 'and thou shalt love thy neighbor as thyself,' constitute a great principle of the Torah." Ben Asai said to him: "There is a greater principle, namely, this is the Book of the Generations of Adam. In the day that God created man, in the likeness of God He created him" (Genesis V, 1).[1] The meaning of Ben Asai's statement is that he tells Akiba that the words in his verse are not explicit enough, as the term *neighbor* may be understood with some limitation—as it usually is—and consequently, in spite of this

[1] *Sifra, Sec. Kedoshim,* Ch. IV.

principle, there may be discrimination. He therefore quotes the other verse where it is explicitly stated that all men have an elemental worth. A later Midrashic remark upon this verse states: "Said Rabbi Tanḥuma, 'Do not say that since I am to be humiliated, let also another man be humiliated.' Know then that God made man in His image, and no effort should be spared to save a man from humiliation or injury if possible." [2]

This concept of the inner worth of man on the basis of his creation is indirectly expressed in the Torah when it forbids the causing of any possible injury to persons weaker and less capable than others. In the Book of Leviticus which contains many precepts both of a purely religious nature and of a social type, the formula "And thou shalt fear thy God" is appended to only five injunctions, namely, XIX, 14, 32; XXV, 17, 36, 43. In all these injunctions, not to curse the deaf, nor to put a stumbling block before the blind, not to cheat, nor to take interest, nor to work a servant too hard, and to honor old age, the people referred to are weak or defective or stupid. The injunctions, therefore, have the appended statement, "And thou shalt fear thy God," namely, know that he also is created in divine impress and an insult or injury to him is like one unto God.

Another phase of the creation of man, as told in the Pentateuch, also served Judaism as a buttress to the doctrine of equality of man. A statement in the Mishnah, the second authoritative book of Judaism, says: "Why was only one man created by God and not several? This was done in order that some people should not say my ancestor was greater or possessed nobler qualities than yours." All men have the same ancestor, consequently, all men have an equal elemental worth.

49. Israel

It is, as stated above, a fundamental tenet in Judaism that the equality of all men follows as a corollary from the view

[2] *Genesis Rabba,* Ch. XXIV, 7.

of the creation of man, and consequently the fatherhood of God is extended to all of them. Yet, it is constantly reiterated in the Bible, both in the Pentateuch and the Prophets and innumerable times in the entire post-Biblical literature, that the people of Israel is selected by God as His people. This selection is first pronounced in Exodus XIX, 5–6: "Now, therefore, if ye will obey My word and keep My covenant, then ye shall be a peculiar treasure unto Me above all people, for all the earth is Mine. And ye shall be unto Me a kingdom of priests and an holy nation." In other places, such as Leviticus XX, 26, Deuteronomy XIV, 1, Israel is again said to belong to God as His own and are called His children. The Prophets speak constantly of the relation between God and Israel in various ways. Ezekiel calls them "the people of God"; Isaiah, though he bestows the title "my people" also on Egypt, still distinguishes Israel by calling them "Mine inheritance."

This election or selection is based on covenants entered into between God and the Patriarchs of the nation and with the nation itself. Thus God said to Abraham: "And I will establish My covenant between thee and Me and thy seed after thee in their generations for an everlasting covenant, to be a God unto thee and to thy seed after thee" (Genesis XVII, 7). Subsequently, we find recorded in the Pentateuch a series of covenants with Israel itself, the first and most important of which is the revelation at Sinai, followed by two executed by Moses, one immediately after the revelation and the other at the end of his life (Exodus XXIV, 7, 8; Deuteronomy XXXI, 14–20). The question arises, what is the meaning of this selection of Israel? Does it mean to impute to them superiority, racial or otherwise, or is it merely a function, a quality? The answer to this question is that as far as we can deduce from the various passages, both in the Pentateuch and in the Prophets which deal with this election, it is primarily of an ethical nature par excellence. It bestows no privileges upon the nation nor does it endow the group with any indigenous superiority, but on the contrary, lays upon it a heavy responsibility and maps out for it a severe way of conduct.

In the passages referring to the covenant between God and Abraham, the following reason is given for the conclusion of the covenant: "For I have known him (Abraham) that he will command his children and his household after him and they shall keep the way of the Lord to do justice and righteousness; that the Lord may bring upon Abraham that which He hath spoken of to him" (Genesis XVIII, 19). We see then the moral purpose of this election. God knows, i.e., selects Abraham in order that he shall command his descendants to act justly and righteously.

The moral purpose of this election is especially emphasized by Amos who says: "Only ye have I known from among all the families of nations, therefore, I shall visit upon you all your sins" (Amos III, 2). The Prophet means to say to Israel, do not think that the divine election is of a racial nature and consequently you will escape punishment for your sins. Nay, just because God selected you as His people, you shall be punished for your transgressions, and even more severely than other nations, for the purpose of this election is the moral improvement of the nation, and it is the duty of Israel to excel all other nations in ethical conduct.

It is, however, true that Hosea injects in this election an element of love between God and Israel. He compares the relation between the two to a relation between husband and wife, and calls a sinning Israel a wayward wife. But this relationship by no means grants any privileges to the nation. Like Amos he chastises the people for their sins and warns them of dire punishment, for the unfaithfulness of a wife is indeed a grave transgression and entails serious consequences. The stern duty and responsibility is thus not lessened by the introduction of the element of the quasi-marital relationship. All that this element implies is the strengthening of Israel's hope for forgiveness and assurance of a loving reception on the part of God when it will repent of its waywardness. The contribution of Hosea to prophetic teachings concerning the destiny of Israel does not consist in his preaching the doctrine of repentance. This doctrine was taught by all Prophets, even by the stern Amos. Its value lies primarily in the emotional glow which the element of love, introduced by him in the God-Israel relationship, imparts to the act of repentance. God is not a stern judge but is described figuratively as a loving husband and father. It is this element which facilitates repentance even for the weak-willed, for they are assured of a warm reception. The doctrine of election of Israel is frequently repeated in the Talmud and Midrash in numerous passages of which the utterance of Rabbi Akiba can be considered typical. Says Rabbi Akiba: "Beloved are the Israelites, for they were called children of God, and because of His love, He called them My eldest son, Israel" (Abot III, 18). The doctrine of the election of Israel supplied the Jewish people with a notion of a special mission in life, the realization of which is certain to come, if not in the present or even in the near future, then in more distant days.

This mission or destiny is greatly emphasized in the Book of Isaiah both in its first part and especially in its second, which most likely contains the prophecies of an unnamed Prophet of the Exile. Isaiah in his famous prophecy concerning "the end of days" visions Israel as the teacher of nations, saying: "From Zion shall go forth Torah and the word of God from Jerusalem" (Isaiah II, 4). The anonymous Prophet adds a poetic touch when he says: "And nations shall journey by your light and kings by your glow" (Isaiah LX, 3). That light and splendor are used here as symbolic expressions for spiritual influence is self-evident. The Rabbis expressed their idea of their people's destiny in poetic language. They liken Israel to oil and say that just as light comes forth from oil, so is Israel a source of light to the world.[8]

It is also this election for a definite destiny which serves as the guarantee for the imperishability of Israel. The belief in the continued existence of the Jewish people is fundamental with all the Prophets. There is not one among them who dared to imagine the total disappearance of Israel. Isaiah, who frequently threatens his people with severe punishment, re-

[8] *Exodus Rabba,* Ch. XXXVI,

peatedly emphasizes the doctrine of the "remnant" or *Sheor Yoshub,* namely, he assumes the possible disappearance of a considerable part of the people, but not all of it, for a portion will always continue to exist. Jeremiah expressed himself more decisively regarding the eternal existence of Israel. To him the timeless continuation of the existence of the people is as certain as the operation of the very elemental laws of nature. Says the Prophet: "Thus saith the Lord who giveth the sun for light by day, and the ordinances of the moon and of the stars for a light by night, who divideth the sea when the waves thereof roar, the Lord of Hosts is His Name. If those ordinances depart from before Me, says the Lord, the seed of Israel also shall cease from being a nation before Me forever. Thus saith the Lord, if the heavens above can be measured and the foundations of the earth searched out beneath, I will also cast off all the seed of Israel for all that they have done" (Jeremiah XXXI, 35–37). The meaning of the verses is that just as it is impossible that these laws be changed, so is it impossible for the Jewish people to disappear from the world.

Ezekiel propounds the doctrine of the eternity of Israel in a somewhat different form. He argues thus: The Jews are the people of God, consequently, their exile conduces to the desecration of the name of God, for the nations believe God powerless since He cannot save His own people. Their redemption from exile will then, on the contrary, bring about the sanctification of His name. He expresses this idea as follows: "They (the Jews) entered unto the heathen whither they went, they profaned the Holy Name, for they said to them, these are the people of the Lord and are gone out of His land. Therefore, say unto the House of Israel, I do not this for your sakes, but for my Holy Name's sake ye have profaned when you came among the nations. I shall therefore sanctify my Name among the nations, and will take you from among the nations and gather you out of all countries, and will bring you to your own land" (Ezekiel XXXVI, 20–24).

The sanctification of God's name is then a guarantee for the eternity of the Jewish people. Were they to disappear from the face of the earth, the name of God would be desecrated. It follows then from the prophetic standpoint that the people of Israel will exist as long as God Himself exists.

50. Reward and Punishment

From all that was said regarding the relation of God to the world, to man, and to Israel, as well as from numerous other passages both in the Pentateuch and in all the books of the Prophets and Hagiographa, it is self-evident that belief in a complete and all-embracive providence of God over the affairs of man is fundamental to Judaism. In fact, neither the Law nor the prophetic utterances could be understood without positing this belief as a major premise.

Integrated with the belief in providence is the one in reward and punishment for good and bad actions respectively. Since it is God who commands men to be good, and conversely, warns them against committing evil and sin, and it is He who exercises providence over human affairs, it follows as a necessary corollary that He rewards the righteous and punishes the wicked. Accordingly, reward and punishment is a basic dogma in Judaism, and in the Torah there is appended almost to every commandment a promise of reward for obedience, and vice versa one of punishment for transgression.

As for the nature of reward and punishment, the matter is more complicated; the concept went through a process of development. In the Bible the promises both of reward and punishment are, on the whole, of a material and worldly nature and are intended primarily for the people as a whole. Thus, Deuteronomy XI, 13ff: "And it shall come to pass if ye shall hearken unto My commandments which I command ye this day to love the Lord, your God, and to serve Him, that I will give the rain of your land in due season, the first rain and the latter rain that you may gather in thy corn and thy wine and thine oil." Similarly, in Deuteronomy XXII, long life is promised as a reward for observing the precept of sending away the mother bird when the young birds are taken from the nest. Likewise, warnings of punishment for transgression of commandments contain threats of national disaster and loss of material possessions. Thus Moses, warning the Jews against making graven images and worshiping them, says: "I will call heaven and earth to witness against you this day that ye shall soon utterly perish from off the land whereunto you go over the Jordan to possess it; ye shall not prolong your days upon it, but shall utterly be destroyed" (Deuteronomy IV, 26). The individual transgressor is frequently threatened by *Karet,* i.e., being cut off from his people.*

The same trend is evident in the prophetic writings. Amos, chastising his people for their sins and foreboding punishment, says: "Therefore now shall they go captive" (VI, 7), or "Gilgal shall surely go into captivity and Beth-El shall come to naught" (V, 5). His promised rewards are also of a material nature, as he says: "Behold the days come, saith the Lord, that the plowman shall overtake the reaper and the treader of grapes him that soweth seed, and the mountain shall drop a sweet wine, and all the hills shall melt" (IX, 13). Jeremiah speaks in a similar vein, saying: "There shall ye come and sing in the height of Zion and shall flow together in the goodness of the Lord, for wheat and for wine, and for oil, and for the young of the flock of the herd, and their soul shall be as a watered garden, and they shall not sorrow any more at all" (XXXI, 12). It is only in the prophecies of Isaiah, both in the first and in the second parts, that the promised rewards assume an intensive spiritual character, such as the famous prophecy of the "end of days" (Isaiah II, 2–4) and the Messianic prophecy (XI, 2–11). In both of these prophecies where the glorious future of Israel is described, there is hardly a reference to material prosperity, the emphasis being laid primarily on peace and the spread of the knowledge of God in the world as a whole with Israel as the bearer and center of these ideals. In the second part again, in numerous passages, promises are made to Israel

* On the meaning of *Karet* see above, Chapter II p. 60 note.

that it shall be the spiritual light of nations, though there is no lack of promises of material rewards in the future.

The predominance of the promises of reward and punishment addressed to the people as a whole found in the Old Testament, inclined a number of critics and scholars, both Jews and non-Jews, to the opinion that Judaism minimizes the value of the individual and takes account primarily of the deeds of the nation. The case, however, is not so. Not only are most of the laws of the Pentateuch stated in the singular, which proves conclusively that they were given as commands to the individual, but also when promises of reward and punishment are attached to them, they are aimed at the individual. Likewise, the Prophets at times address themselves to the individual, promising him reward for good deeds and vice versa. Thus, we read in Isaiah LVI, 1, 2: "Thus saith the Lord, keep ye judgment and do justice, for my salvation is near to come and my righteousness to be revealed. Blessed is the man that doeth this and the son of man that layeth hold of it, that keepeth the Sabbath from polluting it, and keepeth his hand from doing evil." The prophet Ezekiel is especially anxious to emphasize reward and punishment for the individual. He repeats his dictum twice: "The soul that sinneth, it shall die" (XVIII, 4, 20), and devotes a whole chapter to the thesis that there is individual and personal responsibility for one's deeds. This emphasis was meant to counteract a popular opinion that children may be punished for the sins of their fathers, which is derived from a reference in the Pentateuch itself, where God is described as "visiting the iniquity of the fathers upon the children and upon the children's children unto the third and fourth generations" (Exodus XXXIV, 7). Against this popular opinion both Jeremiah and Ezekiel fought assiduously. Both quote the same adage, the former saying: "In those days they shall say no more the fathers have eaten sour grapes and the children's teeth are set on edge. But, everyone shall die for his own iniquity, every man that eateth the sour grapes, his teeth shall be set on edge" (Jeremiah XXXI, 29, 30). And

Ezekiel thunders: "What mean ye that ye use this proverb concerning the land of Israel? The fathers have eaten sour grapes and the children's teeth are set on edge. All souls are mine; as the soul of the father so also the soul of the son is mine; the soul that sinneth it shall die" (Ezekiel XVIII, 2, 4).

However, we cannot escape the fact that there seems to be a contradiction between the statement in Exodus XXXIV, 7 and the teachings of Jeremiah and Ezekiel, especially that of the latter who specifically says: "The son shall not bear the iniquity of the father, neither shall the father bear the iniquity of the son" (Ezekiel, XVIII, 20). Moreover, there is a contradiction in the Pentateuch itself, for we find the statement: "The fathers shall not be put to death for the children, neither shall the children be put to death for the fathers; every man shall be put to death for his own sin" (Deuteronomy XXIV, 16). The Rabbis in the Talmud noted this contradiction and attempted some reconciliation between the opposing statements. Their view is that all children are, as a rule, not punished for the sins of their fathers. But if the son continues in the path of wickedness of his father, he may also receive additional punishment for the sins of his forebears. Similarly, they claim that if he continues the righteousness of his father, he will receive additional reward for the good deeds of his ancestors.[4] They also point out that reward is extended for many generations, for the words in the same verse, "Keeping mercy for thousands," are interpreted as meaning thousands of generations, while punishment is limited at the utmost to four generations.

Turning once more to the question of the nature and type of reward and punishment, we must admit that while there are some references in the earlier books of the Old Testament to the immortality of the soul, the subject is not sufficiently emphasized. For, as said, the reward and punishment spoken of in almost all books are of a material nature and of this world, and even the promised rewards of a spiritual nature are of this world. It is only in Daniel, a book of a later

[4] Talmud Babli *Sanhedrin* 27b et alia.

date, that we are told twice (XII, 2, 13) with definite assurance of the resurrection of the dead at the end of days, an event which *eo ipso* implies the immortality of the soul, for were the soul to die with the body, one could not speak of a resurrection but of a new creation.

Still, we can assert that the prevalent opinion among many scholars, both Jews and non-Jews, that Biblical Judaism did not know of the immortality of the soul, and that this belief as well as the doctrine of resurrection were foreign importations borrowed from the Persians and the Greeks during the early period of the Second Commonwealth, is incorrect. The numerous references in the Old Testament to the *Sheol* and to some form of life there prove conclusively that the belief was prevalent that the souls of the dead continued their existence in that place. However, the nature of that existence is not described, though it may be assumed that the Biblical *Sheol* is not unlike the Greek Hades. Furthermore, it is almost inconceivable that the Jews, a people endowed with strong religiosity, living in a world in which the belief in the immortality of the soul was almost universal, should have been the exception to the rule and viewed the human soul as dying with the body.

The reason for the inexplicit expression in the Biblical books concerning the continued existence of the soul is due to their closeness to life and the deep sense of reality pervading their content. Books of the Old Testament are neither books of theology nor of metaphysical doctrine. Both the Law and the Prophets are concerned with the regulation of life and its improvement, and primarily life in society. In such case, the most effective and the most tangible modes of punishment are those which deal with matters close to life, namely such which are of a material and this-worldly nature. It is this type which is best comprehended by a group struggling desperately towards an ideal religious life set for them as a goal. It was only due to an acute problem, both in the life of the individual and that of the people, which arose in the early period of the Second Commonwealth and which demanded a definite solution, that the notions of the immortality of the soul and resurrection existing hitherto in the subconsciousness of the people were projected into the religious thinking of the Jews of the period. Henceforth, they became powerful and vigorous elements in the spiritual growth of Judaism.

The first phase of the problem was the well known one, "the prosperity of the wicked and the suffering of the righteous." The doctrine taught both by the Law and the Prophets that the righteous is rewarded for his good deeds, and vice versa, that the wicked is punished for his evil, was not in accordance with reality, and gradually this problem began to find expression in literature. Jeremiah cries out bitterly: "Wherefore doth the way of the wicked prosper? Wherefore are they happy all that deal treacherously?" (Jeremiah XII, 1). The Prophet Habakkuk, who prophesied around the time of the Exile, complains woefully: "Why dost thou show me iniquity and cause me to behold grievance? For spoiling and violence are before me and there are those that raise up strife and confusion. Therefore the law is slacked and judgment doth never go forth, for the wicked doth compass the righteous, therefore, wrong judgment proceedeth" (Habakkuk I, 3, 4). It found the strongest and fullest expression in the Book of Job where an attempt is made to offer a solution to this grave problem. However, due to the loftiness of some of the solutions presented in the Book of Job, the disturbance of the turbulent souls was not allayed. A more practical solution was needed. The problem became more and more keen when it entered upon the second phase, namely, when reward and punishment were applied to the nation as a whole. The post-exilic Prophets, Haggai and Zachariah, painted for the returned exiles a bright and glorious picture of the state of the nation in the near future. But these prophecies were not fulfilled, and the stern reality of a limited autonomous government, of a nation living in constant fear of aggression by its powerful neighbors and subjection to them, was not in accord with the promised glory. The question arose then in the hearts of many, where is the promised reward for the chosen people, for the "suffering servant of the Lord?"

It was in such critical times that several ancient ideas embedded in Judaism, but which lacked vitality and influence upon the daily life of the people, were revitalized and supplied with new force and vigor, and to a degree, with new content, as a result of which they became powerful factors in the continued history of Judaism and the Jewish people. These ideas are reward and punishment in the hereafter and the age-old belief of Messianism, which were now furnished with many added features.

The first solved the problem of the individual, namely, that of the suffering of the righteous and the prosperity of the wicked. It said: God is certainly just; He rewards the righteous and punishes the wicked, but neither the reward nor punishment is always carried out in this world, but in the world after death. It is there that justice is carried out in full. In a partial way, however, reward and punishment are also meted out in this world.

While the general solution of reward and punishment being relegated primarily to the hereafter was largely accepted by the great majority of the Jews during the Second Commonwealth—with the exception of the small Sadducean sect— [5] and became in later generations a cardinal belief of Judaism, there is no complete unanimity upon the form of the reward and punishment. First, there is a difference in views as to the length of time of punishment. The last verse in Isaiah LXVI reads: "And they (the righteous) shall go forth and look upon the carcasses of the men who have transgressed against Me; for their worm shall not die, neither shall their fire be quenched; and they shall be an abhorrence to all flesh." From this we may deduce that the punishment is to be eternal and of a physical nature, primarily by fire. However, the accepted

[5] The Sadducean conception of the soul and its destiny in the hereafter is not entirely clear, due to the lack of authentic records of their views. Consequently, various interpretations of that conception are given by different scholars.—See the author's view on the subject in "A History of Jewish Literature," Vol. I, 2nd ed. p. 501ff.

opinion, the verse notwithstanding, is that it is limited. A statement in the Mishnah says: "The judgment of the wicked in *Gehinom* (Hell) is limited to twelve months" (Mishnah Eduyot, Ch. I). Little is told of their fate afterwards. The common belief is that the souls after purification and punishment enter Paradise. Exceptions are made for two classes of grave sinners—one class, after the limit of punishment, suffer the complete annihilation of their souls, and the other suffer eternal punishment.[6] These, however, are individual statements of the School of Shammai and cannot be said to have full authoritative opinion.

As to the mode of punishment, we can see from the above statement in which *Gehinom* is mentioned, that the accepted opinion is that there are two places, *Gehinom* for punishment and *Gan Ēden* for reward. The very names indicate the nature of the punishment and reward. *Gehinom* is named after a valley near Jerusalem where almost constant fires were burning on altars on which sacrifices were offered to idols, and consequently, the punishment is physical, by fire. *Gan Ēden* is named after the first place of residence of Adam, which was a place of comfort and pleasantness, and signifies comfort and pleasantness. This belief, of course, gave free rein to the imagination and a whole literature, which had its beginning in the Apocryphal and Apocalyptic books, arose through the centuries which deals with various phases of the subject. Some of the books describe both the tortures in *Gehinom* and the pleasures in *Gan Ēden* in great detail and in a colorful manner. The belief in the existence of two places was accepted, as is well known, by the two daughter-religions, which acceptance increased the literature manifold. The *Divina Commedia* by Dante is a fair specimen of the Christian mediaeval conception of these places.

However, this belief in the hereafter in its too realistic form, was not accepted by all Jewish religious leaders. There are statements in the Talmud which construe the reward in a spiritual manner, and we may deduce that those who made

[6] *Tosefta Sanhedrin,* Ch. XIII, 4, 5; *Rosh ha-Shanah,* p. 16.

such statements also understood the punishment in a spiritual manner. Maimonides is quite clear on the question of reward which, according to him, is a spiritual pleasure experienced by the soul after death, but not so on punishment. He does not take the *Gehinom* literally as a place where the wicked are punished by fire, but speaks at times of the annihilation of the soul as a punishment. However, this cannot be construed to mean actual destruction, for a soul cannot be annihilated. Other scholars, among them Naḥmanides or Moses ben Nahman (1195–1270), who was more of a mystic than a rationalist, likewise interpreted reward and punishment in the hereafter in a spiritual manner.[7] In view of what has been said we can assert that while the belief in otherworldly reward and punishment belongs to the very warp and woof of Judaism, as expressed through the ages, there is latitude in the conception of their nature and character. Moreover, the doctrine of reward and punishment of the individual was complemented by the doctrine of reward and punishment for the group or the people, which, of course, also affects the individual. This brings us to the solution offered for the second phase of the problem, the national, namely, Messianism and the world to come.

51. The Messiah and the Messianic Age

The Messiah idea is one of the fundamental aspects of Judaism and is as old as the institution of prophecy. There is hardly a Prophet of note who does not refer to it. It is inseparably integrated with the complex conception of Judaism on the relation of the Jewish people to God and on Israel's destiny in the world. It is also integrated with the question of reward and punishment of the people as a whole. It came directly or indirectly as an answer to the problem: Why does the righteous people which was elected by God Himself as

[7] Space does not allow us to enter into the details of the conception. The student, however, who desires further light on the subject should consult Maimonides' Commentary to the Mishnah, *Sanhedrin*, Ch. XI; also his Code, *Hilkot Teshubah*, Chaps. V–X; Naḥmanides, *Shaar ha-Gemul*.

His own, suffer? The greater part of Jewish history, even during the First Commonwealth, passed in strife, attacks by enemies, and subjection to powerful neighbors. True, the Jews sinned, but the suffering outweighs the sins. Where then is the justice of God? The great Prophets, saturated with a deep sense of justice and righteousness and inspired by divine vision, gave the answer to the question. They pictured a glorious future for the Jews as a compensation for the bitter present. This glory did not consist to an Isaiah in physical strength, for it is this very strength which is the source of much evil in the world, but in spiritual and moral splendor.

Spiritual and moral exaltation, however, cannot be actualized in a world of peoples striving against and warring with each other, by one small people alone. Hence the prophetic vision that not only the Jews will rise to heights of the spirit but humanity as a whole. Consequently, Isaiah's vision of the abolition of war is a *conditio sine qua non* for the glorious period in human history of which Israel will form the center. This is the Messianic idea presented in its full brilliance for the first time in the early eschatological prophecy of Isaiah (Isaiah II, 1–4). But soon there entered a more personal element, namely, that of a personal Messiah. The same prophet once more envisions the glorious future, consisting primarily in a universal knowledge of God and a reign of peace, and even speaks symbolically of peace between animals, thereby implying a change in the law of nature (*ibid.* XI, 1–11).[8] He, however, adds an important feature, that of the personal Messiah, a scion of the House of David, who will preside over this remarkable period in the history of humanity. That the Messiah will not inaugurate a period of spiritual

[8] That the peace among animals is only a symbolic figure of speech was already pointed out by Maimonides, inasmuch as in verse 9 of this vision, the Prophet says: "They (the animals) shall not hurt nor destroy in all My holy mountain; for the earth shall be full of the knowledge of God as the waters cover the sea." The acquisition of the knowledge of God surely, says he, cannot be expected of the animals. Consequently, the animals spoken of by the Prophets are only symbols for mighty and weak nations (*Guide of the Perplexed*, Pt. III, Ch. XI).

glory only but also one of material good follows *eo ipso,* for human life will always be the same in its elemental features. The Messianic idea thus combined in the first period of its emergence two elements, material good and national glory, on the one hand, and the spiritual exaltation of Israel and all other nations, on the other hand.

Henceforth, in the development of the Messianic idea and the Messianic ideal there is an oscillation between the two elements. At times, the national good and glory are emphasized, and at other times, the spiritual glory and all that appertains to it. At no time, however, did Judaism during the prophetic period and even after it omit or even neglect either of the two. The best example is afforded in the second part of Isaiah, ascribed by scholars to an anonymous exilic prophet. At one time he says: "Behold, the darkness shall cover the earth, and gross darkness the people; but the Lord shall arise upon thee, and His glory shall be seen upon thee. And the Gentiles shall come to thy light and kings to the brightness of thy rising." But he supplements this immediately by the statement: "Then thou shalt see and be radiant and thine heart shall throb and be enlarged, because the abundance of the sea shall be converted unto thee and the wealth of the Gentiles shall come unto thee" (Isaiah LX, 2, 3, 5). He goes on to describe in detail the abundance of material wealth which will be showered upon Israel in the days of the future. But a little later (LXV, 17), he proclaims: "For behold, I create new heavens and a new earth, and the former shall not be remembered nor come into mind." And again, he follows this proclamation by a description of material good and length of life which shall take place in those days. Yet the words, "a new heaven and a new earth," injected a new note in the entire conception and were destined to call forth exciting thoughts and notions.

With the post-exilic restoration which was, on the whole, a small affair and created much disappointment, the question of the national Job, namely, why does Israel, the righteous people, suffer, became keen and demanded an answer. The answer came through further glorification and deepening of the Messiah idea. The longer the Messiah tarried, the further the Messianic age was removed, the greater and the more glorious became the vision of both. Both elements, the national and the universal-spiritual, received accretions. A whole literature was developed around this solution, and with each book the idea was enlarged and increased in compass. Imagination was given free rein; the future became not only a period of national glory, but one of a complete change in the entire life of the world. Miracles became the order of the day and not the exception, for the very nature of the world was destined to change. Description of the wonderful "good time" in a material sense which will be had in the Messianic days abound in the Apocryphal and Apocalyptic books. In fact, they have their origin in the prophetic words. Do we not read in Isaiah LXV, 20: "There shall be no more an infant of days, nor an old man that hath not filled his days, for the child shall die an hundred years old, but the sinner being a hundred years old shall be accursed." Likewise did the universal spiritual elements expand and become intensified. The words of Isaiah quoted above, "Behold, I shall create a new heaven and a new earth," were taken literally, and suddenly there was injected in the world of spirit and thought the concepts of *Olam hazeh*, this world, and the *Olam ha-Ba*, the world to come.

With the entry of these concepts, new elements entered into the entire idea of the Messiah, which became complex. Some older ideas which had their roots in Prophetic teachings, such as the Day of Judgment (Isaiah II; Joel IV) and the Kingdom of God, received new content. They lost the national connotation. The Day of Judgment with the Prophets is either a day of judgment over the peoples which oppressed Israel or over Israel itself—only once in Isaiah II is it general, but even there the meaning is vague. But later it was understood to mean a judgment over all men which only the righteous and the saints shall escape. The Kingdom of God was no longer understood in the Prophetic sense—the spread of the knowledge of God among all nations who lead a moral but natural life—but primarily in the sense of a society of saints in a world where evil will be no more. This conception is already found in the later part of the Book of Daniel where "people of the saints" undoubtedly refers to Israel, but even there it is used in a limited sense, for a whole people cannot be saints, and its larger part is thus excluded.

Another important element which entered into the concept of the new world, destined to make its appearance at the beginning of the Messianic period, is the belief in the resurrection of the dead which is to take place during that time. Resurrection of the dead is not unknown in the Bible. The miracle was performed once by Elijah and twice by his disciple, Elisha, once when the prophet was still alive, and another time when he was already dead.[9] Ezekiel (Ch. XXXVII) speaks of the restoration of Israel metaphorically as resurrection of the dead, and describes it in great detail, which shows that this idea was not totally strange to him. There are also other references in the Bible to resurrection. However, this idea belonged to the class of ideas which were inactive in life, but at this time it was itself "resurrected" and filled with content. In a way, the incorporation of resurrection in the complex of "the world to come" was a logical deduction from its fundamentals. If the new period and the new world are offered as a reward to the righteous, why should not the righteous of the past generations who have suffered not enjoy it? Resurrection follows then as a corollary.

The national element, though, struck deep roots into the consciousness of the people and could not be dismissed by the great majority of the people. Consequently, during a part of the Second Commonwealth period, attempts were made to retain both conceptions. The Messianic period is to precede the "world to come," and at its end resurrection will take place, and then "the world to come" will begin. Opinions differ about the duration of the Messianic period.

All these views which arose and developed during the

[9] I Kings, Ch. XVII, 17–24; II Kings, Ch. IV, 32–37; XIII, 19–21.

period of the Second Commonwealth, while they were active and effective in life, never received during their formation any definite sanction by a fully authoritative body. The sanction came later, after the destruction of the Temple, when Judaism became more concrete and more crystallized in its views. Then the concept of the Messianic period, while retaining both elements, that of *Olam ha-Ba* and resurrection, which were even raised to the status of dogmas, once more regained its national character. The view in the Mishnah is that all Jews share in the world to come except one who denies the divine origin of the Torah or the doctrine of resurrection—saying it is not an original belief—and a heretic (Sanhedrin X, 1). Furthermore, according to semi-authoritative statements in the Talmud, the Messianic period proper will precede the world to come and the two thus become distinguished from each other. The belief in resurrection was then incorporated in the most important of the daily prayers—*Shemoneh Esré*—and thus received additional sanction.

The sanction spoken of, however, refers only to fundamental concepts, namely, to the coming of the Messiah, *Olam ha-Ba,* and resurrection, but not to details. There is no authoritative opinion on the length of the days of the Messianic age and various lengths are given. Nor is it definite whether resurrection will precede or follow the days of the Messiah. Nor is the nature and character of *Olam ha-Ba* determined, for while miraculous phenomena in the future are frequently spoken of, it is not definite whether they belong to the days of the Messiah or to those of *Olam ha-Ba*. What is definitely connected with the Messianic age is the gathering of the Jews from exile and the restoration of the kingdom in Palestine. There is an opinion expressed by a famous Rabbi in the Talmud that the distinction of the days of the Messiah will consist only in the gathering of Israel to its own land and the restoration of the kingdom. The miraculous phenomena mentioned frequently in the Rabbinic literature as a part of daily life are then relegated to the world to come.[10] This opinion of the

[10] T.B. *Sabbath,* 63a *et alia.*

character of Messianic days is followed by Maimonides.

There is no authoritative description, as said, of the world to come, but on the whole, it is conceived in the Talmud as of a physical nature, namely, that man will enjoy physical good.[11] However, the purely spiritual nature of that world spoken of in some Apocalyptic books is not entirely unknown in the Talmud. Rab, the founder of the great Academy of Sura, expresses that opinion. Maimonides follows his view. Unfortunately, Maimonides is not entirely clear on the term *Olam ha-Ba,* whether he refers to the hereafter or to the world to come.[12]

Disregarding all Agadic embellishments we can say that the beliefs in the coming of the Messiah, a scion of David, who will gather the Jews from exile and restore them to Palestine, in the resurrection, and in *Olam ha-Ba,* became cardinal principles and dogmas in Judaism. Some mediaeval dogmatists, though, relegated them to a second class of dogmas. Notwithstanding this relegation, the influence of these beliefs upon life, especially the belief in the coming of the Messiah, was tremendously great, even greater than some of the dogmas which are considered by all as fundamental. It can be said that the belief in the Messiah was a leading factor in the survival of the Jewish people in spite of the numerous persecutions.

[11] T.B. *Sanhedrin,* 92a; *Ketubot* 112.
[12] T.B. *Berakot,* 17; *Mishnah Torah, Hilkot Teshubah.*

CHAPTER VIII

ETHICAL AND SOCIAL IDEALS

52. TESHUBAH (Repentance)

To the contributions which Judaism made towards the spiritual advance of humanity in general and that of the other great religions in particular belongs also the concept of *Teshubah* or repentance. This does not mean that pagan religions did not know of the importance of atonement for wrong acts committed, or of prayers of supplication to the gods for forgiveness of sins which contained promises for better behavior in the future. But such regrets were mainly external and were primarily expressed by means of a sacrifice intended to propitiate the gods. Repentance as a state of the soul, as a complete change of heart and a renewal of personality is entirely a gift of Judaism. It occupies an exceptionally important place in the Bible. Time and again, prophet after prophet calls his people to repent and thus escape the pending doom decreed for them by God as punishment for their sins. They also emphasize its inner nature, that it must be a change of heart and not demonstrated by external signs only. "Turn ye even to me with all your heart," says Joel. This is the primary condition. It is, of course, accompanied also by visible signs, for he continues, "and with fasting, weeping, and mourning." These actions, however, should not be considered of primary importance, and he calls again: "Rend your hearts and not your garments" (Joel II, 12, 13). Ezekiel has a number of prophecies in which he repeatedly stresses the value of repentance as the only means of avoiding punishment and summarizes its character in the phrase, "and make ye a new heart and a new spirit, for why should ye die, O

House of Israel" (Ezekiel XVIII, 31). That repentance is a divine gift to all humanity is taught by the Book of Jonah, where Jonah is sent to Nineveh, the Assyrian capital, to call for repentance in order to avert the decreed doom. And when his call was heard it was averted.

Repentance, according to the Bible, is efficacious no matter how grave the sin may be, as exemplified in the case of Menasseh, King of Judah, who committed numerous sins and was as a punishment captured by the Assyrians. But when he repented and called upon God, he was released and returned to his kingdom (2 Chronicles, XXXIII, 10–14). The later Agada embellished this act by telling us that the angels, knowing the depth of Menasseh's sins, wanted to prevent the acceptance of his repentance by closing all entries to his cries before the throne. But God, in order to show an example to repentants, opened a channel beneath the throne and accepted it.[1]

In later days, repentance assumed an exceptionally important role in Judaism. Numerous passages in Talmudic and Midrashic literature extol the value of *Teshubah* to a very high degree. One statement says: "In the place (i.e., spiritual degree) where repentants stand, not even the very righteous can stand." [2] Another Midrashic statement counts *Teshubah* as one of the seven things which were created before the world itself was created.[3] In view of the fact that repentance is only a matter of thought and feeling in the hearts of men and has no existence per se, the statement can only mean that it is to be considered as a final cause which was in the mind of the Creator before He proceeded to creation. In other words, were repentance unattainable by man, the creation of the world would not have been worth while. However, notwithstanding the great value which *Teshubah* possesses, it has

[1] Jerusalem Talmud, *Sanhedrin*, Ch. XI.

[2] *Berakot*, 34. Maimonides expressed a somewhat different opinion on the matter and believes that one who has purified his soul to such a degree that he does not desire to commit evil is really on a higher status than the repentant (*Eight Chapters*, Ch. I), but in his *Code* he follows the Talmudic opinion.

[3] *Genesis Rabba*, 1, 4.

certain limitations. According to the Mishnah,[4] *Teshubah* results in immediate forgiveness only for sins for which punishment by court is flagellation. In case of graver sins, repentance supplements the Day of Atonement to procure forgiveness. For the forgiveness of very grave sins for which the legal penalty is death, a third factor is necessary, namely bodily suffering which comes through providence as punishment.[5]

Teshubah, as an instrument for forgiveness, is effective only for sins of a purely religious or ceremonial nature, but if the acts involve an injury to a fellow-man in any way, the injured person must first be satisfied. If it was a matter of damages to property, it must be made good, and if the injury was of a personal nature, such as insult or slander, the forgiveness of the injured party must be procured. The primary condition of *Teshubah* is, as stated, a complete change of heart, a condition which is often described in books on morality as follows: Regret for past actions and a resolve never to commit such acts in the future no matter how great the temptation or the compulsion may be, as long as it does not involve loss of life. But in view of the fact that every change in human life must have external expression, it is usually accomplished by confession, not publicly, and supplication for forgiveness.

Confession as such as an instrument for forgiveness or at regular intervals before a religious representative, as in other religions, is not known in Judaism. Nor is anybody empowered to remit sins except God Himself. Public confession is only recited on the Day of Atonement. This, however, is a standardized formula and the catalogue of sins is too general and too long for any one person to have committed during his life time. A formula of confession is also recited, if conditions permit, before death, primarily as an indication of the sick man's repentance, but not necessarily as a means of forgiveness. Standard Judaism knows no infliction of self-torture as a form of repentance except fasting. Mediaeval pietists and

[4] *Yoma,* 86.
[5] Ibid.

followers of mystical trends, however, introduced such measures and even elaborated a scale of such infliction to correspond with the gravity of the sins. This is sometimes called *Teshubot ha-Mishkal* (The Balance of the Scale of Repentance), but such actions were hardly practiced except by the extremely pious.

53. Torah

Of all the fundamental conceptions of Judaism, that of Torah is of the most unique character and can be considered of a *sui generis* nature, hardly paralleled in any other religion, past or present. The term itself originally meant teaching and was applied to any kind of instruction whether religious, moral, or merely practical. A verse in Proverbs says: "My son, hear the instruction of thy father, and do not forsake the Torah (teaching) of thy mother" (Proverbs I, 8). Here Torah evidently refers to the practical teaching of the mother. In the sense of teaching it is used many times in the Bible. Later, however, it became more and more restricted to the Pentateuch, sometimes with the addition of the name of Moses as *Torat Moshe*, and as such Torah is usually translated, the Law. Around the middle of the Second Commonwealth period the term was expanded to include also all interpretations and explanations of the various precepts which formed a part of the Oral Law. In the first Mishnah in the tractate of *Abot* which hails from early times, we read: "Moses received the Torah from Sinai and handed it to Joshua; Joshua (handed it down) to the Elders, the Elders to the Prophets; and the Prophets to the men of the Great Assembly." In this statement the term Torah includes the Oral Law, for it is the Elders, the Prophets, and the men of the Great Assembly who were the guardians of the Oral Law, while the Pentateuch was in the hands of all the people. In later literature two terms are used, *Torah she-Biktab*, the written Torah or the Pentateuch, and *Torah she-Beal Peh,* Oral Law. But, as a rule, both parts coalesced into one and were denoted by the same term Torah, as evident in this very Mishnah which includes the Oral Law under the same term.

However, the words "Moses received the Torah from Sinai" were understood not in the literal sense that the Torah as a book was in heaven and was delivered to Moses in that form, but that all the commandments, precepts, and even the historical portions were communicated to him by God in the highest form of prophecy, for his prophecy was *sui generis,* different in kind from those of all other prophets. This view was exalted into fundamental dogma by the Mishnah in another place.[6] This dogma is technically named *Torah min ha-Shammayyim,* literally Torah from heaven, i.e., given to Moses by divine inspiration or communication. Maimonides expanded this dogma into two. The first states that the entire Torah which we possess was given to Moses on Sinai. The second asserts that the Torah with all its precepts is immutable. Other dogmatists differed with him in the form of expression of this dogma but agreed in the veracity of the fact that the Torah is divine. The dogma refers primarily to the written Torah. As for the Oral Law, though the belief is general that a large part of it is Sinaitic, and consequently its directions as to the manner in which the precepts mentioned in the Pentateuch are to be performed are considered Biblical—yet there is no definite authoritative view that the belief in the Sinaitic origin of the Law is a dogma (Ikkar).

The role of the Torah as the principal expression of the Jewish national spirit, due to the vicissitudes of life, gradually increased, and its value constantly rose higher and higher until it came to be considered a cosmic power. Such a conception is not paralleled in any other religion or in the culture of any other nation, and can only be compared to the Platonic idea of the Good. Numerous statements through the Talmudic literature of earlier and later periods testify to this exceptionally exalted conception. It is, of course, counted in the Midrash among the few things which were created before the world and which dictum means that it served as a final

[6] T.B. *Sanhedrin* XI, 1.

cause and purpose of creation. But its role is even more distinguished than that of the other things, for according to another statement, noted above (p. 140), the world was created with an expressed condition, namely that if the Jews will accept the Torah, then it shall continue in existence, but if not, it shall return to chaos.[7] The meaning of the statement is clear; the continuation of the existence of the world is valueless unless there is Torah, i.e., religion, morality, and ethical social life. However, a still higher role was assigned to it, namely, that it served as a pattern and blueprint to the Creator in the creation of the world.[8]

With this conception as a fundamental element in the Jewish view of life and the world there is small wonder that the study of the Torah, in the broad sense of the word, became the principal occupation in the spiritual life of the nation and the most potent factor in its survival in spite of all suffering. The Jews are usually called the People of the Book, an appellation which arose from an erroneous interpretation of the words of Mohammed who used this epithet merely to describe the peoples who had a written book containing the principles of their religion. The real title of the Jews should be "people of study." With the destruction of political independence, study became the center of Jewish life to such a degree that it can veritably be said that the Torah through the ages was the portable spiritual fatherland of the Jews. The place of study in Jewish life during the last two thousand years can hardly be estimated. It was the occupation of young and old of all classes and stations in society, and the ideal of the great masses.

Study was not a mere instrument or means of ascertaining the proper way of performing precepts—though it followed from it—but an aim in itself, a self-expression and a goal. At an early conference of Jewish scholars in Lydda, Palestine, which took place in the middle of the 2nd century C. E., the question arose, which is greater in value, study or observation

[7] Talmud Babli, Tr. *Sabbath*, 88b.
[8] *Genesis Rabba*, Ch. I.

of religious precepts, and after some discussion, it was decided that study is more valuable, for study will also result in piety and observance, while the latter, no matter how punctilious, will never be perfect.[9] In fact, it is definitely stated in *Abot* [10] that an ignorant man, no matter how much effort he spends in the observance of the religious precepts, can never be called truly pious. And another Mishnah, after enumerating the most important religious and ethical practices, such as that for which man receives both great reward in this world (only as interest) and many times more in the world to come (as the inexhaustible principal) states: "But the reward of the study of the Torah is as great as that of all of them." [11]

It followed from such a concept that study raised a man to the highest position, no matter how low his descent might be. It is therefore stated that a scholar, though he be of illegitimate birth (*Mamzer*), takes precedence over an ignorant high priest. Consequently, much space is given in Talmudic literature to the exaltation of study. A whole chapter in the tractate *Abot* (Ch. VI) is devoted to this subject in which the study of the Torah and the acquisition of learning are described in the most glowing terms. Torah is, according to its statement, higher and more important than priesthood and kingship, and was first in God's plan of creation. It further enumerates forty-eight steps by which real learning is acquired which, if really followed, make the learned ideal types of men.

The road of the Torah is not an easy one. Among the forty-eight steps mentioned above, satisfaction with very little of worldly goods and still less of pleasure are included. It is a stern taskmaster; it requires continuous pursuit, for it is said in the name of the Torah: "If you forsake me for one day, I will forsake you for two" [12]; and furthermore, if one separates himself from it, he loses his life, i.e., the life of the spirit which is the only one worth pursuing.

[9] T.B. *Kiddushin*, 40.
[10] Ibid. Ch. II, 6.
[11] *Peah*, Ch. I, 1.
[12] Palestinian Talmud, end of *Berakot*.

The result of such a view was that the position of the scholar—called *Talmid Ḥakam* (a wise disciple) and not *Ḥakam* (wise man) which name signifies that one is always a disciple—in Jewish life was of exceptional importance. However, *noblesse oblige,* he had not only privileges but also numerous duties. His whole conduct as a model in many ways of life, at home, in the market-place, in social relations, and even in dress is minutely described. All these ideas gradually impressed themselves upon the masses and moulded the life of the people for centuries. And at least up to the middle of the last century, the scholar, or better still, the man of Jewish learning, was the Jewish ideal social type who served as a center of imitation to all classes. Jews prayed daily and on special festivals that God open the hearts of their children to love the Torah, and parents exerted all their efforts to have their sons learned even if they themselves did not possess much learning. Simple untutored mothers prayed in the vernacular—mostly in Yiddish—at the time they lighted the candles on the Sabbath eve not for riches for their children, though they were desperately poor, but for learning.

It is this set of complex ideas, views, and feelings peculiar to Judaism, integrated with the life of the people in numerous ways, which acted as a potent factor in the survival of the Jews. It may, under the force of circumstances, be changed and modified to a large degree, but it can never be abolished or emptied entirely of its content—for then Judaism itself may lose its force and vitality.

54. Peace

Peace, as we have seen above, is a distinct contribution of Judaism to civilized humanity. It was Isaiah who, in a world of strife where war was the order of the day and the most natural phenomenon, envisioned a condition of human life where swords and spears would be beaten into plough-shares and into pruning-knives. Again, he returns to his subject in his second Messianic vision (Ch. XI) and extends peace symbolically to the animal kingdom. Peace, as an ideal which must be realized in life, runs through the entire Bible like a red thread. Prophet after Prophet emphasizes the blessing of peace. Micah repeats the words of Isaiah about the "end of days." Jeremiah, chastising his people, threatens them with the direst punishment by saying: "Thus saith the Lord, 'Enter not into the house of mourning, neither go to lament nor to bemoan them, for I have taken away my peace from them, even loving kindness and mercies'" (XVI, 5). Similarly, Haggai, when comforting his people, says: "The glory of this latter house shall be greater than that of the former, saith the Lord of Hosts. And in this place will I give peace, saith the Lord" (II, 9). In this vein speaks Zachariah when, visioning the coming of the Messiah, he emphasizes the Messiah's most important characteristic to be "that he shall speak peace unto the nations" (IX, 10). The Psalmist sings: "The mountains shall bring peace to the people and the little hills, by righteousness." Again, "In his days (those of the righteous king) shall the righteous flourish and abundance of peace as long as the moon endureth" (Psalms LXXII, 3, 7).

Peace as an ideal state of social life will undoubtedly come in the future, for otherwise that life is valueless, but there are definite conditions for its realization. The primary condition is the spread of the knowledge of God in the full sense of the term. Isaiah, the first to visualize the glorious vision of universal peace, emphasizes twice its dependence upon that condition. In his prophecy of the "end of days" he says that only when the nations will come to the House of the God of Israel and plead for instruction and receive it, only then will they break their swords and spears into peaceful instruments. Again, in his second Messianic vision (Ch. XI), after picturing the future complete state of peace in the world, he offers the reason for this completeness in the words, "for the earth shall be full of the knowledge of the Lord as the waters over the sea." Knowledge of God spoken of by Isaiah is the general condition and it includes a number of subordinate ones, prominent among which are justice and righteousness. When the

Psalmist sings of the time when the very mountains will bring peace, he concludes that this can only take place when righteousness will grow on the hills. Another singer of Israel chants: "Mercy and truth are met together, righteousness and peace have kissed each other" (Psalms LXXXV, 11). Thus did the prophets and psalmists of Judaism conceive the realization of peace among nations, namely that it will come when men will undergo a complete change of heart.

It cannot be otherwise, for war to the lawgiver, prophets, and historians was only a result of the evil passions of the human heart and the failure of man to live up to the laws of God. The chronicler, in describing King Asa's religious reformation and his abolishing all idolatry in Judah, prefaces it by the speech of the Prophet Azariah, the son of Oded, who said to the king: "Now for a long season Israel hath been without the true God and without a teaching priest and without law. And in those times there was no peace to him that went out, nor to him that came in, but great vexations were upon all the inhabitants of the countries" (II Chronicles, Ch. XV, 3, 5). The Torah correctly recognizes covetousness and greed as the principal causes of war and strife when it promises the children of Israel: "Neither shall any man covet thy land when thou goest up three times a year before the Lord, thy God" (Exodus XXXIV, 24). It is not only a reward for the observance of a precept, but implies the belief that man can overcome his evil inclination and abstain from coveting his neighbor's property. Only then when he will learn to restrain his passions will peace reign in the world.

Moreover, peace is, according to the Talmudists, the goal of the entire Torah for the realization of which it was given, as it is stated: "Her ways are ways of pleasantness, and all her paths are peace" (Proverbs III, 17).[13]

Again, say the Rabbis: "The Torah urges us to pursue peace even more than the performance of the precepts, as it is said,

[13] Tr. *Gittin,* 59b. The verse speaks of wisdom but the teachers of the Talmud always identified the wisdom spoken of in the Book of Proverbs with the Torah.

'Seek peace and pursue it' (Psalm XXXIV, 15) meaning seek it in your own place and pursue it in other places. Hence the children of Israel pursued it even with their enemies." [14] Even the destruction of the enemies of Israel, though at times necessary, is yet bewailed by the Agadists who tell us that on the night when the Egyptians were drowned in the Red Sea the angels were prevented by God from singing His praises, for He said: "My handiwork drown in the sea, and ye want to sing before Me." [15]

Later Talmudic Judaism continued in the same strain and even expanded and widened the conception of peace to include all phases, those of smaller social units as well as of larger ones. The Mishnah emphasizes the value of peace a number of times. It says: "Three things sustain the existence of the world—justice, truth and peace" (Abot I, 17). By the *world* is meant, of course, the human world, and as with the Prophets and the Psalmists, the three elements go together. Peace is placed as the last pillar, for it cannot arise unless the two former precede it. The closing statement of the entire Mishnah reads: "God did not bestow any greater blessing upon Israel than peace, for it is written, 'The Lord will give strength to His people, the Lord will bless His people with peace!' " [16] Another statement reads: "Peace is great, for all blessings are included in it." [17] Furthermore, in the judgment of these scholars, peace is of the greatest importance for the life of a people, for no matter what faults the people may possess, as long as there is unity of effort and peace, it will overcome all handicaps. This thought is expressed in a Midrashic statement: "Said Rabbi Judah the Prince, 'Great is the effect of peace upon the life of a people, for even when Israel worshipped idols, as long as peace reigned among them God did not punish them, for it is said, Ephraim is joined to idols, let him alone' " (Hosea XIV, 17).[18] The verse is interpreted

[14] Midrash, *Numeri Rabba* Ch. XIX, 27.
[15] Tr. *Sanhedrin,* 39b.
[16] Tr. *Okẓin,* III, 12.
[17] Leviticus R. Ch. IX.
[18] *Genesis Rabba* Ch. XXXVIII.

to mean that though Ephraim is worshiping idols, as long as he is "joined" together, God will overlook his sins and not punish him.

Great stress is also laid by Judaism upon peace in smaller social units, such as the family. Numerous statements extol its importance. Says the *Mekilta:* "If a man exerts himself in maintaining peace in the family life of his friend and prevents its disruption, he is promised that he himself will never suffer any grief in his own life." [19] Stories are related of great scholars who suffered grave personal insults at the hands of wicked husbands in their efforts to effect reconciliation between them and their wives. Similarly, many legal enactments and religious customs have their basis in the desire to realize peace in social life. One of the important functions of the scholar is, according to the Rabbis, to increase peace in the world, and the first act of the Messiah will be to declare peace, as it is said: "How beautiful upon the mountains are the feet of one who bringeth tidings and declareth peace" (Isaiah LII, 7), which is understood by the Rabbis to refer to the Messiah.[20]

A prayer for peace forms one of the benedictions of the *Amidah* and is recited by every pious Jew three times daily. The desire for peace in the daily routine of the life of society and the hope for its universal reign in the future form fundamental traits of Judaism inculcated by its teachings and integrated in all its aspects and phases.

55. Labor

There is hardly a religion which has placed so high a value on labor as Judaism. All through the Bible, whenever the occasion occurs, labor is exalted and praised. The Psalmist says: "For thou shalt eat the labor of thy hands, thou shalt be happy; and it shall be well with thee" (Psalms CXXVIII, 2). In the Book of Proverbs the industrious man who attends to his work

[19] *Mekilta,* Section on *Jethro.*
[20] *Leviticus Rabba,* Ch. LX.

is pointed out as the man whose conduct is to be imitated, while the lazy man who shirks work is continually deprecated. Labor, according to the Book, leads not only to material success, but to personal dignity, for, "Seest thou a man diligent in his labor, he shall stand before kings and shall not stand before mean men" (Proverbs XXII, 29). On the other hand, "He that is slothful in his work is a brother to him that is a great waster" (ibid. XVIII, 9).

The Talmud speaks of labor in still more glowing terms. The Mishnah in *Abot* (1, 10) says: "Love labor and hate mastering others." Several great scholars, on their way to the Academy, carried their tools and would say: "Labor is great for it honors the man who performs it." [21] Another Mishnaic statement says: "Just as the Sabbath was commanded to the Jews at the Sinai Covenant, so was labor enjoined in that Covenant, for it is said: 'Six days shalt thou work and perform all thy labor and on the seventh day shalt thou rest.'" [22] In other words, the Rabbis equate labor with the Sabbath, and consider work on the six days of the week a divine injunction just as rest on the seventh. Still another statement raises labor even higher than the merit of the fathers, meaning that a man should not rely on the prestige of his ancestors and go idle, but should rather engage in useful labor and consider it of high merit.[23] Such being the views of Judaism, small wonder then that the Jews, contrary to current opinion, were a people of laborers during more than two thirds of their history. In their own land as well as in several settlements in the Diaspora they were primarily engaged in agriculture. But wherever that was not possible, as e.g., Alexándria and Rome, they engaged in trade. It was only during the Mediaeval Ages, when laws of discrimination were enacted against them, that Jews were forced out of many kinds of labor and pushed into commerce or into finance. Yet even in those times and during the modern period in the large Jewish settlements

[21] T.B. *Nedarim,* 49.
[22] *Abot di Rabbi Nathan,* Ch. XI.
[23] *Genesis Rabba* Ch. LXXIV, 12.

in Eastern Europe the masses engaged to a very large extent in all kinds of labor.

If labor is exalted, it follows that the interest of the laborer must be protected. Accordingly, the Pentateuch twice repeats injunctions regarding the wages of the hired laborer—that he must be paid in the proper time without delay. It says: "The wage of one that is hired shall not abide with thee all night until morning" (Leviticus XIX, 13); and again: "Thou shalt not oppress a hired servant that is poor and needy whether he be of thy brethren or strangers that are in thy land within thy gates. At his day shalt thou give him his hire, neither shall the sun go down on it, for he is poor and setteth his heart upon it, lest he cry against thee unto the Lord and it be sin unto thee" (Deuteronomy XXIV, 14). The Rabbis, in interpreting the statements regarding the speedy payment of wages, noted the change of terminology in the two verses. In the former it says the night must not pass before payment, while in the latter, the limit is sundown. They explained that they refer to two types of laborers. The one who works by the day must be paid before sunrise of the following morning, while one who works at night, must be paid by sunset on that day. In either case, if the limit is transgressed, the employer is guilty of transgressing a prohibitive precept which is a grave offense. The same limit is fixed for laborers who hire themselves out for longer periods—a week, a month, or even a year. No more than twelve hours should pass after they finish their term before they receive their payment.[24] The hired laborer is also given the privilege of eating the fruit of the land on which he is working during the time of his work so that he should not suffer any pangs of pain at not being able to satisfy his natural desire for tasting the fruit he is handling. The law is Biblical, but later interpreters expanded it to apply to many cases. Likewise did Jewish law evolve regulations covering the question of wages and the right of stoppage of work under different conditions. While the question of wages is usually settled by agreement between em-

[24] T. B. *Baba Metzia*, p. 110b (Mishnah).

ployer and employee, the law recognizes a certain standard fixed by custom of the conditions of labor, as for instance, if the number of hours of labor for the day is fixed, no employer can demand of his laborers longer hours even if he offers them higher wages.[25]

In regard to the right of stopping the work after it has begun, the law favors the laborer and allows him to change his mind even in the midst of his labor without loss. For instance, if a laborer hired himself out for the day at the wage of four dollars per day and he stopped work in midday, he is paid two dollars even if the employer will have to pay a higher wage for the work undone. On the other hand, if wages fall and the work can be finished for a dollar, the laborer gets three dollars. This law is subject to certain limitations and modifications, but the rule in general is that the laborer has the upper hand.[26]

Again, if the employer has no work and fails to inform the laborers beforehand, he must nonetheless, if they come to work, pay them wages for the entire day at a lower rate.[27] The rate in such cases is the rate the laborer would accept for a day on condition that he be at leisure. These privileges are given only to the laborer hired by the day, the week, or the month, but when one has contracted to manufacture certain articles or perform a definite amount of labor on a project until it is completed, he can also change his mind, but he has to pay whatever damage was incurred by his act. For example, if prices for labor rise and in consequence the unfinished work will cost more than originally anticipated, he must compensate his employer for the difference in labor cost so that the latter will not suffer loss by reason of his defection.[28] From all this it is evident that Judaism in its legal phase was careful to guard the rights of the laborer and preserve his dignity and position. It has even gone to such lengths as to prohibit a

[25] Ibid. p. 83a (Mishnah).
[26] Ibid. p. 77b.
[27] Ibid. 76b. *Hoshen Mishpat*, Sec. 333, 1.
[28] Ibid. sec. 333, 4.

Jew from hiring himself out to another Jew for a period of more than three years. In this case the opinion is given that it appears as if he assumes the status of a servant—the usual period of one who sells himself as a servant was six years; more than half of that term would give that status—and Jews ought to be free for they are the servants only of God.[29]

[29] Ibid. sec. 333, 3.

Chapter IX

THE DOGMAS OF JUDAISM

Though we endeavored to point out in the introductory chapter of the book that Judaism is a religion *sui generis* and stressed its unlikeness to other religions, yet this difference by no means excludes the fact that like other religions, it possesses dogmas or contains principles the belief in which is incumbent upon every one who is considered among its adherents. The view advanced by Moses Mendelsohn in his book "Jerusalem," that Judaism does not command one to believe, but to know and recognize, and that it emphasizes mainly the performance of deeds and the observance of precepts, a view followed by many others in the 19th century, is now considered by most scholars as obsolete.

In fact, the very contribution of Judaism consists in its proclamation of the belief in one God and one only. The Bible even condemns to death those members of the Jewish people who demonstrate by an act the denial of such belief, namely, by worshipping idols. It insists on an act because it serves as sufficient proof for such denial, for heresy in thought man cannot be certain of; only God alone, who knows all inner secrets, can be aware of it. Such heresy was therefore left to His judgment. We find in Deuteronomy XXX, 17-20 an explicit admonition against heretical thoughts expressed as follows: "Lest there should be among you man, woman, or tribe whose heart turneth away from the Lord, our God, to go and serve the gods of these nations—the Lord will not spare him—and all the curses that are written in this book shall lie upon him, and the Lord shall blot out his name from under heaven." We can see clearly that Judaism took note even of pure belief in the heart or mind.

It is true that the Bible did not emphasize as strictly and as rigorously the belief in certain principles as other later religions do. It is quite doubtful whether we can find in the Biblical books definite attempts at the formulation of a set of dogmas in the technical sense. The case is, however, different with the Talmud, the second great book of the Jewish people after the Bible.

There we find in the first Mishnah of the tenth chapter of the Tractate Sanhedrin a statement which can be considered a real promulgation of a set of principles of Judaism. It reads: "All Israel share in the world to come (Olam ha-Ba) except the one who says resurrection has no origin in the Law (i.e., the Torah) [1], or that the Torah was not given *from heaven, and the Apikoros.*"

In view of the fact that other cardinal principles of belief are emphasized in numerous places in the Mishnah, such as free will (Aboth III, 19, 20), reward and punishment (Ibid. II, 14, 15, and in many other places), providence (Berakot IX, 5), while the discussion on the principle of the unity of God contained in the Shema opens the Mishnah, there is no doubt that these dogmas express class concepts, namely, that each or at least two of them include several dogmas which are subsumed under one concept. Thus, the dogma *Torah min ha-Shamayyim,* i.e., divine origin of the Torah, may include the four dogmas relating to the importance of the Torah

[1] Resurrection is mentioned explicitly twice in the Book of Daniel Chap. XII, 2, 13, and is referred to in Isaiah Chap. XXVI, 19, and in the Vision of Ezekiel. But the Mishnah does not refer to these passages, inasmuch as the passages in Isaiah and the Vision of Ezekiel may be interpreted in a metaphorical manner. In fact, there is a view in the Talmud, Sanhedrin 92b, that the vision of resurrection described by Ezekiel is only a *Mashal,* i.e., a parable, symbolizing redemption from exile. Daniel is a book of a later period than that of the prophetic books. The Mishnah connotes by the word *Torah* the Pentateuch, for certain verses in these books were interpreted by early Tannaim as inculcating the belief in resurrection. See also above, p. 163.

and prophecy enumerated by Maimonides in his scheme of dogmas, and the dogma of the Torah origin of resurrection includes several dogmas relating to divine providence, and to reward and punishment. We cannot accept its literal meaning, for such a disbelief is rather a mild case, for the denial of the origin of a dogma is certainly a lesser heresy than the denial of the dogma itself. It is put in this form in order to emphasize the value of the belief in the dogmas of providence and reward and punishment of which resurrection is an aspect. It tells us that even if one belives in resurrection but does not ascribe to it a Torah origin, he is still a heretic, from which it follows of course that disbelief in resurrection itself or in retribution in general is a greater heresy.

The meaning of the term *Apikoros* in the Mishnah is not quite clear, and there are various opinions as to its connotation. The meaning of the literal term which denotes a follower of the views of the Greek philosopher, Epicurus, cannot be taken here in its strict sense, for the Mishnah hardly expounds or even refers to systems of philosophy. In view of the fact that Epicurus was a materialist, denied immortality and the existence of any guiding reason in the universe, and refuted the belief that the gods interfere in the events of the world—though he did not deny their actual existence— the term Epicurean was used in a later period of antiquity as a synonym for infidel, or a materialist, or for one who has a light attitude towards religion in general as well as to its important doctrines. It is in a similar connotation that the term is used in the Mishnah, but still it requires a more exact meaning since it intends to convey a specific heresy. A number of explanations of its meaning were therefore offered. The Gemarah takes it to mean one who insults (Mebaseh) scholars or in general thinks lightly of them. Maimonides in his commentary to this Mishnah agrees with the explanation of the Gemarah and adds that the term applies also to one who does not believe in the fundamentals of the Torah without specifying which fundamentals he refers to. In the Code [2], he says that the term refers to one who denies the four dogmas concerning the authority of the Torah enumerated by him in his scheme of dogmas (see below). A later Jewish philosopher and scholar, Simon Duran (1361-1444), explains the term to denote one who denies the existence of God.

However, though such connotation of the term was prevalent in Mediaeval ages, and to a degree even later, it cannot be accepted on account of the place of the term *Apikoros* in the Mishnah. It is given third place while atheism is the highest form of heresy, for it undermines all religion and annuls all dogmas. It should have been mentioned first. Nor are the explanations of the Gemarah and of Maimonides entirely suitable. The statement in the Gemarah is made by an individual. Besides, if we take the word *Mebaseh,* the one used in the Talmud, to mean literally insult, it refers to an action which is often due to anger or grievance. It is hardly likely that one should be proclaimed a heretic for an action which may occur frequently. Maimonides' addition in the commentary that it refers also to one who denies fundamentals of the Torah is too general, while the one given in the Code, namely, that it denotes denial of a dogma relating to the authority of the Torah, makes the *Apikoros'* heresy a redundant one, for it is really included in the dogma *Torah min ha-Shamayyim.* I therefore believe that the term *Apikoros* denotes one who denies the validity of the Oral Law. This view may be even supported by the view of the Gemarah if we interpret the term *Mebaseh* not to mean actually to insult, but to hold the teachings of the scholars who interpret the written Torah in contempt. In fact, the Sinaitic origin of the Oral Law or a large part of it is inculcated in the first Mishnah of the

[2] Code, Vol. 1, Hilkot Teshubah, Chap. 3.

tractate Abot, where the term Torah in the opening statement, "Moses received the Torah from Sinai" is understood by commentators to refer both to the written and the Oral Law.[3] We have, then, in this Mishnah the first promulgation of dogmas in Judaism.

That these beliefs are dogmas with all the importance attached to dogmas is indicated by the denying to the disbelievers a share in *Olam ha-Ba*. There is also a difference of opinion as to what *Olam ha-Ba* means. Statements in the Talmud and a great number of later Jewish scholars interpret it to mean the world which is to come after the resurrection, at the end of the Messianic period. Maimonides holds that it is the blissful state of existence in the hereafter which is destined for all Israel. This is not the place to discuss the reasons why Maimonides chose to differ in the interpretation of this term, as the subject needs extensive treatment. In either case, however, a denial of the group of dogmas included in these statements of the Mishnah excludes one from sharing a reward promised to all Israel.

Coming down to the Mediaeval Ages, the first philosopher and theologian who atempted to formulate a scheme of dogmas or a creed was Saadia Gaon (892-942). His *Emunot we-Deot* (Doctrines and Beliefs), though it is supposed to be a work on Jewish philosophy and theology in general, was in reality intended to inculcate the ten articles of faith—for, even Maimonides' thirteen articles really enunciate only ten articles or dogmas as will be seen below—in the nine sections originally included in the book. The tenth section is a later addition. In fact, these sections are arranged according to dogmas. The first two enunciate the existence of God, His unity, the purity of the God concept, and creation. The third establishes the divine origin of the Torah or

[3] See the commentary of Rabbi Jonah, in the Wilna Edition of the Talmud; commentaries on Abot in Mahsor Vitri, and Maimonides in the introduction to his commentary on the Mishnah.

Torah min ha-Shamayyim and its immutability; the fourth, free will; the fifth, reward and punishment, primarily in this world; the sixth, the immortality of the soul; and the seventh, resurrection. The eighth and ninth describe the coming of the Messiah, the hereafter, and the *Olam ha-Ba*. It is interesting to note that Saadia finds the dogmas of the coming of the Messiah, resurrection, and reward and punishment in the hereafter inherent in the conception of the justice of God. Life is too short for the carrying out of complete justice in this world, and its completion must be left to life after death and the last period, or *Olam ha-Ba*.

Saadia's attempt found many followers, and almost all Jewish philosophers with the exception of Gabirol dealt with this question, directly or indirectly, but none as explicitly as Maimonides. To Maimonides belongs the credit of accomplishing the task of systematization and classification of the dogmas of Judaism. His thirteen articles of creed form not only a complete pronouncement of the principal beliefs taught and insisted upon by Judaism, but are also stated in a brief and dogmatic manner. It was the intention on his part to fix them as the fundamentals of Judaism, the denial of which excludes one from the congregation of believers in the Jewish religion. [4] It is for this reason and due to the authority of Maimonides that the Thirteen Articles were tacitly accepted by the Jewries of different countries as the official pronouncement of religious belief. I said tacitly for we have no record that these articles were ever sanctioned by an authoritative body or assembly of representatives of the Jewish religion. On the contrary, as will be mentioned, they became a subject of controversy and an object of criticism on the part of several leading thinkers and scholars during the succeeding generations.

In fact, he calls them *Ikre Da'enu we-Yesodoteho*, i.e., principles of our religion and its fundamentals.

Of this creed there are two versions. The original one is given in his commentary on the tenth chapter of the Mishnah in the tractate Sanhedrin, written first in Arabic and translated by Samuel Ibn Tibbon into Hebrew, and is included in all leading editions of the Talmud. The second one, that of the *Credo,* known as *Ani Maamin,* i.e. I believe, a formula repeated in every article, is printed in all editions of the prayer-book. There are a number of differences between these two versions, and on the whole, the prayer-book *Credo* is not an entirely correct and exact translation of the original. But the divergencies of the *Credo* do not affect the essence of the dogmas but only certain particulars. A detailed discussion of these differences is out of place here. I have dealt with the subject in a special essay which the reader may consult. [5] I will therefore give the content of these articles as they are contained in the original version in the commentary. They pronounce the following beliefs: (1) the existence of God. The formula is purely philosophic and reads in part, "There exists a Being perfect in all ways of reality. He is the cause of all existing things, and the ground of their existence is in Him." (2) His unity; (3) His incorporeality; (4) His priority to all other beings; (5) no intermediation in worship; (6) belief in the truthfulness of prophecy in general; (7) belief in the *sui generis* character, i.e., uniqueness, of the prophecy of Moses; (8) belief that the entire Torah was given from heaven; (9) immutability of the Torah; (10) God's omniscience; (11) God's retribution in this world and in the hereafter; (12) the coming of the Messiah; and (13) resurrection. We can note in the enunciation of these dogmas a tripartite division. The first five articles deal with the concept of God; the succeeding four with the Torah; and the last four with man, his conduct in relation to God, and the destiny of Israel.

[5] See the author's essay in the Year Book of the Central Conf. of Am. Rabbis, 1935.

Examining the Articles more closely, we perceive that Maimonides was very careful to remove any possible misunderstanding of the concept of God which might cast a shadow on its purity and exaltedness, and he therefore did forego strict logical enumeration, for from a logical point of view at least the first three dogmas can be reduced to one, especially if we remember Maimonides' proof of the existence of God and the necessary corollaries he draws from it as given in the *Guide*, Part II, Ch. I, third and fourth arguments. He divided this dogma into three, so that even the belief of a non-philosophically minded man should be of the proper kind. He was especially careful to emphasize His incorporeality, for many expressions in the Bible and in the Talmud, though they are undoubtedly metaphorical, are liable by their literal meaning to mislead people in their belief. The fourth dogma, priority, does not mean to assert eternity for that is included in the first Article and is given in the complete statement where God is defined as the first cause of all existing things. It seems to emphasize God's activity as Creator, meaning by the term priority that He is prior in power, quality, and activity to all other beings. In fact, in the Code version of this Article he says: "God is the *Zur la-Kol,*" i.e., Creator of everything. The fifth Article asserting that there must be no intermediation in worship can be explained only in the assumption that Maimonides wanted to warn against attributing undue value to the function of angels, or as the philosophers call them, separate intelligences who, in the philosophy of the day, and even in his own, play an important part in the guidance of the lower world, especially the active reason, and hence this dogma.

The four Articles dealing with the Torah are likewise intended to obviate any misunderstanding in regard to the principal dogma, the divine origin of the whole Torah and its complete immutability. Article Six is the basis of the three following dogmas, for prophecy is the means by which God makes known to man His wishes. Article Seven, asserting the *sui generis* character of the prophecy of Moses, strengthens the belief in the divine origin of the whole Torah, for the prophecy of the later seers was, as Maimonides explains in the *Guide,* not a continuous process, but intermittent and occasional, and in addition, it was received in dreams and visions and through the mediacy of the active reason. The Torah is too voluminous an affair to be explained by an occasional power of prophecy, nor are there parables or fables which need interpretation. Hence the Article stresses the *sui generis* character of Moses' prophecy. In a chapter in the *Guide* [6] he explains the uniqueness, namely, that it was continuous, i.e., he could communicate with God whenever he wished, and that it took place in a state of waking in the clearest possible way.

The eighth Article therefore asserts that the entire Torah was given to Moses from heaven, he acting as scribe, namely that it was dictated to him while he was in the state of direct communion with God. In the commentary he expresses himself clearly on that point and says: "Moses received it in the way which we call, figuratively speaking, *Dibbur* (i.e. speech)." The ninth Article about the immutability of the Torah is not rendered correctly, neither in the prayer-book *Credo* nor in the translated version of the commentary. Its full implication is given in the original Arabic. It means not only that the Torah will not be superseded by another revelation—claims of the other religions—but also that God will never change even one of its particulars, for since Moses' prophecy was of the highest type, and since he conceived God directly, without any mediation, it follows of course that the Torah should be permanent and of eternal value in all its details. This meaning of the Article

[6] Part II, Chap. XXXV.

is substantiated by a statement of Maimonides in his Code [7]. The last four Articles are clear and need no elucidation.

The promulgation of the Thirteen Articles of faith by Maimonides created a whole literature on the dogmas and their fixation. This discussion was divided into two currents, a Maimunist and an anti-Maimunist. Of the views of the successive dogmatists, those of Simon Duran (1361-1444) and Joseph Albo (1380-1444) are of special importance inasmuch as they contribute toward a clearer conception of dogmas in Judaism.

The first, in reality, accepts all the Thirteen Articles of Maimonides as important and necessary beliefs but divides them into two categories. The first he calls *Aboth,* i.e., principles, and the second *Tolodot,* i.e., corollaries. As we will see, it is not a mere question of logical division but implies an essential difference in regard to the degree of heresy. To the first class belongs belief (1) in existence of God; (2) in divine origin of the Torah; (3), and in reward and punishment. From the first principle there follow as corollaries (4) unity of God; (5) incorporeality; (6) priority to all beings; (7) no worship of intermediaries. From the second principles follow (8) prophecy; (9) uniqueness of Moses' prophecy; (10) eternity of the Torah. From the third principle there follow (11) God's omniscience; (12) belief in the coming of the Messiah; and (13) in resurrection. We see then that he did not add or diminish from the list of Maimonides, but he does make an important distinction between the two classes, the second of which he at times calls branches—though at times he also calls them dogmas (Ikkarim). He says if one accepts any of the beliefs of the second class but ascribes to it a meaning different from the one generally given to it, and he tries to justify his view by interpretation of certain verses of the Torah, he is not a heretic. He quotes proofs for his assertion

[7] Code, Hilkot Teshubah.

from the view expressed by some Talmudic authorities and several Jewish philosophers. This was a daring view and considerably more lenient than that of Maimonides. He was followed in this by Albo.

Albo in his famous book *Ikkarim* (Dogmas) was greatly influenced by Duran and agrees with him in several points. Like Duran, he offers a division of the Articles into classes, but unlike him, he actually differs with Maimonides in the number of dogmas. He denies to some Articles in the list of Maimonides the rank of dogmas and elevates several other beliefs to that degree. His definition of the term principle (Ikkar) or first class dogma serves him as a basis for his division into classes. "That term," says he, "connotes only something on which the very existence of an object depends, and without it the object cannot exist." The *Ikkar* contains subsidiary concepts which emerge on the unfolding of the principal one. Accordingly he divides the dogmas into two classes: (A) *Ikkarim* which contain three dogmas: (1) existence of God; (2) divine origin of the Torah; (3) reward and punishment. (B) *Shoroshim*, i.e., roots which are (1) unity of God; (2) incorporeality; (3) God's independence of time; (4) complete perfection. These four emerge as corollaries from the *Ikkar* of the existence of God. From the second principle in its unfolding there emerge (5) God's omniscience; (6) verity of prophecy; (7) authenticity of the message borne by the one sent by God to deliver it (the messenger or Sheliah). From the third *Ikkar* there emerges only one belief, namely providence. We have eleven dogmas, for all these are dogmas to him; the difference between the classes is really a verbal one, inasmuch as the first three are class concepts, and the roots emerge from them upon analysis.

As can be seen, he omitted from the *Credo* of Maimonides the dogmas of the *sui generis* character of Moses' prophecy, the immutability and unchangeability of the Torah, the coming of the Messiah and resurrection.

These are to him neither *Ikkarim* nor *Shoroshim.*

The reason for his omission of the first two dogmas is, says he, that since the authenticity of Moses' teaching was proved by the personal experience of a multitude who heard God speak to him, [8] the degree of his prophecy is of little importance. Similarly, immutability and unchangeability are no dogmas, for any succeeding prophet who will claim abrogation of the Torah or introduce changes into it will have to prove his message in the same way Moses did. As for the coming of the Messiah and resurrection, he claims that these beliefs are not particular to Judaism, for another religion, i.e., Christianity, employs the same beliefs as an argument for its assertion that the Torah of Moses was abrogated. [9]

There is undoubtedly a polemic ring to his omission of the dogma of the coming of the Messiah, for in the religious discussions at the time the Jews were constantly reminded that the Messiah had already come. Albo, who had himself participated at the great discussion in Tortosa in 1413-1414, claims that the validity of Judaism will not be impaired even if we omit such a dogma. [10] As for resurrection, since there are different views in the Talmud and Midrashim about its extent, namely, whether it is limited to the righteous only or to all Israel, it cannot be considered a dogma.

He therefore places these four dogmas with two others in a special class which he calls branches (Anafim). They are true beliefs and must be accepted, but the one who denies them is only a grave sinner and partakes of heresy but is not a real heretic and may still share in the world to come. [11] Albo agrees with Duran that if one accepts a dogma of the second class but interprets it dif-

[8] Ikkarim Sec. I, Chap. IV, Chap. XVIII.
[9] Ibid, chap. XV.
[10] Ibid.
[11] Ibid, Chap. XXIII.

ferently than is generally accepted, but following his own understanding of certain verses, he is not a heretic.[12]

As we can see, the differences between the scheme of dogmas of Maimonides and those of his critics, Duran and Albo, are not essential. Not only Duran who agrees totally with Maimonides' list of dogmas, but even Albo who omitted several important ones, such as the coming of the Messiah and resurrection, does by no means disparage these beliefs. He merely places them in a lower class, and declares one who denies or doubts them a very grave sinner but not a complete heretic. Of importance is their leniency in allowing one an interpretation of a dogma deviating from the accepted one. They thus allowed an amount of freedom of thought in the realm of dogmatics which was not entirely new in Judaism. The philosopher and Bible commentator, Levi ben Gershom, interpreted *creatio ex nihilo,* i.e. creation from nothing. to mean not from absolute nothing, but from primary matter, i.e., one without qualities, and also placed a certain limitation upon God's knowledge, yet no one thought of excommunicating him, and his commentary on the Bible is placed beside Rashi's.

The great body of Israel, however, was not interested in these keen logical differences and accepted the entire list of Maimonides' dogmas as its *Credo*. It did not take long and a version of this creed was incorporated in the prayer-book and recited by all Jews daily. We do not know who wrote this version and who introduced it in the prayer-book. We know that the Thirteen Articles were originally printed as one of the appendices to the first complete and large edition of the Bible in 1513, and from there they found their way into the prayer-book The oral recitation of the *Ani-Maamin* preceded, however, the printed one by more than a century. Rabbi Jacob Mollin, known as Maharil (1365-1427) speaks of numerous Judaeo-German (Yiddish) versions of the *Ani-*

[12] Ibid. Chap. III.

Maamin which were recited frequently by the people.

It is worth noting that Jewish law does not prescribe any form of physical punishment for a heretic as long as he keeps his views to himself, i.e., does not attempt to persuade others. Jewish law prescribes death to one who acts as a missionary for idolatry (Mesit). Furthermore, in case of idolatry, even a verbal acceptance in public, i.e., before two witnesses, of a certain idol as a god, whether before the image or not, is punishable by death, but the particular idol must be mentioned. Punishment for mere heresy, i.e., denial of a dogma, does not come under the jurisdiction of a human court. As stated, it is left to the heavenly court and its punishment is forfeiture of a share in the world to come. [13] It is true that Maimonides says in the above-mentioned commentary that it is proper to hate a heretic and that we have in the late Mediaeval Ages several famous acts of excommunication for heresy, such as those of Uriel de Acosta and Spinoza. But we must remember that these acts were performed under the pressure of external influence. In addition, the ban pronounced against Spinoza distinctly states that it is done not only for his heretical views, but also for his transgressions of the Jewish law. Nowhere do we find a statement that a heretic should be attacked bodily, whether with intent to kill, or wound, or even to give a severe beating. Zealous individuals might have resorted to such measures and even a Rabbinical court urged by particular circumstances might have subjected heretics to a lashing, but not in *due legal form.* [14] How far such an attitude was from those of other religions by the command of whose courts heretics were burned at the stake for a mere doubt of belief in a dogma, one can judge for himself.

Irrespective of all that was said regarding the Maimonidian creed by later critics, it held sway in the heart

[13] As stated in the Mishnah quoted above.

of Jews in every country of their dispersion, and until the modern period, few, very few, doubted the veracity of the Articles. Even in our own day thousands of Jews went to the crematories and other places where wholesale death was meted out to them with the song of *Ani-Maamin* on their lips.

[14]I emphasized the words *in due legal form* advisedly, for in several statements by Maimonides in his Code (Vol. IV, Hilkot Rozeah, Chap. IV) and in his philosophic work, *Guide for the Perplexed* (Part III, Chap. XLI) he employs ambiguous language from which it may be deduced that it is proper to cause grave injury to one who denies the veracity of the Torah. But on examination, we can see that Maimonides does not deal with mere heresy, but heresy manifested by an action of transgression in public with intent to demonstrate that there is no authentic veracity to the Torah. Nor does he say that this heretical transgressor should be brought to court for sentence, but disinctly says that the injury which is permitted to be inflicted upon him is not a punishment decreed by law, but only as a special measure which may be taken under certain circumstances in order to guard against the undermining of faith. I, therefore, reiterate that mere verbal denial of a dogma does not come under the jurisdiction of a human court, but is left entirely to the heavenly court.

THE ETHICS OF JUDAISM

Introduction

WHAT IS ETHICS?

I

DEFINITION OF ETHICS

Before we can undertake to discuss and describe the nature and character of Jewish ethics and attempt to delineate the practical rules that Judaism laid down for the guidance of man in his way of life, it is proper to offer a brief definition of ethics in general, and note its various traits and aspects.

Ethics is usually defined as a discipline that has as its task the determination of the nature of certain phases of human conduct, whether they are good or bad, right or wrong; in other words, to pronounce upon them a judgment of approval or disapproval. These judgments upon human conduct possess two aspects. While it is true that the area of human conduct connoted by the terms *ethical* and *unethical* lies primarily in the social sphere, for a man alone on an island would have very limited range of action to which these terms can be applied, yet since all conduct stems from the individual, we must pay attention to his views, feelings, and motives or, in other words, the character of the human self. Consequently, we pronounce, on the one hand, judgment upon the self of the acting individual declaring it to be of a moral, unmoral, or immoral character, and on the other hand, judgment upon his actions in relation to and treatment of his fellow men.

However, the formation of a complete set of judgments upon the self, as well as upon the activities of the individual, extends beyond the range of ethics proper, for it must have the help of other sciences, such as psychology and sociology. These sciences will afford us data upon the make-up of the self and its development, and of the influence of the social environment upon human action. Such extension, though, is an encroachment upon the province of other sciences. The scope of the judgments of ethics is more limited. They are concerned mainly with the nature of the choice of action and with the effect of the action, whether upon the agent himself or upon his fellow men. It is in relation to these two aspects that judgments upon actions are pronounced, declaring it good or bad, right or wrong.

II

STANDARDS AND END OF CONDUCT

Judgments are pronounced according to a certain standard of action in order to determine whether a particular act is in agreement with that standard or not. The standard, in turn, is based upon the concept of an end that man strives to attain. In a way, the end in general terms is really contained in the judgment. When we declare an action to be good, we have already supplied its end, for as Aristotle says, "Every action and pursuit is thought to aim at some good." Yet the generality of the term *good* raises many questions as to its exact nature, and through time immemorial it has been asked what is the good that all people aim for. The term *good* employed in the judgment of an action merely signifies that this particular action approaches an end that is also the end of many other actions. But the real good for the sake of which many actions are done, or rather should be done, was a subject of contention, and there have arisen various views about its character and nature.

The variety of conceptions of what constitutes an ethical or moral good deed stems from the very nature of the term *good* when it designates an end or a goal of action. The term, when thus employed, does not aim to describe the quality of an act about to be done, but rather to determine what should or ought to be done. And since human actions are determined by motives that stem from attitudes, beliefs, and ways of reasoning prevailing in the social groups in which men live, it follows that the conception of the ethical end or the designation of actions that ought to be done varies according to spiritual and cultural climates of different social groups or nations in certain ages. These conceptions, however, were, on the whole, not formulated by the groups as aggregate units, but by individual thinkers who evolved theories of ethical conduct embodying the views of certain social groups of their time and impressed them with the stamp of their own thought. In time, a number of these theories acquired popularity and influenced human life in various degrees, and some of them received wide acceptance and became standards of conduct.

III

ETHICAL THEORIES—ANCIENT AND MODERN

On the whole, ethical theories can be divided into two classes, one of which is called heteronomous, and the other autonomous. The former posit an end in the light of which actions are judged, namely, whether they serve as a means to attain that end and are good or, vice versa, lead away from that end and are bad. The latter assert that actions are good when they carry in themselves their end, inasmuch as they issue from a good will and possess characteristics of universal application. Most ethical theories belong to the first class.

The leading end posited by all ancient and most modern ethical theories is happiness, for all men strive after happiness or well-being. The difference between the theories, and consequently between the judgments pronounced on actions, arises from the different conceptions of what constitutes happiness. In the classical or ancient period all theories, especially those pronounced by the leading Greek philosophers, placed great value on knowledge and proportion as characteristics of ethical action and as the best means of attaining the end—happiness. Thus Socrates declared, "Virtue is knowledge." Again, the striving after proportion in human activity was a deep-seated trait in the Greek character, and we are told that the slogan, "Nothing in excess," was engraved on the portals of the Delphian Oracle. However, these two characteristics or qualities are also subject to interpretation.

It is, then, according to the interpretation of knowledge and proportion that the ethical theories varied, for a change in their meaning involved a change in the meaning of happiness that all theories placed as the desired end of conduct. But no theory, irrespective of the interpretation it placed upon knowledge and proportion, failed to stress the importance of these two qualities. In earlier times, when happiness was understood in the materialistic sense, knowledge of the useful was considered a necessary factor in the determination of the proper conduct, for how could one discern what was good and useful, or, vice versa, what is harmful, without knowledge? When Socrates declared knowledge to be virtue, he also spoke of it as being useful. He did not, though, explain the type of its usefulness, whether it leads to pleasure or to some other end. Even Aristippus, the founder of the Cyrenaic school, who taught that the pleasure of the agent should be the good sought, insisted on the virtue of wisdom or knowledge. He asserted that by means of it one will be able to choose the purest and most intense pleasure. He also insisted that pleasure is to be pursued in a measured and proportionate way so as to avoid pain.

In Plato's view of ethics, these two characteristics likewise play a great role, but with him there begins a change in their content, for though he does not disregard the useful, knowledge to him is mainly knowledge of the idea of the good, which is all-embracing. But to make his ethics more concrete, he substitutes truth for knowledge and adds two more elements, beauty and symmetry the most excellent phases of proportion. By making the pursuit of truth, beauty, and symmetry the guides in conduct man can attain a harmonious and perfect life, which is the desired end. This end may be called happiness and even pleasure, but it is of a higher and ideal type. To what extent proportion plays an important part in Plato's ethics can be seen in his conception of justice, which is to him the highest type of virtue. "Justice," says he, "is attained when every part of the soul fulfills its function and does not interfere with the work of the other parts." The parts, as is well known, are desire to satisfy bodily needs, feeling, the force of will, and the power of thought.[1] This proportionate activity is not limited to the individual, but to society as a whole, as illustrated in his Utopian *Republic* where the activities of the various classes of the people are delineated, namely, the activity of the laborers and men of business symbolizing satisfaction of bodily needs; of the warriors, symbolizing courage and strength of will; and of the philosophers, representing the virtue of knowledge and wisdom. Each of these classes must fulfill its own function.

Aristotle's *Ethics also* places happiness as an end. But this happiness is not of the material kind, for though he says pleasure is valuable in that it perfects life, it should be considered only a means and not as an end in itself. Real good consists in the development of man's capacities, which should culminate in an harmonious life. Proportion then occupies an important place also in his view of morality. It is more in evidence in his doctrine of the mean, namely, that man in his action must choose the middle way between two extremes. That one must possess knowledge to ascertain the exact middle goes without saying. Knowledge and proportion are, therefore, the two determining factors in moral

[1] *The Republic,* 443.

conduct. Aristotle knows though of an activity which is an end in itself, namely contemplation.[2] However, the pursuit of this type of happiness is limited to a small and select group.

The Epicureans, as is well known, turned to pleasure as an end of conduct, but the pleasure spoken of was not altogether of the gross type. They emphasized to a large degree the avoidance of pain and also advocated the pursuit of mental pleasures, which, they said, may even exceed bodily pleasure in intensity and range. It follows, of course, that knowledge is necessary in order to choose the right kind of pleasure. Similarly, they valued other virtues, such as courage in order to combat fear and temperance to avoid excess, both of which may lead to pain. For the same reason they even considered justice a great virtue, though not for its own sake, for since man must live in society, he must be careful not to transgress the rights of his fellow men in order that they should not retaliate and cause him pain. Their ethical views may be considered a refined egotism, utilitarian in essence.

For the Stoics the wise man whose conduct is right and ethical is he who understands the fixed order of the universe, which is controlled by universal reason, and who voluntarily subjects himself to this order irrespective of whether it results in pleasure or pain. To obey reason is good and it is proper for man to regulate his conduct in conformity with its dictates. Such a view gave birth to the concept of duty which, though scarcely developed, gave an impetus to the rise of a higher type of morality, for it made its rules and laws originate with the self.

All these theories, in spite of their noble features, possess many weaknesses when applied to a life in society that implies continuous dealing with fellow men. In the first place the moral qualities and even the ends are too abstract and general. Knowledge, proportion, and harmony are noble

[2] *Nichomachean Ethics,* Book X, Ch. 7.

traits, but have little power to restrain fierce emotions when they explode under the hard conditions of life. Secondly, these theories have no real notion of duty. Even the Stoics who spoke of duty did not point out its moral essence. Their duty is more of a submission to natural necessity than an intrinsic trait of human character. Thirdly, classical or Hellenic ethics is primarily class ethics. The virtues of knowledge, symmetry, and harmony can be practiced mainly by an aristocratic caste who have leisure to pursue art and devote themselves to contemplation. Finally, all these systems fail to emphasize the dignity of man as man and allow many breaches of morality. Thus, even Plato sanctions the murder of deformed or otherwise unpromising infants at birth,[3] and not only does he condone slavery as a proper institution, but permits even the enslavement of free men taken as prisoners of war,[4] or of Athenians of an inferior type.[5] Aristotle too considers slavery a normal social institution. Even the Stoics, whose views foreshadowed the notion of humanity, never condemned it. The result is that all these fine theories never produced a moral nation.

Without surveying the numerous ethical theories of the modern period, we can say that most of them follow the ancient pattern with certain modifications arising from the philosophical views of the authors. Even more original philosophers echo in one way or another the views of the ancients in their ethical theories. Thus Spinoza, who displays originality in his conception of God and the universe, echoes in his *Ethics* the Aristotelian and Stoic conceptions of the ends of moral action, such as mental perfection on the one hand and obedience to the law of nature on the other.

The numerous theories of the English philosophers, from Hobbes to John Stuart Mill, notwithstanding their variation, bear a utilitarian aspect and really offer a modern modified

[3] *The Republic,* 460.
[4] *The Republic,* 443 B-C.
[5] *The Laws,* 309.

version of the Epicurean view that pleasure is the end of action. This modification stems from a wider social view, for though happiness in its essence still consists in the attainment of pleasure, it has with the later utilitarians like James Mill and John Stuart Mill lost its egotistic character, and is interpreted to mean the happiness of the greatest number.

Unlike Jeremy Bentham, the founder of the utilitarian school, who posited that all men always act out of consideration for their own happiness, the Mills taught that man possesses two kindly impulses, regard for self and regard for others, and that the latter can be developed as fully as the former. Happiness is, therefore, defined by the Mills as that of the greatest number. John Stuart Mill goes farther and speaks of gradations of pleasures, assigning an important place to the pleasure arising from a motive of disinterestedness when doing good. The materialistic content of ethics is still the central phase of all theories of modern utilitarianism or, as it is often called, Hedonism.

Of the few modern philosophers who consider ethical notions as ends in themselves, the leading one is Immanuel Kant. Kant says that nothing is good but a good will, and that an action which is to be called good or moral must be disinterested and judged on its own merit. His criterion of an ethical action is the famous categorical imperative, which runs as follows: When one is about to perform an act, one should ask oneself whether the necessity to perform it could be a universal law. If so, it is one's duty to perform it; if not, it is one's duty to abstain. In following such a rule, there is no vestige of egoism, for though the act may bring some good to the agent, this is not the motive.

Kant also emphasizes the dignity of man. He says that man exists as an end in himself and he must not arbitrarily be used as a means for the attainment of benefit to any other man, and in all actions, whether they pertain to the performer or to other rational beings, both the agent and his fellow men must be regarded as ends.

There is still another ethical theory that possesses several variations, but whose common feature is intuition. This theory teaches that there can be a certain kind of action which may be known to man as right or wrong by a direct intuitive sense without any reference to the value of its consequences. In other words, the acts have their ends in themselves, whether affirmatively or negatively, i.e., whether they are good and should be performed or bad and should be avoided. The judgment stems from an innate feeling in man. If one commits a wrong action, it is not because he lacks moral intuition, but because he is unable to control his passions, and the desire to do good is overcome in the conflict. This view has, as mentioned, several varieties, which differ in defining the range of moral intuition.

This brief survey of ethical theories will enable us to evaluate the ethical teaching of Judaism. It will show us its special character, how it escaped the pitfalls of other theories, and how it succeeded in delineating a path of conduct for all men. That Jewish ethics exerted influence upon ethical views of other religions and left a mark upon ethical thought of Western civilization is well known, and will be dealt with later.

PART I

PRINCIPLES OF JEWISH ETHICS

Chapter I

SOURCES OF JEWISH ETHICS

1. The Bible

Unlike the Greeks or other peoples of antiquity, who were searching for the good and the end to be attained by action, the Jews were spared that effort. Their religion, divinely revealed to them through Moses at their very emergence into nationhood, and later through the other prophets, supplied them with the ideal of conduct to be followed in the path of life.

The ethical views, commandments, and precepts that serve the Jews as the guideposts in their manifold actions are contained in the Bible, and it is there that we must look for the conception of morality and the principles of conduct.

The Bible is not merely a sacred book or a compendium of laws and commandments, but a book that sustained the life of a people for millennia. There was, through the ages, a continuous mutual relation between it and life. The Bible influenced life and life influenced the Bible, not in changing its text, but in the understanding of its meaning. The Pentateuch, that part of the Bible which contains the laws, is not a detailed code and does not give the particulars of the laws which it states, but briefly states the laws in a general way. Life, however, with its many currents and streams and with its manifold activities, is wide and is in constant need of guidance and rules. Consequently, the very source of ethical conduct had to be widened. Men of spirit, sages, and spiritual leaders from early times and through the ages devoted themselves to the explanation and interpretation of the ethical principles and precepts of the Bible and drew out their deeper meaning, the hidden thoughts, teaching the people a way of life in the light of the new understanding.

2. Talmud and Midrash

There thus grew up what we may call an oral ethical teaching—for all learning in Jewry for many centuries was oral—of many facets and phases. The core of this teaching consisted primarily of the interpretations and deeper understanding of the Biblical ethical commandments and precepts, but it also included additional layers of moral thought and practice that were formulated by the sages themselves. And just as in the field of religious law we have a number of additional ordinances and precepts, known as *Rabbinic*, enacted to serve as fences around the law in order to strengthen its observance, so in ethics there were added rules and virtues called forth by the exigencies of life.[1]

[1] A few additions to a Biblical law as well as its expansion to include a wider range of cases, as introduced by the sages of the Talmud, can serve as examples of the influence of life conditions upon Jewish law and ethics. The law referred to deals primarily with honesty in commercial transactions. It says, "And if thou sell aught to thy neighbor, or buy of thy neighbor, ye shall not wrong one another." *(Al-Thonu)* (Leviticus XXV, 14). In this particular case, the wrong consists in deception in regard to the price of an object, i.e., charging more than the goods are worth, or paying less than its value: in other words, a case of fraud. But the Bible does not state the exact amount that constitutes fraud, nor any other particulars concerning that type of wrong.

The Talmud, however, introduces additions as well as an expansion of the range of wrongdoing. First, it fixes the amount that constitutes a fraudulent deal as being one sixth of the worth of the object or of the price paid. At this amount the injured party, whether buyer or seller, must be paid the difference, but the transaction remains valid. If the injury is higher than a sixth, then the transaction is invalid and either party may retract. There are many other particulars affecting the validity or invalidity of such transactions, and modes of punishment are stated for this type of wrongdoing, but they belong more to law than ethics. What is of still greater importance for us to note is the expansion introduced in the concept of *Oneah,* i.e., a wrong based on deception. The sages of the Talmud say that the prohibition of *Al Thonu* covers not only a wrong causing a loss of money, but also wrongs caused by speech that misleads one's fellow men. It is called *Onath Debarim,* misleading or improper speech. One should not, for instance, ap-

All such interpretations, rules, and views incorporated in the ethical teachings of generations of sages formed a solid ethical tradition that served the Jews in their daily conduct. When these oral teachings were organized into treatises and books, ethical teachings, whether derived from interpretation of laws of the Bible or rules established by sages, formed an important part of these treatises and books. Thus, the extensive Talmudic and Midrashic literature, running into many volumes, forms a second source of Jewish ethics. And though some of the ethical views may be expressed in this literature by individuals, they became an integral part of the ethical view of Judaism, for these books, together with the Bible, form the sources of authority for Judaism and the center of Jewish spiritual life.

3. The Third Source—Tradition of Life

To these two sources there is to be added a third, which may be called the tradition of life. This tradition stems from the life experiences of the nation at large during its long existence. It is true that almost all nations possess such a tradition, but there is a uniqueness attached to the Jewish tradition, inasmuch as the life of that nation, during the last two millennia, was of a character unparalleled in human history. It is the only nation which, though scattered to the four winds of the world, yet maintained a remarkable spiritual and cultural unity. This unity in dispersion could be attained only by a severe struggle for existence, which included a struggle against oppression and animosity and a

---

proach a merchant and ask the price of certain goods without having intention to buy, thus raising a false hope in the heart of the merchant and causing him disappointment. According to the sages, this term really covers a wide range, especially such wrong forms of speech as may cause grief or injury to a fellow man, even though they are not a direct insult, such as reminding a man of his former faults or of his improper conduct in the past. Thus conditions of life brought about from one single word the derivation of numerous prohibitions of all kinds of wrongs to fellow men, whether affecting loss of money, the tarnishing of honor, or any other kind of grief.

struggle to guard the integrity of its spiritual heritage against the influence of the various cultures and views of life with which the people came in contact.

This struggle, which involved power of will and of resolution, not only strengthened the loyalty of the people to its religion and laws, the source of its spiritual life, but also emphasized right ethical conduct as the most important means for its survival. Benevolence, help of the oppressed, and love for fellow Jews were cultivated, exalted, and placed as ideals to be followed by every Jew of whatever station in life. The effort to withstand common suffering and to survive in spite of attacks and massacres strengthened the willingness to make sacrifices on behalf of the people, religion, and God, and the number of individuals who made the supreme sacrifice in order to sanctify the name of God was, as is known, very great. Numerous also were the chosen spirits who distinguished themselves in ethical and religious conduct in many ways. Their conduct was considered exemplary and became patterns for imitation which, though few could achieve, more strove to follow. Legends grew up around their lives, and their deeds were recounted and embellished from generation to generation. In this way, out of the life experiences of the nation and its multifarious vicissitudes, there grew up a tradition of religious-ethical conduct that became an integral part of Jewish life.

This life tradition, like the previous oral tradition, was turned into a written one, and therein lies its strength. The Jewish people, having lost its land and government, had concentrated its energy upon literature, which thus became the main expression of its national genius. As a result, an extensive literature dealing with many subjects was created during the long Middle Age as well as during a part of the Modern period. In these works, the ethical tradition is incorporated and reflected in all its phases. There is hardly a book, no matter what its subject, whether the law, exegesis, poetry, or philosophy, which does not stress the value of ethical conduct. Hundreds of books deal entirely with ethics. In them the virtues are all discussed and exalted, and their practice is inculcated.

This later literature, which left a deep mark in the hearts of the people, thus serves us as another source from which the views of Judaism on ethics and conduct are to be derived.

In attempting to delineate a system of Jewish ethics in its particulars, its choice of virtues and its condemnation of the vices, as well as in its general principles, we have to turn to these sources and by diligent study select scattered statements and thoughts dispersed in a vast literature and join them in a connected whole. But as no system of ethics can be clearly understood without a proper comprehension of the concepts and views of God, the world, life, and the role of man in the world and life as held by the group, or the religion propounding that system, it is necessary therefore briefly to survey these views from the point of view of Judaism and, first of all, to consider the conception of God, which is the very foundation of all spiritual life in Israel.

Chapter II

VIEWS OF GOD, MAN, AND LIFE

4. Conception of God

The main contribution of Judaism is monotheism, which raises the one God above the world and makes Him the source of all existence. But He is not merely above the world and the cause of all existence, a view to which we may find a resemblance in the philosophy of Aristotle; He is the Creator of the world. He is the God, "That created the heavens and stretched them forth. He that spreadeth forth the earth and that which cometh out of it. He that giveth breath unto the people upon it and spirit to them that walk therein" (Isaiah XLII, 5). It is in this activity of creation delineated in the first chapter of Genesis that the uniqueness of the God conception of Judaism lies, and this it is which forms the fountainhead of all the spirituality of life and is the most important condition for ethical conduct.

This conception shattered the position of primacy that nature held with all peoples in antiquity. All peoples, including the most civilized Greeks with all their science and philosophy, could not fathom nature, and it remained a thing unknown, a thing to be feared, to whose laws and mysterious force, which they called destiny, that man was subjected. Judaism robbed nature of its mystic power, for it, like man, is only the handiwork of God. Even its very existence becomes uncertain, for God at His will can change it. Man was liberated from slavery to nature and the fear of destiny, for he was put on a par with nature. In a way, he was even placed above it, as indicated by his position in the process of creation, namely, as the last in the series of created beings, and his spirit was imparted to him by God Himself, events that indicate the value attributed to man by Judaism.

There remain, then, only two forces in the world, God and man. The mystery of the world is concentrated in human nature, and relations between man and God are immediate and direct. Man was equipped for such relations, according to Judaism, with freedom of will, for we are told in the Bible that immediately upon his creation he was given the task of choosing between desire and command. The fact that he succumbed to passion does not take away from man the power to exercise the force of his will or his freedom of action. Otherwise he could not be held responsible and subject to punishment. God's activity in creation, as given in Genesis, supplies, therefore, the substratum and condition for ethical action, as it frees man from subjection to the unknown forces in nature, endows him with freedom of choice, and places upon him the responsibility implying obligation to use the force of his will.

5. Worth and Dignity of Man

From this basic conception of the creation of man there emerge several other conclusions that raise the position of man to a high degree and from which evolve important ethical principles. We read in the Bible that only one man was created. The sages of the nation, to whom every event mentioned in the Torah as well as every word in it were of great significance, pondered upon the subject and asked, "Why was only one man created?" It was, they said, for two purposes: first, that no one should be able to say, "My first ancestor was of a higher type than yours." In other words, the singleness in the creation teaches us the equality of man. In fact, the famous statement, "All men are created equal," incorporated in the United States Declaration of Independence, has its basis in this Midrashic statement. "The second purpose," say the sages, "is to teach us the value of human life, namely, that if one destroys the life of even one man, it is tantamount to the destruction of the whole world. And, on the other hand, if one saves a single life, his act is considered as highly as if he saved a whole world."[1] This exceptional appreciation of human life, taught by the Rabbis, stems from the position of man in the process of creation. He was created last, and by his coming into being creation was completed and perfected. Without him the world would be defective. It follows, therefore, that the life of even one man contributes to the perfection of the world as a whole, and vice versa, his loss makes it deficient. Another statement prevalent in Talmud literature calls a man a microcosm *(Olam Katan)*, for his body represents a world in miniature.[*]

The second feature in the creation of man is, as told in the Bible, that he was formed in the image of God. The statement, of course, arouses much difficulty as to its meaning. How can we speak of the image of God when the basic Jewish conception of the Godhead is that He has neither image nor any kind of form, a statement that the Bible repeats numerous times? Religious philosophers, Jewish, Muslim, and Christian, offered many explanations. However, we are not interested in this aspect, but in the ethical notions involved in the statement. We will later show how deeply this notion affected Jewish ethical conduct. For the present we will merely say that it implies the principle which was later placed by Kant as a cornerstone of his ethical system, namely, that no man should be used as a means but should be regarded as an end in himself.

[1] Babylonian Talmud, Tr. *Sanhedrin,* Ch. IV, *Mishnah* 5.

[*] See *Aboth d'Rabbi Nathan,* Ch. XXXI, where an extensive comparison between the cosmos and man is drawn up showing that all things found in the world, even in a large size, have counterparts in some form in the human body.

6. Jewish View of Life

From the basic conception of the creation of man by God, as given in Genesis, where we are told that He endowed him with freedom of will and with responsibility, there follows an optimistic conception of life unparalleled in the religions of other peoples in the ancient world. Even the Greeks, with all their pursuit of beauty and harmony in life, frequently felt the horror of existence, and from time to time there reverberates in their literature a note of sadness, voicing a fear of life and its tribulations and a desire to escape it. In one of the dramas of Sophocles the chorus sings, "Not to be born is past all prizing, but when a man hath seen the light, the next best by far is that with all speed he go thither whence he hath come." In another drama the chorus watching the miseries of the hero declares, "Therefore, while our eyes wait to see the destined final way, we must call no one who is of mortal race happy until he has crossed life's border free from pain."

In Judaism, on the other hand, life is considered a precious gift granted by the all-powerful and unique God. Throughout the Books of the Old Testament, life is glorified. God Himself is frequently described as the living God. Moses, in his parting speech to his people, standing on the border of the promised land, says to them in the name of God, "I call heaven and earth to witness against you this day that I have set before thee this day life and death, the blessing and the curse; choose therefore life, thou and thy seed" (Deuteronomy XXX, 19). Life, then, is here identical with blessing. Similarly, we read in another place, "For there the Lord commandeth the blessing—life forever" (Psalm CXXXIII, 3), and this view is expressed directly and indirectly in many places in the Bible.

And not only was life considered a precious gift and a blessing, but there is even strong emphasis throughout the Books of Wisdom on the necessity for man to maintain a cheerful attitude toward it. "The hope of the righteous is gladness," says the Book of Proverbs (X, 28), which means that the reward for which the righteous hope will be gladness in life. "Gladdening the heart is the life of man, and joyfulness prolongeth his day," says Ben Sira (*Wisdom of Ben Sira,* XXX, 22). The same spirit pervades even the post-Biblical literature, as the following story in the Talmud shows. Elijah, while standing once in the market-place, was asked by a rabbi to point out to him in the passing multitude men whom he deemed certain to be rewarded in the hereafter. Elijah silently pointed to two men. The Rabbi became interested and asked these men what great merits they possessed. The men answered that their office was to cheer gloomy men, and wherever they noticed a man whose face expressed sorrow, they approached him and endeavored to gladden his heart.[2] This story shows clearly in what esteem Judaism holds cheerfulness in life, namely, that one will receive the highest reward for promoting it.

On the other hand, the responsibility placed upon man by God in his relation to Him and the account he is to give to Him for all his conduct make life a strenuous and serious business. Yet the seriousness by no means counteracts the optimism. Where chance and destiny are eliminated and all life is traced to one source, an omnipotent God whose relation to man is based on man's own will, there is no room for pessimism, as man's fate is in his own hands. Let him but change his conduct and the omnipotent God will change his fate.[3]

[2] Babylonian Talmud, Tr. *Taanit,* 22.

[3] It is true that we have a statement in the Talmud (Tr. *Erubin,* 13b, that the Schools of Shammai and Hillel had a prolonged controversy for three and a half years on the following subject. The former asserted that it were better for man not to have been created, while the latter held the view that it were better for him to have been created. This statement of the view of the School of Shammai, a view that we meet only once in the entire Talmudic literature, is opposed not only by the School of Hillel whose views are generally accepted against those of their opponents, but is contravened by numerous other sages who consider life a gift. In addition, even the

7. The Way of Life

Optimism and seriousness, as said, are not contrary to each other; in fact, they supplement each other. The more precious life is, the more men desire it, and the more serious the pursuit of its attainment becomes, the greater is the effort to overcome difficulties in order to live the proper type of life; for though man was given the power to choose, choice is not always easy. There is the struggle with passion as well as with other difficulties arising from conditions of life. True, Jewish religion through its revealed writings pointed out to man a pattern of conduct delineated in the Torah and in the teachings of the prophets, and the Bible calls that pattern a way of life, stressing thereby that it must be followed continually. Still, man is frequently baffled as to how to follow that way, and in despair often turns to God for help. The Psalmist cries out to God, "Make me know the way of life" (Psalm XVI, 11).

The search for the proper way of life, which is of course an ethical one, requires not only the cultivation of a strong will in order to overcome difficulties, but also knowledge, for without it man can stray even with the best of intentions. This knowledge, however, is different from the knowledge stressed so much in other views of ethics, especially the Greek, which aims at choosing the best pleasures or at acquiring a better understanding of the laws of nature; this knowledge aims at ascertaining the will of God. In the Book of Proverbs as well as in other books of the *Ketubim,* or Hagiographa, the righteous man is identified with the wise man, and instead of being called *Ẓaddik* (righteous) as usual, he is called *Ḥakam* (wise man). To know the way of life in

Shammaites declared that since man was created, it was best for him to live except that his conduct must be ethical. However, the Greeks say, as stated above, "Not to be born is past all prizing; when a man hath seen the light, this is the next best by far that with all speed he go thither whence he hath come." Sophocles, *Oedipus Coloneus,* Eng. Trans. by Jebbs, p. 105.

Judaism means to know how to follow a life of morality and righteousness.

Summary: From what has been said, we can form a conception of the substratum or ground of Jewish ethics. We notice the liberation of man from subjection to nature and the fear of unknown destiny, and that he is presented with freedom of choice of action. We also see that the very account of creation of man, as given in the Bible, stresses his dignity, and tells us that he must be used as an end in himself and not as a means, because he is created in the image of God; furthermore, that equality is the prerogative of all men. This view of life is optimistic, for it emphasizes its preciousness and considers it a blessing, but because of man's responsibility for his conduct, which is demanded of him by God, living a proper life becomes also a serious business, and man must possess knowledge and will to follow the designated way of life. All these views and concepts that are stressed in the Biblical books are not only conditions, but serve also as an incentive for a desire to follow an ethical way of life. With all these, however, Judaism had to fix fundamental principles of morality that should serve as guideposts on the way and constitute the source of a desire and a wish to follow it.

Chapter III

FUNDAMENTAL PRINCIPLES OF JEWISH ETHICS

8. Basis of All Ethical Principles

This basis is no other than the conception of God as the archetype of ethics and morality, from which follow all other principles as well as the rules of conduct. It is true that God is often described in the Bible by many epithets that are anthropomorphic, such as mighty, fearful, warlike, and as exercising many human activities, such as rising, sitting, descending, or thundering. But all these are metaphorical descriptions of His majesty, employing terms of the human language in order to convey to man a notion of His power in exercising His providence over the world. They do not denote His attributes or signify qualities that are in close relation to His essence or character. These latter, whenever they are mentioned, either as a group as in Exodus XXXIV, 6, 7, or as single attributes, are all ethical.

The passage in Exodus reads, "The Lord, merciful and gracious, long-suffering and abundant in goodness and truth, keeping mercy unto the thousandth generation, forgiving iniquity and transgression and sin; and that will by no means clear the guilty; visiting the iniquity of the fathers upon the children, and upon the children's children unto the third and fourth generation." All these attributes, which are traditionally counted as thirteen and are known as *Slosh Esré Midot*, are all ethical and on account of that are frequently repeated in the High Holiday services.

The apparently nonethical statement, "visiting the iniquity of the fathers upon the children to the third and fourth generation," which contradicts another statement in Deuteronomy XXIV, 16, "The fathers should not be put to death for the children, neither the children be put to death for the fathers; every man shall be put to death for his own sin," was noted by the Rabbis and an explanation is offered. They say that when the children are absolutely innocent, they do not suffer for the iniquity of their parents, but when they themselves are wicked, a modicum of punishment may be added for the sins of their fathers.[1] We must, therefore, assume that the phrase is only a deterrent expression, to emphasize that nobody will escape punishment no matter how long-suffering God may be, and is based on a biological conception that traits of character pass from fathers to descendants, and as a rule up to the third generation; and therefore the punishment meted out to evil-doing children really contains a measure of punishment due to the fathers.

That in ancient times the belief that children are punished for the sins of the fathers was prevalent not only among other nations [*] but also among Jews, we learn from the protests against it by the prophets Jeremiah and Ezekiel. Both quote the proverb current among the people, "The fathers have eaten sour grapes and the children's teeth are set on edge," meaning that they themselves are righteous, but suffer for the sins of their fathers. The prophets thunder against such a belief. Jeremiah says, "But everyone shall die for his own iniquity, every man that eateth the sour grapes, his teeth shall be set on edge." Ezekiel is more emphatic and declares, "As I live, saith the Lord, ye shall not have occasion any more to use this proverb in Israel. Behold all souls are mine; as the soul of the father, so also the soul of the son is mine; the soul that sinneth shall die" (Jeremiah XXXI,

[1] Tr. *Sanhedrin,* 27b.

[*] This belief occupies an important place in Greek literature and forms the theme of Sophocles' tragedies. In *Oedipus Rex,* Oedipus is presented as one who suffers greatly and commits crimes unknowingly for no other reason than the curse resting on his family because his fore-father, Laius, angered the gods.

29, 30; Ezekiel XVIII, 3, 4). We can, therefore, rely on the prophets as to the proper meaning of the verses enumerated in the statement of the group of attributes.

In like wise single virtues that constitute a part of His essence are frequently attributed to God in the Biblical books. The leading of these are truth and righteousness. Thus Jeremiah says of Him, "The Lord God is the true God" (Jeremiah X, 10). The Psalmist declares of God, "Thou art nigh, O Lord, and all Thy commandments are truth;" and again, "The beginning of Thy word is truth" (Psalm CXIX, 151, 160; Rosh Dborkho Emet), meaning to say that the very basis of the word of God in His relation to man is truth, for this is His essence. And so is righteousness, for as the Psalmist says, "For the Lord is righteous, He loveth righteousness," and again, "The Lord is righteous in all His ways" (Psalms XI, 7; CXLV, 17), meaning that all His actions are righteous since righteousness constitutes a part of His essence.* Again and again the ethical attributes of God are emphasized in the Bible, and thus the God of the world with whom the Pentateuch starts is transformed into an ethical God, and becomes the archetype of ethical conduct, the only way by which man can come near Him.

* It is also true that there are several passages in the Bible, Exodus XX, 5; XXXIV, 14; Naḥum I, 2; Deuteronomy IV, 24; V, 9; Joshua XXIV, 19, where God is described as *Kano,* which is usually translated as jealous. It is an unfortunate translation, for in Naḥum and Joshua the term is applied in connection with punishment for sins, and Exodus XX, 5 and Deuteronomy V, 9 in connection with punishment for evil deeds up to the grandchildren. Where, then, could the concept of jealousy come in? Only in Exodus, XXXIV, 14 and Deuteronomy IV, 24 it is applied in connection with worshiping other gods or making images. Even here it could not mean *jealous,* for the Bible consistently denies the existence of other gods, and one cannot be jealous of a nonexisting thing. The real meaning is "zealous for His worship and the following of his commandments," hence it comes in connection with punishment for sins of whatever kind they may be.

9. Likeness to God—Leading Principle of Ethical Conduct

From this conception of God as an archetype of ethics, there emerges the leading principle that guides Jewish conduct and is the standard aim or end. This is likeness to God; man must endeavor to conduct himself in such a way that his conduct shall resemble, insofar as there can be a resemblance, God's action as it is conceived and manifested in the world and in life. This is the meaning of all the laws and commandments given in the Torah. God, in order to help man rise in moral conduct and endeavor to follow such conduct, gave him these commandments and ordered him to observe them. As an incentive, reward and punishment are attached to observances and transgressions respectively, but the real end is the continuous endeavor to emulate God.

This constant endeavor is emphasized in the Pentateuch in connection with a number of commandments, sometimes explicitly and sometimes implicitly. Thus, at the end of the set of laws relating to diet—not to eat the flesh of certain animals and especially swarming things—there is appended the statement, "I am the Lord, your God; sanctify yourselves therefore and be ye holy, for I am holy" (Leviticus XI, 44).

Similarly, Chapters XIX and XX in Leviticus, which contain a considerable number of laws bearing upon moral conduct and relating especially to sexual immorality, begin and end respectively with the following statements: "The Lord spoke unto Moses saying, speak unto all the congregation of the children of Israel and say unto them, Ye shall be holy, for I, the Lord, your God, am holy," and "Ye shall be holy unto me, for I, the Lord, am holy and have set ye apart from the peoples that ye shall be mine." Here we have an explicit call or command to emulate God in conduct. To a number of moral commandments of a social nature there are appended the words, "I am the Lord." This certainly does not mean to tell the Jews of His existence and rule of the world, for the same words are attached a number of times in the same section to definite laws. What they imply is a statement to the Jews to observe these commandments for then they will act ethically as God does.

This principle that men endeavor to act in likeness to God is also emphatically stressed in the demand by God to love Him, a command repeated several times in Deuteronomy, primarily in the *Shema* section. But how can one love a being of whose essence one has no real conception except by endeavoring to emulate His actions? In fact, that this is the only way to express love for God is indicated explicitly in another verse, "And now, Israel, what doth the Lord, thy God, require of thee, but to fear the Lord, thy God, to walk in His way, and to love Him and to serve the Lord, thy God, with all thy heart and all thy soul" (Deuteronomy X, 12). It is clear, then, that to emulate God, to walk in His way, is the ideal conduct, and the striving to realize it must become a strong emotion permeating the soul. The word *fear* does not necessarily mean fright. This word *Yirah* in Hebrew also means reverence, and it is in this sense in which it is used in the verse.

The Rabbis stress repeatedly the principle of imitating the actions of God, deriving that principle primarily from God's urging the Jews to be holy like Himself (Leviticus XI, 45). They say that the call to be holy must not be understood as a mere command that can be performed at one time or another, but is to be conceived as the basic reason for man's entire ethical conduct. To inculcate in the heart of their brethren the importance of such rule of conduct, the sages of the Talmud explained the verse, "Ye shall be holy, for I, your God, am holy," to mean the following: God says if you sanctify yourselves, He will consider it as though you sanctified Him.[2] In other words, ethical conduct of man is the highest type of worship and exaltation of God.

[2] *Sifra Kedoshim,* sec. 168.

10. Holiness

The idea of becoming sanctified through ethical conduct will become clearer when we consider the nature and character of holiness, this most frequent attribute of God by which He is described in the Bible. Holiness denotes the supremacy and power of God, manifested either in His punishment of the wicked or in His showing of His favor to the righteous and the downtrodden. The first phase is referred to in such verses as Ezekiel XXXVIII, 22, 23, where the prophet is describing the doom of Gog who will come to invade Israel, and which end with the words, "Thus, says the Lord God, will I sanctify Myself and will make Myself known in the eyes of the nations." The sanctification referred to does not, however, consist in the revelation of the strength of His power to punish the wicked, but primarily in the reason for such punishment, which is God's opposition to all evil. The prophet Ḥabakkuk, protesting against the rise to power of the Chaldeans or the Babylonians, cries out, "O Lord, my God, the holy One. Thou that art of eyes too pure to behold evil and Thou that canst not look on mischief, wherefore lookest Thou when they deal treacherously" (I, 13).

The second phase is indicated in such phrases as the "Lord God is exalted through justice and is sanctified by righteousness" (Isaiah V, 16), or "the neediest among men shall exalt in the Holy One of Israel" (Isaiah XXIX, 19). We can infer from these two types of the manifestations of God's holiness that His activity is entirely different from that of man. Its basis is ethical, for its cause is either opposition to evil or expression of kindness to the righteous. We must, therefore, understand that in His call upon the Jews to be holy or to strive to attain holiness, stated in Leviticus XX, 26, He calls upon them to act differently from other peoples, that is, in as perfect and ethical a manner as possible. In fact, this call ends with the words, "And I set you apart from the peoples that ye should be mine." In other words, the chosenness of Israel consists in this different way of conduct.

Because of this prescribed aloofness and uniqueness of conduct that Israel is commanded to follow, its closeness to God Who is the archetype of such conduct is often stressed by the prophets, especially by Isaiah, who calls Him the Holy One of Israel. Likewise, all commandments that raise Israel above the conduct of other peoples, such as the laws of sexual morality or the prohibition against eating the flesh of animals that are torn by beasts, or of certain types of animals that are unclean or possess cruel habits, are considered as a means of imparting the quality of holiness to character. Similarly, the Sabbath, an unparalleled institution in the ancient world, is called holy because it raises man's life to a higher level by affording him a day of rest, and its extension also to slaves inculcates in the heart of men the idea of human equality and further impresses the stamp of holiness. It is said, "Verily, ye shall keep my Sabbath, for it is a sign between you and Me throughout the generations that you may know that I am the Lord who sanctifies you" (Exodus XXXI, 13).

How far the Sabbath signifies a difference in conduct on the part of the Jews from that of other peoples of antiquity can be seen from the fact that none of those peoples knew of such an institution. They could not even understand it, and mocked at the Jews for observing it. The Roman philosopher, Seneca, says that the observance of that day proves that the Jews are inclined to laziness for they waste a seventh part of their lives.[3] Aristotle did say that leisure is a valuable condition for spiritual development, but the leisure that he advocates is limited to but a small class of people, the owners of slaves. In fact, he even justifies slavery by the argument that the masters require leisure and, therefore,

[3] Quoted by Theodor Reinach in his *Texts D'auteurs Grecs et Romanes Relatifs au Judaisme,* p. 362. The passage is found in a Ms. treatise on Seneca's *De superstitione.*

there must be a class of people to do the work. But the Torah, having stipulated through its view of creation that there is a fundamental equality of all men no matter of what social status they may be, strengthened this view by ordaining that this day of rest should be enjoyed by all who work, whether manservants or maidservants or masters. There may be differences in the amount and type of work men or women may do, but no one can deprive another of resting one day a week. Furthermore, this day is considered by the Torah a condition for a higher spiritual life, as it calls the Sabbath holy, and this aspiration cannot be taken away from any man, for that also belongs to the fundamental equality of all human beings.

Chapter IV

APPLICATION OF ETHICAL PRINCIPLES

11. Practical Expression of Sanctification

All these principles and views discussed in previous chapters, which emerge as corollaries from the fundamental conceptions of Judaism about God, the world, and life are not mere theoretical principles. They were meant to be actually applied in conduct.

The principle of acting in likeness to God connotes primarily a striving to realize a great ethical ideal in daily life. This can also be said about the demand that man sanctify himself,* for holiness in its fullness can never be attained by man, since only God is holy; man can only strive to attain a particle of that attribute. In other words, it is a high ideal that man should place for himself in search for good conduct, and its very unattainability calls forth an endless striving to do good, so that ultimately it may become an attribute of personality and a striving to follow right conduct. As such, holiness, in its practical expression, signifies a continual desire to perform the commandments of God that aim at making good prevail in life. Sanctification is not the share of the few and the select. The commandments con-

* It is worthwhile to note that the ethical ideal to emulate God in conduct is a unique type of ideal of a *sui generis* character, as it leads to a continuous rise in ethical conduct. Every ideal, no matter how high it may be, has a certain limit at which it becomes realized and loses its capacity as a goal. But God's activity is infinite and has no limit. Consequently, man, when he sets before himself the emulation of God as an ideal, assumes an ethical conduct that will continually rise until it reaches the utmost human capacity in action, for there is always a higher degree. This ethical ideal set before man acts as an incentive to maintain moral perfection within the bounds of human ability.

cerning sanctification, such as "Ye shall be holy" (Leviticus XIX, 2), are addressed to the whole Jewish people, and thus everyone can share in it. The realization, though, may be in different degrees.

12. Sense of Guilt or Sin

The human soul is a constant battleground between two forces or motives. One is the pull of the passions that urge man to satisfy his desires, irrespective of whether such action is harmful to his fellow men or even to himself. The other force, whatever its origin may be, whether an intuition or the effect of social life, resists the impulse of passion and restrains man from committing such acts. The character of a man and the course of his actions depend entirely on the result of this struggle.

Judaism recognized the gravity of this struggle and the importance of overcoming the urge to follow the call of passion no matter what the results might be. The Bible says, "The inclination of man's heart is evil from his youth" (Genesis VIII, 21), and hence the commandments and warnings to restrain that inclination. The sages of the Talmud and Midrash deal extensively with that conflict. They named the inclination to evil *Yeẓer ha-Ra,* and the power of restraint that results in an inclination to the good, *Yeẓer Tob.* They spoke of them as though they came into the heart of man from without, and even discussed the exact time when they entered the human heart. The view was expressed that the *Yeẓer ha-Ra* enters into the human heart immediately upon the child's entry into the world [1] as its strength is based upon the reactions to sense data and emotions that even an infant possesses. The *Yeẓer Tob* comes much later when ideas and views begin to develop in the mind of man and

[1] *Genesis Rabba,* Ch. XXXIV.

the influence of education and social contact becomes effective.*

What is interesting, though, is that these ethicists not only recognize the existence of the *Yeẓer ha-Ra,* but even considered its function in the world and life a necessary one. When one reads the story of creation in the Book of Genesis, he notices that the process of creation accomplished by God on each of the first five days ends with the words, "And God saw that it was good." But at the end of the sixth day when man was created, it reads, "And God saw everything that He had made, and behold it was very good." The additional word "very" called forth a comment by a sage, who says, "Good refers to the *Yeẓer Tob,* very good refers to the creation of the *Yeẓer ha-Ra,*"[2] meaning that the existence of the inclination to evil in man's heart and the ensuing struggle to overcome it, the refraining from bad action and specifically doing good, imparts to the good its high value. Were it performed without struggle and effort, it would lose its value and would become a mere mechanical act. Moreover, even if man loses the struggle and succumbs to passion, the effect of that struggle is not effaced for it arouses in man a sense of guilt or sin.

It is this sense of guilt or sin that plays a leading part in the formation of a man's character, for as far as occasional sinning is concerned, the Bible already noted the frailty of

* The *Yeẓer ha-Ra* was even hypostatized as a special angel whose main purpose is to persuade man to do evil, and who even testifies against the sinner on the Day of Judgment. This hypostatization, though widened and expanded in the Talmud, has its origin in the Bible where, under the name of Satan, an adversary appears twice to testify against man, once in Zechariah III, 1, where Satan accuses the high priest, Joshua, of sinning, and a second time in Job I, where he comes before God and attempts to prove that Job is not as righteous as he is supposed to be. In the Bible, Satan merely finds fault with men, but does not persuade them to do evil or sin. In the Talmud, Satan is identified with the *Yeẓer ha-Ra,* and several times even with the angel of death (Tr. *Baba Batra,* 14). These supernatural embellishments with which the sages adorned the natural inclination of man to do evil prove the great importance they attached to the conflict.

[2] Ibid. Ch. IX.

man and declared, "There is not a righteous man upon earth that doeth always good and sinneth not" (Ecclesiastes VII, 20). What is important is that he possesses the sense of sin and strives to the utmost to refrain from repeating such actions. And to buttress this sense of sin, Judaism, like other religions, warns man repeatedly against sinning and even threatens punishment. But Judaism does more than that, for the strength of that sense of sin depends in a great measure upon the very conception of sin. And it is this conception of sin in Judaism, unparalleled in other religious conceptions, which supplies that strength. In all religions of the ancient world, sin was conceived of as an offense against the gods, consisting primarily in neglecting the offering of sacrifices or any other rituals aiming at honoring them. Offenses against fellow men were entirely left to man himself. Jn Judaism, however, there is no dividing line between a purely religious or ritual act and an ethical deed, for God, the object of religious worship, is also the archetype of ethics. The frequently repeated command by God Himself to emulate His ways and sanctify oneself changes the very essence of a good act or of a transgression or sin.

A transgression is not merely an offense against God or against religion, but is primarily an offense against man's own personality and character, for it constitutes a failure in man to use his own powers in order to live up to the ideal placed before him. The sense of guilt or sin is the consciousness of that failure. The commission of a transgression of a religious precept or of an ethical command implies that one's character is defective.

This idea is reflected in the very terms by which Judaism denotes sin or transgression. Thus the most prevalent term in Hebrew for sin or transgression is *Ḥet,* a term derived from the verbal root *Ḥata,* which means to miss the mark. Missing the mark points to a lack of the proper quality in man's character, and such a man is therefore considered defective. The good man is consequently called

Tamim, a whole man, one who has no defects. Again, the term *Avel,* iniquity, derived from a root *Ul,* meaning to bend or fall away, likewise denotes weakness of character, while the righteous man is designated as *Yashar,* straight, one who does not bend under stress of evil desires. The general term *Ra,* meaning bad or evil, stems from the verbal root *Raoa* to break, indicating that performing an act which is bad constitutes a break in the character of the performer.

These derivations of the terms for sin or transgression signify that the Jewish conception of ethical or moral conduct implies the following of a standard of right action that is universally valid, for its source is God Himself, and every action is measured by the degree to which it approaches that standard. That the idea of sanctification or holiness really denotes the ability to follow the ideal conduct is emphasized in the Talmud by a brief statement uttered by the *Tanna,* Pinḥas, son of Yair. Endeavoring to evaluate the various degrees of ethical religious conduct, he says, "Fear of committing sin leads to holiness,"[3] thus stressing that constant carefulness by man not to swerve from the right path of ethical conduct sanctifies his life. On the other hand, the failure to follow the right path or the committing of a sin is considered in Judaism, as was mentioned, a defect in the personality of the sinner.

In figurative speech, sin is called uncleanliness or impurity, as if to say that every sin spots the soul and contaminates it. The following of the right conduct is called purity, and the man who acts thus is called a pure man, *Naki.* These terms are applied to all classes of sins, no matter of what degree of gravity. Not only is adultery called uncleanness (Numbers V, 13, 19, 29), but even slander or any improper speech is dubbed by that name. When Isaiah tries to convey the awe he experienced at his inauguration as a prophet, he exclaims, "Woe is me, for I am undone; for I am of unclean

[3] *Tractate Abodah Zara,* 20b.

lips and dwell in the midst of a people of unclean lips, for mine eyes have seen the King, the Lord of Hosts" (Isaiah VI, 5). In other words, he felt that because of possible sin he might have committed by mere speech, he was unworthy of the prophetic mission. Even improper thoughts are considered unclean, and the Psalmist pleads to God, "Create me a clean heart, O God" (Psalm LI, 12), that is, help me to think the right kind of thoughts. Similarly, in the Bible the righteous man is often called pure of heart, and he who has not done any wrong is called one of clean hands.

Such appellations are of great significance, for they indicate that man must inculcate in himself an abhorrence of committing a wrong act, just as most men abhore bodily uncleanness and endeavor by all means to become clean. The abhorrence must correspond to the special type of impurity, for while bodily impurity can be easily overcome by washing, impurity of soul is more permanent and may take a long time to erase.

13. Moral View of the World

The practical application of the concept of God as the archetype of morality, which resulted in the principle that man must emulate God, was buttressed by another moral theory. This theory can be called morality as the *raison d'être* of the world. It is a view expressed a number of times, both in the Bible and in the Talmudic-Midrashic literature. The prophet Isaiah, in contemplating the instability of the world of sense, enthusiastically exclaims, "For the heavens shall pass like smoke and the earth shall wax old like a garment, and they that dwell therein shall die in like manner, but my salvation shall stand forever, and my righteousness shall not be abolished" (Isaiah LI, 6). This statement, divested of its poetic flourish, means to teach us that in the flux of phenomena in the physical and human world there is one thing constantly permanent, namely, ethical action, for good deeds endure.

The sages of the Talmud injected into this view a still deeper thought. They said, "When God created the world, he laid down a condition for the continuous existence of the heaven and the earth, namely, that if Israel receive the law, it is well, but if not, it will relapse into chaos.[4] There is, of course, much fancy in the statement, and was undoubtedly prompted by the desire to encourage the Jews to observe the Torah in spite of the tribulations they suffered, but under the figurative cloak there remains the thought that the *raison d'être* of the physical world is the realization of morality in the life of the people dwelling therein. Without the Law and without at least one people following its commandments and principles, the world would lose its value, and under such circumstances, chaos, brutality, and their evil consequences would reign in it. That this thought is the kernel of the statement is evident from another Talmudic passage which reads, "He who performs a moral act, as for instance, a judge who pronounces a righteous judgment, associates himself with God in the creation of the world,"[5] meaning that every moral act adds to the worth and value of the existence of the world. A similar thought, aiming to impress men with the value of a single good act, and, vice versa, with the evil effect of a single wrong act, is expressed by the sages in the following way. It is known, they say, that both the individual and the human world are judged by God according to the majority of their deeds. If they are good, the judgment is favorable, but if not, it is unfavorable. A man about to perform an act should, therefore, consider the state of his deeds and those of the world as equally balanced between good and bad. His present deed will throw him and the world as a whole to a one-sided balance, either

[4] *Ibid.*, p. 3a.
[5] Tr. *Sabbath*, p. 10a.

good or bad, according to the character of the act.[6] Thus, one act on the part of a man can either justify him and the entire world or, oppositely, can condemn both.

These and similar statements scattered throughout the wide Talmudic-Midrashic literature reflect the views of the sages of Israel on the role morality should play in the world and in human life. True, such statements are maxims, fragments of teachings, but they were intended to be inculcated in the hearts and minds of the people to serve as motives of action. Having been transmitted from generation to generation, they became a part of Jewish ethics and moulded the attitude of at least a portion of the group toward moral conduct.

14. Human Dignity

This conception of human moral conduct as imparting value to the existence of the world forms another link in the chain of views concerning the dignity of man held by Judaism. Man, according to Judaism, was not only created last in the process of creation and thus became its seal and purpose, but was also impressed with the divine image and endowed with freedom and choice of action, and his conduct gives value to the world as a whole. All this makes him practically the center of the universe and envelops him with a halo of dignity which, arising from the conception of equality of all men, is indigenous to every human being.

This view, while implied in the Biblical story of creation where the statement that man is created in the image of God is twice repeated, was more fully unfolded by the sages of Israel and applied as a rule of action. In a discussion about the most important principle of conduct in relation to our fellow men, the great Akiba said, "Love thy neighbor as thyself" is the great rule of conduct commanded by the Law (Torah). But his disciple, Ben Asai, said that the verse,

[6] Tr. *Kidushin,* 40b.

"This is the book of the generations of Adam. In the day that God created man in the image of God He made him" (Genesis V, 1) is a greater rule of conduct.[7] Immediately after Ben Asai's statement comes an explanation of its import. Says Tanḥumah, "Do not say if I was insulted I shall do likewise and insult my fellow men; if I were cursed by someone, I, too, will curse another man. Know that if you do so, you are insulting and cursing a being who bears the image of God." In other words, though one happens to suffer insult or injury by a wicked man, he must restrain himself from abusing the dignity of another man under all circumstances.

Other sages went deeper into the subject and derived from the Biblical statement that man was created in the image of God an exalted ethical principle that man should not be used as a means, but must be regarded as an end in himself. They applied it in a most rigorous way, maintaining that even when one is about to suffer the greatest injury, he must not try to obviate it by using another person as a means to escape the threatened injury. The Mishnah says, "If a group of captive women are told by their captors to surrender one of them for immoral purposes, lest they all be subject to the same ordeal, they should all suffer the consequences and not surrender a single one for that purpose.[8] Similarly, if a man is ordered to murder a fellow man under the threat of death if he refuse to comply, the sages say he should suffer death and not commit murder. The adage of the obligation is, Do you think that your blood is redder than that of your fellow man?[9] In other words, no person should be used as a means to protect another, no matter how grave the consequences.

[7] *Genesis Rabba,* Ch. I, sec. 13.
[8] Tr. *Terumot,* Ch. VIII, Mishnah 12.
[9] Tr. *Sanhedrin,* 74.

15. Love of Fellow Men

Everyone knows of the commandment in Leviticus XIX, 18, "And thou shalt love thy neighbor as thyself." It was borrowed by the daughter religions of Judaism, Christianity and Islam, and greatly stressed by them, yet its full force and importance cannot be gauged unless we delve into its meaning as the sages of Israel did, and see its relationship to the Jewish view of man, with its concept of the manner of his creation, and his bearing the divine impress. It is frequently misunderstood, as witness the statement of an English philosopher who says, "All agree to the commandment, 'love thy neighbor as thyself'; they differ only in the answer to the question, Who is my neighbor?" In fact, the very translation in the New Testament of the Hebrew word *Reah* as neighbor is erroneous. *Reah* is more inclusive, for it means fellow man. Some non-Jewish Biblical scholars go even further, and limit the meaning of the term, *Reah,* to mean friend or member of the Jewish people and claim that the term *neighbor* in the New Testament is an improvement that widens the scope of the commandment. The sages of Israel, following the fundamental Jewish view that the Torah is the word of God and that there are no unnecessary additions to its commandments, elicited the proper meaning of the word *Reah* in this commandment. They asked why do the words, "I am the Lord," come at the end of this commandment? The answer is that the commandment means to say, "Thou shalt love the *Reah* as thyself, for I am the Lord, thy God, who created both of you." [10] It is evident, as the philosopher Hermann Cohen remarks, that since God did not create two types of men, the term *Reah* does not mean here friend or even neighbor, but fellow man without qualification. That this is the meaning of the term, says Cohen, can be seen from another verse in the same chapter, verse 34, which reads, "The stranger that sojourneth with you

[10] *Abot d' Rabbi Nathan,* Ch. XVI.

shall be unto you as the home-born among you, and thou shalt love him as thyself, for ye were strangers in the land of Egypt; I am the Lord, thy God." [10a] We see then clearly that the commandment, love thy *Reah* as thyself, is not limited to friend, or neighbor, or Jew, but to all fellow men.

There is, however, some difficulty in determining the exact degree of love implied in this commandment. Can we really take it literally that one should love his fellow man exactly as he loves himself? It seems that, at least in certain cases, it is impossible to fulfill the injunction. Such a case is mentioned in the Talmud. We have there a discussion as to what should be done when two persons, while traveling through the desert, have only one measure of water, which can sustain the life of only one man. Ben Patira, an extremely pious man, said that both of them should drink and die together, and let not one man see the death of the other. Taking a rigorist stand, Ben Patira really wanted to take the commandment in its strict, literal implication. But this is really impossible, for were only one to drink, the drinker would love the other less than himself, while the one who would forego the drink for the sake of the other would display more love than that which he bears for himself. And since it is impossible to carry out the commandment in the exact measure, it is evident that Ben Patira's solution results only in a mere waste of human life. Akiba therefore said that one's own life precedes that of his fellow man.[11] It is interesting, though, to note how far Jewish sages carried the fulfillment of ethical precepts: that one sage could teach that a man should be ready to sacrifice his own life in order not to display more love for himself than for his fellow man.

On the other hand, a Mediaeval sage, the famous Moses ben Naḥman, raises another difficulty. He says that it is psychologically impossible that one should love his fellow man exactly in the same degree as he loves himself. Such a

[10a] H. Cohen, *Jüdische Schrifton,* vol. I, pp. 148 and 186.
[11] Tr. *Baba Metziah,* 62a.

demand would be against nature, and the Torah, which is given to man as a guide in daily life, could not oppose nature. Therefore, says he, we have to understand the commandment in the following manner. Man may love his friend exceedingly well, but he still may possess a modicum of feeling of superiority. Usually one sees only few aspects of good in the character of his fellow man while noticing many unfavorable aspects. But in himself he sees many aspects as good, though he may be quite conscious of their limitations both in quantity and quality. Naḥmanides says, therefore, that the commandment, "Love thy neighbor as thyself," while it by no means implies loving him with the same intensity as one loves oneself, tells us to endeavor to see the good in our fellow man from all aspects and not to emphasize his shortcomings.[12] In other words, judge the other man with the same leniency as you judge yourself.

From all such discussions we can see in what high degree Judaism held the love of man and made it a rule and a leading motive in conduct. Verily did Akiba say, "Thou shalt love thy neighbor as thyself" is the most embracive principle in the Torah, for out of it there can be deduced manifold ways of conduct.

16. The Golden Rule

Another rule of conduct that was considered by one of the sages of Israel as the very epitome of morality is the one known usually as the *Golden Rule of Hillel.* When a Gentile who wanted to embrace Judaism asked him for the shortest formula of what Judaism has to teach, he answered, "Do not unto others what thou wouldst not have done unto thee. This," he added, "contains the essence of the teachings of Judaism; the rest is commentary. Go and study."[13] The rule aroused much discussion. Some have wondered why Hillel

[12] *Commentary on Leviticus,* Ch. XIX, 18.
[13] Tr. *Sabbath,* 31a.

did not quote to the would-be proselyte the Biblical verse, "Thou shalt love thy fellow man as thyself." Others claimed that the dictum does not go far enough, as in its negative form it seems only to warn against committing acts that may cause injury or grievance to a fellow man, but does not obligate him to perform beneficent acts.

However, there was good reason for the selection of the maxim instead of the Biblical verse, as the scope of conduct it embraces is much wider than what is attributed to it. The maxim intends to supply the commandment of loving one's fellow man with a special desire to act in the proper ethical manner. It says that one should place himself in precisely the position in which the other man is, and then act as he would have acted toward himself. It is thus evident that the maxim embraces positive acts of beneficence as well. When one sees the other man in a precarious position, whether lying sick or in need of help, or in want of money for the necessities of life, the maxim urges one to place oneself in the stricken man's position. It says, would you have liked not to be offered any help or assistance? Certainly not. Then do not withold from the other man the necessary help he requires.

The actual ethical principle is the same as in the Biblical commandment of loving your neighbor—but the psychological motive injected in the maxim supplies the urge to perform good deeds and abstain from evil ones. The mere imaginary placing of oneself in a precarious position, though it may stem from self-pity, arouses the will to alleviate the misery of the other man. One may argue that the element of self-pity injected in the good deed tarnishes somewhat the purity of the ethical act. Still, the principle that one must love his neighbor as himself is wholly preserved, for the needs of the other man are seldom placed on the same level as those of ourselves, and the urgency to do good is, as stated, strengthened.

17. Duty

The concept of duty that all systems of ethics consider as the very foundation of the moral life, inasmuch as it is the force that impels man to turn toward the right and proper action, occupies an important place in Jewish ethics. Its importance is increased when we consider its source, which endows it with a distinctive character. Moralists and propounders of systems of ethics found it difficult to determine the exact source of that sense of duty of which almost every man is conscious in some way. Some sought it in the feeling that the act must be sanctioned or approved by the social group of which the agent is a member. Others thought that usefulness resulting from the performance of the act is the source of the duty. Still others placed its origin in abstract reason or law. Jewish ethics, which considers God as the archetype of all morality and posits likeness to Him as a guiding principle of conduct, necessarily considers His commands as the source of duty.

Yet though this duty seems apparently a subjection to authority, still, upon examination, its character and inner content will be seen to be essentially autonomous. The Bible constantly insists on employing will in choice of action. It says, in the name of God, "I call heaven and earth to witness against you this day that I have set before thee life and death, the blessing and the curse; therefore choose life that thou mayest live and thy seed" (Deuteronomy XXX, 19). There is emphasis here on choice and exercise of will, for there is no mention of reward and punishment in order to subject the Jews to the authority of God. The terms *life* and *death, blessing* and *curse,* are identified with moral and immoral action. That this is the meaning is evident from the verse which immediately follows, "To love the Lord, to hearken to His voice and to cleave to Him, for that is thy life and the length of thy days" (Deuteronomy XXX, 20). Here there is explicit elucidation of the meaning of the term *life* in the preceding verse. And where there is will, there is no forced subjection. As Hermann Cohen said, "Pure will is tested by the very submission to the command of God. If I consider my will, I demonstrate it through my subjection to the command of God as duty."

Obedience to the command of God by free will and choice, as taught by Judaism, possesses some of the characteristics of the most rational and rigid theory of ethics in modern times, that of Immanuel Kant. This philosopher insists that an act, in order to be ethical, must be done not from any motive of attaining personal benefit or pleasure, but entirely from duty, out of respect to the rational law. Judaism, likewise, insists on such a motive. It is true that Judaism, like every religion, promises reward for good deeds and punishment for wicked ones, but this is merely a concession to the frailty of man; time and again, Jewish teachers through the ages insisted that all moral acts must be done solely from duty, and not from any other motive. It is said, "Know that the reward for performing a divine commandment is the performance itself, namely the will to do good." [14] Again, one of the early teachers taught, "Be not like the servants who minister to their master because of the expectation to receive a reward, but be like servants who minister to their master without expecting any reward." [15] It is even stated that if one performs an act because he is commanded to do so he is preferred to the one who performs it without being commanded,[16] since the latter acts thus out of special inclination for such an act. This statement emphasizes that the performance of an ethical act should be carried out from a pure sense of duty without any egoistic motive. An act done without a sense of duty but by personal inclination may be right and proper and

[14] Tr. *Abot,* Ch. IV, 2.
[15] Ibid. I, 3.
[16] *Kidushin,* 31.

certainly should not be disparaged, but still there is an egoistic element in it.

It is, of course, understood that in practical life such motives are prevalent, but the teachers of Judaism endeavored to point out that acts which do not imply even a vestige of egoism are the highest moral deeds. They say that when a man is faced in life with the problem of acting against all his personal inclinations and he performs the act only because the Mitzvah demands it, he should not hesitate, for this is his duty.[17] In another place it is said, "Precepts were not given for enjoyment."[18] This does not mean that the enjoyment of the performance of a precept is forbidden or improper, but merely that the real motive should be the duty.

The basis of all such views is the fundamental concept of Jewish ethics that God is absolutely good, and, therefore, His commandments are good in their very essence and are identical with the highest law of morality.

[17] Ibid.
[18] Tr. *Erubin,* 65.

PART II

I. VIRTUES AND VICES

CHAPTER V

CHARACTER AND ITS LEADING VIRTUES

18. DEFINITION OF CHARACTER

The total sum of dispositions that a man possesses toward actions done willingly constitutes his character. These dispositions are the result of a number of factors, such as interest, environment, emotional bent, and above all, the reaction of the will to the repeated suggestions of these factors. These reactions by habit become a part of man's personality and on similar occasions call forth similar reactions. Character is, therefore, defined as the habit of the will that a man acquires in life and that conduces him to perform acts judged to be good or, ignoring consequences, to act wrongly. Character plays an important role in human conduct. It is therefore understood that Judaism, in which moral conduct is continually emphasized, laid great stress upon the acquisition of a good character, and conversely, frequently speaks in most derogatory terms of the man whose character is faulty and displays an inclination to evil.

Inasmuch as Jewish ethics is grounded in religion and in obedience to the will of God Who is essentially good and is thus the archetype of all morality, it follows that a man's character is not to be judged solely by the results of his actions, whether they are good or bad, but to a large degree by his inner urge to do good or not. This by no means detracts from the value of a moral act as a beneficent social force. It merely deepens and widens the motive of the agent, not limiting it to mere intention to do good to his fellow men, for intention is frequently based on calculation that at times is erroneous, but demands that the act stem from a rooted desire in the heart of man to do good.

Just as the Bible speaks of God, "The Lord is righteous, He loves righteousness" (Psalm XI, 7), for this is His very essence, so does it speak of the Ẓaddik, "The labor of the Ẓaddik tendeth to life" (Proverbs X, 16), in which the term *life* signifies a desire to increase good. He does not aim at anything else, as it is said, "The thoughts of the righteous are right" (Proverbs XII, 5). The real nature of the kind of character Judaism urges man to acquire is brought out by the Psalmist when, in a mood of helplessness, he turns to God and pleads, "Create me a clean heart, O God, and renew a steadfast spirit within me" (LI, 12). A clean heart means one that habitually loves the good and by its very steadfast nature turns away from evil.

The value of character in a complete practical aspect in life is demonstrated in the Bible in one instance only, namely in that of marriage. In the ode to the ideal woman "whose price is far above rubies" contained in the thirty-first chapter of the Book of Proverbs, the author concludes, "Grace is deceitful, beauty is vain, but the woman who feareth the Lord, she shall be praised." Fear of God, in the Bible, never means fear of His might, but connotes awe and reverence, and that is expressed in obeying the will of God, an obedience that is the ground of Jewish morality as well as of religious piety. In other words, the highest quality in a woman is the right character.

19. Ways of Acquiring the Right Character

The constant insistence of Judaism upon observance of the laws of the Torah and obedience to the commands of God, which contain all morality, spared the sages the task of engaging in the discussion of how character is acquired and established as an integral part of human personality. The way was thought to be known and open to all by the continual practice of the precepts of Judaism. Yet, we find in the ethical treatise of the *Mishnah Aboth (The Sayings of the Fathers),* a discussion on the subject which, though not complete from the psychological aspect, still tells us by what means the right character can be acquired.

We are told that the great teacher, Joḥanan ben Zakkai, said to his leading disciples, "Go forth and see which is the good way to which a man should cleave," meaning thereby what can be considered the surest means for acquiring a moral character that should regulate all conduct. The answers came. Rabbi Eliezer said, "a good eye"; Rabbi Joshua said, "a good friend"; Rabbi José said, "a good neighbor"; Rabbi Simon said, "one who foresees the consequences of his action"; Rabbi Eleazar ben Aroch said, "a good heart." [1]

Eliezer considered that the virtue which ultimately evolves the right character is located in the eye. The eye that sees things in the world and life is considered in Jewish literature an organ in which most of the desires have their origin, as it is the most effective organ. "A good eye" is here used as a symbol for the virtue of contentment or satisfaction. When a man is satisfied with what he has, he will avoid many vices, such as jealousy, greed, and the like.

Both Joshua and José emphasize the social element in the formation of character. Joshua speaks of acquiring the habit of being kind and good to friends, thus laying the foundation for character. José says such a habit must have a wider range and more frequency. Friends are selected on the basis of likemindedness and one does not come in contact with them often. Neighbors are less suited to each other, but one is liable to stumble upon them at any time. Practice in good conduct toward neighbors strengthens the will to do good both by the greater effort it requires and by its frequency. Rabbi Simon, in his answer, emphasizes the good intention of action, namely, that when one is about to perform an act, he should consider the resulting consequences and not be

[1] Tr. *Abot,* Ch. II, Mishnah, 9.

moved by immediate response to impulse and desire. Such a rule will impress the habit of performing good deeds more emphatically than the practice of any other virtue. Eleazar claims that the range must be wider and more embracive, not limited to one form of practice or means, but to the whole personality. This is expressed by the term *a good heart*. The heart, as is well known, is considered, both in Jewish and in Greek psychology, as the seat of the soul and its faculties of desire, thought, and will. A good heart, then, means that a man must so form his character that all he plans to do should be for the good. Eleazar does not specify the means for the acquisition of such a heart, for as stated, the way of the good is already known in Judaism. It is mapped out in the Law, which expresses the will of God, and Eleazar merely informs us that what man is required to do in order to acquire the right kind of character is to make the effort to train his will in all ways for good action or, briefly, to possess a good will.

We can see in this discussion, especially in the opinions of Simon and Eleazar, parallels to the two leading modern moral theories, the one usually called utilitarian which, as pointed out in the Introduction, emphasizes primarily that the consequences of the results of the act should be foreseen and their attainment should form its aim. This is emphasized by Simon's statement that the good way consists in foreseeing the consequences of the act. It does not, however, mean that Simon stresses that the attainment of what is useful or pleasant to the agent himself should be the aim of the action, but he does stress calculation and foresight of consequences. Eleazar speaks not of calculation, but of the inner urge or the will to do good, which is of importance. The master declared himself in favor of Eleazar ben Aroch's view, for he said to his disciples, "In Eleazar's good way your ways are included." Similarly Kant, millennia later, declared, "Nothing is good but a good will," a statement that echoes the content of Eleazar's words. The Jewish basis of the categorical imperative, however, is not reason, but the will of God, which is essentially good.

20. The Character of the Jewish Group

We have discussed thus far the ways and means that conduce to the formation of character in general, which in turn shapes one's moral conduct. This shaping can be considered the concrete expression of character, which takes the form of the practice of a number of virtues and the avoidance of vices. It is through this practice and avoidance that the types of character are distinguished, for while the desire to do good is a general trait and can be possessed by all men, the conception of what is good differs with different social groups. Consequently, there is always a process of selection on the part of the group of certain virtues that are favored by it, and are therefore more frequently practiced. In the course of time, through this selection, types of character associated with different groups or nations are formed in which the individual belonging to the group shares.

It is therefore meet that in discussing the Jewish view of character certain traits be pointed out, which form a part of that which may be called Jewish character. A statement in the Talmud says, "The children of Israel are prone to be meek, merciful, and to cultivate loving-kindness."[2] And while, of course, Jewish ethics does not minimize the value of any virtue, nor are those aforementioned virtues the monopoly of the Jews, they were so frequently practiced through the ages by our people that they can be considered traits of a Jewish character, and hardly any Jew can succeed entirely in divesting himself of them. Having attempted to point out the importance of character and the necessity to use all efforts to acquire it, we will now proceed to delineate the concrete expression of character, namely, the virtues to be practiced and the vices to be avoided. It is in the mastery

[2] Tr. *Yebamot*, p. 79.

of the virtues and resistance to the lure of vices that Jewish ethics comes to full expression.

We referred several times in the preceding sections to the role of habit in the formation of character and even quoted the views of Jewish sages on the desirability of making it a habit to practice certain virtues that conduce to the acquisition of a good character. Now the role of habit in moral conduct is of great importance, and we find it therefore necessary to say something about the acquisition of the habit itself. We must not forget that all that was said about the habit refers to an age in man's life when he is already able to distinguish between good and bad actions, and when by continuous force of will he can acquire the habit to do good. The question then arises whence stems that force of will, for forces or habits do not arise in a vacuum, but must be preceded by inclinations or habits formed earlier in life. The answer is usually given that these early habits are impressed upon the child in his youth by his parents and teachers. The value of training for this purpose was recognized by all religious leaders and moralists, Jewish and non-Jewish. The Book of Proverbs says, "Train a child the way he should go, and even when he is old, he shall not depart from it" (XXII, 6). The sages of the Talmud urge us frequently to pay attention to the moral training of the children. In one of their statements they stress the dire results of the neglect of such training. They say, "Straighten out the branch of a tree when it is soft, for when it hardens you will not be able to make it straight,"[3] which means: form the character of the child early in life, as later you will not be able to do it.

Aristotle similarly emphasized the importance of habit in the formation of character, primarily habits formed early in life. The idea that the formation of man's moral conduct is laid in his very early youth is brought out very forcibly by the contemporary philosopher, Henri Bergson, in his views

[3] *Midrash on Proverbs*, Ch. XXII.

on the origin of morality in life. He claims that this origin lies in the fundamental feeling in the heart of every man from his very youth, that there exists some power or authority which commands him directly or indirectly to conduct himself in a certain way and not do otherwise. And when we ask who personifies that authority, the answer is the father or the teacher. But, says he, the feeling of duty or the obligation to act in one way and not in another, which becomes natural to the children, does not stem from the personality of the father or the teacher per se, but from their position in society. The child feels, though not consciously, that they represent a power or authority that is even above them. As a result, he acquires, through repetition, the habit of acting in a certain way, and thus there develops a general feeling of duty that impels the child, when he grows up, to follow a way of conduct approved by society.[4]

We can, therefore, see the sacred duty of the father to train and to teach the child in such a way that he may feel the power of that authority, for it is this training that will bring about the formation of habits of action, and will thus lay the foundation of character in life.

21. The Virtue of Meekness

Jewish ethics places greater value than any other ethical system upon the virtue of meekness. It urges one to cultivate this virtue consistently until it becomes a fixed trait of the character, and, vice versa, warns exceedingly against the vice of pride. Since morality, according to Judaism, is based upon the recognition of God's greatness and goodness, it follows that man must consider his own position in the world to be of moderate proportion. An exaggerated opinion of one's self involves *eo ipso* a wrong view of the role of the Godhead in the world. Even when a man does not happen to be thoroughly imbued with religion, and his thoughts do

[4] *Les Deux Sources de la Morale et de la Religion,* Eng. Trans., p. 11 ff.

not frequently dwell upon the relation of man to God, yet on contemplating his position in the world and life in general, he will come to a similar conclusion. A modern moralist said, "I am only the vessel in which the power of life works and creates, and I dare not not to be humble at the little I can manage to let come through." [5] Inasmuch as human conduct depends to a large degree on the opinion a man has of himself, it is no wonder that Judaism considers meekness a fundamental virtue from which other virtues stem, and pride a source of improper action.

Both the Bible and Talmudic literature go to extremes in praising the one and in condemning the other. The Bible employs a number of terms for one who possesses the virtue of meekness: *Anav,* meek; humble, *Ẓenua;* contrite, *Daka;* and low of spirit, *Shefal Ruaḥ.* It often contrasts the modest man with the proud one. It condemns the latter as one whom God Himself dislikes, as it is said, "Haughty of eye and proud of heart, him I do not suffer" (Psalm CI, 5); and in another place, one of "haughty eyes" is counted among the six types of persons whom God dislikes (Proverbs VI, 16). Hating pride is even considered a mode of worshiping God (Proverbs VIII, 13). How far this condemnation of pride, which is implied in the Biblical maxims, can be carried out in life is illustrated by the following Ḥassidic story.

Once the Rabbi of Apta came to a city in which two men competed for the privilege of giving him lodging. Both houses were equally roomy and confortable, and in both houses all the rules of dietary laws were observed with pious exactitude. However, one of the men was of evil repute for his sinful doings, and he knew well that he was weak and of little significance. As for the other, no one in the community could accuse him of the slightest breach of conduct. He walked the streets with proud and stately steps, thoroughly aware of his spotless purity. The Rabbi selected the house of the man with the bad reputation. When he was

[5] Ernest Teller in *Letters from Prison.*

asked for the reason of his choice, he answered, "'Concerning the proud,' God says, 'I and he cannot live together in the world'; and if God, blessed be He, cannot share a room with the proud, how can I? Furthermore, we read in the Torah that God dwelleth with the Jewish people even in the midst of their uncleanness, and if God takes lodging with the sinners, why should I not do likewise?"

The Rabbis on their part offered proof for the comparatively limited position of man in the universe from the fact that the whole universe with its infinite number of creatures preceded man's creation. They ask, "Why was man created on Friday, on the day when the process of creation was completed?" The answer is given, "This was done in order that in case one is inoculated with pride and considers himself the very center of the world, tell him, behold, even an insect preceded you in existence."[6]

On the other hand, God is very close and near to the modest and the humble, as stated, "I dwell in high and holy place, and with him also who is of a contrite and humble spirit" (Isaiah LVII, 15). And of the three demands that God makes of man, according to the prophet Micah, the last and most important is to walk humbly with God (Micah VI, 8).

All these harsh judgments of the proud man and the praises bestowed on the meek man stem from the assumption indicated above, that the virtue of meekness leads to reverence of God, as it is said, "The reward of humility is the fear of the Lord" (Proverbs XXII, 4). The Hebrew term *Yirah* does not always mean fear of punishment, but more often means awe and reverence. Modesty and meekness inculcate in the heart of man the proper reverence for the greatness of God, but the proud man cannot possess such deep feeling for any other power, for he is too much engrossed in himself and his own aggrandizement. His very piety is tainted with egoism.

[6] Tr. *Sanhedrin*, p. 38a.

22. Meekness as a Social Value

Since, in Judaism, the proper relation to God also involves the right relation to man, the Bible emphasizes the beneficent social results brought about by one's possession of meekness on the one hand, and the detrimental consequences of the possession of pride, on the other hand. It says, "When pride cometh there comes shame, but with the humble there is wisdom" (Proverbs XI, 2), which means that the conduct of the proud man often brings shame to others, as he cares little for the other man's feeling, while the humble or the meek man wisely respects his fellow man. It furthermore points out that not only does man's pride bring inconvenience and discomfort to those with whom he comes in contact by his rude manners, but that frequently it lowers his own social position, for people resent his manners. The meek man, on the other hand, or as the Bible calls him, low of spirit, by his pleasing social manners, attains honor (Proverbs XXIX, 23). It must be understood that the Biblical term, low in spirit *(Shefal Ruaḥ)*, must not be taken literally to designate a characterless personality, but to designate one whose estimate of himself is moderate and who does not aspire to be known as great or powerful, or to overwhelm others with his personality.

Modesty or humbleness is not a virtue to be practiced only by ordinary men or men without ability, but, according to the sages, it should be the share of the very great. Joshua ben Sira advises in his *Book of Wisdom*, "My son, go on with thy business in meekness; the greater thou art, the more shalt thou humble thyself" (Wisdom III, 17), for the greater a man is, the more is he aware of his limitations. As an illustration, it was pointed out by the Rabbis that praise bestowed by the Bible on Moses was that he was very humble, for it says, "And the man, Moses, was very meek, above all the men that were on the face of the earth" (Numbers XII, 3).

The Rabbis went further in emphasizing the need of cultivating the virtue of meekness in both its aspects, religious and social. Thus, in a list of virtues, each of which brings man to a higher grade of religious and moral perfection, modesty or meekness is considered as the one which results in the fear of sin, in that it arouses the practice of carefulness not to deviate from the right path. A statement by a leading Rabbinic scholar adds that meekness is the greatest factor in attaining that perfection.[7] The Rabbis in urging the practice of meekness say, "Be extremely low in spirit in relation to any man for the ultimate fate of all men is the same—death." [8] It follows that because of the ultimate common fate there is no reason for anyone to be proud and to treat his less fortunate fellow man as a lower being.

Time and again, the Jewish moralists urge man to cultivate the virtue of meekness in relation to his fellow men, no matter what their status is. A certain scholar was observed by his students to show honor to every man, irrespective of the amount of knowledge he possessed or of his social position. They asked him the reason for such exceptional conduct. He replied, "I have never come across one in whom I failed to recognize superiority over myself; therefore I have shown him respect. Were he older, I said he has done more good than I; were he richer, I said he has been more charitable; were he younger, I said I have sinned more; were he poorer, I said he suffered heavier trials than I; were he wiser, I honored him for his wisdom; were he not wiser, I said his fault is lighter." [9] Thus, the man who has a moderate opinion of himself can find good in every man.

[7] Ibid.

[8] Tr. *Aboth*, Ch. IV, 4.

[9] Testament of Judah ben Asher in *Hebrew Ethical Wills*, ed. Israel Abrahams, Vol. II, p. 178.

23. Other Aspects of Meekness

Meekness is also considered a factor in the pursuit of knowledge, for the meek man feels his limitation and endeavors to attain more and more knowledge. Meekness also serves as a guard against any attempt to speak evil *(Lashon ha-Ra)* of one's fellow man.[10] With keen psychological penetration into human nature the Rabbis taught the social value of the virtue of meekness in apt maxims, thus: "Lowering myself will result in my rise, and vice versa, raising myself will ultimately lower me."[11] The revelation at Sinai was cited as an illustration of the worth and value of the virtue of meekness. God chose to reveal Himself not on any other of the numerous high mountains, but on the low Mt. Sinai and thus taught a lesson in conduct.

Even the very designation of Israel as a chosen people was ascribed by the sages to the practice of the virtue of meekness by the leaders of the nation. They said, "God said to Israel, I favor you, for even when I bestow greatness upon your leaders, they humble themselves before Me. I made Abraham great and yet he said to Me, 'I am but dust and ashes' (Genesis XVIII, 27). I made Moses and Aaron great, yet they said, 'What are we?' (Exodus XVI, 7). I raised David into Kingship, still, he said, 'I am only a worm and no man' (Psalm XXII, 7). Thus do great men in Israel act."[12]

Consequently, the practice of meekness is insisted upon by every great teacher of piety and morality through the ages. One of them even remarked that if a man possess all virtues but lack modesty, he can be compared to food that is well cooked and prepared but is lacking in salt. It is this one virtue that enhances the entire personality of a man.[13]

The great Jewish moralist, Baḥya Ibn Pakuda, considers

[10] *Kalah Rabbati,* Ch. III.
[11] *Exodus Rabba,* Ch. XLVIII.
[12] Tr. *Ḥulin* 89.
[13] *Book of the Pious,* sec. 15.

meekness a fundamental factor in man's relation to both the Godhead and his fellow man. It is this quality that makes it possible for him to be kind to all men, for, by knowing his own limitations, he may see good points in other men, no matter how little good they may possess. Furthermore, says he, it is this virtue that enables one to acquire peace of mind, for the possessor of the virtue of meekness is usually temperate in his habits and is less grieved when suffering happens to come his way, while the grief and mental anxiety of the proud man are deep and painful.[13a]

What is more, if one practices the virtue of meekness, his relation with his fellow men will not be disturbed under any circumstances. He will not attempt to wreak vengeance upon the man who offends him, nor will he display pride if he is not honored, and even if he attains power and great social position, his attitude toward his friends and fellow men in general will undergo no change.

It must be understood, however, that in Judaism and its teachings, in spite of the exceptional value placed on meekness and the continuous urgency manifested to practice it, there is no denying that it is right for a man to know his worth and to hold the proper estimate of his personality. The meaning of the Biblical term *low soul (Shefal Nefesh* or *Ruaḥ)* does not designate humbleness or humility, but is merely used as a name for the quality opposite to that of haughtiness. The term *broken spirit (Ruaḥ Nishbarah)* (Psalm LI, 19) designates mainly the spirit of the penitent as evident from the content. The prevalent term *Anavah* connotes mostly the virtue of the type described by Maimonides as a way of conduct that is midway between haughtiness or pride and modesty or self-depreciation; in other words, a way that avoids the two extremes. Pious people, however, were not satisfied with the middle way and inclined toward extreme meekness. It is their views that are reflected in many statements found in the Talmud, Midrash, or moral

[13a] *Duties of the Heart,* portal VI, Ch. 10.

treatises, but the general Jewish conception of the normal virtue of meekness is very close to that of Maimonides.

24. The Vice of Pride

The deprecation of the vice of pride by the Rabbis, both in Talmudic and post-Talmudic literature, is extremely severe. It is compared to the sin of idol worship.[14] Even the Shekinah, i.e., the divine presence, is grieved for the proud man who is sometimes threatened with losing the reward of resurrection shared by all Israel.[14a] Another statement asserts that the Messiah will not come until proud men will disappear from Israel. In other words, the existence of such men in Jewry retards the coming of the redemption.[15] The causes of the prevalence of pride among men are spiritual and intellectual poverty,[16] and one of its evil effects may at times be shortening of the span of life, for it is said that the grievances of the proud are deep and frequently bring about disease.

Two stories about Jewish sages, one of whom lived in the Tannaitic period and the other in the middle of the 19th century, illustrate such extreme and exceptional effort in avoiding any taint of pride. It is told of the *Tanna*, Rabbi Tarphon, a colleague of the great Akiba, that once he passed a garden where various fruit trees grew, among them fig trees. The time was at the end of fruit gathering when little fruit remains on the trees, and as a result, permission was granted to gather a few of the leftovers. The owner, who had suffered that season from many attempts to rob him of the fruits of his labor, suspected Rabbi Tarphon to be one of the thieves, wherefore he seized him and placed him in a sack in order to throw him into the river or ditch. Tar-

[14] Tr. *Sotah*, 4.
[14a] Ibid., 5.
[15] Tr. *Sanhedrin*, 98.
[16] Tr. *Sabbath*, 33.

phon did not disclose his identity because he did not want to save himself by means of his knowledge of the Torah and was ready to suffer even death. Luckily, the owner overheard his muttering, "Tarphon, Tarphon, woe is thee for that man will kill you." When the man heard the words, he dropped the sack and fled.[17]

The second story tells of Rabbi David of Talna whose habit it was to spend a half hour each morning reading his letters in his private room. A friend asked him why he did that before the prayers, which should be recited first. The Rabbi answered, "I wish to commence the day right. As you know the higher the social position a man occupies, the harder are his struggles against evil thoughts. Hence, when I look over my letters and read in them salutations in which I am called a Ẓaddik, a leader, a holy man, and the like, I pray to the Lord, 'You and I know that I do not merit these titles of honor. But since so many good men believe them in all sincerity, I beseech Thee to aid me to avoid the snares of Satan so that these men may not feel shame.' "

There is no doubt that threats to the proud man uttered by some of the Rabbis were never meant to be taken literally. They are merely exaggerated to denote an abhorrence of vice. The Jewish position throughout millennia as a group subject to persecution and animosity by proud oppressors might have served as a stimulant to the feeling of abhorrence at this particular vice. A group in such a situation needs a common feeling of fortitude and a common strength of resolution to withstand all storms and tribulations through a willingness to make sacrifices for the good of all. The proud man who maintains his egoism in his relations with his fellow men is a disturbing factor in the life of such a group, and hence, the exceptional condemnation of this vice.

[17] Tr. *Nedarin*, 62.

25. The Importance of Veracity

Telling the truth, or veracity, is considered one of the cardinal virtues in Jewish ethics. To the question asked by the Psalmist, "Lord, who shall dwell in Thy Tabernacle, who shall sojourn in Thy holy mountain?" the answer is given, "He that walketh uprightly, and worketh righteousness, and speaketh truth in his heart" (Psalm XV, 2). It is quite evident that these virtues are primarily fundamentals in an ethical life, and are really to be understood as classes of virtues, each of which subsumes a number of subordinate virtues. A number of these individuals virtues, embraced in the general or class name, are later discussed in this and subsequent chapters. Veracity, then, is a virtue which, when carried out in all its phases, embraces a fair section of ethical conduct. Its wide scope is marked even in the verse quoted. To the words, "and speaketh the truth," there is attached an additional phrase, "in his heart." This addition aims to convey the idea that not only must a man speak the truth, but also think the truth. There must be no contradiction between his thoughts and his words.

The importance of the virtue stems from the God conception taught in Judaism. When Judaism proclaimed to the world the idea of only one God, it indirectly enunciated the philosophic conception of truth, which usually runs as follows: A statement that is true agrees with or corresponds to the reality of the object it describes. When Judaism decried all gods worshiped by other peoples as false, it either denied their existence, implying that there was no reality to them, or that they did not correspond to the concept of God. Only the one God, Creator of the world, is the real God and corresponds with the widest conception of a God that men may have. Hence, truth has become an important attribute of God, as Jeremiah says, "The Lord God is the true God" (Jeremiah X, 10).

The conception of the close relation between the one God

and truth can best be gained from a story found in one of the earliest apocryphal books, III Ezra. We are told there of a contest in oratory held before King Darius where the subject of the discourse was a description of the strongest force in the universe. One participant in the contest spoke about wine as being the strongest; the second participant proclaimed the might of the king as the strongest; the third, who at first spoke of the great power of woman, turned around and declared that truth is the strongest force in the universe. It abideth forever, for it is closely related to the true God whose existence is eternal. From the identification of truth with God, it follows that He is the very guardian of truth and is really called by the Psalmist, "He who keepeth truth forever" (Psalm CXLVI, 6), and again, "Truth and justice are the works of His hands" (Psalm CXI, 7). Even the very revelation of God to man began with truth, as it is said, "The beginning of Thy word is truth" (Psalm CXIX, 160). A similar thought is expressed in the Talmud in a brief statement, "The seal of God is truth." [18] And what does one guard more than his seal? In fact, the cosmos in all its variety is the seal of God, for therein His greatness is reflected, and it is He who guards its existence.

Judaism, positing God as the archetype of all morality, and declaring that the way of the good is to imitate Him, raised veracity which, according to its view, is the very essence of the Godhead, to the position of a leading virtue that man must practice all his life. In fact, knowing and speaking the truth leads ultimately to a knowledge of God. As a Medieval sage said, "Know truth and you will know its source—God—for He is the Creator of all reality.[19] It teaches man to guard against uttering falsehood and speaking guile for this is the way to a perfect life. (Psalm XXXIV, 13, 14). And one who does not heed this advice estranges himself

[18] Tr. *Sabbath*, 54.
[19] Shem Tob Ibn Palkira in *Iggereth ha-Vikuah*.

from God and cannot enjoy His favor, for such conduct opposes the very nature of God.

To inculcate the importance to man of cultivating the virtue of truth, the Bible repeats again and again that the false tongue is hateful to God and is considered as one of the great vices (Proverbs VI, 16). To be able to make veracity a leading trait of conduct is considered an important constituent of an ideal life. In one of the short prayers given in the Book of Proverbs, the text of which later served as the basis for what is known in Christianity as the Lord's Prayer, man pleads that God grant him two things before he dies—to remove him from falsehood and lies, and to give him neither poverty nor riches, but merely to supply him with his daily bread (Proverbs XXX, 8). To live in truth and to have enough for life's sustenance is the Jewish ideal of a perfect life.

26. Agreement Between Speech and Thought

As stated above, veracity contains a number of phases, and therefore the sages of the Talmud devoted much attention to the task of widening the scope of truth-telling and pointing out its various applications. To be truthful does not mean only to tell the truth at a certain time, when at that moment the statement agrees with facts, but under all circumstances and conditions. To the truthful man the statement must be in inner agreement with his thought. A man may make a true statement, as when he praises a man who deserves praise, but if he thinks differently, the difference between speech and thought brands his statement as a lie. His praise is not exactly a form of flattery, for he may not have any reason for flattering this particular man except that he does not have the courage to express his own opinion, and his praise records only the opinion of others. Under the circumstances he should refrain from making any statement.

The rift between speech and thought is usually designated in the Talmud as duplicity, one thing being said by the mouth and another thought by the heart. It is considered by the Talmud as one of the things hateful to God.[20] The avoidance of such duplicity has a wide range of which the following is of great importance, for it assures the permanence of truth even in the future. An injunction is therefore given by the Rabbis, based on the repetition in the verse, "Justice, justice shalt thou pursue" (Deuteronomy XVI, 20) which injunction reads, "See that thy yes shall be just and thy no shall be just, that each of your statements shall be kept in the future." In other words, no change of mind shall take place, for when one makes a statement, whether of promise or of agreement, he must decide in his heart that it will be permanently true. If one breaks an oral promise, though it does not come under the jurisdiction of a human court, he is subject to a form of divine punishment. The technical term for that threatened punishment in the Talmud is *Mi she-Porah,* which means to say that God who punished transgressors in the past will not forego the moral transgression of this man either. The ethical demand that man maintain unity of word and thought covers a large variety of transactions and its full observance brings about a most exemplary conduct that can be achieved only by a few.

The following story related in the Talmud will illustrate the point. A scholar by the name of Rab Safra had certain wares to sell, and once, while reading the *Shema,* a man came and offered to buy them at a certain price. Rab Safra, not wanting to interrupt his prayer, did not answer. The man thought that he was not satisfied with the price and offered a higher amount. When Rab Safra finished his prayer, he told his customer that he would get the goods for the first price offered, for that was the one he had decided to sell the wares for, even before anyone appeared on the

[20] Tr. *Pessahim,* 113.

scene. Once he agreed to the price in his mind, it held good under all circumstances.[21] Such conduct is based on the interpretation of the words of the Psalmist quoted above, "He who speaketh the truth in his heart."

27. Veracity as a Social Value

The practice of veracity is not merely a virtue that perfects the individual character and brings man nearer to God, but as evidenced from the above examples, affects the relations of man with his fellow man. This aspect is an absolutely necessary condition for the stabilization of social life as a whole, without which it could not develop and progress. Were men not expected to practice it, no social life could exist, for no one would trust his fellow man or would have confidence in his word. Neither proper family life, nor friendship, nor business relation, nor even government could exist and function properly. This wide and ramified virtue of telling the truth is summarized by the Rabbis of the Talmud in one short sentence in which truth is placed as one of the three pillars that support the world, meaning of course the social world.[22] Were these pillars to fall, the entire social structure of human life would crumble.

As such, as one of the three props of a social ramified life, veracity, as well as its opposite, falsehood, have a number of phases that are at times considered special virtues, or vice versa, special vices. For the present, we deal with veracity in its limited function as a very important trait in human character. Judaism, through the mouth of its thinkers and scholars, continually inculcated the importance and value of truth, even in minor matters. Thus, we are admonished in the Talmud that when one promises a child to give him something, one must by all means keep that promise, for

[21] Tr. *Makot,* 23.
[22] Tr. *Aboth,* Ch. I, 18.

otherwise it will cause injury to the character of that child, and it will learn the ways of falsehood.[23]

One of the great teachers of piety and right conduct warned that when one discusses with his friend a certain matter, he should strive only for the establishment of the truth and not attempt to gain his point by the use of arguments which, though they display keenness of mind, are basically untrue. Likewise he admonished that when one hears from a friend or teacher words of wisdom of any kind of instructive statement, one should not repeat it to others in his own name, but should mention the name of the man from whom he heard it. In other words, he should neither contribute to the minimizing of the worth of the man who first uttered these words, nor give the impression that he, himself, has wisdom or knowledge that he really does not possess. Though such conduct is frequently of an innocuous kind, the omission of the name of the man who offered the instruction or made the statement constitutes a falsehood. The same teacher also advised that if a man asks another for a loan and the supposed lender doubts whether the borrower will repay the loan, he should not tell him that he has no money, but should tell the truth even at the risk of incurring his anger or animosity.[24] This rigorous demand is based on the assumption that once one utters a lie, he will undoubtedly repeat it, and ultimately it will become a habit and eventually one will turn to other kinds of falsehood as well.

28. The Vice of Falsehood

There is no wonder, then, that just as Judaism considers the practice of truthfulness to be one of the precious virtues that man must cultivate, so does it condemn the vice of uttering falsehood. We have already referred to several

[23] Tr. *Succah,* 46.
[24] *Book of the Pious,* sec. 752, 789.

Biblical verses which declare that God hates and abhors a lying tongue. Actually the Bible is untiring in its condemnation of that vice, turning to it again and again and pointing to its devastating effect on social life. It asserts that the practice of the vice of uttering falsehood destroys friendship between man and man. It says, "Lying lips hide hatred" (Proverbs X, 18), meaning thereby that the one to whom the falsehood was uttered will ultimately discover the lie, and as a result animosity will break forth between him and the man who lies to him. Moreover, it warns the liar that this practice will frequently bring him misfortune. It says, "The bread of falsehood is sweet to a man, but afterwards his mouth shall be filled with gravel" (Proverbs XX, 17), for when his lies will become known he will be punished and hated in one way or another. It even claims that falsehood undermines the foundations of the government, saying, "If a ruler hearkeneth to falsehood all his servants are wicked" (Proverbs XXIX, 12), and it is well known that a state ruled by wicked men must ultimately fall.

The Rabbis went even farther than that and threatened those who practice falsehood with severe punishment even after death, saying that hell (Gehinom) waits for them.[25] They counted utterers of falsehood among the four groups whose company the Divine Presence (*Shekinah*) avoids. Like the Bible, the Midrash warns those who practice the vice that they will gain very little and will be bitterly disappointed with that practice.

This warning is conveyed in a fine parable. It is told, they say, that at the time of the flood, falsehood wanted to enter the Ark in order to save itself from destruction. Noah, however, refused it admittance for it had no companion, and only pairs were admitted to the Ark, as it is said, "Of every living being of all flesh two of every sort shalt thou bring into the Ark (Genesis VI, 19). Falsehood then went in search of a companion, and the only one it could find was "bad

[25] Tr. *Sotah,* 41.

luck." This companion asked for remuneration, and they made an agreement to share their earnings. After they left the Ark, falsehood came to bad luck asking for his share of what bad luck had made. But bad luck laughed and said, "You know well that I only take but never return, for I lose everything I take in and have, of course, also lost what I took from you."[26] Falsehood had nothing to reply, for that was the agreement. The moral is, of course, that falsehood brings little gain to the one who practices it, for it loses in one way or another.

The teachers of Israel warned time and again against lying in any form. Even keeping silent when an untrue statement is uttered is considered a sin by Jewish moralists. A story in the Talmud serves as an excellent illustration of this view. Two Rabbis were taking a walk outside the gates of the city. Another Rabbi, who was just entering the city on a visit to the community, believing that they came to greet him, thanked them for their kindness. One of the Rabbis said to him, "We do not deserve your gratitude, for we are simply taking a walk." His companion was surprised at his conduct, thinking that he should not have disillusioned the visitor, but the other answered, "Even causing one to be deceived is a kind of lie."[27]

The scholars inveighed against the vice of falsehood, emphasizing the sinfulness of such conduct and the divine punishment that would follow. Some of them went to extremes. One said that when one is in the habit of lying, he will die before his appointed time, for such conduct is opposed to God's will and nature, since the eternal God is the God of truth. This form of punishment seems to be based on the norm of divine punishment, often emphasized in the Talmud and called *Midah Keneged Midah,* i.e., measure for measure, namely that God deals with man in the same way that man deals with his fellow man. In this case, when a man is lying,

[26] *Yalkut on Genesis,* 57.
[27] Tr. *Ḥulin,* 94.

he estranges himself from truth, which is permanent, and prefers lying, which is passing and ephemeral. He will, therefore, be punished by dying before his proper time.

However, these moralists, rigorous as they are against uttering any falsehood even of the most innocuous kind, allow its use when it is uttered for the purpose of saving the dignity of man. In other words, one is permitted to make an untruthful statement in order to prevent a fellow man from being put to shame. We are told in the Talmud that once a number of selected members of the Jewish High Court were invited to discuss an important matter. When the meeting was opened, it was discovered that the gathering contained one more than they expected. When the president asked who came there uninvited, a leading scholar by the name of Samuel rose and said, "I am the man." He made the statement in order to save another man, whom he did not even know, from being insulted. It is, of course, unnecessary to say that a lie may be used in order to avoid any injury to oneself or to a fellow man. These are the only conditions when a falsehood may be uttered in any form according to Jewish ethics.

A story told by a great ethical teacher, Judah ben Asher, in his moral Testament to his children, will illustrate the great value placed by Jewish ethics upon truth as a preventative of all sin and transgression. A man who repented from his evil ways came to a rabbi asking for a penance for his sins, and the rabbi told him to abstain from lying. The man, whose repentance was not genuine, cheerfully accepted such light penance, thinking that he could still continue his former conduct and yet be forgiven. He proceeded to commit a theft. However, on the way to the place where the theft was to be accomplished, he bethought himself of the difficulty of carrying out his act and yet cling to the penance. Suppose, said he, if one were to meet me and ask me whither I was going. If I tell him the truth, I will be prevented from carrying out the act and even be punished. If

I lie, then I am not observing the imposed penance. He thus changed his mind and restrained himself from all evil acts and became an honest and righteous man.[27a]

29. Contentment

Virtue is defined by Aristotle as a state of character which serves as the incentive to moral action. It seems that by the term "state" he means to designate an inclination in the person's character to do certain actions which are good, and on the contrary, to avoid those which are declared bad. Aristotle, thus, like Judaism, lays more stress upon fixed traits in human character than on the calculation of the end of the results of actions. Such inclinations are many, and their sum constitutes the entire character. However, though all virtues tend toward good action, yet the extent of their influence is not equal. Some possess a wider range, and the range of other virtues is narrower. Several of the first class can be considered fundamental virtues, though their manifestation is primarily in the field of the negative, namely abstaining from wrong acts. As such they serve as a power restraining men from ever possessing too numerous common vices.

Such a virtue, emphasized more by Jewish ethics than many another system, is the one which for the want of a better name Judaism calls satisfaction with one's lot or position *(Someaḥ be-ḥelko)*. I say for want of a better name, for virtues akin to this one, bearing the name of self-control or temperance, were much emphasized by the Greek systems of ethics as well as by the modern ones. But those virtues, as they are interpreted by the ethical teachers, are limited in their range. Aristotle limits temperance primarily to restraint in pursuit of bodily pleasures. Similarly, the virtue of self-control that played a great part in Greek ethics was either limited to restraint of excesses of conduct, primarily

[27a] *Hebrew Ethical Wills*, ed. I. Abrahms, vol. II, p. 176.

as relating to the pursuit of pleasure, or to withholding from acts of violence. Plato's definition of self-control as a harmony of all parts of the soul is too general and possesses little concreteness.

The case is different with satisfaction with one's lot or contentment. It not only restrains men from pursuing vice or committing wrong acts, but is also conducive to peace of mind and restfulness of spirit. It thus not only restrains one from committing wrong actions, but also from having evil desires that arouse improper passions.

The Bible, in inculcating this virtue in a very practical way, emphasizes especially its value for the attainment of peace of mind. Thus, "Better is little with the fear of the Lord than great treasures and turmoil therewith" (Proverbs XV, 16), or "Better is a dry morsel and quietness therewith than a house full of feasting and strife" (Proverbs XVII, 1). There is expressed in these statements the view that excessive desire for pleasure or greed for money disturbs the mind, for treasures cannot be obtained without resulting in turmoil, either spiritual or otherwise. Likewise seldom does a great feast run off without strife, either actual or in thought and feeling.

The *Mishnah* gave a general ethical maxim aiming to guide man in conduct and the acquisition of the proper character. Taking satisfaction as its basis it says, "Who is rich? He who rejoices in his portion." [28] The richness referred to is not of material things, but a quietude of mind and the lack of disturbance from unsatisfied desires. We already noted above in a preceding section that a leading sage, Rabbi Eliezer, said, "That satisfaction with one's portion is the very basis of a moral life, expressing his view symbolically by saying that the surest way to ethical conduct is the possession of a good eye," i.e., an eye that does not serve as a means to arousing desire for all that its sees.

This view is also inculcated by the Talmud through a fine

[28] Tr. *Aboth*, Ch. IV, 1.

legendary story about Alexander the Great, the king who greatly impressed the peoples of the East by his conquests and became the subject of many legends. It is told that on one of his expeditions he reached the gates of Paradise and knocked at the door, demanding admission. He was told that this is the gate of the Lord; the righteous shall enter it (Psalm CXVIII, 20). Alexander declared that he was the king and should at least get something for remembrance. He was given an eye socket with an open eye in it. This he placed on one scale, and on the other scale much gold and silver. The scale with the eye upon it overbalanced the other. Alexander became desperate and piled all his gold and silver on that scale, but in vain; the eye was still heavier. Asking his sages for an explanation of this peculiar phenomenon, he was told that this was the eye of a man who was never satiated with what he had, but whose eye always looked for more. They advised him to close the eye and put some earth on it. He did so, whereupon the scale on which the eye lay immediately rose upward. The story concludes with these words, "Verily, it is written, 'the nether world (Gehinom) and destruction are never satiated so is the eye never satiated,'[29] (Proverbs XXVII, 20), until it is closed forever."

It must, however, be understood that the contentment urged by no means tends to lessen man's effort to improve his economic or social position by proper means. It merely teaches that man's mind should not be disturbed by the inability to rise higher and higher in honor, nor to be grieved by envy at observing the great wealth that other men possess; and certainly it warns against committing wrong acts in order to obtain more wealth or social honors. The practice of this virtue prevents one from such vices as envy and dishonesty in business, for it abolishes greed, since the one who possesses that virtue is devoid of the passion to strive for wealth. Furthermore, this virtue leads to moral purity, as one who is satisfied with his position holds in check improper

[29] Tr. *Tamid,* 32b.

desires and prevents them from taking root in his heart. Desire is the source of action. Not in vain is the commandment, "Thou shalt not covet or desire" considered by a Rabbinic moralist as the most important one in the Ten Commandments, for improper desires are the fountain head of transgressions and crimes. The verse, "A merry heart hath a continual feast" (Proverbs XV, 15), was skilfully interpreted by the Rabbis as meaning that the term *merry heart* does not refer to light-minded merriment, but designates a man who rejoices in his portion, whose peace of mind is not disturbed, and whose spirit is calm.[30] His life, then, can be compared to a feast where serenity reigns.

30. Mercy

The virtue of mercy can be considered one of the fundamental virtues from which many others stem. It is, like the preceding one, contentment and satisfaction with one's lot, a trait of character. In common parlance, we distinguish between the terms *mercy* and *pity*. The first, as a trait, has wider range of application and is more enduring, and serves as a means of doing good in many ways. The second denotes primarily a feeling aroused in us at the sight of suffering experienced by our fellow men.

The Bible mainly uses the terms *Raḥamim*, which is usually translated as *mercy*, and *Ḥemlah*, which is translated as *pity* or *compassion*. That Judaism places high value on this virtue is unnecessary to stress for, as is known, mercy is a leading attribute of God who is the archetype of morality. In the list of divine attributes of God given in Exodus XXXIV, 6, 7, "merciful and gracious" are given as the first of God's attributes, and God's mercy is referred to numerous times in the Old Testament. This leading attribute of God stems or rather emanates from His fundamental relation to the world and man. He is the Creator and the Father of all being.

[30] Tr. *Sanhedrin*, 101a.

Mercy is, therefore, a kind of emanation from His very being and is as permanent as a father's mercy for his children, which is hardly distinguished from love. In fact, the Psalmist says, "Like as a father hath compassion upon his children, so hath the Lord compassion upon them that fear Him." (Psalm CIII, 13). It is, of course, true that the object of mercy may be, in a way, inferior to the one who exercises that mercy, especially man as compared to God, yet it is not true that mercy differs in essence from love or kindness, as some ethicists aver. From the Jewish point of view mercy is saturated with love, and divine mercy is identical with divine love just as a father's mercy is not different from his love.

Inasmuch as the basis of Jewish ethics is the striving to be like God, it follows that man must make mercy a leading trait of his character. Hence, the Jewish ethical teachings embodied in the Talmud constantly reiterate the statement, "Just as He is merciful, so shalt thou, man, be merciful." It follows also, as pointed out, that human mercy must be saturated with love just as is divine mercy; in other words, man must be permeated with the desire to do good. The source of mercy and the fact that Judaism makes no distinction between mercy and pity also do away with the selfish aspect of pity as presented by numerous moralists, especially the English. They say that pity for the sufferer arises from self-pity, for the onlooker pictures himself as being in the same position and, therefore, his pity is aroused. We certainly cannot apply such a presentation to God. Consequently, the Jewish view of mercy, whether as a divine attribute or as a human trait of character, is wider, deeper, and is saturated with a love of man expressed in the desire to do good, especially to the needy.

31. Mercy to Animals

According to the Jewish view of mercy, it is the duty of man to display mercy to all men, Jews and non-Jews. The Bible repeatedly warns against any mistreatment of the stranger and distinctly says, "And thou shalt love him as thyself, for ye were strangers in the land of Egypt" (Leviticus XIX, 34), And just as God's mercy extends to all creatures, as it is said, "God is good to all, and His tender mercies are over all His works" (Psalm CXLV, 9), man's mercy must likewise extend to all creatures, including animals. The Torah therefore commands and prohibits the slaughter of a cow or ewe and its young in one day, or taking the mother bird with its young. These commandments aim, first, at preventing suffering even to animals and, second, to inculcate in the human heart the trait of mercy. But Jewish ethics goes farther and teaches that it is prohibited for a man to taste any food before he feeds his animals,[31] as these can neither provide their own food while in the stall, nor can they ask for it. They might, therefore, suffer hunger before man becomes aware of it. Their feeding, therefore, comes first.* There are numerous warnings in the Talmud and in Jewish ethical works against causing any suffering to animals (*Ẓaar Baale Ḥayyim).* We have selected the most extreme. In view of what was said, the statements of a writer on ethics that only under the teaching of Christianity pity has been extended to embrace also the animal world [32] seem a bit strange.

A story told in the *Midrash* will illustrate how highly Judaism values an act of mercy even when it is displayed only

[31] Tr. *Gittin,* 62.

* This Rabbinic ordinance is based again on the principle that man must act in likeness to God. The Rabbis derive their prohibition from the words of the Torah. It is said, "And I will give grass in thy field for thy cattle and thou shalt eat and be satisfied" (Deuteronomy XI, 15). We see, then, they say, that the food of the cattle is mentioned before the food of men, and this points the way to human action.

[32] Article "Pity," in *Encyclopaedia on Religion and Ethics,* Vol. X, 49.

toward animals. It tells that once when Moses was pasturing his sheep near Mt. Sinai, he noticed that a young lamb had run away from the flock. He ran after it in order to return it to the flock. When the lamb stopped to drink at a brook of water, Moses said, "Poor lamb, I did not know that you ran away in order to quench your thirst and consequently you are tired. I shall therefore carry you back to the flock in my arms." A voice from on high was then heard. "Moses, you displayed the quality of mercy in shepherding flocks belonging to men; I shall therefore appoint you as the shepherd of my own flock, the people of Israel." [33] The Rabbis teach us that no matter what fine qualities a man may possess, he does not deserve a position of leadership if he does not possess the quality of mercy in the highest degree. Only when he displays it in the finest manner as Moses did, does he deserve to become a leader of men.

No wonder that the trait of mercy was considered by Jewish teachers of ethics as a mark that distinguishes the character of the Jewish people, a kind of ethnic trait. They even said that any person who displays mercy to people proves thereby his descent from the seed of Abraham, and one who is not merciful denies thereby this same descent.[34] The statement is, of course, somewhat exaggerated, for it does not mean that doubt is cast upon the purity of his Jewish descent, but it connotes that this man fails to possess that typically Jewish trait of character. Since mercy is a leading attribute of God, and man in practicing the virtues acts in imitation of God, it follows, say the Rabbis, "If one displays mercy to his fellow men that God will have mercy upon him." [35]

Important as the trait of mercy is, it has some limitation and does not interfere with justice. Punishment of the wicked must take place, nor should a court decision be with-

[33] *Exodus Rabba,* Ch. II.
[34] Tr. *Betza,* 32.
[35] Palestinian Talmud, Tr. *Baba Kama,* Ch. VIII.

held even if it will cause suffering to one of the litigants. The law distinctly says, "Thou shalt not favor a poor man in his cause" (Exodus ch. XXIII, 3), a commandment greatly admired by moralists. Jewish law established the following maxim, "No mercy should divert the pronouncement of a legal decision," [36] as a rule for judges to act by. But excessive mercy is not countenanced by some ethical teachers, and is even considered one of three things that embitter a man's life,[37] for the world is full of suffering and a man who carries a feeling of mercy to excess will be constantly grieved.

[36] Tr. *Ketuboth*, 84.
[37] Tr. *Perjaḥim*, 113.

Chapter VI

SOCIAL VIRTUES

32. Gratitude

To have a feeling of thankfulness to the one who confers upon us some kind of benefit and to express this feeling to the benefactor, either by word or deed, is a fundamental social virtue. In its essence gratitude can be defined as the emotion of love felt by the recipient of kindness to him who bestowed the kindness. Judaism places a very high value upon the practice of this virtue. It, therefore, follows that Judaism, which places upon us a duty to love our fellow men in general, considers it a still greater duty to be grateful and express that gratefulness in one way or another to the benefactor.

Still, the Bible does not stress the practice of gratitude as much as it does the performance of other ethical acts. The reason for this lack of stress by the Bible is that it considers this virtue so fundamental to human nature that its practice needs no urging. Moreover, gratitude or thankfulness lies at the basis of the duty to observe all the commandments of God, which are often repeated in the Torah. In fact, God is the archetype of benefactors. He, the Creator of the world, the One who bestows upon us life, health, and all possible benefits, is the benefactor par excellence. Our worship of God, observing His commandments, and our prayers are all forms of expression of gratitude. Consequently, there is no need to place special emphasis upon the duty of expressing gratitude toward a fellow man.

A proof of the high value placed by the Bible upon gratitude is the commandment, "Thou shalt not abhor an Egyptian, for thou wert a stranger in his land" (Deuteronomy XXIII, 8). It means to say that in spite of the fact that the Egyptians enslaved and oppressed the Jews in many ways, yet as long as this suffering was tempered by some benefit, that benefit must be remembered, if not in a positive way, at least in a negative one. A Jew must restrain himself not only from doing harm, but must consider the Egyptian or any stranger like a human being, and if he needs help to offer it to him.

The magnitude of the benefit conferred should not serve, according to the view of the Jewish moralists, as the determining factor in either the feeling of gratitude or in its expression. It is, of course, understood that the amount of benefit bestowed affects the type of gratitude, but no matter how small the kindness displayed, one should always feel grateful and express the feeling. The sages therefore said, "One who partakes of a meal supplied by his friend, even if it was only a piece of bread dipped in salt, should feel grateful to him." [1] The statement means to tell us that the quantity of the kindness is of great importance, but the spirit accompanying it is still greater. In displaying kindness toward a fellow man, one is often liable to exaggerate the deed and exaggerate the demand from the recipient. Jewish ethicists warned against entertaining such feeling. They said, "If you did a favor to a friend, even if it was a great favor, look upon it as if it were a small one. On the other hand, if your friend did you a favor, though it might have been small, think of it as if it were a large one." [2] Such advice is given in order to avoid any ill feeling between benefactor and recipient that may result from some error in the expression of gratitude by the recipient or in its inception by the bestower of the favor. In case the expression of gratitude takes the form of returning a favor, it is advised that the returned favor should exceed the one received. They said, "If your

[1] *Tanna d' be Elijahu*, Ch. XVIII.
[2] *Aboth d' Rabbi Nathan*, Ch. XL, 1.

friend invited you to a meal consisting only of a dish of lentils, you invite him to a meal where meat will be served for he showed you kindness first." [3] This is another statement that stresses the spirit in which a favor or kindness is bestowed rather than its magnitude.

33. Ingratitude

And just as gratitude is valued highly by all systems of ethics, so its opposite, ingratitude, is condemned in harsh terms by all moralists. Shakespeare portrays the harshness of the vice of ingratitude by saying that it is greater than that of the winter wind. Speaking to the wind, He says, "Blow, blow, thou winter wind, thou art not so unkind as man's ingratitude," [4] meaning thereby that the sting and coldness of ingratitude penetrate deeper into the heart of man than does the winter wind penetrate into man's body. The Talmud says that ingratitude is as severe a transgression as denying the existence of God.[5] This statement, though expressed in an excessively exaggerated form, contains a deeper meaning. As pointed out previously, gratitude or thankfulness is the very basis of religious worship and obedience of God's commands. It follows, then, that when a man practices the vice of ingratitude, he simultaneously undermines the basis of man's relation to God, whether he does so consciously or unconsciously.

Jewish morality views the virtue of gratitude as one of the strongest bonds of social solidarity and as the basis of the proper appreciation of the advance of civilization through common effort and mutual help. Says Ben Zoma, "Observe how much toil and physical effort did Adam, the first man, undergo until he succeeded in tasting a piece of bread. He had to plow, sow, reap, thrash, winnow, knead the dough

[3] *Genesis Rabba,* Ch. XXXVIII.
[4] *As You Like It,* Act II, Scene 7.
[5] Palestinian Talmud, Tr. *Berakot,* Ch. IX.

and bake, and only then could he eat it. But I rise in the morning and find it all prepared for me. Similarly, in order to cover his nakedness with some kind of clothing, he had to shear the wool, whiten it, dye it, spin, weave, sew and then put it on. I find it all ready for me by the common effort of a group of laborers."[6] This short statement contains an embracive view of the entire history of human civilization and teaches us how thankful we should be for the help extended to each one of us by groups of fellow men.

From all that was said about the value placed upon gratitude by ethics in general, and Jewish ethics in particular, we infer that it is our duty to cultivate that virtue and practice it in our daily life.

34. Loving-Kindness

Out of the important trait of character which is the love of fellow men there stems a group of virtues that possess great value for social life. Their general name is loving-kindness, better known among Jews as *Gemillut Ḥassadim.* These virtues relate to various aspects of human life and affect all classes of society. The specific virtues will be discussed separately. For the present we want only to indicate the common characteristic of the group, as well as the importance attached to their practice, as expressed many times in the Bible, the Talmud, the Midrash, and other Jewish ethical works. This common characteristic is the possession of human kindness that values every man as an equal and preserves his dignity, and urges one to perform for any man any service of which he may be in need. Without this group of virtues, social life could not be carried on in any dignified way. Judaism had always valued this group of virtues in the highest degree, and had incorporated in the Mishnah, the book second in importance to the Torah, that loving-kind-

[6] Tr. *Berakot,* 61a.

ness is one of the three pillars which support the world.[7] It implies that without the practice of this group of virtues, the social world would not exist in the proper manner.

That Judaism considers the term *loving-kindness* as being more embracive than the term *charity* is indicated in a Talmudic statement regarding its wide scope. It says, "Loving-kindness exceeds the range of charity in three ways. Charity is dispensed by offering help only to poor people by presenting them with gifts of money or goods, and only when they are alive. Loving-kindness offers help to all people, rich or poor, and finally it can be dispensed to the dead." [8] From this statement we deduce that loving-kindness embraces the following form of exercising kindness toward fellow men: the practice of giving nonprofit loans to poor and rich alike when they are in need; the performance of personal service that relieves the pain of the sufferer or comforts him in his grief, such as visiting the sick, comforting the mourner, and the like; and finally such services as relate to preserving the dignity and honor of the dead.

35. Gemillut Ḥassadim

In the foregoing reference to the extension of nonprofit loans, we noted that one of the distinctions between charity proper and loving-kindness is that the latter can be extended also to the rich. In considering it on that account higher in value than the practice of charity, there is an emphasis on the importance of maintaining human quality when performing a moral action. In giving charity, no matter how much the giver attempts to remove from his heart any feeling of superiority, a modicum of that feeling always remains, and more than a modicum of feeling of inferiority remains in the heart of the receiver. But in extending loans to the rich or even to the poor the feeling of equality is maintained as long

[7] Tr. *Aboth,* Ch. I, 2.
[8] Tr. *Succah,* 19.

as the giver expects a return and the receiver hopes to give it.

For that very reason loving-kindness, while it includes a number of social virtues, was and usually is conceived in a narrower way. It is limited in use to the extension of loans to whoever is in need at the moment.

It is therefore said by ethical teachers of Judaism that the extension of a loan, especially to a poor man, is more important than charity. This practice is greatly lauded by them. They said that, by performing such an act, man is putting not only the borrower under obligation, but even God Himself. For it is written, "He who is gracious unto the poor lendeth unto the Lord" (Proverbs XIX, 17). Helping the poor graciously can be accomplished only through a loan.

These teachers, being anxious to guard the high morality of the act of a loan extension in time of need also took care to protect the borrower from grief and shame under certain conditions. A loan is, of course, to be repaid, but if the borrower suffers an unexpected reverse and cannot repay the debt for a time, his dignity must still be guarded. They therefore said, "If one loans money to his fellow man and he knows that he cannot repay him, it is forbidden for the lender to appear before him so as not to cause the borrower to experience a feeling of shame. It is told of a certain scholar that if he knew that his debtor was tarrying in a certain street, he avoided passing through that street at that time in order not to meet him even by chance." [9]

To buttress the value of loving-kindness and to emphasize the importance of its practice, the Talmud points to the exceptional role that this virtue occupies in the Torah. It is said, "Come and see that at the very beginning of the Torah we meet with an act of loving-kindness, and also at the end of the Torah we are told of such an act. And what is more, both acts were performed by God Himself. We read in the

[9] Tr. *Baba Metziah,* 75. Palestinian Talmud, Tr. *Tannet,* Ch. III, sec. 1.

Book of Genesis (III, 21) that after Adam and Eve ate of the fruit of the Tree of Knowledge, they began to feel shame at their nakedness as a result of their loss of innocence. God, though he reproached them severely for their sin of eating of the forbidden fruit, relieved them from this grievous sense of shame by making for them garments of skin and clothed them. Again, we are told in the Book of Deuteronomy (XXXIV, 5, 6) that when Moses ascended Mt. Nebo and died there in loneliness, God Himself performed the act of burial of his body.[10] The insertion of these two stories at the beginning and at the end of the Torah demonstrates that the Torah as a whole is saturated with the spirit of loving-kindness. It urges man to make its practice a leading aspect of his kindness, for thus he follows the fundamental principle of Jewish ethics, which bids man to act in imitation of the actions of God Himself.

That Judaism views the repayment of a loan as the prime duty of the borrower goes without saying. Failure to fulfill such a duty is considered a wickedness of the first magnitude. One who does not repay a debt when he is able to do so is called a *Rasha,* a wicked one, a name bestowed in the Bible on the person who commits a grave sin. It is said, "The wicked borroweth and payeth not" (Psalm XXXVII, 21). It is further said in the Mishnah, "One who borrows from a man and does not repay commits a sin as if he borrowed from the All-Present God." [11] What the sages intend to emphasize is that people should always bear in mind the Jewish view that God is the source of morality and any failure to live up to His ethical command is an offense against God. There is also a veiled threat in the statement. It seems to say, remember that man's life, health, and wealth are loans from God, and, therefore, beware, for if you do not fulfill your duty and pay your lender, God may call in his loan.

[10] Tr. *Sotah,* 14 a-b.
[11] Tr. *Aboth,* Ch. II, 9.

It is no wonder, then, that through the ages this particular form of loving-kindness was extensively practiced by the Jews. There was hardly a Jewish community, no matter how small it was, that did not have a *Gemillut Ḥassadim* office, whether it was maintained by the community at large or by a free loan association. To refuse a loan to a man in need was considered a sin. Even today, notwithstanding the many opportunities for borrowing offered by banks and public and private loan institutions, there is still room for the practice of this virtue in the genuine Jewish way.

36. The Jewish Conception of Charity

Charity, one of the leading phases of the group of virtues known as loving-kindness described above, is considered by Judaism to be of the greatest importance. The very name given it, *Ẓedakkah,* the primary meaning of which is justice, testifies to that. The name *charity,* though derived from the Latin word "caritas," which means love or affection, does not express the proper degree of importance of such action. Real love can only be between equals, but where the social or economic position of the persons differ, where one is the giver and the other the receiver, there is no equality, and the supposed love is more or less superficial. The case is different when the obligation is termed *justice;* the sting of inequality is removed; the giver of charity performs only an act of justice. The act is attributed in the Bible to God Himself a number of times, and though He is always the giver and man the receiver, yet His giving is called *Ẓedakkah,* justice, as it is only just for the good to give. Jewish ethical teachers, however, were aware of human frailty, knowing that even involuntarily the giver might still feel the inferiority of the receiver. They, therefore, warned time and again against entertaining such feelings. As a comment on the verse, "When thou seest the naked, cover him, and that thou hide not thyself from thine own flesh" (Isaiah LVIII, 7), the Rabbis said, "Consider his flesh as thy own flesh, that is, use all efforts to cover thy fellow man's flesh as if it were thy own." [12]

The value of giving succor to the needy is emphasized both in the Bible and in Rabbinic literature. The Bible continually stresses the merit of such action, and promises the highest reward, as it is said, "In the way of dispensing charity, there is life, and in the pathway thereof there is no death" (Proverbs XII, 28). The reason for this statement is that it is through these deeds of charity that man is remembered after death. The Rabbis, on their part, exalted the act of charity to the highest degree. They said, "The dispenser of charity thinks that he confers a favor upon the poor man, but in reality the favor the poor man confers upon the giver is greater since he provides him an opportunity for performing a good deed for which there is a great reward." [13] To make the matter more emphatic, they added, "When the poor man stands at your door, God stands at his right. Know then, when you help the poor, who is the one that stands at his right and guarantees your reward." [14] They went even further and said that the fulfillment of the precept of charity is as great as the fulfillment of all other *Mitzwot* (*Precept*).[15] This last statement must, of course, not be taken literally, for giving charity does not release one from the duty of fulfilling all other religious *Mitzwot*, though some modern Jews think so. It is merely a way of expressing the great value and merit of charity.

The Jewish laws of charity distinctly reflect the fundamental conception implied in the very name *Ẓedakkah*, especially the laws relating to the type of charity prescribed by the Bible. We know that the owner of fields and vineyards is obligated to allow the poor to share with him in

[12] *Leviticus Rabba*, Ch. XXXII.
[13] Ibid., Ch. XXXIV.
[14] Ibid.
[15] Tr. *Baba Batra*, 9a.

the reaping of the grain and in the vintage of the vineyard. The owner of the grain fields must leave *Peah,* i.e., some part of the grain to be reaped by the poor; also, he must allow them to gather the stalks that fall out of the hands of the reaper. This is known by the term *Leket,* i.e., gathering. Likewise, when a sheaf of grain is forgotten in the fields, the owner is not allowed to go back and bring it in the barn, but must leave it for the poor. This is called *Shikhah.* Similarly, the poor may gather the grapes or all other fruits that fall out of the vintner's hand, and are allowed to pick the grapes when they are not joined in clusters (Leviticus XIX, 9, 10; Deuteronomy XXIV, 19). All these gifts belong to the poor, and the owner cannot withhold them. He even has no right to select to whom to give the gifts. They must be shared by all the poor who come to the fields or gardens. Similarly, the owner cannot even dedicate his vineyard to the Temple once the gleanings that belong to the poor have become evident.[16] The reason for the limitiations of the rights of the owner is that these gifts are the property of the poor, and the owner has no right to say who should get them.

Besides the perennial dispensation of charity to the poor by any owner of fields and vineyards, the Bible also commands that every third year the poor be given a special tithe of all the products of the fields after they have been thrashed and gathered into the barn (Deuteronomy XXVI, 12). Taking into consideration the fact that agriculture was the principal occupation of the Jews in early times and their main source of sustenance, we can assume that the share of the poor in the national income of the people as a whole was considerable.

As the dispensing of charity is an important factor in ameliorating social life, for there are always many who need help, Jewish ethical teachers exalted the one who devotes his time and energy to persuading people to do their duty

[16] Tr. *Peah,* Ch. V, Mishanah 6; Ch. VII, Mishnah 8.

to charitable institutions. The Rabbis have declared, "Greater is the merit of the man who makes people give charity than the one who gives himself." [17] This statement must not be taken literally, and one must not be satisfied when others give and he himself does not.

Even persons who reside in a city temporarily must contribute to the charitable institutions of the places of their temporary abode, irrespective of what they contribute to the institutions of their permanent residence.[18] The Talmud laid down the following rules in such cases. One who resides in a city for thirty days must contribute to the public kitchen *(Tamḥu)* where the very poor get their daily bread. If he stays in a town for three months he must also contribute to the charity fund from which the poor get their weekly support *(Kupah);* if for six months, he must also contribute towards clothing the needy; if for nine months, toward the burial of the poor.[19] The Jewish view that no one is exempt from the duty of giving charity is emphatically expressed in a Rabbinic statement which says, "One who refuses to contribute his share to charity can be compared to an idolator." [20] This harsh statement is based upon the fundamental principle of Jewish ethics that was stressed above, repeated time and again in Rabbinic literature, that man is to act in likeness to God. Just as He is gracious and merciful, so must man be. It follows, then, that if one refuses to give charity, he undoubtedly has a wrong conception of the God of Israel, and his worship of God is as erroneous as that of an idolator.

37. Charity as an Act of Love

From such a conception it also follows that the dispensation of charity must be Godlike, accompanied by friendship

[17] Tr. *Baba Batra*, 9.
[18] Ibid., p. 8.
[19] Ibid.
[20] Ibid., 10.

and love for the poor. It must not be distributed in a cold manner as if one wished to get rid of an unpleasant task. Such a manner of giving charity is condemned by the sages, who said, "When one presents a poor man with the costliest gift but in an impersonal and cold manner, it is considered valueless as if he gave him nothing." [21]

Even a poor man who is himself a receiver of charity must also give some charity, for there is always one who is still poorer and needs help. It is, therefore, understood that charity is not measured by the amount one gives, provided it is according to the ability of the giver. In order to encourage poor people whose ability is very limited, charity was compared to a coat of mail, for the Bible depicts God attiring Himself with *Ẓedakkah* like with a coat of mail (Isaiah LIX, 17). The comment is accordingly made that just as in such a coat every link, no matter how small, adds to the strength of the coat, so does every amount, even a penny count when given to charity.[22] And when a poor man gives a penny for charity his reward is greater, for by this act he comes nearer to God.

As an illustration of this view there can serve us two stories in the Midrash. The first story tells of a rich man who was leading a large and fat ox to the Temple as an offering for a sacrifice. At a certain place, the ox stopped and refused to move. All efforts to make him continue his journey were of no avail. A poor man passed by, and observing the obstinacy of the ox, went out and brought a handful of grass and offered it to the ox, and thus succeeded in moving him from his place. Elijah then appeared to the rich man and said, "You undoubtedly think that the sacrifice you offered today was very pleasing to God. I want to tell you that the small offering of the poor man, a handful of grass, outweighed your offering, for it was all he had." [23]

[21] Tr. *Aboth d'Rabbi Nathan,* Ch. VIII, 1.
[22] Tr. *Baba Batra,* 9b.
[23] *Leviticus Rabba,* Ch. III.

The second story relates that a poor woman once brought to the Temple a handful of flour as an offering. The priest who received the gift mocked at the smallness of the offering. He was later reprimanded in a dream with the following words, "Mock not at the poor for their small gifts. These stem from the very soul and their offering is an offering of the soul." [24]

38. Charity and the Dignity of the Receiver

Great care must be taken in dispensing charity to preserve the dignity of the human personality so as not to cause the receiver grief or shame. The Bible says, "Happy is the one who considereth the poor" (Psalm XLI, 2). The sages interpret the word *considereth* in the sense of considering the dignity of the poor and said, "If one who is supposed to receive charity is the one who possesses dignity and is ready to suffer rather than to receive charity, devices should be used to make him accept it without losing his dignity. It is advisable to ask him casually whether he is in need of a loan. He will then accept it without feeling that he is a recipient of charity." [24a]

Another way to spare the receiver the feeling of inferiority is to dispense charity anonymously. In such a case, the receiver does not face his benefactor and is not placed in the role of an object of pity. The term for this form of dispensing charity is *Matan Besether* (giving in secret). This form is extolled by the Bible and by the Rabbis. It is said, "A gift in secret pacifieth anger" (Proverbs XXI, 14). The Rabbis interpreted this verse to mean that when a man offers charity anonymously, this deed pacifies the anger of God that he incurred on account of his transgression and obviates the punishment due him. The sages have gone even further in magnifying this form of charity, and said in their enthusi-

[24] Ibid.
[24a] Ibid., Ch. XXXIV.

astic manner of speech, which does not mind exaggeration, "He who gives charity secretly is even greater than Moses."[25] They proved their assertion homiletically as follows: Moses with all his greatness said, "I was in fear of the anger of and displeasure wherewith the Lord was wroth" (Deuteronomy IX, 19), while regarding charity given anonymously, it is said that it pacifieth anger.

We know that this form of *Ẓedakkah* became prevalent in Israel as early as the period of the Second Temple, for we are told that there were two separate rooms in the Temple building where two types of donations were deposited. One was called the chamber of secrecy where the pious people anonymously placed their money that was distributed to the poor weekly. The second chamber served as a depository for donations of vessels to be used in the Temple service. Every thirty days, this second chamber was opened and the collected vessels were examined. Those that could be used in the Temple service were consecrated, while those that could not be used were sold and the money was turned over to the Temple treasury.[26] Another source informs us that Jewish communities throughout the Diaspora followed the example of the Temple and established similar chambers for secret donations to charity.[27] The same custom was practiced throughout the ages up to modern times in all Jewish synagogues, where a box with a sign reading *Matan Besether* (anonymous gift) was placed in the corridor.

However, more indicative even than these practices of the high value placed by Jewish moralists on *Matan Besether* are the actions of certain scholars in this matter. We are told in the Talmud that a certain scholar by the name of Mar-Ukbah would go to the home of a poor neighbor early every morning, and would put four dinars under the door and depart without being seen. One day Mar-Ukbah, ac-

[25] *Baba Batra,* p. 8.
[26] Tr. *Shekalim,* Ch. V, Mishanah 6.
[27] *Tosefta Shekalim,* Ch. II, 16.

companied by his wife, happened to come on his mission later than usual. At that time, the poor man was awake and watching for his benefactor. Ukbah and his wife rushed away, but the poor man ran after them. To escape detection the pair hid in an oven that had been heated some time before and, of course, the man did not follow them. These people were ready to suffer the heat and even risk their lives in order not to cause the receiver of their charity any shame. Another scholar, Rabbi Abba, used to tie an amount of money in a scarf and walk among the poor and throw it over his back so that they would take the money without facing him.[28] We see from such actions to what extent the sages went in order to avoid grief or shame to their fellow men.

39. The Importance of Keeping Promises

Much warning was given by Jewish moralists throughout the ages against cheating in charity, whether on the part of the giver or the receiver. If one announces a donation and does not pay it, he will ultimately lose the sum promised and even more as punishment for the sin. Again, if one does not need charity and takes it, he is threatened with punishment of the type called measure for measure, that is, he will not depart from this world until he becomes poor and actually needs charity.[29] Again, in the maxim, "The house which is not open for collectors of charity or for the poor will be open for the physician," is a warning against those who abstain from giving charity. The teachers well knew human frailty in the reluctance to part with money; hence these threats of punishment, which are not as frequent in regard to the observance of other precepts.

[28] Tr. *Ketuboth,* p. 67.
[29] Ibid., p. 68a.

40. Distribution of Charity According to Need

How large should the amount of charity be? Should it be limited to a sum sufficient to take care of the essential needs of the receiver or should it occasionally be expanded to provide the receiver with some luxuries? The sages of Israel speak definitely on the subject. As guardians of the dignity of human personality, they took care to point out that even in the case of a person in need of help, his dignity must be preserved to the extent that the recipient enjoyed in better days. They quoted the Biblical verse regarding a poor man, "Thou shalt surely open thy hand unto him, and thou shalt surely lend him sufficient for his need in that which he wanteth" (Deuteronomy XV, 8). They observed that the commandment stresses his need and his want, and from such stress it is to be concluded that the need of the receiver of charity is to be provided according to his standard of living in better days. If a man was used to certain luxuries, he should be provided with them even if he has recourse to charity. In certain cases, when a man of probity and integrity who held a high social position, and who used to travel in the streets on horseback or even had a slave marching before him to facilitate his making his way on the crowded streets, is reduced to receiving charity, he is to be provided with the same luxuries. The story of the action of the famous sage, Hillel, is told as an illustration. Hillel once met a poor man of high quality and character who had seen better days and was used to such luxuries. He provided him with a horse to ride upon and a servant to march before him. Once when no servant could be found Hillel performed the service himself.[30]

Such service to the poor is, of course, exceptional and cannot come under a common rule. Nor can we take the extreme declaration of the sages in this regard as mandatory either upon individuals or representatives of charitable in-

[30] Ibid., p. 67.

stitutions. But they teach us the spirit and manner in which charity should be distributed. By no means should it be limited to primary necessities, but should include provision of certain comforts in proportion to what the receiver was accustomed to in better days. The rule quoted above, which looks upon the needs of the receiver as needs of the donor, should prevail.

Small wonder, then, that the collection and distribution of charity was considered the most important function of Jewish communities and the prime care of communal leaders through the ages. No matter how small a Jewish community was, it was not lacking in one or more charitable institutions. These were probably less methodically organized than in modern times, but what they lacked in mechanical organization, they made up in personal contact and warmth of attitude.

This attitude should by all means be preserved in modern times to whatever degree possible. It is true that in present-day life when communal affairs are organized on a large scale and charitable institutions are administered like any large business with directors, assistants, and numerous clerks, and the number of people who apply for help is large, it is almost impossible to maintain the attitude of friendliness and personal interest in the needs of the receiver. Still, all efforts should be made to make that attitude prevail even in public institutions by introducing a courteous and friendly relation between the distributors of charity and the needy receivers.

Greater effort should also be made to cultivate that attitude in private charity. We must always remember that the high value placed by Judaism on charity takes into account not only the actual giving, but also the way and manner in which it is given.

41. Hospitality

We know that the extension of hospitality to strangers is, among the Semitic peoples, one of the most important virtues, and is, of course, valued very highly by Judaism. The pleading of the patriarch, Abraham, to the three wayfarers whom he noticed at a distance that they should not pass him by, but should allow him to offer them hospitality, and the great efforts he made to please them as told in Genesis XVIII, 1–8, prove how deeply that virtue was rooted in the heart of the fathers of our nation. And the practice of this virtue also struck deep roots in the soil of Jewish life throughout the ages, for the sons of our people knew the tribulations of wandering and valued the attempt to alleviate its misery.

There is actually no special precept in the Pentateuch commanding the practice of hospitality as such. The reason for the lack of special precept is that Jews took the practice of hospitality as a matter of fact, stemming from a racial trait. The Bible was not satisfied with the command merely to extend hospitality to the stranger, but insists rather on an all-embracive relation to him, a relation that is saturated with warmth and exalted by placing value on his dignity. It therefore placed the relation on a more inclusive basis of which hospitality is only a phase. It demands love for the stranger and says, "And thou shalt love him as thyself, for ye were strangers in the land of Egypt" (Leviticus XIX, 34). The same admonition is repeated in Deuteronomy X, 19, "And ye shall love the stranger, for ye were strangers in the land of Egypt." It is not pity that is demanded, but love, which places the stranger on an equal footing with oneself, irrespective of his economic status, or manner of appearance, or degree of mental power. He is to be loved as a person. The repeated reminder to the Jews that they, too, were strangers is employed in this commandment as a means of inculcating that virtue in their hearts. The Bible is aware of how difficult it is for men to rise to a high level of ethical conduct—to love the stranger. It therefore adds the reminder of their own suffering at the hands of strangers and their neglect by them, in order to arouse the Jew to act well toward a stranger in the spirit of this commandment.

The sages who influenced and guided Jewish life through the ages, however, paid attention to the humbler phase of the general injunction, to love a stranger, namely, to hospitality, and exalted its value to a high degree. A Talmudic statement says, "Receiving and accommodating strangers in their need takes precedence to meeting the *Shekinah,* i.e., the Divine Presence itself." They based the statement on the action of Abraham to whom God revealed Himself (Genesis XVIII, 1), but who, on seeing the strangers passing at a distance, rushed out to meet them.[31] Hospitality is also counted among the ten precepts *(Mitzwot),* the reward for whose performance is so great that only its interest is paid during man's life in this world, while the capital, the real reward, is preserved for the hereafter.[32] One of the sages compared the value of extending hospitality to that of offering sacrifices, saying, "In the time when the Temple was in existence, men brought sacrifices in order that their sins be forgiven. In later times, the table in the house at which strangers in need are served food and drink serves in the same capacity as the altar, as a means for obtaining forgiveness for sins.[33]

In post-Talmudic works, the virtue of extending hospitality is likewise glorified and the duty of its practice repeatedly urged. One of the moralists compares the offering of hospitality to the planting of a tree, the beginnings of which are small, but which grows and develops into good fruit. Hospitality may consist of a night's lodging or the offer of a meal or two, yet its fruits are valuable for they foster kind-

[31] Tr. *Sabbath,* 127.
[32] Tr. *Peah,* Ch. I, Mishnah 1.
[33] Tr. *Berakoth,* 55.

ness, friendship, and love between man and man.[34] Another moralist stresses the extent of sacrifice one is to make in order to comfort the weary wanderer. Commenting on the words of Isaiah when he urges the people to perform good deeds instead of declaring a fast-day, saying, "Is it not preferable to God to break thy bread with the hungry and that thou bring the poor that are cast out to thy house" (Isaiah LVIII, 7), the moralist points to the lesson that we can draw from the words of the prophet. Isaiah, says he, does not employ the words, "Give thy bread," but "break thy bread," which means that even if you have only one bread, break it and give a half to the hungry. Again, says he, the prophet says, "Bring the poor to thy house" and not "take them in," which means that one must not wait until the poor come begging for shelter, but one must go out and find them and bring them into the house.[35]

42. Behavior of the Host and of the Guest

Other moral teachers insisted that attention should be paid not only to the actual offering of hospitality but also to the refined ways of such offering. Says one, "When you entertain a stranger, avoid looking at him when he eats, for he may be hungry and will be embarrassed by displaying his eagerness for food, and will feel ashamed by your noticing it." [36] Another one issues a warning to scholars, saying, "Do not start a scholarly discussion with a stranger whom you feed or give lodging to unless you are sure that he possesses this kind of knowledge, otherwise you may put him to shame.[37] A third one says it is the duty to receive a traveler with friendliness, not only by offering him food and drink, but also, if necessary, to guide his way in a strange

[34] Eliezer of Worms, in his book *Rokeaḥ*.

[35] Bahya ben Asher in his ethical work, *Kad ha-Kemaḥ*.

[36] Testament of Rabbi Eliezer the Great in *Ethical Wills*, ed. Abrahams, Vol. I, 41.

[37] *Book of the Pious*, sec. III, 14.

environment by proper advice given smilingly and with the expression of friendship.[38]

Thus far, Jewish ethics admonishes the host anent his duties, but it also pays attention to the duties of the guest. With keen psychological observation, it distinguishes between two types of guests, the ungrateful and the grateful. The ungrateful one says, "What has the host done for me? He added a few spoons of soup or a few pieces of bread for my sake, but primarily he took care of himself and family." The grateful guest says, "All preparations for this meal or meals were made on my account." [39]

This statement is made by Ben Zoma, a leading scholar of the second generation of *Tannaim* and a contemporary of the great Akiba. We quoted another statement of his regarding the feeling of gratitude one is to entertain for the benefit he derives from social life. It seems that this last statement of Ben Zoma about the good guest intends to express a deeper thought than the plain meaning that the words imply. Thus, if one is to be grateful to the host who provides him with some comfort, how much more grateful should he feel toward God, the great Host, the Creator of the world, who provides all of us with so many of the things we need and at whose great table we are all guests. From this feeling follows also the duty of offering hospitality to the one who is in need of it, for nothing is as pleasing to God as when man attempts to imitate Him in his relation with his fellow men.

Owing to this exaltation of hospitality, it quickly became a leading feature of Jewish social life throughout the generations. There was not a Jewish community that did not have a hospice for strangers where all their needs were taken care of. There was hardly a Jewish family in times gone by that did not invite a guest for the Sabbath. Suffice it to say that the famous organization known as *Hias* (He-

[38] Bahya ben Asher in his ethical work, *Kad ha-Kemah*, Art. *Ger*.
[39] Tr. *Berakoth*, 58.

brew Immigrant Aid Society), which saved thousands of immigrants abroad and provided not only shelter and food for tens of thousands of immigrants, but also helped them to adjust themselves in a new country, had its origin in the modest hospice known as *Hachnasat Orḥim.*

Times have changed and with them all ways of life, including the older form of extending hospitality. Yet there are still enough opportunities to practice that age-hallowed Jewish virtue. What is more, in the modern world with its overpopulated cities and the noisy life prevalent in them, in which each one looks out primarily for himself and cares little for his fellow men, the stranger may be in greater need of hospitality than is a traveler in the desert. True, his need may not be for food and drink or even lodging, as such things are often provided by charitable institutions, yet his need is keen. He feels great loneliness in the tumultuous crowd where everyone passes him by with a cold look. He longs for a warm greeting, for a friendly smile, and interest in his situation. It was a prevalent Jewish custom to greet every stranger by extending the hand and uttering the words *Shalom Aleikem,* peace be with you. Frequently this formal greeting led to the establishment of friendly relations and to the extension of help, whether in the form of guidance in the way of adjustment to the new environment or any other assistance. Such a form of extending hospitality is as valuable as that of offering food and lodging. It is high time that the old Jewish custom of greeting every stranger with the traditional *Shalom Aleikem* be revived, that we not be satisfied with merely uttering the words, but endeavor to help the stranger attain peace of mind by lightening the burden of his loneliness.

43. Visiting the Sick

We have seen how far Jewish ethics is concerned with the welfare and dignity of fellow men, and how it repeats the injunctions to cultivate those virtues that urge one to come to the assistance of his fellow man who is in need either of financial help or service. It follows, of course, that it places great value on offering service to the sick no matter of what station. Visiting the sick in order to cheer and comfort them and to raise their spirits is therefore constantly enjoined by all ethical teachers of Israel. Like hospitality, this virtue is counted among the more important ones, the practice of which earns for a man the complete reward not only in the world to come, for, as stated, whatever reward he may get during his life is considered only as the interest on this good deed.

Repeated admonition by Jewish moralists is given to practice this virtue, as are warnings not to neglect it. The great Akiba even said that one who does not visit the sick commits a grave offense, almost comparable to murder,[40] for by his neglect to give comfort, he contributes to the aggravation of the disease, which may lead to death. These ethicists were not physicians, but they had a fair knowledge of human psychology and of the way a sick man reacts when given kind attention. They knew that a visit by a friend who shows interest in his state raises the power of resistance of the sick person and enables him to put up a stronger fight for recovery. They put this thought in an adage, saying, "Anyone who visits a sick person takes away a sixtieth part of his sickness," meaning thereby that the visit contributes toward the sick person's recovery.[41]

These teachers even offered advice on the way and manner in which the visits should take place. Said one, "When you visit a sick person do not overstay if his disease is serious, for in such a case he may be embarrassed by comparing his state with yours and will not display his suffering." He further advised, "When you go in to see a sick person come with a smile and a cheerful mien, for he scans the faces of

[40] Tr. *Nedarim,* 40.
[41] Bahya ben Asher, Ibid., 39.

the visitors to gauge their view of his state."[42] These Mediaeval Rabbis possessed much intuitive psychology to understand that whether the patient is in need or not, a little present, whether it be flowers or some other thing, is a symbol of concern for his state of health that buoys the spirit of the sufferer.

Another teacher taught, "When two people are sick, and one is rich and the other poor, it is the duty to visit the poor one, for many will visit the rich person, while few will visit the poor one.[43] Be then of the few to visit the poor."

Great emphasis was therefore placed by these moralists upon the duty of visiting the sick and exempted no one from fulfilling it, no matter what his social or scholarly status might be. We are told in the Talmud that in early times it was the custom in Jewish communities, when a member fell sick, to make a public declaration of the case and to call upon every one to visit the invalid.[44] In later times, up to the end of the last century, there was in almost every Jewish community, especially in smaller towns where hospital facilities were limited or not to be had at all, a special society by the name of *Bikkur Ḥolim* (visiting the sick), which undertook to offer comfort to the sick and help them recover. There was hardly a member of the community who did not belong to it. In some of the communities, since the office of nurses was unknown, there existed a special branch of the general society that devoted itself to the task of coming to the house of the sick at night in order to relieve the fatigued family from watching the patient during the night. It bore the name of *Linat Haẓedek* (righteous lodging).

Times have changed and the burden of the sick is much lightened by the modern improvements and devices of the great hospitals and their excellent nursing service, yet nothing can take the place of the cheer and comfort that the

[42] Testament of Eliezer the Great, Ibid.
[43] *Book of the Pious,* sec. II, 61.
[44] Palestinian Talmud, Tr. *Peah,* Ch. I, sec. I.

visit of a friend or an acquaintance can bring. The value of a visit to the bedside of a patient is still great and the practice of the virtue is still meritorious.

44. Comforting Mourners

We quoted above that loving-kindness is more embracive than charity, for while charity is limited to helping the poor, loving-kindness offers help to the rich and poor alike, as it also includes acts of personal service of which the rich may be in need as well as the poor. It follows therefore that comforting the mourners is, like visiting the sick, an act of loving-kindness and is accordingly valued highly by Jewish ethics.

There is, however, no special precept in the Bible enjoining the practice of this virtue. It is true that it is said in the Book of Ecclesiastes (VII, 2), "It is better to go to the house of the mourner than to the house of feasting." But this is only an advice and not a command. The reason for the neglect to enjoin this practice is similar to the one stated by us in regard to hospitality, for comforting the mourners, like the former, also stems from a racial trait. It was practiced in Israel as well as among other Semitic peoples from time immemorial as evident from the story of Job.

We read in that book that, "When Job's three friends heard of the evil that was come upon him, they came every one from his own place to "bemoan him and to comfort him" (II, 11). The use of the different words "bemoan" and "comfort" shows that they came for a double purpose, to express grief at his being smitten "with sore boils from the sole of his foot even unto the crown," and to comfort him in his mournings at the death of his children. We are also told (verse 13) that "they sat down with him on the ground seven days and seven nights," which shows clearly that comfort in mourning was the important purpose the friends came for, as this form of mourning is the very one practiced through the ages.

More attention was paid to this kind deed by the sages of the Talmud and Midrash. They even ascribed its practice euphemistically to God Himself, deriving such assumption from the verse in Genesis XXV, 11, "And it came to pass after the death of Abraham that God blessed Isaac his son." The fact that the verse states that this blessing took place immediately after the death of his father seemed, according to them, to tell that God revealed Himself to Isaac at that time and blessed him in order to offer some comfort to the mourning son.[45] This remark is made in order to inculcate in the hearts of men the importance of the practice of this virtuous act. Emphasis is also laid on the social value of this virtue and it said, "Comforting mourners brings good to the world," meaning the human world.[46] Advice is also offered as to the way and time such comfort should be extended. It is said, "Do not comfort the mourner in the hour when his dead lies before him,"[47] that is before burial when his grief is at its highest point. Another sage said, "The reward of a visit to a mourner's house is silence,"[48] meaning that the reward one receives for this act is not for his comforting speech but for his silence in the company of the mourner. The silence expresses deeper sympathy and greater participation in his grief.

As mentioned above, the practice of this good deed in Jewry dates from very early times. A number of statements in the Talmud and also in post-Talmudic Midrashim testify to its extent and to the great value placed upon it by the people as a whole. We are told in the Mishnah, "All people who entered the Temple Mount entered on the right side and on leaving turned to the left, but a mourner turned im-

[45] Tr. *Sotah,* 14.
[46] *Aboth d'Rabbi Nathan,* Ch. XXXIX.
[47] Tr. Aboth, Ch. IV, Mishnah 18.
[48] Tr. *Berakoth,* 6b.

mediately to the left. He was asked, why do you enter on the left? He answered, because I am a mourner. All the people around him called out, "God who dwelleth in this Temple shall comfort you." [49] In those times the performance of this deed was a public affair, and in Judean cities the people who accompanied the funeral on the return from the cemetery formed themselves in two rows and the mourners passed between them while comfort was offered.

Later, customs changed. In one Midrashic source, which hails from Palestine, we are told that the mourners used to repair after the burial to the synagogue, and the people that were there sat for a while with them on the ground expressing their condolence "in order to discharge their duty of performing an act of loving-kindness." [50] Another source limits the visit of the mourners to the Sabbath. It says that after the morning service was completed, the mourners left the synagogue, tarried for a time in the entrance, where they recited a special mourner's benediction and afterwards the *Kaddish,* while the people stood around silently expressing their participation in the mourners' grief.[51]

From the beginning of the Middle Ages the practice was and is still continued in orthodox synagogues that the mourner repairs on the eve of the Sabbath during the week of mourning to the synagogue, but stays in the lobby until the introductory part of the service known as *Kabbalat Shabbat* (Reception of the Sabbath) ends with the recitation of the last verse of the hymn, *Lekho Dodi.* The cantor then calls upon the people to meet the mourner and they turn to face him. All these customs were introduced in order to afford as many people as possible the opportunity to participate in an act of loving-kindness.

The proper way, however, to discharge this duty of offering comfort to mourners is by visiting them in their homes

[49] Tr. *Midoth,* Ch. II, Mishnah 2.
[50] *Midrash Pirke d'Rabbi Eliezer,* Ch. XVII, 12.
[51] *Maseket Sofrim,* Ch. XIX, Mishnah 12.

during the week of mourning and showing participation in their grief. So highly did the Rabbis value such visits that they even allowed one to perform this act, though reluctantly, even on the Sabbath, the day when the mourner himself is freed from laws and customs relevant to the state of mourning.

Chapter VII

VIRTUES AND VICES THAT AFFECT THE DIGNITY OF MAN

45. Insult

We noted above the great emphasis that Jewish ethics lays upon the dignity of man and its preservation. It is from this view that there followed a number of rules of conduct; some deal with prohibitions not to act in any way that directly or indirectly lowers that dignity and causes grievance or injury. Others, on the other hand, commend those actions which help fellow men in time of need, with strong admonitions to preserve human dignity in such circumstances.

Of the vices included in this group, insulting a fellow man in public is considered a very severe moral offense. In Talmudic sources, the act is described by the effect it has upon the one who is thus insulted, namely that his face goes white from such mortification. The act is therefore called "whitening the face of a fellow man in public." It is considered an exceptionally grave moral sin by Jewish sages, and they have gone to extremes in warning against such a practice. They compared it in gravity to murder. "The murderer," said they, "sheds the blood of his fellow man, and likewise the one who insults his fellow man causes a temporary recession of the blood in the face of the one who is insulted. The redness passes and whiteness succeeds." [1] The statement is of course metaphorical, but the underlying thought is that a public insult to a man lowers his dignity and undermines his self-esteem. It thus causes a deep injury to the soul of the man from which he may never recover.

[1] Tr. *Baba Metziah*, 58.

Since, in Judaism, there is no distinction between a religious sin and a moral transgression, both being deviations from the standard of conduct commanded by God, insulting a fellow man is considered among the gravest of sins. According to the view of some sages, the man who commits such an action is denied participation in the world to come, in which every Jew as well as righteous non-Jews are supposed to share.[2]

Another moralist has gone further and said, "It is prescribed for a man even to suffer death rather than to insult or cause shame to a fellow man."[3] The statement is based on the story of Tamar (Genesis XXXVIII, 25–26), who though she was about to be burned for adultery by the decree of her father-in-law who was the guilty person, yet did not reveal his name publicly, but informed him by means of a sign that he was to bear the guilt.

And so careful were the Rabbis to preserve human dignity that they even warned against mere intent to insult a fellow man, though the actual insult was not carried out. The example in this case is as follows. A man may get used to a derogatory nickname and as a rule is not fully conscious of the insult implied by that nickname, yet when the name is applied to him it is considered a sin, for there is the intention on the part of the one who calls him by that name to insult him. Similarly, we are warned not to say to a penitent whose present conduct is flawless, "Remember your former actions," for though the penitent himself may in his heart be ashamed of his former conduct and other people may also know of it, the reminder will aggravate that shame.[4]

There is no doubt that there is much exaggeration in such statements and that their aim is to deter people from committing such acts in greater or lesser degree. Since the commission of such acts is frequent in social life and causes for

[2] Tr. *Aboth,* Ch. III, 11.
[3] Tr. *Baba Metziah,* 59.
[4] Ibid., 58.

such commissions are numerous, a severe warning against it was deemed necessary. In addition, the psychological factor is to be taken account of. Men usually place little value on words and do not calculate the evil effects of a wrong utterance. Hence, the repeated warnings in Jewish ethical literature against insulting fellow men in public and the severe divine punishment promised for such transgression. In reality, the injurious effects of an insult may be more severe than a physical attack, for one may more easily recover from the latter while the result of the former, as said, may undermine self-confidence and thus leave a lasting impression upon the soul.

A story related in the Talmud and quoted by us above illustrates the extreme carefulness exercised by the Rabbis in avoiding the slightest insult even indirectly. A pious scholar took the shame upon himself in order to save an unknown scholar who acted improperly by coming uninvited to the high court session. He felt that he could bear the shame more easily than the unknown one whose reputation was not as well established as his.

A Mediaeval moralist goes even further and says that when one happens to hear a scholar expounding Biblical verse or a passage in the Talmud, but finds some flaw in the explanation, he must not express his opinion publicly for he may cause the scholar shame. The same moralist warns employers of servants, whether men or women, Jews or non-Jews, to be especially careful not to offer them the slightest insult, for because of their inability to retaliate, their suffering is severe and their grief deep.[5]

46. Admonition as a Duty

Insulting a fellow man is, as stated, a grave moral transgression when done in public, but chiding and admonishing him not to stray from the right path of conduct is, on the

[5] *Book of the Pious,* sec. 137, 784.

contrary, considered an important virtue. It is, of course, understood that the admonition must be given privately, for otherwise it may result in shaming the friend. The purpose of performing this act of admonition is to prevent a man from suffering insult, and aims at preserving his dignity. Were the man to persevere in the kind of conduct for which he is chided by his friend, he would ultimately lose his dignity by being insulted, and often even suffer injury and great loss. And as Judaism considers every Jew responsible in a degree for the welfare and conduct of fellow Jews, as it is stated, "All Israel are responsible for one another," admonition is considered a duty and its performance is repeatedly urged in the Bible and by the sages.

The importance of performing the duty of admonition is clearly expressed in the Biblical commandment, "Thou shalt admonish thy fellow man so that thou not bear sin for him" (Leviticus XIX, 17). It means to warn the one who sees his fellow man committing a wrong act and does not admonish him to refrain from repeating or performing a similar one that his silence in this matter will be considered a sin.

The Book of Proverbs does not tire of urging the duty of admonition and uses various devices to impress its importance and social value. As a general statement it declares, "Open reproof is better than secret love" (Proverbs XXVII, 5), namely, let no one refrain from reproving his friend whom he loves, for such act will bring the friend more good in life than the love that is borne. It promises reward to those who undertake such act as, "To them that admonish, delight and blessing shall come upon them" (XXIV, 25), and urges one not to refrain from reproving his fellow man, "For he that rebuketh a man shall in the end find more favor than he that flatters with the tongue" (XXVIII, 23).

The Rabbis, having a fair knowledge of human psychology, well understood that admonition possesses value and that the attempt to guide fellow men in moral conduct can be effective only when there is co-operation on the part of the recipient of the admonition. They, therefore, urged men to cultivate the ability to take reproof or censure in a calm manner and to improve their ways. They even included such an ability among the virtues that a man should acquire saying, "A liking to listen calmly and attentively to reproof and censure when one happens to commit an improper act will ultimately bring him to choose the right path of conduct." In another place it says, "As long as censure and admonition are effective in social life, there will be peace and comfort in life." [6] They further emphasize the value of this virtue by observing that a kind of love between friends that restrains the expression of mutual censure can really not be called true love or even friendship.[7]

47. Limitations of Admonition

As a result of the demand for co-operation on the part of the recipient of the censure, namely willingness to listen to reproof, they said that when one is certain that his admonition will not be heeded, it is best that he should not offer it.[8] These moralists, however, insisted that the uselessness of the reproach should not merely be assumed but must be proved by evident signs. On the nature of this reproof there are various opinions. One sage asserted that the reprover must continue his admonition until the recipient makes a move to strike him. Another one said that he need not go so far, that the uttering of a curse by the recipient frees the reprover from his duty, and a third one averred that a mere rebuke suffices for desistance.[9]

These statements may seem to us somewhat extreme in demanding that one fulfill his duty of admonition to his fellow men not to stray from the right path of conduct until

[6] Tr. *Tamid,* 28.
[7] *Genesis Rabba,* Ch. XLIV.
[8] Tr. *Yebamot,* 65.
[9] Tr. *Erukin,* 16.

he meets strong resistance, expressed in rebuke, or curses, or even attack. They do, though, prove the high value these ethicists placed upon morality, and especially on the attempt that must be made to make morality prevail in social life. They taught that one must assume responsibility for the acts of his fellow men and must make all effort to prevent his following the wrong way of life. Hence the insistance on the duty of admonition.

There are certain limitations to admonition. First, that the reproof must be couched in proper language. It must not contain rebukes or derogatory words that may shame the recipient; second, that the admonition must be given, as said, privately, and not in the presence of others. Under such circumstances, the duty prescribed by the Torah to admonish a friend not to follow the wrong path of conduct really serves as an incentive for the moral improvement of the admonisher or censor himself. The idea of such incentive is very convincingly presented by an 18th-century Jewish moralist. He says, "A man cannot pronounce judgment upon the proper form and shape of the physical organs of his body, for his vision of himself is limited to the frontal part of his body, and he cannot see his own back, and if any injury occurred to any part of his back, he must have the help of his fellow men to tell him about it. The other man sees his body from all sides. Similarly, man cannot pronounce complete moral judgment upon himself as he is not fully conscious of the flaws in his own conduct. It is only when he judges his friend that he notices all the flaws. The Torah, therefore, says he, makes it a duty to admonish your fellow men. 'Thou shalt surely admonish your neighbor and not bear sin because of him.'" This precept, according to our ethicist, means to say that, when a man attempts to rebuke his neighbor or friend for moral flaws that he notes in him, he will, as a result, examine himself first lest he possess the same flaws, and will thus avoid sin; or, in the language of the Bible, not bear himself the sin which he sees in his friend.[10] Only after such severe examination of himself does he have the right to admonish others. The sages of the Talmud put this warning in a short aphorism which reads, "Ornament yourself morally and then you will attempt to ornament others." [11]

The philosopher Spinoza who, on the whole, was estranged from Judaism, yet echoes the Jewish spirit in regard to admonition, and even gives it a wider scope. He says, "A man who desires to help others by counsel will refrain from dwelling too much on men's faults and will speak but sparingly of human weakness. But he will speak at large of man's virtue and power and the means of perfecting the same, that thus men may endeavor to live by the commandments of reason (ethics)."

48. Forgiveness

Man, as stated above, is a creature in whom good and evil struggle for mastery, or as the Talmud sees him, as one who harbors within himself two wills, one to do good, and the other to do evil, euphemistically called the *Yetẓer Tob* and *Yetẓer Ra,* i.e., good and evil spirits. It is therefore impossible for any man in the course of life not to injure or insult some man with whom he comes in contact. Were there no way to repair these wrongs, it would be very difficult to carry on any form of social life, for animosity would rage among groups and individuals. To avoid such a state of affairs, religion and morality insist upon the duty of man to refrain from harboring in his heart a feeling of grievance against the one who caused him any injury and to cultivate the virtue of forgiveness. Judaism, which stresses so much the love of fellow man, considers forgiveness one of the leading virtues and even instituted an annual holiday in which forgiveness is the principal feature, namely *Yom ha-*

[10] Jacob Kranz (Dubner Maggid), in his ethical works, *Sefer ha-Midot.*
[11] Tr. *Baba Metziah,* 107.

Kippurim, the Day of Atonement or, in its literal meaning, the Day of Forgiveness.

49. Anger

But before we can discuss the Jewish view of forgiveness, we must touch upon the vice that is the source of all the grievances between men which call for forgiveness, namely anger. The Bible condemns anger in harsh terms, and names the one who harbors it a fool. The Hebrew term used for the foolish one, namely *Ksil,* connotes more than mere foolishness, but identifies it with wickedness. The Book of Proverbs, like Socrates, who repeatedly asserted that ignorance is vice and knowledge is virtue, dubs the wicked by the name *fool,* and the righteous by the name *wise.* It says, "A stone is heavy, and the sand weighty, but a fool's anger is heavier than both (Proverbs XXVII, 3). In other words, it is difficult to lift loads of stones and sand, but more difficult than the weight of both is to bear the anger of your fellow men. In another place we are warned, "Be not hasty in thy spirit to be angry, for anger resteth in the breast of fools" (Ecclesiastes VII, 9), that is, fools or rather, wicked men, cannot control their anger.

The sages of the Talmud condemned the inability of a man to restrain his anger as a grievous sin and said that he who displays anger can be compared to an idol worshiper,[12] a comparison frequently used by them when desiring to indicate the severity of a certain transgression. With keen insight these moralists pointed out the futility of anger, for not only does the angry man usually make errors, both in his statements and his actions, but the anger usually results in some form of suffering for the irascible man himself. They expressed this warning in a fine adage. They said, "Just as when the pot boils over it spills the water on the side which is hottest, so is the irascible man. Whatever spilling or in-

[12] Tr. *Sabbath,* 105.

jury will result from his anger will strike himself."[13] The punishment for a display of anger was the threatened loss of the knowledge and learning acquired during a lifetime, for irascibility disturbs the mind, and not only does it prevent the delving in the recesses of learning and the increase of one's mastery of it, but ultimately brings about the loss of what was acquired.[14] Furthermore, it was observed that anger may lead to all kinds of sin and transgression, for in his fury the irascible man may commit actions that he will later bitterly regret.[15] And verily did a Mediaeval didactic poet say, "The beginning of anger is a kind of insanity and blindness, and its end is regret and loss."[16] The frequency of irascibility in human life and the necessity to urge men to restrain its outbursts moved the Jewish sages to declare that the degree of a man's anger, or vice versa, that of its restraint, is one of the three things by which a man's character is to be judged for good or bad.[17]

Possessing such an all-embracing view of the value of restraining oneself from such a display of anger, it is no wonder that Jewish moralists repeatedly praised those that practiced the virtue of restraint. Of those who forego to repay an insulting fellow man in his own measure and calling him similar names, it is said that their reward will be great. They are called the lovers of God and to them is applied the Biblical statement, "They that love Him, God, will be like the sun when he goeth forth in his might" (Judges V, 31), that is, they will shine in their spiritual and moral glory. Mediaeval moralists are untiring in urging the practice of the virtue of restraint of anger, and one of them even proclaimed that "There is no virtue greater in excellence than restraint of anger."[18]

[13] *Koheleth Rabba,* Ch. VII.
[14] Tr. *Pesaḥim,* 49.
[15] Tr. *Berakot,* 28.
[16] Immanuel of Rome in *Mahberet,* Portal 11.
[17] Tr. *Erubin,* p. 65.
[18] Eliezer of Worms, in *Book of Rokeaḥ,* p. 10.

50. Vengeance

All this condemnation of anger, the urging of its restraint, and the praise of the practice of this restraint refer primarily to the phase of immediate outburst of wrath and its restraint. There is, however, another phase of the vice of anger as well as its virtuous opposite. This phase is expressed by retaining anger in one's heart against the man who caused injury or grief, while the opposite virtue is called forgiveness after the grievance was accomplished. This phase of the vice, namely retention of anger or animosity toward the offender, may lead to worse results than a mere flare or outburst, for it may lead to vengeance. A hatred retained or anger preserved may become stronger with age. Again, a flare of anger with the resulting action is done impulsively, but vengeance is planned and calculated. Against retention and its possible results the Torah speaks out explicitly, "Thou shalt not take vengeance nor bear a grudge against the children of thy people, but thou shalt bear love for thy neighbor as thyself" (Leviticus XIX, 18). The bearing of a grudge prohibited in this statement is explained by the authors of the *Halakah* to refer to the following case. At one time A asked B for a loan of money or a utensil; B refused. However, later, B was in need of the same favor and came to A to ask for it. A said, I shall grant you the favor but remember what you did. This bearing a grudge, this verbal chiding that accompanies the grant of the favor, is considered a grave sin. Judaism demands full forgiveness, wiping out any ill-feeling. It is for this purpose that the statement ends with the words, "But thou shalt love thy neighbor as thyself," meaning, place yourself in the position of your fellow man. Suppose you commit an error, do you not forgive yourself? Act, therefore, in the same way toward your fellow man.

51. Forgiveness Must Be Complete

The duty to practice forgiveness stems from the fundamental conception of Judaism and of the Godhead, as well as the relation of man to God. Forgiveness is one of the thirteen attributes of God given in Exodus XXXIV, 7, where He is described "as forgiving iniquity and transgression and sin." This attribute, which reveals a part of the essence of the Godhead, is emphasized in the Bible numerous times, and since Jewish ethics is based on the principle that man must endeavor to imitate God in conduct, it follows that just as God is forgiving, so must man forgive his fellow man for any grievances he may have against him. In addition, since, as was pointed out, man often turns to God and pleads for forgiveness of his sins, how can he refuse such a favor to his fellow man? The Rabbis have therefore urged man to practice forgiveness by pointing out that just as he acts toward his fellow man, so will God act toward him and forgive all his sins.[19]

We are told in the Talmud of numerous exemplary acts of the sages in the practice of this virtue. One sage by the name of Mar Sutra was wont to say every night before he went to bed, "I forgive every one who might have caused me any grievance in any way or form." He was thus careful to remove any taint of grudge in his heart against any of his fellow men. Another exemplary case of such conduct toward fellow men is given to us in a statement by an 18th-century pious man in the testament to his children. He says, "When I found myself in a group of men, I used to scan it from one end to the other in order to find out whether I loved every one of them, and as a rule I found that I did. If it happened that one of the assembled did offend me at one time, I immediately forgave him. If my heart found it somewhat dif-

[19] Tr. *Rosh ha-Shanah*, 17.

ficult to love a particular man, I made all effort to overcome the disinclination until I succeeded." [20]

However, such conduct is the share of only a few chosen spirits. In ordinary life forgiveness must be asked for. Just as it is the duty of the one who suffered the grievance from his fellow man to forgive, it is also the duty of the one who caused the grievance to ask for forgiveness. It is stated in the Mishnah, "All transgressions that man committed against God, namely transgressions of purely religious practices, which are prescribed by Jewish law, are forgiven on the Day of Atonement when man repents and pleads to God for forgiveness. But transgressions that involve the relation between man and man are not forgiven, even if the sinner repents in his heart, but he must come to the one against whom he sinned and ask for forgiveness." [21] It does not matter how slight that offense was; it might have been only a wrong expression at which the friend took umbrage. The one who uttered it must ask for forgiveness. In severer cases of offense, such as the case of a man striking his fellow man in a burst of anger, we are told that any amount of recompense he may offer to the sufferer is not sufficient. The offender must personally come to the one he struck and plead for forgiveness.[22] Money cannot pay for the abuse of human dignity. It is the evident manifestation of a change of heart on the part of the offender, demonstrated by his pleading, which effects the reconciliation. Pleading for forgiveness, however, has a limit. In case the one who is to grant it is obstinate and refuses the plea after it has been made three times, no further beseeching is necessary on the part of the offender.[23]

The emphasis thus placed by Judaism on the duty to practice the virtue of forgiveness, on the one hand, and on

[20] Testament of Joel ben Shemaryah in *Ethical Wills,* ed. Abrahms, vol. II, 34b.

[21] Tr. *Yomah,* Ch. IX, Mishnah 9.

[22] Tr. *Baba Kamah,* 92.

[23] Tr. *Yomah,* 87a.

the duty to ask for forgiveness, on the other hand, helped greatly to stabilize social relations in Jewish life. This practice was strengthened by the aforementioned statement from the Mishnah that the transgressions of man against man are not forgiven on the Day of Atonement unless a reconciliation is effected. Until recently it was the custom in Jewish communities that, on gathering in the synagogue on the eve of the Day of Atonement before the service began, people asked their friends, neighbors, or anyone with whom they usually came in contact, for forgiveness for offenses they might have caused each other during the year. It is a custom worthwhile preserving.

52. Slander

Of the group of vices severely condemned by Judaism for the reason that they tend, in one way or another, to impair the dignity of man and undermine the value of human personality, that of slandering a fellow man or bearing tales against him is one of the gravest.

The Pentateuch contains a strict prohibition against slander or talebearing, saying, "Thou shalt not go up and down talebearing among thy people, neither shalt thou stand idly by the blood of thy neighbor, I am the Lord" (Leviticus XIX, 16). The gravity of the offense of slandering is emphasized in this verse in two ways, first, by coupling it with the command not to stand by the blood of a fellow man. This implies that slander may cause as deep an injury to a fellow man as standing idly by when seeing him threatened with death and not moving a finger to save him. Second, the closing words, "I am the Lord," which are not frequently inserted in commandments, seem to tell us to remember not to act in either of these two ways toward your fellow man, for God who created both of you will hold you responsible whether for injury to the human personality by wrong speech, or for the loss of life by your neglect. The Psalmist and the author of the Book of Proverbs are equally zealous in stressing the importance of avoiding this vice. "Who is the man that desireth life and loveth days that he may see good therein?" asks the Psalmist. He is certain that every man desires it and immediately supplies the means for attaining life and the good of days, "Keep thy tongue from speaking evil and thy lips from speaking guile" (Psalm XXXIV, 13, 14). In a similar vein declares the author of the Proverbs, "Whoso keepeth his mouth and his tongue keepeth his soul from trouble" (Proverbs XXI, 23). They thus endeavored to point out the dire results that may follow from practicing the art of slander or talebearing to the bearer himself.

The Rabbis, whose purpose it was to maintain on a high level, social life in general and Jewish life in particular, and who had a deep knowledge of human nature and its frailties, paid great attention to this particular vice. Observing that men, on the whole, have a particular inclination to talebearing or slandering their fellow men remarked, "There are three sins which few men escape from committing daily, and the most prevalent is slander in one form or another." [24] They warned against it time and again, and emphasized its gravity continually. They even went to extremes, saying, "One who slanders his fellow man, his transgression is as great as if he denied the existence of God." [25] One scholar expressed the same idea in a more striking manner. Basing himself on the interpretation of a Biblical verse, he said, "God and the slanderer cannot live in the same world." [26] The underlying idea of such statements is that slander in any form, even in a milder phase, gossip, is bound to injure the one who is the target of such talk, damaging his reputation and lowering his dignity and personality in the eyes of his fellow men. It thus contradicts the very purpose of God

[24] Tr. *Baba Batra,* 164b.
[25] Palestinian Talmud, Tr. *Peah,* Ch. I.
[26] Tr. *Erukin,* 15.

in creating the world and placing man in it, for He aimed at solidarity and stability of human activity.

53. Evil Effects of Slander

The gravity of this vice is aggravated by the fact that it is frequently committed without any benefit to the talebearer. This phase is beautifully illustrated by the sages. Referring to the verse in Ecclesiastes X, 11, "Surely the serpent will bite if he is not enchanted, and the master of the tongue is no better," they said, "The Serpent was asked, 'All animals, the wolf and other carnivorous animals kill in order to eat. What profit hast thou of your striking and poisoning other creatures?' " Answered the snake, "Go to the slanderer and ask him the same question. He, likewise, has no gain from his action; maybe he will offer a reason for his action." [27] The implication is that the biting of the serpent and the injury of the slanderer stem from the same bad inclination.

The comparison of slander with the bite of a serpent was exploited by the Rabbis in another manner to point out the extent of its effect. "The serpent," say they, was asked again, "Why is it that thou strikest only one organ, but thy poison affects all other organs?" Answered the serpent, "Ask the slanderer to offer an explanation for the fact that he utters his slanderous words in Rome, but the injurious effect is felt by a man who lives in Syria, or vice versa." [28]

Another sage threatened the slanderer with severe punishment and said, "The one who slanders his fellow men will ultimately be smitten by leprosy." [29] The statement seems to imply that the punishment follows the rule of measure for measure, for slandering is considered a kind of moral leprosy. The punishment for it will be a physical leprosy.

[27] Palestinian Talmud, Tr. *Peah,* p. 16.
[28] *Deuteronomy Rabba,* Ch. V.
[29] Tr. *Erukin,* 16.

And just as the slanderer is guilty of a breach of morality, so, in the view of the Rabbis, is he who hears the slander, accepts it as truth, and judges the one who is slandered according to the report given him. They, therefore, say that slander injures three persons—the slanderer, the one who is slandered, and the one who accepts the slanderous report.[30]

To prove the gravity of accepting the report of a slanderer, they analyzed the dire results of such an acceptance. Referring to the verse in Psalms CXX, 3, 4, which reads, "What shall be given unto thee, and what shall be done unto thee, thou deceitful tongue? Sharp arrows of the mighty with coals of broom." They pointed out that the comparison of slander with the coals of the broom has special significance. The coals of this plant possess a special quality for preserving heat. When externally the fire in them seems to be totally extinguished, internally it is still burning, and woe to the one who judges the coals by their external appearance. On touching them he is badly burned. Similarly, for one who accepts the evil report of the slanderer that his friend or neighbor plans to do him harm or thinks lightly of him, even though externally he does not show signs of animosity toward that friend, internally hatred will burn in his heart and for a long time he will bear him a grudge.[31]

In order to warn people to beware of the great sin of slander, the Rabbis point to the Biblical story of Miriam who spoke evil of her brother Moses, and who in spite of her great righteousness, for she is considered a prophetess in Jewish tradition, was immediately punished for this act by being smitten with leprosy. Only after her brother, Moses, pleaded on her behalf was she cured (Numbers XII, 1–16).

There are, of course, various degrees of talebearing or slander, but the Jewish sages warned even against the lighter grade, such as is commonly called gossip. They la-

[30] Tr. *Erukin*, p. 15b.
[31] *Genesis Rabba*, Ch. II.

beled this type by a special name, calling it the "dust of slander" *(Abak Leshon ha-Ra).* They included in it the apparently innocent remarks that people often make after a visit to a friend's house, remarking upon the extravagance in conduct of the home or ménage. They refer, as usual, to the Bible, which is the source of religious and moral conduct. When Sarah, the wife of Abraham, heard the angel promising her husband that within a year his wife would give birth to a son, she smiled to herself, thinking that she was past her youth and her husband was old. But when God revealed to Abraham her view of the matter, He said that she thought, "Shall I of a surety bear a child who am old?" (Genesis XVIII, 13), and made no mention of her inner thought, "My lord is old," so as to avoid even a remark that might contain a particle of "dust of slander," and in this way not arouse any ill feeling.[32]

There is, however, one exception made in regard to this particular vice. If the man who is the object of the evil tale has himself told its content in the presence of three persons, anyone else may retell it. It is assumed that by telling it to three persons he made it a public matter, and therefore it no longer comes under the category of slander or talebearing. With this exception, any phase of talebearing, no matter how light, is time and again condemned by Jewish ethicists.

The Rabbis, in order to wean people away from practicing this vice, described the most important event in Jewish history—the Exodus, the very birth of a people—as a partial reward for abstaining from talebearing. I say a partial reward, for three other factors that brought about this great event are mentioned, namely abstaining from idolatry, from sexual promiscuity, and from murder.[33] Oppositely, the divine decree that the generation which left Egypt should wander almost forty years in the desert and ultimately die there was declared solely because the people who were sent

[32] Tr. *Erukin,* p. 16.
[33] *Leviticus Rabba,* Ch. XXXII.

to spy out the land slandered the chosen land, and spoke evil of it.[34] This statement is even incorporated in the Mishnah, the book considered by tradition second in authority to the Law or Torah.

From what was said we can conclude how much Judaism values social solidarity, good will between fellow men, and the dignity of man, for any form of speaking that may in any way impair the social and ethical values is considered a grave vice. This continual warning to abstain from this attractive and, at times, apparently an innocent vice is not limited to Talmudic and Midrashic literature, but throughout the ages in almost every work in the extensive ethical literature, at least one chapter and frequently more are devoted to the discussion of the evil effects of that particular vice.

A Mediaeval Jewish moralist, stressing the evil effects of slander even in its mildest form, advised people not to praise a rich man in the presence of another wealthy man, since such praise would arouse jealousy in the heart of the other man and cause him to make a slanderous remark.

Another moralist said that the injury caused by slander is greater than that caused by shooting an arrow, for the latter strikes only one man, while slander strikes injury to more than one man and undermines the solidarity of social life. These continual warnings and demands for restraining the tongue from speaking evil run like a thread throughout Jewish literature, from the Bible to the recent past, and left an influence on Jewish life.

54. Exemplary Restraint from Slander

The following anecdote about the conduct in this matter of the famous Rabbi and moralist, Israel Kagan will serve as an illustration of how far the restraint from causing any reflection upon the character of a fellow man can be carried.

[34] Tr. *Sanhedrin,* Ch. XI, Mishanah 2.

That Rabbi was hardly known by his name, but by the name of his book, *Ḥofetz Ḥayyim (One Who Wants Life)*. This book is devoted entirely to the discussion of the importance of avoiding any form of *Lashon ha-Ra* (slander), and the title taken from Psalms XXXIII, 13, 14, "He who wants life, etc., keep thy tongue from evil and thy lips from speaking guile." On one occasion, at a conference of representatives of the Orthodox Jewish communities called by the Russian government in the days before the First World War, when the election of officers for the conference came up, the *Ḥofetz Ḥayyim* refused to vote and left the hall. In vain did the outstanding scholars and Ḥassidic rabbis, leaders of the conference, plead with him. He was adamant in his refusal. His argument was that since there were several candidates, were he to vote for one, it would indirectly imply that he considered the others unworthy for the office, and this might be considered a species of the "dust of slander." While of course we cannot follow such conduct, nevertheless, such an all-embracing feeling for the dignity of fellow men evokes our admiration. It proves to us to what depth the ethical teachings of Judaism penetrated into the hearts of some Jews.

55. Jealousy

The vice of jealousy can be considered a double-edged evil trait in a man's character. Its effects are injurious both to the man with whom the envious one comes in contact and to himself. It is this aspect which is stressed by Jewish ethics, as it is reflected in its literary sources, and it makes a great effort to warn against this vice. The Book of Proverbs declares that "envy is the rottenness of the bones" (Proverbs XIV, 30), meaning that this feeling only causes such suffering to its possessor that his very bones are affected. Similarly, Solomon, in his Song of Songs, pronounces the evil results of jealousy or envy saying, "Jealousy is as cruel as the grave" (VIII, 6). One who is envious or jealous may display cruelty toward the object of that envy and this cruelty will ultimately react upon its perpetrator.

The same idea that envy hurts its possessor more than its object is frequently referred to in post-Biblical ethical sources. The Mishnah, in the *Sayings of the Fathers,* says, "Envy and cupidity and pursuit of honor cause man to die prematurely." [35] Ben Sira, the famous moralist says, "Envy and anger shorten a man's life." Another statement carries this idea to exaggeration by saying, "Better to die a hundred times than to live a life with envy in the heart," [36] for this feeling makes life miserable. All these harsh statements against the vice of jealousy that warn the envious man of the evil which will befall him if he continues to entertain this feeling are really based on keen psychological analysis of the nature of jealousy and its possible effects. Jealousy is not one vice but really an amalgam of several and the cause of the acquisition of new vices. First, it is accompanied by hatred of the person envied. The envious one continually wishes that some misfortune may overtake the person or persons who are the objects of the envy. Verily did a Mediaeval philosophical moralist say, "Envy is a disease for which there is no cure." [37] Second, this vice frequently brings about the acquisition of new vices, as another sage observed, saying, "Jealousy causes covetousness, and covetousness conduces to many immoral acts, even stealing or robbery in various forms." In fact, the envious one may at times be instrumental in causing misfortune to the person he envies, and thus the character of the jealous man gradually deteriorates, his peace of mind is disturbed, and his life is embittered. In fact, the very vision of life is distorted as observed

[35] Tr. *Aboth,* Ch. IV, 21.
[36] *Deuteronomy Rabba,* Ch. IX.
[37] Bahya ben Asher in his work *Kad ha-Kemaḥ.*

by a modern Jewish sage, "Envy has a thousand eyes, but not one sees right." [38]

Only one form of envy is permitted and that is when a scholar envies another scholar for the latter's achievement and tries to imitate him in diligence. It is therefore said, "The jealousy of scholars may increase knowledge." [39] This type of envy, which results in a striving to reach a certain standard, is permitted also in other walks of life, in business, and in skilled crafts. In fact, a statement in the Midrash asserts that, "Were it not for envy, the world would not exist," [40] meaning that if not for a striving in man's heart to imitate the skill and diligence of other men, there would be little progress in the world. This type of envy possesses neither bitterness, nor jealousy, nor hatred against the one who possesses higher skill and talent, but only admiration.

56. Flattery

Flattery is a species of falsehood and in its essence is a form of lying, but it has a graver aspect than lying, for it has a definite purpose. The desire on the part of the flatterer to deceive the one who is being flattered has the aim to obtain gain, whether monetary aid, honor, or position. The endeavor on the part of the flatterer is strong, and the results of this device may be grave, including the effect upon the flatterer himself.

Jewish ethics therefore condemns this vice severely. In the Bible it is equated with all kinds of evil, and is frequently paired with them by the prophets. Isaiah, threatening the people with dire punishment, offers as a reason for this, "For everyone is a flatterer (or hypocrite) and an evil doer, and every mouth speaketh wantonness" (Isaiah IX, 16). The verb *Ḥanif*, which usually means *to flatter*, is used

[38] *Mishle Issachar*, Ch. II.
[39] Tr. *Baba Batra*, p. 21.
[40] *Midrash on Psalms*, Ch. XXXVII.

both by Isaiah and Jeremiah in the sense of *to defile,* and both describe the moral degradation of the people with the words, "And the earth is defiled under the inhabitants thereof" (Isaiah XXIV, 5; Jeremiah III, 1). The Bible also points out the uncertainty of the results expected by the flatterer, for it is confident that the hope of the flatterer shall be ultimately lost and his joy will last only for a moment (Job VIII, 13; XX, 5).

The sages of the Talmud condemned the vice exceedingly. They even counted flatterers among the evildoers who cannot be in the presence of God,[41] for God is the source of truth. And like the writer of the Book of Job, they were confident of their ultimate fall. They said, "One who flatters his fellow men will ultimately be unmasked by the son of the flattered who will revenge the deception of his father."[42] In reality, the flatterer hates the man upon whom he fawns, for when his words have borne fruit and people begin to honor the man upon whom he bestowed much praise, the flatterer who knows that the man is undeserving of that honor begins to entertain a strong feeling of animosity toward him. Therefore the Jewish moralists say of this type of man, "His mouth drips honey, and his words are as smooth and soft as butter, but in his heart there flows anger and jealousy.[43]

Flattery also has a devastating effect upon the character of the one who practices it. Being used to the employment of false statements, he will gradually lose all distinction between truth and falsehood, and as a result will commit many acts of dishonesty without any compulsion.

The Jewish ethical teachers, penetrating deeply into the essence of this vice, pointed out the deteriorating effect of its prevalence upon the social life of the group. One of them said, "When flattery and hypocrisy prevail, judgments of

[41] Tr. *Sotah,* 41.
[42] Ibid.
[43] *Mishnah Hadashah,* by Yehiel Michal ben Yididiy, Ch. V.

law are distorted and conduct is degraded, for no one can rise and reproach evildoers for their acts since flatterers declare the worst type of man as righteous and good." Another sage went further and declared that "Any community or group in which flattery is tolerated deserves contempt."[44] And in order to stem the spread of the vice and restrain its devastating effect upon the life of the group, the Jewish moralists endeavored to attack this vice at its very source. The strength of flattery consists in the fact that the one who practices it hides his real intention which is, as pointed out above, not to pay honor to the one he praises, but to gain something for himself. He only deceives the recipient of the flattery, and verily did a Mediaeval sage say, "The flatterer is worse than a thief, for the latter steals money and the former steals or takes way from the man upon whom he practices his art right views and opinions." The way to curb him, then, is by uncovering his real intention. The moral teachers therefore declared that it is the duty of the leaders of a community to publicize and unmask flatterers and hypocrites so that the name of Israel should not be desecrated by their actions.[45]

[44] Tr. *Sotah,* 42.
[45] Tr. *Yomah,* 86.

PART III

BUSINESS, FAMILY, AND GROUP ETHICS

Chapter VIII

BUSINESS ETHICS

57. The Importance of Business Ethics

Special emphasis was laid by Jewish ethics on right conduct in business relations, which relations were interpreted by the teachers of morality in a wide manner embracing many phases. Such relations are, as is well known, the very woof of the social fabric of the life of a group. And since the Jews, according to the Bible, were chosen from among all the other nations to be a morally distinguished people, it follows that their social relations must be conducted on high ethical levels. Accordingly, there were numerous commandments given in the law regulating conduct in such relations as well as warnings against transgressions of those commandments. The post-Biblical teachers of ethics have done their share in inculcating in the heart of every Jew the inclination to live up to the desired standard and to avoid any deviation from it.

The very terminology employed by them for such deviations proves the importance attached by them to such conduct. The harsh term of robbery *(Gesel* or *Geselah)* is used in the wide Talmudic, Agadic, and ethical literature as a generic term indicating not only the limited form of taking things away from a fellow man by force, but also for all forms of unfairness in business dealings. It is said, "One who takes from his fellow man anything, directly or indirectly, even something that is worth only a *Peruta* [smallest coin in existence, worth about a tenth of a cent] is considered as if he robs him of his soul." [1] It is also asserted that

[1] Tr. *Baba Kama,* 119.

the destruction of the generation of the flood was decreed primarily for the prevalence among them of all forms of robbery.[2] How far these moralists urged people not to take from anyone in any form that which does not belong to them can be seen from the fact that the laborers are allowed not only to shorten their prayers during working hours, but to read the *Shema* while they stand on top of a tree, even when engaged in pruning the tree. This permission is given in order not to spend the time that belongs to the employer in descending and ascending, in order to recite the prayer on the ground.[3] We are told of a sage named Rabbi Hilkia who, when working as a hired laborer, did not reply to the greetings from friends or passersby in order not to detract a second from the time due his employer.[4] Such conduct is of course extreme, but even from an extreme view we can learn the high value placed by Jewish ethics as a whole upon carefulness in avoiding wronging fellow men in any way.

A remark by an 18th-century moralist will illustrate this value. In interpreting Job's assertion of his righteousness, which ends with the words, "If any spot hath cleaved to my hands, then let me sow and let another man eat," he says, "The word *spot* refers to a light form of *Gesel* that is generally not intended, but if one is not careful, it cleaves to the man."

Another term, *Onoah,* is likewise generic in character; it denotes several phases of dishonesty in business. In its strict connotation when used in a legal sense, it is equivalent to the English term *cheating,* but in an ethical sense it embraces all kinds of dishonest action in business by which the perpetrator aims at his own gain and the other man's loss. Since, owing to human frailty, most men endeavor to increase their wealth and are inclined to use all efforts in order

[2] Tr. *Sanhedrin,* 108a.
[3] Tr. *Berakot,* 16.
[4] Tr. *Taanit,* 23b.

to accomplish that purpose, Jewish ethics does not tire of warning people against acts of dishonesty.

58. Forms of Business Dishonesty

Of the various forms of business dishonesty, the first and most evident is overcharging the buyer who does not know the value of the object he buys, or on the other hand, endeavoring to buy something at a lower price than the object is worth when the seller is ignorant of the market price. The Bible in discussing selling and buying says, "Ye shall not deceive one another, but thou shalt fear thy God, for I am the Lord, thy God" (Leviticus XXV, 17). The words "Thou shalt fear thy God, for I am the Lord, thy God," attached to this commandment are attached to but four more commandments dealing with warning against wronging a fellow man. "These cases are not to curse the deaf, nor to put a stumbling block before the blind" (Leviticus XIX, 14); "to rise before the hoary head, and to honor the face of the old" (verse 32); not to take interest or increase on loans (XXV, 36), and not to rule with rigor over a Jewish servant (verse 43). As we can see, four of these commandments are prohibitive, and only one, honoring the old, is affirmative. In reality, however, not paying honor to an old man is also a form of wronging him. In the entire ancient world, it was accepted that honor is due to age and not honoring the man is witholding what is due him. All these cases have one trait in common. The persons spoken of are all weaker than the perpetrators of the act. Not only is the weakness of the others, such as that of the deaf, the aged, the servant, and of the borrower evident, but also the one who is deceived in a transaction possesses weakness, be he the buyer or seller, either because of inexperience or ignorance. And since men are usually prone to take advantage of the weak, the Bible attaches to the warning against wronging them the extra statement, "Thou shalt fear the Lord, thy God." We may also explain that the special attachment of this statement aims to emphasize the dignity of man, for as is well known, weakness often arouses in the heart of a man contempt toward the one who possesses it, which feeling indirectly arouses the desire to mistreat the possessor of the weakness. The words, "Thou shalt fear the Lord, thy God," seem to imply a warning not to wrong anyone, whether weak or strong, for both were created in the divine image and hence no one's dignity may be impaired, his weakness notwithstanding.

The sages of the Talmud, therefore, warn repeatedly against dishonesty in business dealings, whether done by the buyer or seller. It is said that when a man is brought for judgment in the hereafter, the opening question is, "Did you deal honestly in business?" [5] Honesty is thus the prime factor in determining the future state of man, whether he be rewarded or punished. And in order to encourage people to cultivate this virtue, the ethicists raised the value to an exceedingly high degree, saying, "One who deals honestly in business, and people are pleased with his conduct, he is considered as if he observed all the commandments of the Torah." [6] This assertion, which is frequently inserted in regard to the practice of a number of ethical precepts, does not mean, of course, as in many similar statements, that the one who follows such conduct is free from observing all other commandments. It is only a form of expression meant to stress the great importance of dealing with complete honesty in business and its high religious and ethical values.

Another form of dishonesty in business dealings *(Onoah)* is when one prices things placed on sale with no intention of buying. Such an act of deception, technically known as *Onoat Debarim* (deception by words) is severely condemned by the sages for the reason that pricing or offering to buy the articles may cause a loss to the seller, inasmuch as oth-

[5] Tr. *Sabbath,* 30.
[6] *Mekilta,* sec. Beshalaḥ.

ers may abstain from bidding in order not to raise the price, and thus the seller may not be able to sell his goods. It is, of course, understood that the loss resulting from such an action is prevalent in a limited market and does not apply to modern ways of trade, yet even under modern conditions the practice of such bidding without any intention to buy may cause in certain deals a loss and grievance to the seller and can be considered a form of wrongdoing. The ethicists of the Talmud gave a much wider application to the term "verbal deception" and included under it many wrong acts, such as causing grievances to a fellow man by words as in the case of making promises to men who ask a favor, whether in business matters or for other purposes, and not keeping them. Such deceptive promises cause much grief to the one who relies on them and often bring about a monetary loss. The emphasis, though, is laid primarily upon the feeling of disappointment and the resulting mental anxiety. It is said, "The sin of verbal deception is greater than that of the deception in the price of goods." The reason given is that the latter can be rectified by returning the sum overcharged, while there is no return for the pain of disappointment and mental anxiety.[7]

A grievous form of dishonesty in business is the practice of deception in weights and measures. The Bible warns against this vice and commands the observance of correctness in weights and measures. It says, "Thou shalt not have in thy bag diverse weights, great and small. A perfect and just measure shalt thou have that thy days may be long upon the land which the Lord giveth thee" (Deuteronomy XXV, 13–15). The special promise of reward of length of days attached to this commandment points to the importance placed upon the observance of this particular aspect of honesty in business. Moreover, the promise attached to this commandment speaks more to the nation than to the individual, for it ends with the words, "Upon the land which

[7] Tr. *Baba Metziah,* 59.

the Lord giveth thee." It seems to say that such conduct must become a national trait and thus elevate the social life of the nation and strengthen the body politic. Warnings against this kind of deception are also given in the Book of Proverbs. "A false balance is an abomination to the Lord, and a false balance is not good" (XX, 23). The repeated warning points to the gravity of the offense.

The later moralists have gone to extremes in warning against the vice and said, "The punishment for employing false weights and measures is even severer than that of the sin of adultery." [8] The statement is, of course, an exaggeration, but its purpose is evident, and that is to deter people from falling into a practice which, owing to its prevalence, seems so attractive. Another Agadic statement says that practice of this vice was one of the leading causes that brought about the exile of the Jews from their land.

The Rabbis laid down a number of rules for dealers to follow in selling their wares by weight and measures in order to avoid any wrongdoing even when not done intentionally. Thus, with measures used in liquids the wholesaler must wipe them out once a month in order to clean them from whatever liquid has accumulated there, which accumulation may lessen the amount measured; as for the dry measure, the retailer must clean them at least twice a week for these measures are used more often. Similarly, the weights must be wiped at least once a week so that particles clinging to them may not lessen the actual weight of the goods sold, while scales must be cleaned every time they are used.[9]

There are numerous other indirect acts that may result in deceiving the buyer in one way or another and that are prohibited, as, for instance, when one sells an animal he should not comb its hair carefully so as to raise it and make the animal look fatter, nor use various means to make ves-

[8] Tr. *Baba Batra,* 88.
[9] Ibid., Ch. V, Mishnah 10.

sels look more valuable than their actual worth.[10] Even what was considered in olden times unfair competition is taken care of. One sage prohibits a storekeeper from distributing free nuts and fruit to the children of the neighborhood in order to cause them to make purchases in his store and thus diminish the sales of other storekeepers. This view, however, is not accepted, and in our day it seems quite naïve. However, the principle that unfair competition must be avoided is expressed through the condemnation of its practice by Jewish moralists and even in modern times there are numerous ways to practice it, all of which may be considered Jewishly unethical. From what has been said it can be seen how strongly Jewish ethics condemns any form of dishonesty in business. It is no wonder, then, that in addition to the deterring statements quoted above, the moralists issued a general warning covering all cases of dishonesty. It says, "All pleas by men to God against wrongdoing done to them by their fellow men may at times not be heard immediately, except the plea against deception in business in any form. It is always heard and punishment will follow." [11]

59. Interest

It is well known that the taking of interest on loans is explicitly prohibited by the Torah. It says, "And if thy brother be waxen poor and his means fail with thee, then thou shalt uphold him; as a stranger and a settler shall he live with thee. Take thou no interest or increase with him, but fear thy God that thy brother may live with thee. Thou shalt not give him thy money on interest nor thy victuals on increase" (Leviticus XXV, 35–38). In these verses there are included besides the brother, i.e., an Israelite, also the stranger *(Ha-Ger)* and the settler *(Toshab).* The meaning of these two Hebrew terms is not quite clear. The usual translations

[10] Tr. *Baba Metziah,* 60.
[11] Ibid.

of *stranger* for *Ger* and *sojourner* or *settler* for *Toshab* are not correct. The Bible always seems to make a distinction between the two, and the distinction is not based on the length of time that those denominated by these terms dwell in the land of Israel. According to the translation, the *Ger* is a visitor who stays for a short time, while the sojourner or the settler is the non-Jew who dwells permanently in the land. But the Bible always places the *Ger* first and the *Toshab* next where both are mentioned, which proves that the *Ger* holds a more important place in the community. It also speaks of the family of the *Ger* as distinct from the *Ger* proper. The distinction could, under the circumstances, be only in the religious status of the *Ger* that is different from that of the family. It seems that the traditional explanation of the terms *Ger* and *Toshab* is the correct one. According to it the term *Ger* designates a non-Jew by race but a convert to Judaism, and *Toshab* is a non-Jew living in the land of Israel who has abjured paganism and observes the seven Noachide laws,* which contain a number of the fundamentals of Judaism, but who has not embraced Judaism completely.

The plain meaning of the verse seems to be that not only is a Jew prohibited from taking interest from another Jew, but also from a proselyte and from the non-Jew living in the land who has abjured idolatry and observes a number of the fundamentals of Judaism. This view can be supported by the commandment regarding interest given in Deuteronomy XXIII, 20–22 which reads, "Thou shalt not lend upon interest to thy brother, interest of money, interest of victuals, interest of any thing that is lent upon interest. Unto a *Nakri* thou mayest lend on interest, but to thy brother thou shalt not lend on interest." Again, the Hebrew term *Nakri*, in certain Bible translations that identify it with *foreigner*, is not

* The seven Noachide laws are: 1. not to worship idols; 2. not to blaspheme God; 3. not to murder; 4. not to commit incest; 5. not to rob; 6. not to practice injustice; 7. not to eat flesh torn from living animals.

rendered correctly. *Nakri* is not identified with *Ger* or *Toshab,* but is a term used in the Bible primarily for pagans or idolators. From the fact that the Law uses this term especially, it can be deduced that the Jews are allowed to take interest only from pagans, but not from non-Jews who are not idolators. However, the majority view of the sages is that as long as a non-Jew is not completely converted to Judaism, a *Toshab,* one is allowed to charge him interest on a loan.[12] This subject will be discussed again in the next section where the general Jewish attitude toward non-Jews, especially the members of the two great monotheistic religions, the daughters of Judaism, will be dealt with.

Strict, however, as the Bible and the Talmud are in regard to a Jew charging interest to another Jew, this law could not be carried out in life in full rigor, especially when Jewish life lost its original agricultural economy, and business became an important factor in the economy of the group. As early as the Talmudic period, a device was worked out that enabled one to offer a loan to a fellow Jew and legally obtain some gain from this transaction. The device consisted in making the lender a silent partner in the business and under the circumstances holding him liable for a part of the loss that the undertaking might sustain. Under these conditions, the transaction was considered not a loan but a partnership. In late Mediaeval times, a special form of note was worked out for all loans whereby the transgression of charging interest was legally obviated.

However, where such device is not employed, the charging of interest is considered a grievous sin and a vice. The Talmudic, Agadic, and Midrashic literatures are replete with warnings against it, and with condemnation of the practice in severest terms. One such statement even denies to the lender who charges interest resurrection in Messianic times, a reward that is promised to all Jews.[13]

[12] Tr. *Baba Metziah,* Ch. V, Mishnah 6.
[13] *Leviticus Rabba,* Ch. XXXIV.

The sages of the Talmud gave to the term *interest* a very wide connotation, including all kinds of favors that the borrower might bestow upon the lender. One source even states that when the borrower was not accustomed to being the first to greet the lender previous to the transaction, but began to do so afterwards, such a greeting is considered a form of interest and is prohibited.[14] Whether all this rigor in transactions of money lending was carried out in life is a subject of doubt, but that great efforts were made by Jewish moralists in all ages to guard as much as possible the principle that money should be lent without a charge of interest, of this there can be no doubt.[15]

60. Sanctification and Desecration of the Name of God

Time and again the Jews are warned, both in the Bible and in the Talmud, to beware of desecrating the name of God, and are repeatedly urged to do their utmost to sanctify it. Both of these terms refer to the conduct of the Jews. The first relates to such conduct as is disapproved by fellow men, and through the derogatory remarks that such behavior calls forth the names of Israel and God are desecrated, for the two are closely connected. On the other hand, when the conduct is praised by the people, it is said that such action by a Jew sanctifies the name of Israel and of God. These two concepts have exerted great influence upon the conduct of the Jews and were instrumental in bringing out the application of ethical rules in life, especially in business transactions with non-Jews.

The basis of the exceptional admonition against desecrating the name of God through improper conduct is the emphasis placed throughout Jewish religious and ethical literature upon the idea of the election of Israel. The Jews, standing before Sinai, on the point of receiving the revela-

[14] Tr. *Baba Metziah,* 75b.
[15] *Tosefata Baba Metziah,* Ch. VII.

tion that was supposed to decide their destiny through history, are told by God through Moses, "Now if ye will hearken unto my voice indeed and keep my covenant, then ye shall be my own treasure indeed from among all peoples, for the earth is mine." The meaning of the additional words, "for the earth is mine," is that, though I am the God of the world and all men and nations are mine, you are chosen as a special treasure for a distinct purpose. The purpose is stated immediately. "And ye shall be to me a kingdom of priests and a holy nation" (Exodus XIX, 5, 6). We have already explained above that the Biblical meaning of holiness of life means nothing else but distinguished ethical conduct. The election of Israel is, therefore, primarily an election to be the most moral people.

The sages even asserted that the right conduct toward all people is the very essence of the love of God, which is strongly urged in the Biblical passage later incorporated in the daily prayer and known as the *Shema*. It is said there, "And thou shalt love the Lord, thy God, with all thy heart and with all thy soul and with all thy might." They interpreted the commandment, "And thou shalt love the Lord, thy God," as though the verb were written in the causative form, namely, make people love Him. In other words, act so that through thy actions the name of God will be loved by all people, that is, carry on all business transactions in the most honest way and generally speak kindly and pleasantly with people. Such conduct on the part of Jews will enhance the glory of the God Who chose them as His people.[16]

61. Transactions with Non-Jews

It is no wonder, then, that the Rabbis of the Talmud and the sages of the post-Talmudic age declared any infringement of honesty in transactions with non-Jews, whether it

[16] *Sifre Deuteronomy*, Ch. VI, 4-9.

be included under the generic term *Gesel,* i.e., robbery, or cheating, or giving short weight, or false measure, is not only a sin but a most grievous one. They said, "Any act of *Gesel* toward a non-Jew is even a severer transgression than that committed toward a Jew, for it constitutes a desecration of the name of God." [17] Similarly, in acts of dishonesty that may be included under the name *Geneva* (theft), there is no distinction whether they be committed against a Jew or non-Jew, no matter how small the loss involved may be, even if be only a *Peruta.*

The great Akiba said, "One who manipulates the accounts when dealing with a non-Jew in order to charge him more than the goods are worth commits a grievous sin, just as if he did this to a fellow-Jew." [18] Maimonides says, "A merchant who uses false weights or measures in his transactions, whether with a fellow Jew or non-Jew, thereby transgresses an explicit prohibitive precept of the Torah and he must make good all loss the buyer sustained thereby." Likewise must a Jew, if he finds an article that belongs to a non-Jew, return it, for if he retains it, there results by such conduct a desecration of the name of God of Israel.[19] How far this prohibition goes may be illustrated by the fact that a Jew is warned not to sell to a non-Jew meat from an animal that died from disease or was killed as though it were meat from an animal slaughtered by a Jew; though it makes little difference to him as far as the question of using it for food is involved. The reason for this injunction is the general principle that no kind of deception must be practiced upon either Jew or non-Jew, and since there is a possibility that even a non-Jew may like that type of meat better, either because he considers it fresher or, since the Jew uses it, the animal had no severe disease (for otherwise it would be *Terefa,* i.e., disqualified for Jewish food), it is considered a

[17] *Tosefta Baba Kamah,* Ch. X.
[18] Tr. *Baba Kama,* 113.
[19] *Code of Maimonides,* sec. on Theft, Ch. VII.

deception. In such cases, he must tell him the exact state of the animal from which the meat comes, whether it was *Nebelah,* i.e., had died from disease, or that it was disqualified by Jews because of *Terefa* after slaughtering it.[20]

Mediaeval codifiers have continually warned Jews of the great sin of acting toward non-Jews in any improper manner in any business transaction. Says Rabbi Moses ben Yacob of Coucy, France, in his code, "Those who lie to non-Jews or cheat them belong to those who desecrate the name of God. Therefore, in business one must not deceive even if such deception does not entail any loss but is only a verbal one, no matter to what religion the party belongs. If a Jew sells any merchandise to a non-Jew, it is his duty to inform the buyer of any defects the merchandise contains when such defect is not openly evident." [21] A famous Mediaeval moralist, Judah the Pious *(Hassid),* says, "A non-Jew who follows the seven Noachide laws, such as a Christian or a Moslem, must not be deceived in any way, even if the disclosing of the defect involves a loss to the Jew. In general, no disrespect must be shown to a non-Jew, and if he is deserving of honor, it must be accorded to him." [22] How far deception must be avoided is evident from the following statements: "If one, whether Jew or non-Jew, asks for a loan but you do not want to lend him the money for fear he may not return it, still you should not tell him that you haven't the money, better tell him the reason for your hesitation openly. He may then succeed in reassuring you against loss, but you will not deceive him with words." [23] Of according honor to those who deserve it, whether Jew or non-Jew, he says, "If one praises righteous people who are dead for their good deeds, it does not matter whether the righteous man was a Jew or non-Jew, he must always

[20] Tr. *Hulin,* 94a.
[21] *Sefer Mitzwot Gadol.* Vol. II, p. 170.
[22] *Book of the Pious,* sec. 358.
[23] Ibid.

add the words 'Of blessed memory' after the name of the man spoken of." [24]

62. Interest on Loans to Non-Jews

There is one exception in which non-Jews are treated differently from Jews. It is the aforementioned case of charging interest on loans. In order to present the different treatment of non-Jews in regard to the charging of interest on loans in the proper light, it is best to review the subject briefly from the Jewish point of view.

We know that the Torah distinctly prohibits the charging of interest to a fellow Jew (Leviticus XXV, 35–38), as quoted above. Besides these verses there is also another prohibition that says, "If thou lend money to any of my people, even to the poor with thee, thou shalt not be to him as creditor, neither shall ye lay upon him an interest" (Exodus XXII, 24). We note differences in these commandments. In the one given in Exodus there is a general statement not to charge interest to a Jew. In that in Leviticus, there is an additional statement relating to a *Ger* and a *Toshab,* and as we pointed out above, Jewish tradition, i.e., the oral law, understands the term *Ger* to designate a complete proselyte, while *Toshab,* often called *Ger Toshab,* refers to a non-Jew who follows the seven Noachide laws. It was also noted by us above that according to the plain meaning of the verse in Leviticus (XXV, 35) one who observes the seven Noachide laws is included in the prohibition to charge interest on loans. In fact, the personal opinion of Judah the Prince, the redactor of the Mishnah, is that he should not be charged interest. However, the Mishnah that represents the view not only of the redactor, but of the majority of scholars associated in the editing of this work, permitted charging him interest as well as borrowing from him on interest.[25] Still, in spite of

[24] Ibid.

[25] Tr. *Baba Metziah,* Ch. V, Mishnah 6.

the view expressed in the Mishnah, there seems also to have prevailed in early times another opinion that supported Judah the Prince in prohibiting the charging of interest to the *Toshab.* An old collection of laws relating both to complete proselytes and partial proselytes, i.e., *Toshab,* called *Maseket Gerim,* distinctly prohibits such a charge even to the *Toshab.*

In addition to these two statements regarding the charge of interest, there is a third statement (Deuteronomy XXIII, 20–21), where there is a distinct permission to lend money on interest to the *Nakri,* and to borrow from him on interest. The term *Nakri* means one who is a total alien, whether one who does not live in the land but visits for commercial purposes or one who does not even visit but transacts business from a neighboring land. At any rate, he is different from the *Toshab,* being a pagan who has not accepted even the fundamental laws of the land, which are in fact laws of humanity, nor is he domiciled, but belongs politically to another land and country. In this case, in charging interest to him, one cannot see any discrimination against a non-Jew. As is well known, all nations of antiquity allowed interest, and this was the ordinary practice in all business transactions. The permission to charge interest to foreigners who do not submit to the law of the land is therefore logical and constitutes no infringement upon morality. A business transaction must be two-sided. If the Jew could not charge interest to the *Nakri,* it follows that the *Nakri* should not charge interest to the Jew. But as long as he will not agree to that, the Jew must also charge him, for otherwise the Jew will always be the loser. The case is different with the *Toshab;* if he really submits to the law of the land, he will also not charge the Jew. This must have been the reason of the scholars who held that the *Toshab* is included in the prohibition to lend money on interest. Those who decided to exclude him from the prohibition thought otherwise. Their view was that the law regarding not charging interest on loans could not be forced upon him, for a man has the right to withold from lending money. He may prefer to follow the general way of the Gentile. Thus, there cannot be a two-sided reciprocity to money transactions, and therefore it is quite logical to assume that the *Toshab* was not included in the prohibition. It is evident, though, that there is no intended discrimination against the non-Jews, whether pagan or those of the class of *Toshab;* this would also apply to Christians and Muslims, who are of the same status as the *Toshab*.

Still, in spite of the fact that the Bible allows charging of interest on loans to a non-Jew, primarily a pagan, there was great hesitation by many scholars to carry out the practice. A number of them prohibited it. They said that the verse, "He that augmenteth his substance by interest and increase gathers it for him that is gracious to the poor" (Proverbs XXVIII, 8), which means that wealth thus obtained will not remain with the owner, but will be given away to charitable institutions, includes also the loss of wealth by lending money on interest even to non-Jews. It seems that there was, on the whole, a strong aversion to such practice among the scholars of the Talmud. It is even mentioned that there is an ordinance against charging interest on loans to non-Jews. And while this ordinance was not fully accepted, efforts were made to limit such practice. One sage said that the practice is allowed only when the man has no other source of income to supply life's necessities. Others limit it still further and allow it only to a scholar who devotes himself to study, deriving an income sufficient for a modest living from such practice. There were scholars who said just the opposite, that a scholar whose conduct should be exemplary must not engage in such practice at all.[26]

Throughout the ages there has gone on among the codifiers and Jewish sages a continual wavering between granting permission for this practice and prohibiting it. In general, it is to be noted that the sages who lived in those

[26] Ibid., 70b-71a.

countries where the Jews were not forced to occupy themselves solely with business transactions, but were engaged in agriculture and manual trades, prohibit lending money on interest to non-Jews. On the other hand, where the Jews were forced out from agriculture and manual trades by law, as in the Mediaeval Ages in most European countries, the codifiers allowed that practice but with great reluctance. In fact, there is a statement in the Talmud that the words, "He that putteth not out his money on interest" (Psalm XV, 5), which form one of the qualities of a pious man worthy of dwelling in the Tabernacle and the holy mountain of God, refer not to the man who refrains from taking interest only from a Jew, but also from a non-Jew.[27] Every permission for charging interest to a non-Jew is worded with many apologies stressing the economic conditions and the burden of taxation and special contributions to which the Jew in the Mediaeval Ages was subjected.

From all that has been said can be seen the groundlessness of all attacks that were made against the Jews through the ages by the numerous Gentile scholars, writers, and dramatists, charging them with greediness for demanding interest from the non-Jew. We can also note the high morality of Judaism and its tradition when even the fundamental law, i.e., the Torah, permits such charging and, as pointed out with perfect justice, allowed it with reluctance and limitations. Only because of the conditions forced upon them was the permission grudgingly given.

[27] Ibid., 70b.

Chapter IX

JUSTICE

63. Jewish Conception of Justice

As is well known, justice is a virtue that is emphasized in every system of ethical conduct, whether ancient or modern. It is considered the very cornerstone of morality. This had already been recognized by Aristotle when he said that justice in its complete form is not a virtue but morality itself, yet we will see later that, in its application in life, most moral systems limit it to a large degree. The case is different in Judaism. Its very conception prevents the narrowing of its range, whether in theory or in practice. The great advantage of Jewish ethics is, as was pointed out, that its basis and source are not knowledge or proportion, or mere human law, but God Himself. As mentioned, He is described in the Bible time and again in moral attributes. But none of the other ethical attributes are emphasized as much and as often as is His justice. From this repeated emphasis we can learn the Jewish conception of justice as such, the necessity for men to cultivate it as a part of their inner personality and also the mode of application of its various phases.

A fundamental element in the Jewish conception of justice as reflected in its literature is that it is the basis of the order of the world established by God, which conduces, as pointed out, to a moral view of the world. The Psalmist in his religious fervor exclaims, "Righteousness and justice are the foundation of Thy throne" (LXXXIX, 15), meaning that these attributes form the essence of God's rule in the world of which the throne is symbolic. It is no wonder that Bildad, in refuting Job's charge that he is treated unjustly, exclaims amazingly, "Doth God pervert judgment or does the Almighty pervert justice?" (Job VIII, 3). Such a thing is inconceivable and would destroy the order of the world.

A second element in that conception is that justice is identified with truth, as in the verse, "Thy justice is everlasting and Thy law is truth" (Psalm CXIX, 142). The emphasis is here laid on the idea that justice and law, the essence of both of which is truth, are the staying powers of the world and make it endure eternally. And since justice is the foundation of the divine order in the world as well as its staying power, it is no wonder that all the commandments and precepts given by God to man to guide him in life are saturated therewith. We thus see that the conception of justice in regard to its source in the divine nature is really the sum of all ethical precepts.

We have thus far seen the all-embracing role that justice or righteousness plays in God's conduct of the world. It follows that justice, from the point of view of Judaism, must occupy an exceptionally important place in human conduct. In other words, man in imitation of God must make it the foundation of his own world, and cultivate it as the principal trait of his personality. It will then conduce to the practice of other virtues, for the range of justice is wide. As we have seen, truth constitutes a part of its essence, but there are other virtues included in that range. Some of them are pointed out by the Psalmist who, in drawing the picture of the ideal king whose rule is just, says to him, "And in thy majesty prosper, ride on behalf of meekness, truth, and righteousness" (Psalm XLV, 5), meaning that the king must endeavor to practice all these three virtues that really form a unity, for each of them constitutes a facet of justice. Justice also helps man to refrain from the practice of a number of vices: for instance, pride, which is a form of injustice, as it lowers the other man in the eyes of the proud. And just as God loves justice, so should man love it; but not only must the ethical man love justice, it must, as mentioned, become a part of his personality and be always with him. The Bible, wanting to express the idea that justice must always be present in man's relations with fellow men employs figurative language and says that man must be wrapped in it. Job vindicates himself by proudly asserting, "I put on righteousness and it clothed itself with me as a robe and as a diadem (Job XXIX, 14). Similarly, the prophet Isaiah, in describing the Messiah, the redeemer of Israel and of all humanity, finds no better figure of speech to picture the ideal man than "And justice shall be the girdle of his loins, and faithfulness the girdle of his reins" (XI, 5).

64. Justice as Applied in Life

We noted the high value placed by Judaism on justice, considering it as the embracive virtue that man must cultivate in order to follow ethical conduct. We turn now to justice in a somewhat narrower sense as carried out in society. As such, it presents two phases, the right treatment of your fellow man in all kinds of business transactions and the rectifying of wrong done by means of judicial action, called by Aristotle distributive and corrective justice respectively. As far as the first phase is concerned, its application presents numerous facets that are usually subsumed under business ethics in its various angles and were dealt with by us previously. It remains then for us to point out the emphasis placed by the Bible and the Rabbis upon several general features. The Bible commands, "Justice, justice shalt thou pursue that thou mayest live" (Deuteronomy XVI, 20). The repetition of the word *justice* and the term *pursue* mean to convey that it is not enough for one who seeks to lead an ethical life merely to act justly, but that he must go out of his way and make all efforts to attain it, and at times even balance the scale in favor of his fellow men. The Rabbis deduced from this verse a rule for businessmen, namely that if they sell merchandise by weight, they should always add a little more than the exact weight.[1] Similarly they laid down a rule for the view that a man should form of those with whom he comes in contact and watch his actions. They said that the verse, "In justice shalt thou judge thy neighbor" (Leviticus XIX, 15) is not limited to the righteous dispensation of court justice, but also implies a rule for judging the actions of fellowmen, namely, one must assume that the other man acted from a right motive, even if the motive is not openly evident, and withold his condemnation until proved otherwise.[2]

As for the second phase, namely dispensation of justice in correcting wrongs done, or court justice, excessive emphasis is laid by Judaism on its most rigid ethical procedure. There must not be the slightest partiality on the part of the judge. The litigants must appear in the presence of the court in an equal way, and the Rabbis took care that the equality be preserved as far as possible. They ruled that if one of the litigants is dressed in fine clothes and the other shabbily, the judge must say to the one who is better dressed, "Either dress your opponent like yourself, or you put on clothes similar to his." The old rule was that both litigants stand before the judge. The court, however, had a right to seat both of them. Later the rule was adopted that both litigants are usually seated while the case is argued. They must stand when decision is pronounced.[3]

65. Equity

Modern systems of law have, besides the regular courts for administration of justice, also courts of equity, the purpose of which is to apply certain principles of justice to adjust particular cases where the law by its universality is deficient. In Judaism there are no such courts, but the urgency

[1] Tr. *Baba Batra,* 88.
[2] Tr. *Shebuoth,* 30a.
[3] Ibid., b.

to act in a way that endeavors to avoid any possible injury or grief to a fellow man, though the law cannot compel such action, is taken over by Jewish ethics. The Hebrew term for this type of ethics is *Lifnim Meshurat ha-Din,* which designates actions above the rule of the law. As such, it calls for superfairness and begins where the law ends. The basis of such a line of ethical action is the Biblical verse, "And thou shalt teach them the statutes and laws, and shalt show them the way wherein they must walk, and the work that they must do" (Exodus XVIII, 20). The sages interpret the verse as follows. The words, "the statutes and the laws," covers all cases to which all legal justice should be applied. What then do the additional words, "shalt show them the way wherein they must walk and the work that they must do," mean to convey? They say we must assume that the way in which they should walk designates the superjustice line of action, while the work that they must do refers to special deeds of loving-kindness.[4]

Since actions of this type or of equity are fairer than the law requires, it follows, of course, that their performance is carried out primarily by the few, the specially pious and ethical. Yet some moralists felt that such action should spread among larger strata, and they pity a community that adheres strictly to the law and does not go beyond it. One such moralist even said, "One of the causes of the destruction of Jerusalem was that it followed the exact line of the law and never ventured beyond its limits."[5]

As the practice of equity is primarily an individual affair, there cannot be any fixed rules to be followed, nor any limit to the cases when equity is to be applied. There are many instances when a man of a deeply ethical character can practice it. We mention several cases cited in the Talmud to illustrate the nature of the character of such acts.

The Bible states, "If thou seest the ass of him that hateth

[4] Tr. *Baba Metziah,* 30b.
[5] Ibid.

thee lying under its burden, thou shalt not forbear to pass him by; thou shalt surely release it with him" (Exodus XXIII, 5). And again, "Thou shalt not see thy brother's ass or his ox fallen down by the way and hide thyself from him; thou shalt surely help him to lift them up" (Deuteronomy XXII, 4). These verses were expounded by the sages in the following way. It is explicitly stated that one must help another Jew, even if he is an enemy, to unload the burden of wares from the back of the animal as well as to load them on. These, they say, are two precepts that every Jew must obey. But if the one who passes by is an old man and cannot carry loads, or if he is a respected leader in the community and such work is not in accord with his position, the law releases him from the duty and he may pass on.[6] It is here where equity comes in. If he is imbued with the spirit of Jewish equity, he goes beyond the limit of the law and either hires someone to help his brother in need or discards his dignity and offers the needed help.

An extreme case of performing a superlegal deed is told in the Talmud. A certain scholar, Rabba, the son of Hona, hired men to move casks of wine from one place to another. Through carelessness they broke several of the casks and, according to the law, were liable for the loss. Rabba in anger took some of their garments in order to guarantee the loss. When the great scholar, Rab, heard of it, he ordered him to return the garments immediately. When the workers finally completed the job, Rabba wanted to retain their pay, which covered only a part of the loss, but the laborers pleaded, "We worked a whole day and we are hungry, and even our families have little to eat." Rab then ordered the scholar to pay the full amount he had promised, for this is the way wherein Moses told the Jews to walk.[7] This is Jewish equity, which it is urged that ethically imbued Jews should follow at any time when the occasion arises.

[6] *Code Shulhan Aruch,* Vol. IV, sec. 272.
[7] Tr. *Baba Metziah,* 83a.

Chapter X

FAMILY ETHICS

66. Basis of Happy Marriage

The importance of marriage as an exalted phase of human life is highly stressed in Judaism. According to the prophet Malachi, God Himself is the witness of that union and He accuses the husband who breaks the union in a treacherous manner. He says, "Ye say, 'wherefore?'" that is, you ask why He should refuse you offerings. "Because the Lord hath been witness between thee and the wife of thy youth against whom thou hast dealt treacherously, though she is thy companion and the wife of thy covenant" (Malachi II, 14).

The last statement, naming the wife the husband's companion, points not only to the equal position of the wife in the union, but also to the very purpose of married life. This is expressed in the fidelity and loyalty that the partners bear each other. Throughout the Bible this trait is exalted. The very close relations between Israel and God is symbolically represented as a married union. And when the prophet chastises Israel for turning away from God's worship, they speak of the breach as that of an unfaithful wife, an idea that is especially emphasized by Hosea. The Song of Songs, which sings of the lover and the beloved, is a part of the Scriptures, for Jewish tradition always considered it as a work depicting symbolically the relations between God and Israel. It was said by the great Akiba, "If all the Biblical books are holy, the Song of Songs is the holiest of the holy." [1] He thus expressed the view that the love which is the highest and finest relation between man and wife deserves to be

[1] Tr. *Yadayim*, Ch. III.

considered as the symbol of closeness between God and Israel. In the closing chapter of the Book of Proverbs, an ode is devoted to the faithful and loyal wife who is thus described: "Her price is above rubies." And while beauty is highly estimated in the Bible, as evidenced in the passages in the Song of Songs, yet the most important factor in a happy marriage named in this ode is right conduct. It is said there, "Grace is deceitful, beauty is vain, but a woman who feareth the Lord shall be praised" (Proverbs XXXI, 30). We know already that in the Bible fear of the Lord stands for ethical conduct. The verse seems to say that grace and beauty are not permanent and are subject to change, but the right character, once acquired, is the proper foundation for a happy marriage.

The Rabbis have gone further in the evaluation of the benefits of marriage and its blessed state. They said, "Man's life is not complete in the state of singleness. Both must be united in marriage, and then only does the Divine Presence enter their lives.[2] Another sage said, "The life of an unmarried person lacks joy, blessing, and goodness."

67. Mutual Duties of Husband and Wife

Numerous passages in the Talmud emphasize the importance of respect and honor a husband is to pay to his wife. It is said, "One who loves his wife as he loves himself and honors her even more than himself, of him the Bible says, "And thou shalt know that peace is in thy tent" (Job V, 24),[3] for by such conduct peace will reign in the household. Another sage warns the husband to be careful to pay due respect to his wife,[4] for says he, blessing enters a man's house only on account of his wife.

Knowing the natural desire of women for fine clothes,

[2] *Palestinien Talmud,* Tr. *Berakoth,* Ch. IX, sec. 1.
[3] Tr. *Yebamot,* 62.
[4] Tr. *Baba Metziah,* 59a.

these sages said, "A man should spend on his own clothing less than he can afford, dress his sons and daughters in accordance with his income, but spend on his wife's clothing even more than he can afford." [5] This advice is offered in order to maintain peace and harmony in the home. The sages, valuing highly a successful marriage, do not tire in praising the good wife and her contribution to the happiness of her family. Joshua ben Sira, an earlier Jewest moralist wise in the ways of the world, said, "A good wife is an exceptionally good gift to the husband." [6] A later scholar, interpreting the verse, "All the days of the poor are evil, but he that is of a merry heart has a continual feast" (Proverbs V, 15) said that the term *poor* refers not to the poor in wealth, but to the one who has a bad wife, for she embitters his life all his days, while the phrase "one who is of a merry heart" refers to the man with a good wife who treats her husband in such a way that life seems to be a continual feast.[7] And just as the sages lavished praises on the good wife, they were not sparing of the bad wife. It is said, "A man can bear all kinds of evil, but not life with a bad wife." [8]

The goodness of a wife consists primarily in her character and her right actions. The sages advise a man to be careful in choosing a life partner, to pay attention to the family whence she comes, and to her upbringing. But above all they warned against marrying for money. It is said, "Do not take a wife for the sake of her wealth, for she will consider you a dependent upon her and treat you as one." And furthermore, the end of such a marriage may result in poverty for, relying on his wife's wealth, a man may neglect his own business and gradually fritter away his wife's riches.[9]

Good advice to the wife for right marital conduct is also offered in Jewish ethical literature. She is warned not to re-

[5] Ibid.
[6] Tr. *Yebamot,* 63.
[7] Tr. *Baba Batra,* 145b.
[8] Tr. *Yebamot,* 63.
[9] *Taanna d' be Eliyahu, Zuta,* Ch. II.

veal things that her husband wishes to keep secret, not even to her father and mother. Nor must she show disrespect to the husband's family, and certainly not to the husband himself, though his social status may not be high and though he possesses little education.[10]

68. When Divorce Is Proper

Since, according to the Jewish view, fidelity and loyalty to each other is the very foundation of a happy married life, it follows that when for certain reasons these conditions are lacking, marriage loses its value, and it is better that it be dissolved by divorce. Judaism, therefore, considers divorce not only a necessary remedy for an unhappy marriage, but also does not place strict limitations on its attainment. There was, however, one school of scholars, that of Shammai, which insisted that a divorce should be given only when the wife commits a breach of fidelity. This view was not accepted, and mere incompatibility or any other condition that undermines happiness suffices for the granting of a divorce. However, Jewish law generally limits the power of giving a divorce to the husband alone, even without the wife's consent. This power, though, was restricted by later sages who enacted an ordinance that no divorce could be granted without the consent of the wife.

There are several instances in which the woman can apply for divorce and the court forces the husband to grant it. Such cases arise if the husband refuses to perform his marital duty, if he is smitten by leprosy or any other contagious disease, or if his occupation is such that because of it his clothes exude an unpleasant smell.[11]

Yet, notwithstanding the extenuating legal conditions in regard to divorce, Jewish scholars and moralists were against divorce. Beginning with the statement of the prophet Mal-

[10] Isaac Al-Makaveh, in his *Menorat ha-Maor*, Pt. X, p. 45.
[11] Tr. *Ketubot*, Ch. V, Mishnah 6; Ch. VII, Mishnah 10.

achi, quoted above, throughout the ages they raised their voices against divorce. One says, "He who divorces his wife he married in his youth, even the very altar in the Temple cries over such an act." [12] It is therefore considered an ethical duty of the one before whom the application for divorce is presented to prevent a rift in the family and to make the greatest effort to reconcile the couple before the application is granted. The separation from the wife whom one married first, whether by divorce or death, is considered a great misfortune. One rabbinic statement declares there is no substitute for the wife of a first marriage. Another statement says that when the wife dies, the world is darkened for the husband.

69. Mutual Duties of Children and Parents

Just as Judaism insists upon the exemplary conduct of the husband toward his wife and the wife toward the husband, so does it urge right and proper conduct of all members of the family toward each other. In no other religion or social group does the family occupy such an important place as in Judaism and Jewry. The very origin of the nation is traced to one family. It is no wonder that the family is considered the very cornerstone of the Jewish social fabric. This view is reflected in the numerous statements in the Bible and in Talmudic and Rabbinic literature. It is true that the Book of Proverbs advises one not to spare the rod, but tempers the advice with moderation and with love, and for the purpose of training a child to follow a moral life, as it says, "He who spareth the rod hateth his son, but he that loveth him chastiseth him (Proverbs XIII, 24). And again, "Thou beatest him with the rod and wilt deliver his soul from the nether world" (Proverbs XXIII, 14). The Rabbis, however, lay stress upon kindness and continually urge upon the father, as the head of the family, to conduct himself in

[12] Tr. *Gittin*, 90.

a very gentle manner toward his children. They warn him against introducing rigorous discipline in his house and against causing fear of his authority. Such conduct, they say, can bring grave results as fear may induce the family to use even improper devices in order to escape punishment.[13]

A later ethical treatise, while urging gentle and even humble conduct toward all men, said, "But most of all toward members of one's family," and threatens with dire punishment in hell one who displays temper toward his family and conducts himself in a quarrelsome manner.[14]

Exceptional emphasis is laid in Judaism upon children honoring their parents. As is well known, this duty is the subject of the fifth commandment in the Tables given to Moses at Mt. Sinai and heads the list of all ethical commandments contained therein. Its very place in the Tables points to the fact that it was considered the foundation of all social ethics.

The Mishnah considers the performance of the precept of honoring parents among the few *Mitzwot* for which men receive only the interest of their reward in this world, while the expected complete reward is paid in the hereafter.[15] The Rabbis vied with each other in magnifying the importance of this duty. Said one, "Honoring parents is as great as honoring God, for it is said, 'honor thy father and mother,' and it is said, 'Honor the Lord with thy substance.'" The same term, *honor,* is used for both, which means that there is equal value to the performance of both precepts. He continues, "When one honors his father and mother, God says, I consider your act as if I dwelt in the midst of you and paid you honor."[16] Said another Rabbi, "Honoring parents is even more important than honoring God, for in regard to

[13] Ibid., p. 6b.
[14] Tr. *Derek Eretz,* Ch. IV.
[15] Tr. *Peah,* Ch. I, Mishnah.
[16] Tr. *Kiddushin,* 30b.

God it says, 'Honor thy God with thy substance,'" which means that if one is poor he is released from that type of honor, but to the parents the commandment is unqualified, and one must honor his parents by supporting them even if he is poor and is forced to go begging for that purpose.[17] According to Jewish law, the needs of one's father precede the needs of one's son, and when the father and his own son are in the same trouble, it is his duty to help the father first and then the son.[18] These sages were not satisfied, however, with merely praising the performance of this duty but actually specified ways in which this duty is performed. Some of these duties are affirmative and some prohibitive, namely, things that the son has to do and things that he must take care not to do. To the first group belong such duties as providing the parents with food, drink, a home, and clothing if they are in need. A son must also receive them with great joy when they come to visit him, and accompany them when they leave. To the second group belong such actions as indicate the avoidance of any kind of disrespect. The son must not sit in the father's seat, nor when the father carries on a discussion should he participate without asking the father's permission, nor contradict his statement publicly, even when he thinks it erroneous. It was added, though, that if the discussion refers to a subject covered by Jewish law, the son may offer a different opinion based on his mastery of the subject, for otherwise, one who hears the father's statement may accept it and act not in accordance with Jewish law. It is, of course, understood that such differences must be uttered in the most gentle and respectful manner.[19]

The ethicists also placed special obligations on the father toward his son. He must teach him a trade or provide him with some profession so that he should be able to support himself; he must also help him to get married, and a more

[17] Palestinian Talmud, Tr. *Peah*, sec. III.
[18] Ibid.
[19] Tr. *Kiddushin*, 31.

practical sage added another duty, namely to teach his son the art of swimming. But the most important parental duty is to provide his son with an education.[20]

[20] Ibid., 29b

Chapter XI

ETHICS OF THE GROUP

70. The Duty of the Individual to the Group

Inasmuch as every individual is a member of a social group or a people, it follows that every ethical system contains a number of duties covering the relation between him and the group. These duties are of a double aspect, duties of the individual toward the group, and duties of the group toward the individual. Jewish ethics is not only no exception, but lays great stress upon their fulfillment. The particular situation of this group, forced upon it by historical destiny, demanded that the relation between the individual and the group as a whole should be of the closest. Dispersed as the Jews were during a great part of their history, and subject to all kinds of suffering and tribulations, they could not have survived and withstood all attacks were it not for the fact that the fulfillment of these duties in both aspects was insisted upon in the most rigorous manner.

Jewish moralists demand not only the mechanical performance of certain public duties which, in a measure, are forced upon the individual Jew by the community, but also an inner and wholehearted interest in the fate and welfare of the people as a whole. It is said that when the nation is suffering, every Jew must share in its grief and must consider it as his own misfortune. For such feeling great reward is promised, namely that one who identifies himself with the fate of the nation as a whole will live to participate in the comfort and joy that will come to the people.[1] Another moralist promises the participant spiritual elevation, sym-

[1] Tr. *Taanit*, p. 11.

bolically expressed by saying that he will be saturated with the holy spirit. On the other hand, the one who does not make the grief of the nation his own is threatened that he will be excluded from participation in the comfort and joy that will come to the people.[2]

Therefore, identification by the individual Jew with the grief of the nation and making it his own is a generic duty. It includes numerous subsidiary duties, all of which aim to relieve the nation in its grief and suffering. It also demands that all actions aiming at that purpose must be performed, not in a mechanical manner, but with love and with a willingness to make the greatest sacrifice for the sake of the nation.

A second duty of the individual toward the nation as a whole is so to act that his actions in no way reflect unfavorably on the name of the group. In other words, he must know that the group is held responsible for the actions of its individuals. The Talmud says all Jews are responsible for one another.[3]

This responsibility and the care that every Jew must take that his acts should not reflect unfavorably on the group as a whole are stressed by the Jewish moralists by an analogy borrowed from the animal world and buttressed by a fine parable. They say, "Why does the Bible call Israel 'scattered sheep' (Jeremiah L, 17)? It means merely to point out that just as a sheep when struck on one of its organs feels the blow on all the organs and its whole body begins to tremble, so is Israel." If one Jew acts wrongly, the effects are felt by the whole group. Such a wrong act by an individual Jew and its effects on the group can be likened to the act of a member of a company traveling in a boat, who began to bore a hole in the bottom of the boat under his own seat. When the other members of the company protested at his action, he said, "Do I not bore under my own seat?" "Yes,"

[2] *Taanna d'be Eliyahu.*
[3] Tr. *Shebuot,* 39.

answered the others, "but the waters will flood us all and the ship will sink." [4] The parable is well chosen, for the life of our people in dispersion through the millennia very much resembled a journey in a boat on a stormy sea, and every slight leak in the boat might be the cause of danger to all the travelers.

Any act on the part of a Jew that might reflect unfavorably on the name of Israel is branded by Jewish ethics as a *Ḥilul ha-Shem,* a desecration of the name of God. We pointed out above that any ethically improper act of a Jew toward a non-Jew bears the stigma of that name. But in reality the term covers a much wider range than merely relations between Jews and non-Jews. It also includes wrongs done by Jews to Jews. The chosenness of Israel frequently repeated in the Bible is designated there by such terms as a *kingdom of priests* and a *holy nation,* which terms imply nothing else but the duty to conduct themselves in such a way that their conduct should be considered ethically exemplary. That this chosenness does not confer any particular advantages upon Israel, but rather many duties the nonfulfillment of which are considered sins, becomes evident from the words of the prophet Amos who says, "You only have I known of all the families of the earth. Therefore I will visit upon you all your iniquities," (III, 2), which means that all deviations from the expected conduct will be severely punished.

Opposed to the term *Ḥilul ha-Shem* is the term *Kiddush ha-Shem,* sanctification of the name of God which, though frequently applied to martyrdom for the sake of the Jewish religion, yet embraces acts the performance of which calls for admiration and brings honor to the name of Israel and to the Jewish religion. Such acts are not matters of everyday affairs and usually their performance requires great sacrifice, involves even suffering, and may not be undertaken by many. But for the chosen spirits, sanctification of the name

[4] *Leviticus Rabba,* Ch. IV, sec. 6.

is a high ethical ideal that they strive to realize when the occasion occurs.

71. Primary Duty of the Group to the Individual

The group or, in its narrower form, the community, likewise has numerous duties toward the individuals of whom it is composed. These duties cover the various phases of the virtues of charity and loving-kindness, the performance of which on an organized and effective basis can be accomplished in modern times only by the community. Some aspects of the duties and their fulfillment were referred to above. The most important duty of the community toward the individual members, however, was hardly touched upon. This duty is the endeavor by the community to provide an adequate Jewish education for the children of its members. When properly performed, it is the best guarantee for the survival of the community, or rather the nation as a whole, and the stress of its value and the necessity is in itself an ethical duty.

The Hebrew name of the Pentateuch is not the Book of the Law or Code, but Torah, which means teaching. It signifies that these books are not to be consulted occasionally like a code of law, but are to be studied and taught daily. It is explicitly stated therein, "And these words which I command thee this day shall be upon thy heart, and thou shalt talk of them when thou sittest in thy house, and when thou walkest by the way, and when thou liest down, and when thou risest up" (Deuteronomy VI, 6–7). Thus, the Torah was supposed to become the companion of the Jewish people immediately upon their ascending into the arena of history. Each Jew has the sacred duty to teach Torah and transmit it to his children. Education is a household occupation.

This was the ideal placed before the people of Israel at its birth as a nation, an ideal that was to determine its destiny through history. But the greater the ideal, the more difficult the way and the longer the time of its realization. Thus, it happened that the young desert-bred nation, coming into the Promised Land, was blinded by the glare of the old civilizations of the nations around it and fell under their sway. Then began the long dramatic period in the history of Israel in its land, a period of ups and downs. At times, Israel deviated from the ideal set before it and strayed from the Torah and from its God, and at times it turned back to both. The zigzag line ended in catastrophe—exile into Babylonia. Out of it the nation emerged physically divided, part returning to its ancient land, and part remaining in the lands of its exile, but united by an endeavor to come closer and closer to its ideal.

There began then the period of the Second Commonwealth, another dramatic period in the history of the people, distinguished by glory and by subjection, and all the time coming closer and closer to the realization of the ideal. As the period was drawing to its end the realization came. From then on, the Torah became the very soul of the Jewish people, and when the final catastrophe came and Israel lost again its state and land, the Torah became, as the great scholar Zunz expressed it, the portable fatherland of the scattered people. The most important function of the Jewish communities throughout the dispersion was to provide education and means of study for its children. A great Jewish scholar remarked that the usual title bestowed upon the Jews, "The People of the Book," is not an entirely adequate one. That title was bestowed by a non-Jew, Mohammed, founder of the great religion of Islam, and it meant only that this people have a book or law that contains the principles of their religion. In fact, he bestowed the same title upon the Christians with reference to the Gospels. The real and true name by which the Jewish people can be characterized is "the people of study."

It is said that Torah, divine worship, and loving-kindness

are the three pillars on which the world is based,[5] and the world is, of course, the world of the Jewish people, namely its very life and existence. In reality, though, Torah was almost the only pillar, for without the knowledge, proper worship as well as the practice of loving-kindness cannot be carried on. And it was said by a sage, "The world continues in existence only through the breath that the scholars exhale while studying the Torah." [6] It is this breath, thin and vapory as it is, that yet has enough strength to keep the Jewish world in existence. Consequently, study and education took precedence over every other activity in Jewish life, and a scholar, endeavoring to emphasize its importance, even ventured to say that we never take children away from school even for the building of the Temple,[7] for important as the Temple, the center of religious worship, may be, study and education are of greater importance. It follows, then, that if one is asked simultaneously to contribute a sum of money for the building of the Temple and for a school for children, the school takes precedence, and the first duty is toward Jewish education.

The duty of educating the children in reality rests upon both the individual, the father as the head of the family, and the community. As mentioned above, the Torah says, "And thou shalt teach them diligently unto thy children." In early times, teaching was primarily entrusted to the father, and the Talmud states, "It is the duty of the father to teach his son Torah as soon as he begins to talk." [8] But as the means at the disposal of the individual are limited, education very early became the responsibility and prime duty of the community.

In times gone by, there existed in the ghetto, a division of the educational duties between the father and the com-

[5] Tr. *Aboth*, Ch. I, 2.
[6] Tr. *Sabbath*, 119b.
[7] Ibid.
[8] Tr. *Kiddushin*, 29.

munity. Elementary education was primarily the task of the father; he turned his son over to a teacher who maintained a private school and was paid by the parents. Even the poor saved enough from their meager income, to pay the teacher. In those days, Jews were not satisfied with just elementary education. They wanted higher learning, which they considered the very soul of their existence, and thought that it should become the share of every young Jew. To provide learning became the task of the community. Academies or *Yeshibot* were built where scholars taught and students gathered. Communities not only paid the teachers, but maintained the students. There was then hardly a Jewish community, no matter how small its numbers, that did not maintain a *Yeshibah,* though frequently of modest size. We are told by a Polish scholar who lived in the 17th century and witnessed the massacres of Chmelnitzki in the years 1648-50 that in his time every Jewish community in Poland that had only fifty families maintained an academy for thirty students with a scholar at its head, and paid the salary of the scholar and maintained the students.[9]

Learning provided social prestige. To be learned meant belonging to the nobility of the nation, for Jews knew no other type of nobility. Parents, therefore, strove with all their might to have at least one learned man, or as the scholar was usually called, a *Talmid Ḥakam,* a wise student, as a member of the family. The father did his best to train as many of his sons as possible, as scholars, or at least one of them. He also used all efforts to marry off his daughters to scholars.

Learning was not a profession for it became a part of the personality of the one who delved in it. Nor did it have a limit or end. The very name for scholars, *Talmid Ḥakam,* proves that one must remain a student all his life and continue his study to the very end, for no material reward is expected. It is true that some learned men served as Rabbis

[9] Nathan Hanover, in his work *Yeven Metzulah.*

in communities or engaged in teaching, but this was not their aim. In fact, the view of the Talmud was that a scholar must not take payment for his services to the community or for his teaching, as only the teachers of the very young were to be paid.[10] Most great scholars, from the beginning of the Talmudic period until the Middle Ages, were engaged in various occupations or trades in order to make a living. Scholarship was an art, and its mastery, the pleasure and joy experienced by the learned, were real reward, irrespective of any other rewards that the pursuit of learning might have brought.

The spread of learning and the effort to attain it during the ages became traits of the national character. And rightly did Leopold Zunz consider the pursuit of learning one of the few activities that expressed the nationality of the Jews during the millennia of dispersion. The results of this agelong activity are collected in an extensive literature in many languages covering many subjects, reaching in quantity hundreds of thousands of volumes.

Times have changed and the pursuit of Jewish learning is no longer an elemental trait of the character of the Jewish group, nor do the conditions allow the parents to take upon themselves the task of supplying even elementary education. As a result, Jewry may face spiritual deterioration. In such a time, the duty to save as much as possible of the heritage of Israel by providing education for Jewish children is increased tenfold in importance and necessity. The fulfillment of this duty is obligatory upon both the individual Jew and the community or the group as a whole.

Great is the ethical duty to save a brother's life or health or to relieve him from suffering, but still greater is the duty to save the Jewish spirit and soul of a generation. The Mishnah offers a list of ethical deeds. It is said there that these deeds have no limit in their performance or in their reward. Whatever reward a man may get during his life is only the

[10] Tr. *Nedarim*, Ch. IV, Mishnah 3.

interest, but the capital comes in the hereafter. The Mishnah concludes, "Greater than all these deeds is the study and teaching of the Torah."[11] If ever there was a time in the long history of the Jews when this maxim should be taken in its literal meaning and carried out with the greatest effort and sacrifice, it is the present. And in performing this duty of Talmud Torah, both individuals and the community should remember that it has no limit. It can by no means be limited to elementary education, but must embrace all of learning, for on the day when the Torah and learning will cease in Jewry, Jewry will exist in name only.

[11] Tr. *Peah,* Ch. I, Mishnah 1.

Chapter XII

THE ETHICAL ASPECT OF JEWISH HISTORY

72. Leading Factors in Jewish History

Ethics, or morality, has an important function in any social group. In fact, no society, even a primitive one, can exist without some code of ethics, which sets limits to the actions of the individual and tames his greed and lust and his passion for violence. Otherwise there would be a state of *Bellum omnium contra omnes,* a war of all against all, and no social life could ever exist. But in the life of no other group or nation did ethics play such an important role as in that of the Jew. Its long history is unique in this matter.

Already in its early life, on its very emergence on the scene of history, it was in the possession of a religion that taught not only the existence of one God, only one, but also invested Him with an ethical essence, and He thus became the archetype of morality. It is irrelevant whether that exalted religion became immediately the share of the whole nation or only of the few. But it was there embedded in the consciousness of the nation, even though not clearly understood by the masses.

The exaltedness of the religious conception, on the one hand, and the inability of the masses to grasp it and live up to it, on the other hand, precipitated, as mentioned above, a struggle in the life of the people in the first centuries of its existence.

The chosen spirits among them who urged and pleaded for a return to God threatened punishment in the name of God if there were no return, and promised reward if a return were to take place. The threat was exile, and the reward restoration and a glorious future. Both of these, though their original expression was only in words, were destined to become powerful factors in the long history of this people and they practically form its warp and woof. The threat was realized and became a fixed state in Jewish life for millennia; the reward was and still is in the distant future. Yet all the multifarious vicissitudes of the existence of the nation are to be viewed in the light of these two factors, exile and redemption. The basis of both, the threat and the reward, in fact their very essence, is primarily ethical. The first was threatened mainly as punishment for the transgression of precepts of morality, and the second is portrayed as the attainment of a complete ethical life. Of course, there were also purely religious transgressions, but the emphasis is laid by almost all prophets on the moral transgressions. Similarly, there are other features, material ones, of the reward, but again the strongest emphasis is upon moral perfection. It is in these ethical features that the strength of both factors and the power of their shaping of history lies.

The first time that the threat of exile is mentioned in the Torah is found in a section that lists prohibitions of incestual relations as well as of all other immoral acts, and then concludes with the words, "Ye shall therefore keep all my statutes and all my ordinances and do them, that the land whither I bring you to dwell therein, vomit you not out" (Leviticus XVIII, 28). On the very entrance into the Promised Land, the weary wanderers of forty years in the desert are warned that their long hope for final settlement will be shattered if they will be morally unclean. The very soil will rise against them, for morality is the very essence of the God who created it.

Again, when the first of the great prophets, Amos, makes his appearance in Beth El, a leading city in the northern kingdom of Israel, he first thunders against the neighboring nations of Israel and chastises them for their immoral crimes against His people. But turning to Moab, he says, "Thus saith the Lord, 'for three transgressions of Moab, yea, for four, I will not reverse it because he burned the bones of the King of Edom into lime. So I will send a fire upon Moab'" (Amos II, 1). Both Moab and Edom were enemies of Israel; Edom was a bitter enemy of Israel, and is one who was chastised by this prophet for its murderous attacks against Israel. Yet so inflamed was the prophet by the barbarous act of Moab in desecrating the holiness of the human body and burning its bones that he pronounces doom upon the perpetrator, forgetting all other evil deeds of Moab.

Finally, when turning to Israel, Amos glosses over the worship of idolatry of which Beth-El was the center and cries out, "Thus saith the Lord, 'for three transgressions of Israel, yea, for four, I will not reverse it, because they sell the righteous for silver and the needy for a pair of shoes. That pant after the dust of the earth on the head of the poor and turn aside the way of the humble" (II, 6, 7). He continues to list other immoral acts and prophesies the doom of the nation for such conduct. The crux of that doom is exile. He was the first of the prophets to inject exile as a factor into the history of the Jewish people and reverts to it again and again, thus, "For Gilgal shall go into captivity, and Beth-El shall come to naught" (V, 5). And turning to the rich who are so confident of the continuance of their good fortune that they spend their time in search after pleasures, he warns them, "That they shall go captive at the head of them that go captive, and the revelry of them that stretched themselves shall pass away" (VI, 7). This threat was made not in time of stress and insecurity, but in the very period of glory of the kingdom of Israel, the reign of Jeroboam II, when the boundaries were extended and things looked bright. But the prophet knew that immoral actions and unethical conduct cannot go unpunished and the doom must come, if not in the form of destruction, for Israel must live, then in the form of exile.

The threat of exile and the emphasis that the cause of its

realization is primarily ethical transgressions winds like a dark thread through the entire prophetic literature. The prophet Micah, after chastising his people for their transgressions, sums up God's demands from his people and outlines the way He wants them to follow. Says Micah, "It had been told thee, O man, what is good and what does the Lord require of thee"—to do justly, to love mercy, and to walk humbly with God" (VI, 8). Jeremiah, who knew that the doom of exile was imminent, for the Babylonian forces were already in the land, yet hoped that he might avert it if the people would prove their willingness to repent by observing at least one ethical precept, namely freeing their Hebrew men and women slaves at the end of six years as it is written in the Torah. The King Zedekiah made a covenant with the nobles and all who possessed Jewish slaves to free them. However, the covenant was immediately broken and the freed slaves were again pressed into service. Jeremiah then told the king and the people that this transgression of the ethical precept sealed their fate, and that the capture of Jerusalem and the destruction of the Temple were inevitable (Jeremiah XXXIV, 16–22).

From what was said we can see how exile, which forms such an important factor in Jewish history, had such a close connection with moral conduct. Of course, moral transgressions were not the only ones that the prophets made the targets of their chastisement, but the emphasis was laid on moral acts for, as Micah says, "Justice, loving-kindness, and humbleness are the main things which God expects from His people" (VI, 8).

And when the later sages, who lived after the destruction of the Second Temple, searched for the cause of the second catastrophe, they were at first baffled in their efforts. This catastrophe, accompanied by a new exile, concluded the period of the Second Commonwealth, which had none of the great flaws of the preceding period. It had no traces of idolatry nor any of the other grave sins. The people clung to the Torah and fought for its preservation. Delving deeper into history, they discovered the old cause of exile, the lack of right moral conduct. Said one sage, "Jerusalem was destroyed because there were quarrels among factions and animosity toward fellowmen increased." [1] Another sage was asked, "Why did the Second Commonwealth close with exile?" And the answer was, "Because the Jews at the time were greedy for material wealth and instead of love, animosity was prevalent in society." [2] There was learning and also observance of purely religious precepts, but there was a lack of proper moral conduct, and this lack determined their fate—to go once more into exile.

The ethical aspect of Jewish history is not limited to the fact that it was repeatedly threatened with punishment primarily for moral transgressions. The very realization of the threat, the duration of the exile, the hope for redemption, and the consequent glorious future that would follow the return from exile are all drawn against a background in which ethics plays a leading role. All these form points in one long process of ethical progress and improvement for the Jewish people in particular and for the human world in general.

73. Ethical Purpose of Exile

Punishment, as such, plays a subsidiary role in the event of exile. The main purpose is that it serve as a means of purification of the spirit of the people, and prepare them for the great role they are to play in the future. Of course, prophet after prophet called to his people to repent and thus avoid exile. But when repentance did not come it was hoped that, in the strange land and under the stress of subjection, not only would repentance come, but a real change of heart and a rise to great spiritual and ethical heights. All

[1] Tr. *Yoma,* 9b.
[2] *Ekah Rabba,* Ch. 1.

the prophets refer to that purpose of exile, but the thought is more explicitly expressed by Jeremiah.

In the midst of the siege of Jerusalem by the Babylonians, God tells Jeremiah to buy a piece of land from his cousin Ḥannanel as a symbol that the Jews will return from exile and will again buy fields and vineyards in their own land. Jeremiah says to God, "Thou hast said unto me, O Lord God, 'buy thee the field for money and call witnesses,' whereas the city is given into the hands of the Chaldeans" (Jeremiah XXXII, 25). In these words there is an indirect complaint. Why send the people into exile and then redeem them? Why not postpone the very exile and wait for repentance? The answer is also given indirectly by God (Ibid. 36-40). He says the exile will take place and so will the redemption or the ingathering, but at their return He will give them "one heart and one way" (Ver. 39) to obey all His commandments. The meaning is that the exile will prepare them for the future when the eternal covenant between God and Israel will be made (Ver. 40). All prophets assume the efficacy of the exile to effect a change of heart, for they all speak of it as temporal and emphasize the returns from it. Jeremiah, however, was not satisfied with a general statement about the temporalness of the exile, but fixed a specific date for its termination—seventy years (Jeremiah XXIX, 10), so convinced was he of the effectiveness of the exile in bringing about a change of heart. The acme of progress toward spiritual and ethical improvement is reached in the third link of the process, the redemption of the future. It is this future, or rather the hope for it, that was deeply imbedded in the heart of the Jews for millennia and preserved it in spite of all tribulations in the long dispersion, and its ethical aspect is dominant in its portrayal.

74. Ethical Character of Redemption

That portrayal, of course, contains glorious features of a material nature, political power, wealth, length of life, and similar things, but the highest rung in the ladder of happiness is spiritual and moral perfection. The great painter of this picture of the future is Isaiah. He begins by asserting that every dweller in Jerusalem in the future will possess spiritual and moral perfection so that he will attain holiness (Isaiah IV, 3). He continues by drawing the character of the future king, the redeemer or the Messiah who will come forth as a shoot from the stock of Jesse, father of King David. He will be saturated with the spirit of knowledge and the fear of the Lord. His reign will be the very incarnation of justice for the poor and the meek of the land. And what is more, "The earth shall be full of the knowledge of the Lord, as the waters cover the sea" (Isaiah XI, 9). In other words, this time of the future in which ethical perfection will take place is not limited to the Jews, but all men will share in it. To make matters clearer and more specific, Isaiah completes the picture of the future by his vision of "the end of days" when war will be abolished and eternal peace will reign among all nations. Zion will be the spiritual capital of the world whither nations will flock in order to learn the ways of God and ethical conduct. The prophet concludes his exalted vision by an appeal to the Jewish people, who are destined to be the center of that future, to begin the long march toward that distant ideal goal and says, "O, House of Jacob, come ye and let us walk in the light of the Lord" (Isaiah II, 1–5). The people accepted that duty, but human frailty and the vicissitudes of life prevented their living up to the ideal or even coming close to it, though it was always in their consciousness.

Prophet after prophet reminded them of their destiny and in glorious terms drew the future that awaited them. The successors of Isaiah never reached his exaltedness, and some dwelt much on the glory of the material phase of that time. None, however, failed to emphasize the spiritual and ethical aspect of life in the promised future. Jeremiah, speaking to his people on the verge of their departure into exile, presents before them a vision of the time to come, saying, "Behold the days come, saith the Lord, that I will raise unto David a righteous shoot. And he will reign as king and excel in knowledge and shall execute justice and righteousness in the land. In his days Judah shall be saved and Israel shall dwell safely. And this is his name whereby God shall call him, "Our righteousness" (Jeremiah XXIII, 5, 6). Speaking again of the future glory of Jerusalem, he says, "This is the name which the Lord will call her—Our righteousness" (XXXIII, 15, 16). Righteousness, then, is the basic quality of the king and of life, and Jerusalem will be filled with it.

The people went into exile and a part of them returned to their land, but the glorious future did not come. The present fell even lower than the past, for those who returned and lived in their own land were still subjected to a foreign power. Yet the glow of the vision of the future was not dimmed. The hope for and the striving toward it became a part of the character of the nation. The darker the present, the brighter glittered the vision of what was to come. A vision seen by one who witnessed the persecutions of Antiochus Epiphanes but integrated in an earlier work included in the Bible, namely the Book of Daniel, stresses that the time is coming when transgressions will be finished and there will be an end of sin and everlasting righteousness will be brought in. It further states that rule and power and kingdom that will be everlasting will be given to the people of Israel. The seer does not call them Israel, but "the people of the saints of the Most High" (Dan. VII, 18; IX, 24). This places a condition on the attainment of their future—to rise in the spiritual and moral exaltedness so that they will deserve to be called the people of the saints of the Most High.

Eventually prophecy ceased and the Biblical Canon was

closed, but the literature in which the nation expressed its hopes and aspirations did not cease. It increased, and a great popular literature began to be produced. Some were called *Apocryphal,* i.e., hidden books, for they were supposed to have been written early, but were hidden for a time and later made public. Others were named *Apocalyptic,* which means revelations of what is to happen in time. In all these works, the web of portrayal and visions of the glorious future are woven further and further, new strands are added and new colors and hues injected, the supernatural encroaches on the natural, boundaries between worlds are removed, for this world may be succeeded by another one, and death loses its terror for belief in resurrection is dominant. But one thing remains constant in all this whirl of ideas, views, and visions, the ethical and spiritual exaltedness that the Jewish people must attain in order that the future may be realized. Work after work stresses that in the period of glory sin will be abolished and evil powers destroyed, and righteousness and justice will reign supreme in the Messianic Period.

This magnified vision of the future, purged of certain elements, crept into the popular literature, was absorbed in the wide stream of literary activity carried on by the sages and scholars, and became a basic phase of beliefs and views of Judaism. And when the nation went once more into exile and was scattered to the four corners of the world, it took with it the Torah in both its aspects, written and oral, together with the hope for and aspiration toward that glorious future as guardians of its existence.

Millennia passed, suffering and tribulation were the share of the nation, but the distant light of the future was until the last centuries not dimmed. Time and again Messianic movements broke forth. False Messiahs stirred the enthusiasm of the masses of Jews and made them believe that the promised future was about to be realized. Bitter disappointment followed, but the hope in the heart of the people as a whole remained, and it continued to believe in the reflection of that luminous future. This hope for a better world and a better life in which goodness will reign is also clothed in the form of ethics, for ethics emphasizes not what is but what ought to be, the change for the better that constitutes progress. And so did Jewish life through the ages always strive to the ideal, and thanks to that striving it did overcome all obstacles and survive. Thus did Jewish history continue the ethical aspect that it assumed in the early period.

Chapter XIII

JEWISH CONTRIBUTION TO WORLD ETHICS

Casting a glance upon what was said in the preceding pages, we must come to the conclusion that the Jewish contribution to world ethics is considerable. First, by positing God as the archetype of morality, it placed moral law upon the highest level—to be obeyed for its own sake with no attention to any other factors, such as usefulness or personal benefit. The believer considers it his sacred duty to obey that law as it is an *imitatio Dei,* and an endeavor to act in the likeness of God. Also, the skeptic or even the disbeliever must agree that such law contains truth since it is considered the essence of the most perfect being imaginable, and, consequently, action according to it must be the best that the human mind can conceive.

Second, Judaism, considering man to have been created in the image of God, endows his personality with a high degree of dignity, making any abuse of it a gross sin and a gross immoral act. It also teaches that man must be thought of as an end in himself and not be used as a means. Along with dignity, it also emphasizes the equality of all men since they are all descendants of one pair of ancestors. It buttresses the ideal of equality by the institution of the Sabbath, which stresses the fundamental right of all men of whatever status to share in the benefit of rest from work for one day a week. All these things were unknown in the ancient world, and Western humanity borrowed them from Judaism.

Third, Judaism, by conceiving of justice as a leading attribute of God's activity, also makes it the basis of the view of the moral order of the world, since He created it and keeps it in existence. It also demands that by his conduct man make justice the basis of his own world.

Fourth, the ethical character of the future portrayed by the prophets, picturing it as an age in which all moral aspirations of humanity will be realized, thus created a great ideal for all mankind to strive toward. Millennia may pass before that ideal will even partially be realized, but its very existence in the sacred books and in the minds of men of spirit may act as an incentive in speeding the progress of humanity toward the ideal goal.

It is true that all these postulates, beliefs, and ideas are no longer the monopoly of the Jews and are shared by a great part of humanity, but it cannot be denied that the origin lies in the Jewish moral tradition. Hence the claim of Jewish ethics to an important contribution to the moral rise of humanity is rightfully founded.

GLOSSARY

1. Abot di Rabbi Nathan

Abot di Rabbi Nathan is an enlarged ethical treatise extraneous to the Mishnah. It contains the same material as the Mishnaic tractate with many supplements and extensive comments upon the ethical statements, eliciting their full value, together with many Agadic remarks and stories. The authorship is ascribed to Rabbi Nathan, the dean of the Sanhedrin during the presidency of Simon ben Gamliel, the father of Judah the Prince; a number of his statements as well as those of his colleagues, not quoted in the Mishnaic tractate, are given in this tractate. It is divided into forty-one chapters.

2. Agada

Agada is a general name for a diversified mass of Jewish teachings aiming to supplement those of the *Halakah.* It embraces views, opinions, and ethical maxims touching both on the life of the individual and that of the nation in all their phases, as well as ancillary subjects. Much of this mass of teachings was derived, like the *Halakah,* by interpretation of Biblical verses, and for this purpose all the books of the Bible, and not only the Pentateuch, were utilized. The method of interpretation was the same as that of the *Halakah,* namely *Midrash.* The verses were searched and analyzed, and whatever pertained to ethics, theology, history of the people in the past, its destiny and hopes for the future, was extracted and used in instruction. In time much extraneous matter of heterogenous character was absorbed and included in that current. The word is derived from the Hebrew root *Nagad* which in its *Hiphil* (causative) form means to say, or impart instruction. The Hebrew form of the word is *Hagadah* and the Aramaic form which is more commonly used is *Agada.*

3. Amoraim

The name *Amoraim* is given to the scholars of the generations succeeding the redaction of the Mishnah, whose statements and discussions make up the content of the *Gemara.*

4. Book of the Pious

The *Book of the Pious* or *Sefer Ḥasidim* is a classic in Jewish ethical literature. It is of a practical nature; no ethical theories are taught there, for they were considered unnecessary, as it is all based on the teachings of the Talmud and Agadic literature, and is permeated with a deep religious spirit. It does contain detailed instruction of the conduct in daily life, covering practically every part of it. It is ascribed to Judah ben Samuel of Regensburg (*ca.* 1200 and named ha-Ḥassid.)

5. Derek Eretz

Derek Eretz, literally *the way of the world,* came to be used as a term for *good manners.* It was therefore given as a name to a small tractate on ethics and good conduct. It is included in the series of small tractates *(Kalah Rabbati,* q.v.). Like the tractate *Kalah,* it has two versions, shorter and longer.

6. Halakah

The term *Halakah* is used in two ways, as a wide connotation of all laws and regulations which relate to various phases of life resulting from the activity of the bearers of the Oral Law and tradition, and also as a name for a single statement embodying a law, or a regulation, or an ordinance abstracted from the interpretation of the original source in the Pentateuch or from the discussion of the motive for the ordinance. The meaning of the word seems to be derived from the Hebrew root, *Halak*, i.e., to go, namely a rule of conduct which the people should follow.

7. Iggeret ha-Vikuaḥ

The *Iggeret ha-Vikuah (Letter of Discussion)* is a work by Shem Tob Ibn Falquera (1129–1225), wherein a debate between a philosopher and a Ḥassid is presented by the author. The philosopher attempts to prove that the teachings of philosophy do not oppose the principles and beliefs of the Torah. It contains also a number of ethical apothegms.

8. Kalah Rabbati

Kalah Rabbati is one of the tractates of a group called "small tractates" *(Masekot Ktanot)* appended to the Talmud, but not included in it. These tractates were compiled in Palestine after the redaction of the Talmud and deal with various subjects. This tractate opens with a chapter on marital relations, and therefore its name *Kalah,* i.e., a bride. The larger part, however, deals with ethical matters, especially of the conduct of scholars. There are two versions of this tractate, a shorter and a longer. The longer is called *Kalah Rabbati,* i.e., the larger.

9. Kad ha-Kemah

The *Kad ha-Kemaḥ,* literally a jar of flour but figuratively the substance of truth, for truth supports spiritual life as flour the physical, is an ethical book by Bahya ben Asher of Toledo or Saragossa, Spain (d. 1291). The subjects are arranged alphabetically and are treated briefly though adequately. In addition to the articles on ethical subjects the work includes a number that bear on the principles of religion.

10. Maseket Sofrim

Maseket or tractate *Sofrim* is one of the small tractates (q.v.), which deals primarily with ways of the writing of the Holy Scrolls of the Torah, portions of which are read in the synagogue on the Sabbath and the Holy Days. It also deals with prayer and its various forms and order. But in many of its passages numerous ethical statements are integrated.

11. Midrashim (Agadic)

There are a number of collections of Agadic nature containing diversified matter—homilies, religious and ethical teachings, proverbs, interpretations of historical events, folk legends, and other subjects. Since a great part of the content is based on interpretation of verses of the Bible by the method of *Midrash* they are also *Midrashim.*

These *Midrashim* are likewise arranged on the Books of the Bible. The material contained in them dates from various times. In parts it can even be traced to the early period of the Second Commonwealth, while other parts belong to much later times, as late as the 6th and 7th centuries C. E. The compilation of the books began late, probably not before the 6th century C. E.

There are two principal orders of such *Midrashim,* the

Rabba, i.e., the large one, and the *Tanḥuma.* The former contains two divisions, one on the Pentateuch as follows: (1) Genesis or *Bereshit Rabba;* (2) Exodus or *Shemot Rabba;* (3) Leviticus or *Wayikra Rabba;* (4) *Numeri* or *Bemidbar Rabba;* (5) *Deuteronomy* or *Debarim Rabba.* The second division is on the five Scrolls (Megillot) as follows: (1) *Canticles* (Shir ha-Shirim) *Rabba;* (2) *Ruth Rabba;* (3) *Ekhah Rabba* or Lamentations; (4) *Kohelet Rabba;* (5) *Esther Rabba.* The Scrolls, like the Pentateuch, are read in the synagogue and they were thus likewise a subject of exposition and much of the material was preserved.

The *Tanḥuma* order consists of five books arranged on the Pentateuch only. There are two versions of these books, a shorter and a more elaborate one. The name *Tanḥuma* is given to it because many of the passages or homilies begin with the words: "Said Rabbi Tanḥuma or Rabbi Tanḥuma preached." Rabbi Tanḥuma was a Palestinian *Amora* who lived in the 4th century C. E. and distinguished himself as an Agadist.

12. Midrashim (Tannaitic)

As stated above, the method which was used by the early interpreters of the texts of all the Biblical books, Pentateuch and others, was called *Midrash,* i.e., search and investigation. It was applied in a very broad way for *Halakah* as well as for *Agada.* The result was a large number of motivated statements, namely, the Biblical basis was given for the legal deduction, or the ethical, religious, or historical teachings.

This way of study received an impetus from the time of Hillel and continued along with the Mishnaic way. Consequently, attempts were made at the end of the Tannaitic period to collect also these motivated statements and arrange them, since the larger part of the content is Halakic, according to those Books of the Pentateuch the legal passages of which serve as a basis for the discussions. Accordingly, we have four of such books, called Tannaitic *Midrashim,* as the motivated statements therein were made by *Tannaim,* and the method is that of *Midrash.*

These books are: (1) the *Mekilta,* i.e., literally measures or rules, supposed to have been compiled originally in the school of Rabbi Ishmael (first half of 2nd century); (2) *Sifra* or *Torath Kohanim* (the teachings concerning the sacrifices and the functions of priests) on Leviticus; (3–4) *Sifré,* i.e., books, two collections on the Books of Numbers and Deuteronomy. The last three books emanated from the school of Akiba, the first collected chiefly by Rabbi Judah, and the two latter by Rabbi Simeon ben Yoḥai, his disciples. A part of these books contain also Agadic statements deduced from the verses in the way of *Midrash.* In addition, there have been discovered of late two minor collections of this type, a *Mekilta* on Exodus compiled by Rabbi Simeon and a smaller *Sifré* on Numbers. All these books as we possess them contain numerous additions from the hands of later editors.

13. Mishnah

All this mass of teachings of both phases was carried on for centuries orally and not in an organized and systematized way. But the time came for systematization and organization, a task which was undertaken by generations of scholars and which resulted in various works of a collective nature. The most important of these works was the Mishnah. It is in reality a work of generations, for some of its layers hail from times preceding the destruction of the Temple, and it also includes parts of collections made by such leading *Tannaim* as Akiba and Meir. The final redaction of the Mishnah, however, which became the standard one, was undertaken by Judah the Prince, head of the Sanhedrin in Palestine, around the year 210 C. E. His purpose was to organize and systematize the thousands of statements, primarily of an Halakic nature, into a definite order and give them an authoritative character. It consists of six orders (Sedarim) as follows: (1) *Zeraim,* i.e., seeds, dealing with all laws, precepts relating to agriculture and to plants and fruits. It includes also a treatise on prayer and benedictions as an introduction to the work as a whole, for it is God who supervises the life and labor of man. (2) *Moed,* i.e., festivals, containing all laws pertaining to the Sabbath and the holidays. (3) *Nashim,* i.e., women, covering all laws and regulations concerning family life and some ancillary subjects. (4) *Nezikin,* i.e., damages, dealing with civil and criminal laws in all phases and ramifications. (5) *Kadashim,* i.e., holy things, comprising laws and regulations regarding the Temple service, sacrifices, including dietary laws. (6) *Taharot,* i.e., matters of purity, including all laws of purity and impurity.

Each Order is divided into tractates (called Masseket, literally a web, hence a text), each dealing with a phase of the general subject of the Order. There are sixty-three in all. The tractates are subdivided into chapters, and the chapters into sections, each called a Mishnah or *Halakah.* The Mishnah contains, as stated, mainly Halakic matter, but a small portion of *Agada* is also included. There is one tractate, *Abot* or "The Sayings of the Fathers," devoted entirely to the teaching of ethics and proper conduct. Besides, there is a number of *Mishnot* or statements scattered through the collection which inculcate the principles of Judaism, and indicate the sanctity of certain institutions, or preserve records of historical events and of ancient customs.

The name Mishnah is derived from the root *Shano,* which originally means to repeat, and later signified to study. It came to be used as a general term to designate the activity of scholars in its various phases and ultimately for the great collection, the result of this activity.

14. Oral Law

The term *Oral Law* employed many times in this book is a wide one. It embraces numerous laws, statutes, traditions, customs, and usages, as well as ordinances, enacted by bodies of scholars in early times, which became a part of the Jewish religion. However, the greater part of this law bears, as stated above (p. 173), the nature of both a supplement of the written law and an unfolding of its meaning. The laws of the Pentateuch are, on the whole, stated in too general a manner. To carry them out in practice and in their full meaning they needed much interpretation. As mentioned, Jewish tradition aserts that a supplementary law which contains to a great extent interpretations of the written law was given to Moses on Sinai and he handed it down to future generations.

Little is known about the fate of the supplementary or Oral Law during the First Commonwealth, but on the return from the Babylonian exile, an activity of interpretation of the written law bloomed forth in full glory. Old explanations were revived, new ones added, and the legal portions of the Book of Moses were scrutinized carefully, and each law was unfolded to its full capacity. This activity went on for generations and was carried on orally. That the number of laws and regulations was considerably increased goes without saying. While according to a statement in the Talmud,[1] the Pentateuch contains only 613 precepts, the number is several times that amount if we should count the particulars stemming from each precept and unfolded by interpretation. We must not forget that Judaism embraces not only such laws of a purely religious nature, but all social, civil, and criminal laws as well. The method of interpretation was called *Midrash,* i.e., search and investigation of the Mosaic text. Besides, as mentioned, life and history often called forth the necessity of new enactments either to meet

[1] Tr. *Makkot,* 23b.

exigencies or as fences around the law, or even to establish new institutions, as for example, the semi-festivals of Hanukkah and Purim. Such enactments are called Rabbinic precepts or regulations. The number of such precepts is small, only seven, but regulations and "fences" are numerous.

This activity which went on for generations, first by *Soferim* (scribes), then by scholars who bore the name *Zugot* (Pairs), inasmuch as each pair headed the High Court known as *Sanhedrin,* resulted in two currents of intellectual productivity, *Halakah* and *Agada,* q.v.

15. Rokeah

Rokeaḥ (a compound of spices) is a code written by Eleazar of Worms (1160-1238). The code opens with a number of chapters on the principles and ideals of the Jewish religion, including those of ethical conduct.

16. Sefer Mitzwot Gadol

The *Sefer Mitzwot Gadol (The Large Book of Precepts)* is a code composed by Rabbi Moses of Coucy, France (1200–1260). It is arranged according to the six hundred and thirteen precepts contained in the Pentateuch or the Torah. It is divided into two parts according to the two kinds of precepts, affirmative and prohibitive. The first treats of the former (affirmative), the number of which is 248, and the second of the prohibitive, 365 precepts. The author shows the way the precepts are to be practiced, which of course implies a survey of all opinions of earlier codifiers and his own decisions.

17. Shulḥan Aruk

Shulḥan Aruk (The Prepared Table) is the name given to the code written by Joseph Karo (1480–1575). Due to its form, namely, its brevity and decisive character, as well as the authority of the author and the conditions of the time, it became the final and accepted code of Jewry, especially after Moses Isserlis (1520–1572) added his glosses embodying the customs and rules of Franco-German Jewry. It consists of four parts: (1) *Oraḥ Ḥayyim* (Way of Life) covering laws relating to the religious conduct of the Jew at home and in the synagogue, such as laws of prayer, benedictions, synagogue ritual, and those of the Sabbath and festivals; (2) *Yoreh Deah* (Teacher of Knowledge) dealing with prohibited and permitted things, such as all phases of dietary laws and other subjects which need the advice and decision of a scholar; (3) *Eben ha-Ezer,* embracing all family laws. The name is a euphemistic one, taken from 1 Samuel III, 13. (4) *Ḥoshen ha-Mishpat* (Breastplate of Judgment) contains all civil laws in their various phases. This name is taken from Exodus XXVIII, 15, and is also used euphemistically, meaning that its decisions are as correct as those which were given by the High Priest by means of the letters on his breastplate.

18. The Talmud

The Talmud includes both the Mishnah and the long commentary upon it which exceeds many times the quantity of the Mishnah, and which is known by the name of *Gemara.* The term is derived from an Aramaic root *Gmar,* to learn or to study. The Mishnah in itself is not entirely explicit in many places, nor does it always offer a decision indicating which of the several opinions it quotes is the adopted one. In addition, there are also at times statements which either contradict or oppose statements on the same subjects in other Tannaitic collections (see Midrashim [Tannaitic]). All these matters had to be straightened out, explained, and clarified. This work was undertaken by schools of scholars, both in Palestine and Babylonia, whose activity lasted for several generations. These schools did not always consider the statements of the Mishnah sufficient and, in order to make the Oral Law as well as the views and general teachings of Judaism adaptable to life and its conditions, added much of their own in matters of *Halakah* and *Agada,* and as a result, the *Gemara* was expanded to thousands of pages.

As the activity of the expounders was carried on in both Palestine and Babylonia, we consequently have two Talmuds or Talmudim, the Palestinian or Jerusalem Talmud (Yerushalmi) and the Babylonian or Talmud Babli, which differ from each other in character. The difference, of course, is limited to the *Gemara,* but the Mishnah is the same in both.

The redaction of the Babylonian Talmud was undertaken by Ashi, the son of Shimi (352–427), head of the Academy of Sura. He was engaged in the work for a period of close to thirty years. At his death, the Talmud was left almost complete, but there were, however, a number of lacunae, both in matter and in form. These were filled by the scholars who followed him, chief among whom were his son, Tabumi, and Rabina, the son of Huna. Upon the death of the latter in the year 499, the Talmud was complete, and in the following year (500) his successor José closed it officially.

The redactor of the Palestinian Talmud cannot be identified definitely. It might have had several editors, but it is accepted by scholars that this Talmud was closed or redacted around the year 425 C. E. The stress of the times and persecution which the Jews of that country underwent made its redaction a matter of necessity. These conditions are reflected both in its content and form, inasmuch as its *Gemara* is shorter and the organization of the material is less systematic than that of the Babylonian.

Originally there must have been *Gemara* on each tractate of the sixty-three of the Mishnah, but due to various reasons, we possess only *Gemara* on thirty-seven tractates of the Babylonian Talmud and on thirty-nine of the Palestinian.

19. Tanna dibe-Eliyahu

Tanna dibe-Eliyahu (The Studies of Elijah), or as it is often called, *Seder Eliyahu (Agadic Order of Elijah),* is the name given to a religious and ethical work par excellence. Some pious souls thought that the prophet Elijah is the author of the work, but research and careful study of the book prove a more humble origin for the author of this work, namely a scholar named Elijah, or as he is called in the book itself, Abba Eliyahu. It was written, according to the testimony of the author himself, at the end of the 10th century and most likely in Palestine.

20. Tannaim

Since *Tné* is the Aramaic form of the verb *Shanah,* the name *Tanna* (plural Tannaim) was given to the several generations of scholars whose statements or discussions are given in the Mishnah. The period of the activity of these scholars lasted about 250 years, from the time of Hillel, ca. 30 B. C. E., to Judah the Prince. The name is limited to scholars of these generations. The earlier bearers of the Oral Law were called by other appellations. (See Oral Law.)

21. Tosefta

Tosefta, literally an addition, is the name of a large collection of *Halakot* (q.v.) that were omitted from the Mishnah by the redactor either because of his different view on the matter or because of their length, and they were recast in shorter form. The later scholars, interested to preserve as much as possible of the teachings of the *Tannaim* (q.v.), collected the omitted *Halakot,* arranged them in the same six orders of the Mishnah, divided into tractates, chapters, and paragraphs, giving this collection the name *Tosefta.* The longer versions of the group of *Halakot* given in the *Tosefta,* instead of the shorter in the *Mishnah*, often serve as commentaries on their Mishnaic groups. The earliest text of the *Tosefta* was organized by Rabbis Hiyya and Hoshayah, contemporaries of Judah the Prince, redactor of the Mishnah. The *Tosefta* contains also many Agadic statements that are either enlargements upon those quoted in the Mishnah or new ones.

22. Tractate Abot

This tractate, included in the fourth order of the Mishnah called *Nezikin,* in distinction from all other tractates does not deal with law or *Halakah,* but with ethics and right conduct. It is called *Abot,* literally Fathers, but it means the teaching of the Fathers or the leading scholars of the generations. It contains ethical rules and moral apothegms uttered by these scholars or the Fathers of the generations arranged in the following order. Chapter I and several *Mishnot* or sections in Chapter II contain the sayings of the president and some also of the vice-president of the Sanhedrin, or the high court. This series begins with the sayings of the high priest, Simon the Just (*ca.* 200 B. C. E.), and ends with the patriarch, Gamliel the Third, son of Judah the Prince (ca. 210–230 B. C. E.). The series that follows begins with the patriarch Hillel who was quoted earlier, and ends with the fourth generation of *Tannaim* (q.v.). The fifth chapter contains a number of anonymous statements in groups, i.e., each statement begins with a number, such as four things or five things, etc. The statements deal with many subjects, things that were created at the end of the process of creation, types of characters of students, degrees of sin, and several other matters. However, several statements in the chapter bear the name of the person who uttered it. There is also a sixth chapter called *Kinyan ha-Torah* (acquisition of the Torah) devoted to the glorification of the study of the Torah and the ways to master it. It is an addition, external to the Mishnah, and its authorship is ascribed to the *Tanna,* Rabbi Meir, disciple of Akiba.

23. Yalkut

The *Yalkut* is the largest Agadic compendium on the Bible. It contains thousands of Agadic statements, scattered in the entire literature, both versions of the Talmud (q.v.), numerous Midrashim, and many more sources, arranged in such order that each statement explains or interprets a verse or part of a verse in the Bible. The compiler was Simon Caro, an 11th-century man.

24. Yeven Metzulah

Yeven Metzulah (The Deep Mire) is the name of a chronicle of the persecutions and massacres suffered by the Jews of Poland during the years 1648–49, from the hand of the rebellious Cossack led by Bogdan Chmelniki. The author, Nathan Hanover, was an eyewitness of these massacres.

INDEX